CW00751800

Sam's for the Hills

DONEGAL'S ALL-IRELAND ODYSSEY

Sunday, September 20, 1992: Anthony Molloy raises the Sam Maguire

Sam's for the Hills

by Dónal Campbell & Damian Dowds

Published November 2003 by
Dónal Campbell & Damian Dowds

© **Dónal Campbell** & **Damian Dowds**
Speenoge, Burt, Co. Donegal

ISBN 0-9546313-0-7

Design and layout *by* Dónal Campbell

Printed *by* Brookfield Printing Company
Stillorgan Industrial Park, Blackrock, Co. Dublin

Cover design *by* Keith Dalton

Photographs *by* Inpho Photography, Dublin

website: www.samsforthehills.com
email: samsforthehills@eircom.net

PJ McDermott
CONSTRUCTION LTD.

Building for the future
Putting Donegal on the map

BOHILLION, BURT, CO. DONEGAL
Tel: 074-9156055 Fax: 074-9156033
Email: pjmcdermott5@eircom.net

PROPERTY – DEVELOPER – CONTRACTOR – CIVIL ENGINEERING

Contents

A Word from the Authors

Dónal Campbell   Damian Dowds

I first saw Donegal play football as a youngster of eight or nine in the late 1970s. My uncle – Danny Dowds of Burt, a man who seldom missed a Donegal match – carted me all over Ulster and beyond in his pursuit of the boys in green and gold. Omagh and the slenderest of wins over Derry is the first match I remember with any clarity. Even as a wain I sensed the tension radiating around the ground. It was the championship of 1979, and with seconds remaining a Donegal player elected to boot the ball out over the heads of spectators to waste time. My eyes were wide open in amazement as I watched that ball sail out of the ground. As a time-wasting ploy it worked a treat, the whistle blasted moments later and Derry were beaten.

I was starstruck by Sandy Harper and Martin Carney (who we'd lost by 1979). Big Martin Griffin was a hero to me. Landmarks occurred in my life thanks to Donegal football. In 1982 Danny took his son Damian and myself to that year's under-21 championship. Wee McHugh was soon up there with Big Griffin in my book. We ended up in Carrick-on-Shannon on a rainy Sunday in October and celebrated our first All-Ireland title. Damian and I could rhyme the names of every player from one to 15 and the panel too at the drop of a hat. Several days later we manned a struggling bonfire along the Burt roadside and were awestruck to shake the hands of Donal Reid, Joyce McMullan, Sylvester Maguire, Marty Carlin and Sean Bonner. Michael Kelly, Donie McCole and Maurice Carr were there too as they carted the Tadhg Ó Cleirigh cup around the county. I still have a picture of

1

the boys and us somewhere.

And so it went. Little extracts and stills of games over the years. Highs, lows, joy and despair, but always entertainment. Countless hours of excitement. Val Daly's goal which churned the gut. PJ McGowan and the boys of 1987. Sunburn in Clones. Tyrone supporters! Hitching lifts outside the Regional in Letterkenny off Tom Conaghan and talking football all the way home. Watching Brian McEniff in action at County Board meetings.

On Sunday, September 20, 1992, Damian and I watched the All-Ireland together from high up in the old Cusack Stand. Only when the clock at the Canal End indicated two minutes remaining did we dare utter the words "we're going to win!" We bolted from our seats and cleared three and four steps at a time in the race to the lower deck. In the pandemonium we didn't get to see Bonner stroke over that last insurance point. By the time the whistle sounded I was already poised precariously on the perimeter wire and as it happened was early to reach McEniff. Mick Dunne of RTÉ was just about to interview the Donegal manager. I took a quick snapshot as McEniff uttered his initial thoughts as an All-Ireland winning manager. Suddenly, a wall of Donegal fans swept us up the field in a wave of joy. Such memories . . .

In time, we in Burt established ourselves as more than hurlers and I had the privilege of marking the likes of Matt, James McHugh and Barry McGowan. I got to tussle often with Martin Shovlin, Tommy Ryan and Declan Bonner. More often than not my admiration grew. Shovlin, who once took the disciplinary-heat off Naomh Ultan following a particularly heated football match by accusing us Burt men of producing hurleys, I came to greatly admire. Declan Bonner won more frees off me than anyone I know with his craftiness. Indeed, a couple of times he clipped me but I always clipped him back!

I always wanted to write a book about these boys. I mentioned it to Donal Reid years ago but between the two of us nothing ever came of it. It is such a story that it shouts to be told. This year the time was finally right for me to attempt the telling of it. And no better man to tell a story with than Damian Dowds! Many's the collaboration we've been involved in but this one leaves them all standing in terms of pure enjoyment.

It was a Gael's dream job. And the players – the boys who were there in 1992 – were the voice we choose to tell the inside story of a great footballing journey that began in 1980 and finally reached the summit 12 years later when Sam came to the Hills. As with all Donegal folk, we saw the players as superstars when they played and it was a privilege when they chatted football with us and shared precious memories.

Sometimes the story is raw in the telling, but then sometimes football is raw. Occasionally some of them choose to set the record straight 11-odd years down the road. Occasionally they glossed over football matters they deemed better left locked in a dressing-room somewhere in the last decade. Always, this was their prerogative. This is purely a story about football.

To all the boys who told their yarn and the three magnificent men – Tom Conaghan, PJ McGowan and Brian McEniff – who steered them to three glorious All-Irelands – thank you. Hopefully you will find that we have done your story justice.

Footballers of years gone by may wonder why we choose to write our book in the main from 1980 onwards, after all, there was football – and good football at that – played in Donegal long before 1980. True, but the reasoning was simple – 1980 marked the beginning of the road to Sam and it also marked the beginning of our own "living memory" of Donegal football. Perhaps someday, someone will see fit to devote the time and energy to put between the covers of a book the exploits of Donegal footballers from the first day a ball was kicked and right up to 1980 and beyond. Now that would be some book.

At the end of each chapter you will find the main scorelines pertaining to the games discussed within. Hopefully these will be of use to you in matching accounts of games with the bare facts.

To the many people who have contributed to this book we say thanks – hopefully we mentioned you in the acknowledgments. We are delighted to publish it in association with PJ McDermott Construction Limited. PJ has always been a good friend and a good Burt man and we wish him continued success.

A special thanks to my wife Darina Eades for her unstinting encouragement and support and to my folks back in Burt who are simply unbelievable as always. I know that Damian wants to thank his partner, Denise McLaughlin, and his family for all the support and help he received.

Finally, thanks to my co-author Damian Dowds who can only be described as a chip off the old block! – a mighty GAA man altogether. His commitment to *Sam's for the Hills* has been phenomenal. I already look forward to our next GAA project.

Dónal Campbell
October 12, 2003

Acknowledgments

Abook such as this brings one into contact with numerous people and it is the quality of that contact which determines the final product. Such was the number and quality of contributions to *Sam's for the Hills* that it is difficult to know where to begin saying thank you.

Needless to say this book would have been bereft of its depth had it not been for the willingness of every one of the squad of 1992 to talk to us in detail. Thanks to every single one of them and to Tom Conaghan, Brian McEniff and PJ McGowan. And thank you to other halves for the space to chat football and for the many, many cups of tea!

We are particularly grateful to Donna Quinn and the staff of the Central Library in Letterkenny for their courtesy and professional help in the long trawl through miles of microfilm. They were very helpful indeed and never failed to facilitate when an extra hour here and there was requested.

To our panel of experts – PJ Buggy of Ballyshannon, Danny Dowds of Burt and Feargal McGill of Dromod and Dublin (son and heir of the Follower) – who read the drafts and made many useful and incisive comments which we were more than happy to take on board. Thank you for your huge effort – our book is most certainly the better for your input. We are indebted to Rosaleen Campbell who took on and completed the huge task of checking the main statistics against sources. She also spent many hours on our behalf in front of the micro-film machine in Letterkenny.

On the topic of statistics – there is no way anyone could even attempt to publish a book on Donegal football without delving heavily and often into the statistical volumes of Fr Seán Gallagher. The man is a treasure to Donegal GAA. Thank you Fr Seán for your statistics.

We are much obliged to Pat McArt, Group Editor of the Derry Journal Group of Newspapers for permission to quote from the *Donegal Democrat*. Was there ever a better provincial newspaper the length and breadth of Ireland for Gaelic games coverage? Doubtful. The writing of Tine Sí, Gerry McDermott, Connie Duffy, Michael Daly, Peter Campbell, the Follower and others on the subject of Donegal football down the years is a precious record.

It was also hugely beneficial to trawl through the Gaelic games pages of the *Irish Independent, Irish Times, Sunday Independent, Sunday Tribune, Irish News* as well as the now sadly defunct *Irish Press* and *Sunday Press*. Thanks to all those writers, past and present, local and national, whose words on Donegal football we've dropped in here and there.

Thanks also to Packie Keeney who supplied a priceless tape of the All-Ireland with the commentary of *Highland Radio*, and to Charlie Collins for both that commentary and the permission to use it. Thanks also to Keith Dalton, a Kildare-Dub, for his cover design. Our gratitude to: Bill Breslin and all at WNS in Derry for their help and advice; Sally Blake, Letterkenny; editors of Donegal GAA Yearbooks down the years; Seamus Cashman, formerly of Wolfhound Press in Dublin, who continues to dispense wise words we always listen to; Seán Ó Ceallaigh, President of the GAA, for his foreword; North West Tourism for the photograph of Errigal; Ian Richardson of DBA Publications; and Derek Murphy for rerecording tapes. Thanks are also due to Brigid Conway, Brian Finnegan, Olive Murphy, Finin O Driscoll and Paul O'Brien for their help in transcribing interviews.

Our sub-editor hails all the way from Emyvale, Co Monaghan – Claire McGinn had a big job in the final couple of weeks and as always could be counted on when the going got tough. Thanks Claire and no, we didn't take your advice to put more stuff in about Monaghan! Ciaran Dowds from Burt deserves a special mention. Ciaran, a footballer and hurler of note, weighed in and helped out with interviews in fine style. Thanks also to Cormac Campbell for typing up those interviews, and Kathleen Bell, Irish News.

As mentioned in our introduction, this book would not have been possible without the generosity of PJ McDermott Construction Limited. PJ was quick to come on board and it is indeed an honour to publish this book in association with him. We wish him continued success in everything he does. PJ was a good hurler and Gaelic footballer himself down Burt way until an accident when a teenager halted his career. That didn't stop him hurling again in later years and becoming the undisputed king of yarns at the back of the bus! Move over Declan Bonner, we had our own legend in Burt and his name was PJ McDermott!

We are thankful to David Robinson and all at Brookfield Printing in Stillorgan who were a pleasure to work with from start to finish. And thanks also to Norman McCloskey of Inpho Photography on Baggot Street, Dublin, who made life very easy in the sourcing and supply of the vast majority of the photographs of the boys who brought Sam to the Hills.

Finally, a special word of gratitude once again to Darina and Denise and to our respective families in Burt who have had to put up with nothing but Donegal football for a very long time. It was and is much appreciated.

There is always the danger when compiling acknowledgments that someone will unintentionally be left out. Our apologies if that has indeed been the case and go raibh maith agat to everyone who helped in any way.

✻

A Message from the Sponsor
(PJ McDermott Construction Limited)

PJ McDermott

As a long-time supporter and participant of Gaelic games in Donegal, I am absolutely delighted to be associated with a publication that chronicles the meteoric rise and rise of Donegal football from 1980 onwards. A journey which brought the most famous piece of silverware in the country to the North West for the first time ever.

Dónal and Damian have called their book *Sam's for the Hills* and that phrase alone holds special memories for Donegal people. The book really does track – kick for kick – the story of those players who started that journey from scratch in 1980 and culminated some 12 years later in Anthony Molloy climbing the steps of the Hogan Stand to lift the Sam Maguire and uttering those immortal words.

What a day! I watched the game in a bar by the name of 'The Top Hat' in Ealing, London, and I will never forget the feeling of pride that swelled inside when it became apparent that this was it – this was the day that Donegal was going to join the footballing elite. As one of many Donegal people earning a living on a foreign soil I understood exactly what a difference that historic win made not only back in the Hills but in Britain, America, Australia and everywhere you find the Donegal diaspora.

Funnily, I remember a Dublin fella standing outside the bar when a group of us were going in. He was selling Dublin hats and scarves. When we were coming back out again he had discarded the Dublin stuff entirely and was now selling Donegal stuff! You could say that his business acumen inspired me because I struck out on my own shortly after that. Not, I hasten to add, selling hats and scarves!

PJ McDermott Construction Limited has been in operation for the best part of ten years now and during that period my business interests have brought me into frequent contact with several of the boys from 1992. I couldn't agree more with the authors when they say that the 1992 lads are a special bunch. Once they were the most celebrated footballers in the country – they are still the most celebrated footballers in the county – yet their collective feet remain very firmly on the ground. As I say, it is a great pleasure to be involved in a publication that salutes the achievements of a special team.

It is also with great pleasure that I extend my support of Gaelic games beyond club boundaries. I am currently Chairman of CLG Beart and have been involved – as much as time permits – for a number of years. The GAA is one of the most important organisations in the country in how it binds people together for life, be that in the pursuit of an under-12 divisional medal or the Celtic-cross of All-Ireland glory.

I would like to congratulate Dónal and Damian on a fabulous book. *Sam's for the Hills* should be on every bookshelf because it really is a special story. It makes for fascinating reading.

PJ McDermott

Teachtaireacht an Uachtaráin
(Sean Ó Ceallaigh)

Seán Ó Ceallaigh

Is mór an onóir domsa an deis seo a fháil cúpla focal a scríobh ar fhoilsiú an leabhair seo. It is indeed a great honour for me to be asked to pen a few lines on the publication of *"Sam's for the Hills"* which chronicles the historic breakthrough made by Donegal on winning their first All Ireland in 1992. In the 11 years since then, their Northern neighbours in Derry, Tyrone and Armagh have followed the example of Dún na nGall and created their own little bit of history by making the big breakthrough.

When Brian Mc Eniff began his love affair with Donegal and guided them to their first Ulster title in 1972, it marked the beginning of a 20-year personal crusade to place his native county at the pinnacle of Gaelic football. There were many disappointments and even tragedies along the way, but his determination and that of the many players, coaches, managers, officials and supporters of Donegal GAA ensured that the dream would one day become a reality.

The achievement of this Donegal team in winning the All Ireland has to be put in context to be fully appreciated. When they took to the field to face Dublin in the 1992 final, the weight of history was very much against them. No new name had been added to the list of All Ireland winners since Offaly in 1971 and indeed no team had triumphed on a first final appearance since Down in 1960. In fact it had only been a few weeks since Donegal had recorded their first ever victory in Croke Park.

That they would face one of the great traditional powers of Gaelic football and with a scintillating display plant the green and gold flag firmly at the peak of the county's very own Everest is a story in itself, but this particular story is about more than just those manic 70 minutes. It traces the struggle for success from the early 1980s through good days and bad; it follows the trials and tribulations of Donegal football between the county's first under-21 All-Ireland in 1982 and the ultimate glory of 1992. Most of all it is a tribute to the countless thousands of players and supporters who kept the dream alive in the preceding century when at times all hope seemed dead.

I hope you enjoy the read as we welcome yet another excellent addition to the ever growing library of Gaelic Games related publications.

Ráth Dé ar an obair,

Sean Ó Ceallaigh,
Uachtarán, CLG

Brian McEniff

Prologue

Barely 40 seconds had elapsed in the All-Ireland senior football final of 1992. Martin McHugh, the greatest Donegal footballer of his era, had just kicked a free that had drifted to the right and wide of the Dublin posts. As McHugh jogged back into position on the half-forward line, his marker, Keith Barr, seized the opportunity to indulge in a little psychological warfare with the Kilcar man. He suggested to McHugh that he hadn't got the balls to do it.

McHugh was a seasoned footballer of 11 championships and the remark rolled off him. The Donegal number 11 had been around the block a few times and had heard and seen everything football had to throw at him. McHugh retorted, "We'll see who has the balls at the end of the match."

Nonetheless, a fundamental question had been posed by the burly Dubliner. He might well have been posing the question on behalf of football followers everywhere, the county of Donegal included. Had McHugh, on football's greatest stage, got the balls? Had Donegal? Donegal were arguably Ulster's most consistent football team of the previous four years and eight of the starting 15 that day had All-Ireland under-21 medals in their pockets. Yet, over the years, they had never delivered on the hallowed sod of Croke Park – the home of the Dubs.

Most of the Donegal players had already experienced the misery of defeat at the penultimate stage in the All-Ireland series. Galway in 1983 was a painful memory for Anthony Molloy, Donal Reid, Joyce McMullan and McHugh. All but a handful of the others experienced the same pain seven years later when Meath ended the dream in 1990.

Now, on this, the third Sunday of September 1992, 70 minutes of football and 15 players from the capital city stood between this Donegal team and sporting immortality.

It had been a long road for McHugh. Was he to end his career like so many other great footballers of his ilk, never to receive the holy grail that is an All-Ireland medal? Or would he create history and secure his legend?

Many questions remained unanswered as Dublin goalkeeper John O'Leary blasted the ball towards midfield for the first time...

1

In The Beginning

(– 1980)

> "We knew before Ireland knew.
> We saw things Ireland never saw."
>
> FR SEÁN GALLAGHER

Neutrals in the crowd sat up and paid rapt attention. Those from Kilcar merely nodded in appreciation because they had known for a very long time. Ardara, if they hadn't already known, were finding out. For many in MacCumhaill Park on county final day 1980, it was the first time they had seen the youngster from Kilcar in action. He was here and there everywhere throughout the hour and his scintillating runs through the Ardara defence was a thing to behold. He kicked ten points in total that day and – with a magnificent Michael Carr – was instrumental in Kilcar claiming the county championship for the first time since 1925.

Donegal's foremost GAA historian, Fr Seán Gallagher, later wrote, "We knew before Ireland knew. We saw things Ireland never saw."

The name of this youngster exploding spectacularly onto the Donegal football scene on Sunday, August 31, 1980, was Martin McHugh. Aged 19, he had been a sub with the county minors but had never lined out in the green and gold of Donegal. That, however, was all about to change. At MacCumhaill Park that day was one Brian McEniff. McEniff duly noted McHugh's performance and when he became Donegal manager for the third time in his career the following month he resolved to bring young McHugh onto his panel. It would be the beginning of a partnership which would change the face of Donegal football and pay the ultimate dividend some 12 years later.

❉ ❉ ❉ ❉

In The Beginning

In September 1980 the name Brian McEniff was synonymous with Gaelic fooball in Donegal. Again the manager of his county – once an All-Star half-back – McEniff's reputation carried well beyond his native county. Owner of the Hollyrood Hotel in Bundoran – McEniff was a man who had done well for himself. People who had made a pound in the lean 1970s were few and far between but McEniff had carried it off and with panache. Even then, in the autumn of 1980, the word "aristocratic" could be applied to McEniff. Well educated and articulate, McEniff was a man who had made it and had still the ambition to build an empire for himself. Tanned and immaculately groomed, the soft spoken McEniff exuded success and caused heads to turn. Proverbial caps would be proverbially doffed in his direction by his peers on the terraces of MacCumhaill Park.

There was good reason why McEniff the football man was respected on the terraces. He had earned it. This was the man who had played school's football with Macartan's College in Monaghan, who had been an outstanding player on the legendary St Joseph's side that had dominated Donegal football like no other for a decade, who had been a Railway Cup player of distinction, a man who had won two Ulster medals with his county – both as player-manager, and was one of only two Donegal men to hold an All-Star award. In the minds of most, Brian McEniff was representative of a football culture that was a step or two above the norm.

❄ ❄ ❄ ❄

Hiúdaí Beag Gallagher, one of the legends of Donegal football, was in his heyday for club and county when Brian McEniff was born in February 1943. Growing up in Bundoran, McEniff had little chance to shine on the football field. It wasn't until he went to Macartan's College in Monaghan as a boarder in the late 1950s that McEniff the footballer was born. He played extensively with the prestigious school side and the experience shaped him as a player. It was in 1959 at the age of 16 that he pulled on the county jersey for the first time with the minors, and was there again in 1960 and 1961.

By the time the young McEniff made his senior debut in 1961, Donegal football had greatly underachieved. The GAA organisation in Donegal had been slow to gain a foothold and it was 1919 before it was properly organised in the county – some 35 years after the GAA had been founded. Ironically, it was Bundoran who won the county championship of 1919-20. Forty-two summers had come and gone since and there had been precious little cheer for the county. Reasonably good Donegal teams in the 1930s and 1940s had been swallowed up in Ulster by the likes of Cavan and Antrim. Cavan were the undisputed kings of Ulster. The blue and whites won All-Irelands in 1933 and 1935 – although they barely escaped from Bundoran in 1935 in the first round with a two-point win over a spirited Donegal side that included the aforementioned Hiúdaí Beag Gallagher. In a 15 year period between 1932 and 1946, Cavan dumped Donegal out of the Ulster Championship on no less than ten occasions. More often than not victory was achieved by a sizeable margin and on 13 of those years, Cavan won Ulster.

There was some success in the shape of three junior titles in Ulster in 1930, 1933 and 1939. An illustration of Donegal usefulness against the might of Ulster in that period was two back-to-back Dr Lagan Cup titles in 1936 and 1937. But when it came to the all important summer and the white heat of championship Donegal were found wanting year after year.

The 1950s too were lean for Donegal who never emerged from the long shadows cast by their Ulster neighbours. A brace of Ulster junior titles, an Ulster minor title and a solitary Dr Lagan Cup was all that came Donegal's way. They got a first ever run to Croke Park in 1952 for a national league semi-final but succumbed to Cork by five points. In the championship Down, Antrim, Tyrone, Cavan and Monaghan all enjoyed superiority over Donegal and between them ensured that no Donegal man experienced Ulster final day as a player. Six Ulster teams shared provincial honours in that decade – with only Donegal, Monaghan and Fermanagh failing to win Ulster. Worringly for Donegal, they had yet to contest an Ulster final. And this despite the presence of quality players. Hughie Tim Boyle, the Gweedore man, whose career straddled a decade either side of 1950 was there. So too were Jim Gallagher, Peadar McGeehan and Frank O'Donnell. All served with distinction but got nothing to show for their efforts. Perhaps fittingly, it was Cavan who closed the decade on Donegal's championship hopes with an 11-point hiding in Ballybofey.

A year later, they repeated the performance, this time in Cavan, and by ten points. It seemed that even the changing of the decade brought no relief from Cavan for a beleaguered Donegal. The championship of 1961 was lost to Derry in the first round. A few months later in that winter's league, 18-year-old Brian McEniff made his senior debut. Coincidentally or not, the timing of McEniff's arrival on the scene heralded a new era for Donegal football.

The 1960s did not prove to be ultimately successful for Donegal, indeed the team would fail to win Ulster. But for the first time, hope glimmered. Donegal assembled a team and an attitude that could compete with the best in Ulster. And, for the first time since 1919, they removed themselves from the bottom rungs of Ulster football.

Names that are still revered made the county jersey their own. Seamus Hoare, the legendary goalkeeper from Letterkenny. Bernard Brady, a full-back of renown, from Bundoran. PJ Flood from Pettigo. Sean Ferriter of Dunfanaghy. Sean O'Donnell of Dungloe. John Hannigan of Letterkenny who rarely had a bad game. Mickey McLoone from Ballyshannon. From these outstanding players and others modest success and great hope sprang. The Dr

In The Beginning

McKenna Cup victories of 1963 and 1965 signalled Donegal's new status in Ulster. In 1963 they demolished Cavan 2-8 to 0-5. This was the great Cavan team that had won Ulster in 1962 and would do so again in 1964. In those days the McKenna Cup was a prestigious title contested every bit as fiercely as the championship. Donegal had arrived on a new plateau. Success filtered through the grades. Two minor football leagues were captured in 1962 and 1963, the vocational schools took the Ulster championship in 1964 and 1965, and the under-21s won the inaugural Ulster title in 1963, retained it in 1964 and won it again in 1966.

Indeed it was Donegal who dethroned the Ulster champions in 1963. Having accounted for Fermanagh in the first round, Donegal inflicted a 4-5 to 0-6 defeat on the Breffni men. A small measure of revenge for the misery of the war years. The reward was a first ever Ulster final appearance. Down, the Ulster team of the decade and All-Ireland winners in 1960 and 1961, provided the opposition and seared through Donegal by 2-11 to 1-4. Nonetheless, despite the losing margin, an important landmark in Donegal football had been arrived at. The match had generated unprecedented hype around the county and attracted a huge crowd on an extremely hot day to Breffni Park. The minor team also lost their Ulster Final but introduced future senior stars Pauric McShea, Mickey McLoone and Declan O'Carroll.

For the first time Donegal supporters had got a taste of the big time and wanted more. Cavan, the only team to trade provincial honours with Down in the 1960s, proved a steadfast obstacle. In 1964 they avenged themselves on Donegal with a five-point victory in the semi-final. In 1965 the sides played out an epic first round struggle over three matches with Cavan finally emerging with a single point to spare in the third game. However, that same year a Dr Lagan Cup title was achieved for the first time since 1952.

✳ ✳ ✳ ✳

It was an exciting new era for the game in Donegal and a good time to be a county player. One potential player who missed out was Brian McEniff. The Bundoran man's sojourn in the county jersey had been short. Having staked his claim for a place in the winter of 1961, McEniff made the decision to emigrate to Canada in early 1962 to pursue an apprenticeship in hotel management. He was to spend the best part of four years on the other side of the Atlantic, based in Toronto. Football remained a passion for the youngster and he accumulated an unusual collection of North American and National Football League medals. He won a national league medal with New York in 1964 against Dublin. "I have the unique honour of being a Donegal man with a national league medal," he remarked in 1980. It is an honour that remains solely his to this day. He also won five Toronto championship medals with Clan na Gael – three for football and two for hurling.

McEniff played his New York football with Cavan. "It was great to be flown down and come back up again – it was exciting." Heady times for a young man who had known only a handful of dreary winter games for his native county. He also played for a Toronto team which competed in the Mid-West League. McEniff found himself in cities like Cleveland, Chicago, Buffalo, Detroit and Montreal. It was glamourous in a way he had never imagined Gaelic football could be.

In late 1965, McEniff came home. He found that things had changed utterly since his departure. Donegal now had a football team that ranked perhaps third in Ulster. A degree of success had been achieved in his absence and a very established team had emerged. It wasn't going to be easy to reclaim his county jersey. "I made my way back on to the county team through the junior team," he later said.

In 1966 the senior team were back in their second Ulster final. Having defeated Cavan and Fermanagh, Down accounted for their aspirations with two points the margin in Belfast. The team was rightly labelled unlucky but had again dragged Donegal football to new heights. McEniff had fought his way back onto the team for the Fermanagh match, lost out against Cavan, and was a substitute in the final against Down.

The Dr Lagan Cup had been retained the previous March in Dungannon when, ironically, Donegal had accounted for Down by 1-10 to 1-3. A year later this great Donegal side completed a remarkable trio of successive Lagan Cup titles when beating Derry by a single point in Irvinestown. In 1967, they brought their Dr McKenna Cup tally to three.

McEniff wasn't playing in the national league semi-final against Galway in 1967 – a match that entered Donegal footballing folklore. It was the day of the Neilly Gallagher penalty incident. Donegal were three points up and coasting with five minutes left before half time. Des Houlihan put the ball in the Galway net but the referee – Eamonn Moules of Wicklow – called back play and awarded a penalty. As Neilly Gallagher stepped up to hit the ball the wind blew it off the spot. It was replaced by the referee but as Gallagher ran up a second time it was once again blown off the spot. Gallagher retrived the ball and put it back. To the utter disbelief of everyone present the referee awarded a free out. Galway went straight up the field and scored a point – 2-1 to 0-5 instead of 3-1 to 0-4. The Connacht men went on to win by three points. Heartache for Donegal and the mother of all hard-luck stories.

When Donegal ran on to the field against Down in the 1967 Ulster semi-final McEniff was not on the starting 15, although he was a member of the panel. Donegal were beaten and McEniff decided to opt out of the county scene. It seemed an inglorious end to a career which had shown much promise but had yet to ignite while wearing a county jersey. McEniff's undoubted footballing prowess was there to be seen with the great St Joseph's side that had already begun their domination of Donegal football. McEniff had returned to Ireland in time for the replayed county final of 1965 when St Joseph's won their first county title. It was the first of seven county titles he would win with the legendary Ballyshannon/Bundoran side. Speaking extensively to Fr Seán Gallagher in 1981, McEniff said:

> Joseph's were a most amazing side with very little coaching, very little training but with natural footballing ability. They knew each other's play. They were a group of lads that came up through De La Salle in Ballyshannon (I was an outsider because I went to school in Monaghan) ... we had a great understanding – McLoone, Granaghan, McShea, Peter Quinn, Thomas Quinn. They were a marvellous side to play with.

McEniff contended in 1981 that St Joseph's were the most balanced club side he had ever seen, "a uniquely good side." Many agree. McEniff, at right-half back on the team, was an accomplished and stylish defender. St Joseph's won their first Ulster Club Championship in 1966, without having been crowned Donegal champions because of a fierce row with MacCumhaills over venue and timing. Unperturbed as controversy raged in Donegal, they went on to defeat Dunmore McHales of Galway in the final to become the first, but unofficial, All-Ireland club champions. Because of the example provided by teams like St Jospeh's, an All-Ireland club championship was sanctioned at the GAA Congress of 1970 and first contested in 1971. McEniff captained St Joseph's to victory in Donegal in 1968 and again in 1976 – the last championship this great side claimed before it broke up.

❄ ❄ ❄ ❄

In 1967, when he called it a day with the county, McEniff still had some interest in playing soccer. Sligo Rovers and Celtic were two teams he followed as a youngster. He had little time to indulge himself in soccer however. One day, at the tail-end of 1967, Donegal were short when playing Sligo. Hugh Daly, the long-time secretary of the County Board, put in a call to McEniff. The Bundoran man duly obliged the Ballyshannon man. After a retirement that lasted a few short months, McEniff was back on the county scene.

He made his championship return against Down in the Ulster semi-final of 1968. It was another unsuccessful outing against the Mourne men who went on to win Ulster and add to their All-Ireland successes of 1960 and 1961. Donegal lost three successive first round matches: in 1969 and 1970 to Antrim and to Down in 1971. The big names that McEniff had found on the Donegal team on his return from Toronto had now been joined by the likes of Pauric McShea, Anton Carroll, Declan O'Carroll, Neilly Gallagher and Seamie Granaghan. McEniff himself was a fine player at his peak. The years of playing tough football in New York had stood to him and he came back the better for it. Yet Donegal had not delivered on their promise. Indeed, if anything, the team seemed to have stalled after peaking in the mid-1960s. Several of the players, including McEniff, thought maybe the key lay in getting a manager from outside the county. As it happened, the man who would unlock Donegal's potential was within their ranks.

Three years earlier, the Donegal minor team of 1969 had attracted scant interest from potential managers within the county. McEniff – hotelier, club star, county man and workaholic – took up the challenge. "I said I would have a go at it," he recalled. "I never had any experience of it except managing a team in Toronto." McEniff spent two years with the minors, working with the likes of Martin Carney and Kieran Keeney. His teams did not experience Ulster success but McEniff had cut his managerial teeth at inter-county level.

Now in 1971, with the seniors yet again out of the championship at the first hurdle, things were becoming desperate. The point of no return was reached a fortnight before Christmas in Carrick-on-Shannon. Leitrim had inflicted a nine-point defeat on Donegal. The players called a meeting. McEniff recalls:

> We decided we would go as players together to County Convention and that we would put forward proposals to them that we would want an outside man to take an interest in the team.

In 1971 this would have been seen as radical. It was an era long before expenses and mercenary management. McEniff, whose profile was high thanks to his club, county and Railway Cup exploits, talked to Mick Higgins of Cavan to inquire if he would be interested in the Donegal post. Higgins declined but indicated he was prepared to offer assistance. St Joseph's duly proposed McEniff and when Austin Coughlan – his only competitor for the position – withdrew, McEniff at the age of 28 found himself holding the managerial reins of his county.

Mick Higgins, Columba McDyer and Austin Coughlan made up McEniff's team of selectors. With the championship of 1972 looming ahead, theirs was an onerous task. For McEniff however, the glass was definitely half full. As far as he was concerned, it was all down to application. "I knew we had the players but we hadn't got the commitment up to then." McEniff rightly believed that he had the team in 1972 to turn the corner. His encyclopaedic football knowledge was even then to the fore. He understood why the famed men of the mid-1960s had failed. "We had a better quality player in 1966 but again we hadn't the total commitment to win from all the players." McEniff was onto something. It was a truth that was also dawning in football brains in Dublin and Kerry.

McEniff set about changing the Donegal ethos. He led by example. Even then, at the relatively young age of 28, no one could question his utter commitment to Donegal football. The players responded. Just six months after the misery of Carrick-on-Shannon, McEniff the player-manager led his team to a first ever Ulster football championship title. As an achievement by a football manager anywhere it has seldom been equalled.

Ulster champions Down came to Ballybofey and were dispatched in the first round, 1-8 to 0-8. It took a second match to shake off Cavan – they eventually went down by five points in Clones. Tyrone awaited in the final but this time Donegal were destined for the top rung in Ulster. The scoreline read 2-13 to 1-11. "Unbelievable" stated McEniff with good reason. His place in Donegal football folklore was assured. He had turned this team of talented but unfulfilling footballers into Donegal's biggest ever achievers. Not only had he orchestrated their campaign but he had also played a huge role on the field of play from his berth at right half back. A few months later his exploits were recognised nationally when he landed the county's first ever All-Star award. Not even the harshest critics begrudged this recognition.

McEniff had tapped the potential that had been there all along. It was no mean feat. He had succeeded in cajoling a new approach from a formidable bunch of his inter-county peers. Men who had been there before him, who might have considered themselves at least equals on the field of play – Railway Cup stars, the cream of Donegal football. Men he had played with as an ordinary player. Not everyone could have pulled that trick off, but McEniff did:

> For 1972 there was a great commitment from the players. There was no outstandingly good player among the 1972 team in comparison to the mid-1960's team. There was a great commitment and a great feeling of being a Donegal man instead of being a St Joseph's man or a Gweedore man or a Letterkenny man. This is what I tried to instil into the team. We were as one.

It was an extraordinary achievement. Donegal met Offaly in the All-Ireland semi-final. It was a first journey into the promised land for McEniff. He failed by just four points against an Offaly team defending their All-Ireland crown – 2-10 to 1-17 was the final score. Consolation of sorts was gleaned some weeks later when Offaly won their second All-Ireland.

McEniff's Donegal repeated their Ulster success in 1974. By the time the first outing against defending Ulster champions Tyrone came around that summer a few big names had gone. Midfielder Frankie McFeely and forwards Declan O'Carroll and Mickey McMenamin were no longer available to McEniff. He responded with a new panel of players and steered them past Tyrone, Antrim and, at the second asking, Down. If anything it was possibly an even more significant managerial achievement than 1972 as it had been achieved with what McEniff acknowledged was "not as good a set of players".

McEniff's second Croke Park experience at the helm of his county was disappointing. Donegal lost a match they might have expected to win. By McEniff's own admission they were beaten by a poor Galway team and he felt that they should have made it to the All-Ireland that year. The great Dublin side which would gain fame as Heffo's Heroes awaited Galway and a date with their own destiny. Could Donegal have lived with the Dublin of Doherty, Mullins, Hanahoe, Hickey, Doyle and Keaveney had they steered a course past Galway? How would Dublin have dealt with the Donegal of Monaghan, McShea, McEniff, Ward, Bonner and a speedy little forward by the name of Carney?

McEniff never did find out if he could guide his county to compete with that Dublin team who, with Kerry, made the 1970s their own. He lost the Donegal job in early 1975. He maintains that his ousting had its origins in New York. McEniff's New York connections stretched back many years when he frequently flew there from Toronto to play for the Cavan side in the early 1960s. When a Donegal team was organised in the Big Apple in the mid-1960s, it seemed natural that McEniff would be an automatic choice, even after he had returned home to Ireland. "I was playing very good football during that period," he recalled, "and I was never asked out to play for Donegal. I felt a little aggrieved."

The offer did come eventually but by that time things had soured a little. McEniff didn't avail of the offer. From 1971 to 1974, at the behest of the legendary John Kerry O'Donnell, McEniff made the 6,000 mile round trip to line out in the green and gold of Kerry. As luck would have it McEniff never had to pit himself against his native county, a slice of good fortune of which he was glad. That was to change in 1974.

Even before the Ulster final, McEniff had bargained a trip to New York for Donegal if they won Ulster from John Kerry O'Donnell. O'Donnell duly obliged his Donegal friend who had served his Kerry team so well and McEniff's newly crowned Ulster champions were feted in the Big Apple. Things went wrong for McEniff before that trip ended. Seeds were sown that would eventually cost him his job. He says:

> Typical of O'Donnell he saw a great opening to play the Donegal team against a New York team but also the same Sunday to put on the New York championship final between Donegal and Kerry. And I was playing with Kerry that day against Donegal. It led to an awful lot of contention – I had a very good game that same day. I think it spilled over back home. I would say that was one of the reasons I lost my job as manager at the 1975 Convention.

The man who had delivered two Ulster titles in the space of three years was gone. John Hannigan, a Donegal legend himself, beat McEniff in the vote at

Convention. McEniff was not bitter towards Hannigan, that was football. He had much cause to be miffed at the Donegal football fraternity who had voted him out of a job. "At the time I was sore but the soreness would have passed possibly after the first game."

Many would have considered hanging up their county jersey. Not McEniff, he was there again in 1975 when Donegal surrendered their Ulster title at the first calling. Cavan came to Ballybofey and emerged with two points to spare. McEniff was at full-forward and making his final championship appearance for Donegal. It was also the beginning of a slide in the fortunes of Donegal football. The rest of the 1970s were divided between Derry, Armagh, Down and Monaghan. Donegal exited from the championship at the first hurdle every year except 1979 when Seán O'Donnell led them to an Ulster final against Monaghan where they lost 0-11 to 1-15. A McKenna Cup was all that came their way in that period.

Significantly, McEniff had taken the reins of Donegal very briefly between the end of John Hannigan's tenure as boss and the appointment of Seán O'Donnell. It says something for McEniff's personality that he was prepared to place himself in the firing line again for the job that had been taken from him a few years earlier. Donegal football apparently came ahead of ego for McEniff.

McEniff had garnered much from his exploits in kicking a ball on two continents. The All-Star award in 1972 was one of four times he travelled abroad with the All-Stars. He travelled around the world with the New York team in 1975. He won two Railway Cup medals with Ulster, playing in 1970 and 1971 and was captain in 1973. He won four Ulster Club Championships (one, in 1975, was official) and one unofficial All-Ireland Club title in 1968. When the legendary St Joseph's team broke up in 1977 and Bundoran decided to break away from Ballyshannon, McEniff was disappointed to see the end of possibly Donegal's greatest ever club side. However, in typical McEniff style, he bounced back and won an incredible eighth Donegal senior championship medal with Bundoran in 1979. The high profile he enjoyed in the county was a result of his status as a footballer. He had even been tempted to dabble in politics and became a county councillor. His flirtation with politics was short lived however and he revealed that he had no political ambition. His ambition was limited to football and Donegal.

❊ ❊ ❊ ❊

In May 1980 at Irvinestown, Donegal fell to Tyrone in the first round of the Ulster Championship. The final score was 0-9 to 1-17 but had Tyrone capitalised in front of goal the margin of victory would have been much greater. The *Donegal Democrat* was frank in its assessment, "They were outclassed, it was like putting Shanks mare against Monksfield in his prime." Only Jim Brennan and Sandy Harpur emerged with their reputations intact for Donegal. No-one yet knew it but sadly it was the last time Sandy Harpur would play championship football for Donegal. The immensely popular Castlefin man would die tragically on February 12, 1981, as the result of injuries sustained in a car accident a few days earlier.

Martin McHugh was only getting to know Harpur and was as shocked as anyone:

> He was a tremendous footballer and a lovely fella. I used to go to games with my uncles or my parents and I would have looked up to Sandy Harpur. It was great to have played with him.

It (1980) was a terrible year for Donegal. The championship exit only reflected league and McKenna Cup form. The conclusion was inescapable – Donegal were back at the bottom of the rung in Ulster. Pundits within and outside the county accepted that there was potential. A seminar was held in Glenties in August when football men gathered to discuss the problems the game faced in Donegal. Lack of fitness of players, the influence of soccer and general apathy were mused upon. One delegate said that the standard of football suffered in the county because Donegal had never made the big breakthrough at inter-county level. Yet the team that lost to Tyrone eight weeks earlier included players of the calibre of Martin Griffin, Brendan Dunleavy, Michael Lafferty, Michael Carr, Finian Ward, Seamus Bonner and Sandy Harpur. A man was clearly needed who could unlock the potential.

Seán O'Donnell, in the hot seat since 1977, had stood down. His was the job that Brian McEniff got in September 1980.

❄

2
The Bottom Rung
(1980 – 1982)

"Nice boys do not win football matches."

DONEGAL DEMOCRAT

By the time Brian McEniff faced into the first championship of his third tenure at the helm in Donegal, he was fully aware of the mountainous task he faced in transforming the fortunes of the county. He had, after all, endured the National Football League over the bleak winter months.

Division Three of the national league was not Gaelic football at its most glamourous. Neither was Donegal Gaelic football's most glamourous team. Seven league games were contested over the winter of 1980 and the spring of 1981. The outcome flattered to deceive – three wins, two draws and two defeats. The quality of opposition was questionable – Tipperary, Louth, Fermanagh, Cavan, Wexford, Sligo and Clare. Even by Christmas promotion seemed unlikely. A two-point defeat by lowly Sligo in the muck of Ballymote in the penultimate game two months later confirmed that promotion to Division Two was beyond Donegal's grasp. Third place in the league table behind promoted Fermanagh and Cavan resulted. The *Donegal Democrat* wasn't so sure if that wasn't a bad thing anyway and pondered on the team's ability to stay put in Division Two if ever that summit was reached. Donegal's lethargic performances betrayed their ability to lift their game beyond the norm.

McEniff's eyes were wide open. He knew the problems and he knew the players. He had even been involved as coach with Sean O'Donnell the previous summer. His first selection as manager was the team that faced Tipperary in the national league in Ballyshannon. It showed five changes from the championship defeat to Tyrone earlier in May with debutant Martin McHugh having an impressive hour in Fr Tierney Park. Starting his career at right-half forward, McHugh's most vivid memory is of the bespectacled Tipperary full back but it was a gentle enough introduction as Donegal won by 1-15 to 0-5.

McEniff had little time to investigate new talent between his appointment as manager and the onset of the league. He had inherited the core of a team from the tail end of the 1970s. On paper and in reality he had formidable talent already there in the guise of Noel McCole, Big Martin Griffin, Brendan Dunleavy, Michael Lafferty, Michael Carr, Seamus Bonner, Finian Ward, Sandy Harpur and Kieran Keeney. All quality players. But with nothing to show for their efforts. What McEniff needed was fresh blood.

The McHugh lad from Kilcar was a big find. In fairness his club displays with Kilcar had been a unique form of self-selection. McEniff had a look at some potential players at a trial in Ballybofey in mid-September. Anthony Molloy from Ardara, a big strapping county minor and under-21 was promising. Indeed McEniff was aware of a bunch of promising 1980 county minor players that included Molloy, Tommy McDermott, Sylvester Maguire, Paul Carr, Joyce McMullan, Matt Gallagher, Sean Bonner and Brian Tuohy. Many believed that the minors could have won that year's Ulster championship – they had crashed out to Derry in the semi-final. Most onlookers agreed that it was the best Donegal minor team in many years. It augured well for an under-21 side a few years down the road and possibly even the senior side by the mid-1980s. However, McEniff did not have that kind of time at his disposal and for now the minors were too young for the man's game required to extricate Donegal from the mire of Division Three.

❊ ❊ ❊ ❊

Perhaps mindful of his previous experiences at the hands of county delegates, McEniff had been cagey at the County Board meeting at the beginning of September 1980 when pressure descended on him to take the manager's job. Three names, including his, had been nominated for the post. PJ McGowan and Francie Cunningham had withdrawn and the delegates in Ballybofey pushed back their chairs expectantly to hear McEniff's acceptance speech. McEniff put the ball back in their court. He had family commitments and he'd like to hear what they had to say before he decided – one way or the other.

It was a clever ploy by McEniff, one worthy of a shrewd businessman. He wrong-footed the entire floor. A lengthy debate ensued and the delegates themselves exposed the fact that any manager taking the Donegal job was starting from absolute scratch. The outgoing manager, Sean O'Donnell, assured the meeting that "availability of playing talent" was the problem. Lack of discipline was mentioned by an outgoing selector. Too much input from selectors was discussed at length. The attitude of players came under scrutiny.

Sean Boyle, the County Board PRO, got stuck into the players in a colourful outburst:

I have seen players training and there are 12 and 14 year-old girls in athletic clubs in this county who do more training than our players do for important games. There are players [I] had seen coming off with smiles on their faces after being defeated and their interest was in seeing what travelling expenses they would get. Even if it meant putting out a third class team, [we] should leave players off if they were not pulling their weight.

It was clear that expectations were not high among the delegates. Yes, they expected a change in approach and would require progress but, essentially, the tone of the meeting lessened the pressure on an incoming manager. If, by the delegates' own admission, Donegal football was at such a low ebb, then any incoming manager would require time and patience to address the problems. McEniff's tactic had paved the way for a management brief that would allow precious time to build a new Donegal team from scratch. An uninterrupted three-year term which would allow him build and experiment had just been bought for him by the delegates themselves.

There was some exasperation too. At one point an irritated Michael Gillespie, the County Board chairman, asked McEniff – "Do you want these people to force you?" One delegate reminded McEniff that if he was not able to give the required time to the position then they would have to look outside the county for an alternative.

In the end it was even agreed by the delegates that the incoming county manager could pick his own advisers. What did McEniff think of that, wondered Michael Gillespie? McEniff was favourable. So, was he withdrawing his name or not? McEniff kept delegates waiting for a further ten minutes while he consulted. He received loud applause when he eventually confirmed that he would take the post.

❋ ❋ ❋ ❋

McEniff's big problem as the 1981 Ulster Championship loomed was the lack of quality competitive matches. Donegal needed to be tested by Division Two teams – it was the only way to advance. McEniff recognised that promotion to Division Two was of paramount importance if Donegal was to compete seriously in Ulster and become a football force beyond the province. That opportunity had been missed for another year but McEniff was happy that some progress had been made. Already his team was playing attractive football and the high-speed short-passing game that was to become a trademark of Donegal sides under McEniff was evident. And, slowly but surely, he was introducing competent new faces into the starting 15. Letterkenny's Eunan McIntyre had been a revelation in the closing stages of the league and McEniff's old number five shirt seemed in good hands.

Gary Walsh

Donegal got an opportunity to test themselves against Down in the McKenna Cup some eight weeks before their opener against Armagh in the championship. They lost by five points in Newry but consolation could be gleaned from the fact that it was their best performance in some time and against a good Down team that would go on to win Ulster in 1981.

The Athletic Grounds in Armagh proved to be the graveyard of 1981's championship aspirations. A score of 0-13 to 2-15 was in favour of an Armagh team that included aging legends Joe Kernan and Jimmy Smyth. Same old story, the scoreboard indicated. An eight-point margin in the defeat – only three less than against Tyrone the previous year. But there was room for optimism. Even in difficult times the county had recognised a glimmer of hope. The core number of players from great Donegal team of the 1960s eventually went on to win Ulster in 1972 and 1974. This Donegal team wasn't remotely in that league, but knowledgeable onlookers did recognise definite potential as Donegal stretched the defending Ulster champions much more than the final scoreline suggested. Mix-ups in the Donegal defence, a brace of excellent saves from McAlinden in the Armagh goal and an uncharacteristic goal miss by Seamus Bonner all contributed to defeat. Individually there were several above average performances in Donegal sectors of the park but this was a team that hadn't yet gelled as a unit.

McEniff always knew he couldn't turn things around in nine months. He was still team-building and it was going to take time. Realistically his team weren't expected to defeat the reigning champions, they would crawl before they would walk. They had caused Armagh problems and Joe Kernan and Jimmy Smyth were both substituted before the game ended. And two of his championship debutantes, Martin McHugh and a bustling figure by the name of Charlie Mulgrew from Letterkenny had shone.

Charlie Mulgrew had discovered his selection for the game in the pages of *The Irish Press*.

I found out I was on the team by looking in *The Irish Press* on the Wednesday before the match. I didn't think I was going to be near the team. Friends of mine were at Thomond College and I went down to see them. I saw the paper in the canteen and my name was at left-half back. I had to hightail it back to Donegal.

❄ ❄ ❄ ❄

The National Football League of 1981-82 opened as badly as it possibly could have for Donegal. Having defeated Tipperary by ten points in the corresponding game 12 months earlier, Donegal lost 0-10 to 1-10. Already, in early October, promotion hopes had taken a dent. They got back on track with a shaky but comprehensive home win over Louth with Mulgrew enjoying an outstanding hour.

Sam's for the Hills

A narrow defeat followed at the hands of Antrim – a game that was notable on two accounts. It was the day that the Ulster footballing press sat up and noticed Martin McHugh. His magnificent kicking astounded not only the scribes in the press box but also the Antrim supporters who rewarded him with sustained applause as he single handedly attempted to kick their team out of contention. And McEniff made his mark that day too – signalling that he would be giving youth their chance by finishing the game with no less than eight under-21s: Eunan McIntyre from Letterkenny, Brian Tuohy and Tommy McDermott from Ballyshannon, Martin McHugh, Charlie Mulgrew, Joyce McMullan and Paul Carr from Donegal Town and Pat McCrea from Pettigo. Not everyone was impressed. The *Donegal Democrat* reported, "Donegal must surely have hope for the future at inter-county level but little hope for the immediate future." The same writer intimated that Donegal might expect senior success around 1984 when the young talent had matured.

Wins over Laois and Westmeath saw Donegal safely to the Christmas break with promotion a distinct possibility. Victory in their remaining matches away to Wicklow and Wexford would assure them of a place in Division Two. Matt Gallagher, a county minor and under-21 player from Ballintra, was now also on board. McEniff gave him a league debut against Laois and he retained his corner back berth against Westmeath. Gallagher had played his under-age football with Ballyshannon and was a product of De La Salle in the town with an array of national and Ulster titles to show for it. A long and illustrious career stretched ahead of him.

At County Board level, McEniff had a strong ally in Bart Whelan, the county secretary. Whelan took the opportunity to back McEniff to the hilt at the County Convention in Milford in the New Year:

> Last year I asked all clubs to be patient and give our team manager Brian McEniff a chance to build his team as he saw fit, and I know that clubs feel he is going in the right direction. With a very young side he is proving that the future is assured and while we are in with a chance of promotion to Division Two of the national league it is not our most urgent need. With a little time his present panel should be a strong force in the 1983 senior championship.

Prophetic words from the Ardara man. The County Board was also struggling to budget for the long journeys and overnight stays which Division Three was presenting. It was going to cost an extra £20,000 per year if people wanted to see Donegal in Croke Park, warned chairman, Michael Gillespie. He added that if the dedication was right, "our target of an All-Ireland in 1984 or shortly after will be achieved." Brian McEniff was not there in person to acknowledge prophecies nor problems. He had lined up one of many challenge games against league champions Galway in Ballyshannon. Training had been stepped up to two nights per week as the bid for promotion gathered pace. McEniff had succeeded in generating commitment to training from old and new players – something not always to the fore in years past.

It all fell apart in Wexford. Only a point separated the sides but that point banished Donegal to Division Three for another year. It was a very physical encounter and Donegal's seven players under the age of 21 could not cope. "Small boys," remarked the *Democrat's* man, "who were taught a lesson in the basic requirements of the Gaelic game by the first-timing hard-hitting Loch Garman outfit." McHugh, who had a fine game, was hit hard at the earliest opportunity. Martin Griffin avenged this and made himself known to several other Yellowbellies. "The man who hit me was carried off," recalled McHugh. "Nobody knew who hit him. We went for a pint after the match and I asked Griffin about it. 'Jeez Marty,' he said, 'whatever way my hand came back I must have connected.'"

McEniff was incensed at the dirt in Wexford's play. That game also reconfirmed something he had publicly stated as far back as July 1981. McEniff said that the game in Donegal had to become more physical. Leaving no stone unturned, he later addressed the Donegal referees board in a bid to change their attitude to what constituted a foul. McEniff wanted the Donegal game to fall into line with the tougher brand of football that was commonplace in the southern half of the country. He had hit on another truth. If Donegal were ever to clamber out of Division Three they would have to discover a new ruthlessness. Their game lacked aggressiveness, collectively and individually.

McEniff himself would claim to be a ruthless individual when it came to football. Commenting on his perceived ruthlessness to Fr Seán Gallagher in 1981, McEniff advanced the theory, "it is a part of me that made me successful as a player and possibly a businessman." He added:

> I'll go out and try to win it no matter what I have to do to win it. If I can play at a venue that would suit us better than someone else, if I can get a referee that might suit us better than someone else, if I can do anything at all to upset a player on the other side by talking to him or by annoying him I'd do that or advise a player to do that. But when it's over it's over.

As McEniff acknowledged himself, there was no maliciousness in his actions. He merely needed to win. It was a trait he badly needed to pass onto his young and indeed old charges. "Nice boys do not win football matches," agreed the *Democrat*, ahead of the last league game away to Wicklow. Donegal could not fashion a win there either but as the *Democrat* reported, "It was a brave showing, meriting a far better return" by a team weighed in favour of under-21 players. And Martin McHugh, with 0-32 accumulated over that league campaign, was the top scorer in the country.

Sam's for the Hills

✻ ✻ ✻ ✻

Another summer lay in wait for McEniff's boys. Another hard luck story, albeit a genuine one. Armagh came to Ballybofey in May and at the end of a pulsating encounter during which the teams were level on eight occasions, a point in the last minute of normal time by corner forward Mickey McDonald put Armagh through.

Armagh would go on to clinch Ulster but were relieved men leaving MacCumhaill Park with a win under their belts. Donegal had actually led by two points with seven minutes to go. It was as much as McEniff could have expected from his young team – he had again fielded seven under-21 players. They had displayed spirit and tenacity. And they had developed a never say die attitude. Several times Armagh could have skipped away, Donegal never let the margin go beyond two points. It was another tentative yet reassuring step forward.

And they'd attracted a huge crowd to sundrenched Ballybofey. This was a team that carried an aura of possibility and Donegal folk came out to see – a new departure as support had plummeted after the glory days of early 1970s.

McEniff, agreed the pundits, was on the right track. His team would be a handful for anyone in Ulster this time next year. All applauded his team-building efforts and McEniff publicly appealed for patience. The public and the Donegal football fraternity made the right noises in response but no-one – absolutely *no-one* – knew better than McEniff just how fickle that support could be. He knew as he planned for another league campaign and looked ahead 12 months to his third Ulster championship at the helm that the pressure of expectation would soon begin to descend upon him. He had another year to deliver, he could count on that but no more. He had taken Donegal off the bottom rung but unless they were seen to achieve in 1983, McEniff's own future as manager would be very much at stake.

✼

National League 1980-81	National League 1981-82
Donegal 1-15, Tipperary 0-5	Donegal 0-10, Tipperary 1-10
Donegal 1-5, Louth 1-5	Donegal 1-12, Louth 1-5
Donegal 0-4, Fermanagh 0-4	Donegal 0-11, Antrim 2-9
Donegal 1-7, Cavan 1-8	Donegal 0-10, Laois 2-3
Donegal 1-9, Wexford 1-4	Donegal 0-16, Westmeath 0-8
Donegal 0-8, Sligo 0-10	Donegal 1-6, Wexford 0-10
Donegal 0-9, Clare 0-4	Donegal 0-7, Wicklow 1-7
Ulster Championship 1981	**Ulster Championship 1982**
Donegal 0-13, Armagh 2-15	Donegal 0-13, Armagh 1-11

RESULTS

3
Conaghan's Boys of '82
(1982)

"We've Won It! We've Won It! We've Won It!."

Fr Seán Gallagher

Tom Conaghan played a bit of football in his time with Four Masters, trading in those days as Clan na Gael – an amalgamation of Four Masters and St Nauls. Played with the likes of Donal Monaghan, the county man who, in 1974, became Donegal's second All-Star. Seven years later and Monaghan had an unfulfilled ambition – he yearned a first Donegal senior championship medal. That seemed unlikely as the 1970s slipped into the 1980s and the legs that once carried him as the best right full back in the land began slowing down. Four Masters were going nowhere.

By the summer of 1981 Tom Conaghan had long since hung up his boots. His ambitions had never been met as a player. He'd pulled on a county jersey as a minor but injury curtailed his prospects. His days as a senior with Four Masters were nothing out of the ordinary and he'd pulled the plug on his playing career in the early 1970s. Yet in 1981, out of the blue, he had taken on the job of Four Masters manager and astounded Donegal Town by guiding his team all the way to the county final. Although defeat followed at the hands of Ardara, it brought the majestic Donal Monaghan one step closer to his dream and showcased an elegant Joyce McMullan on Donegal's biggest stage. For a first foray into management it was pretty impressive. Tom Conaghan remembers it well:

I had a good record in athletics and was approached about the Four Masters job towards the end of 1980. We stayed in Division One in my first year involved and I wondered how I could improve as a manager. I approached Mick O'Dwyer and asked him to our dinner dance that year. He took the players the day after the dinner dance, put them through their paces and told them what they should expect.

31

Conaghan's Boys of '82

One summer later and Conaghan delivered Donal Monaghan that precious county medal and incredibly led a bunch of Donegal under-21 players to the promised land of an All-Ireland title.

❋ ❋ ❋ ❋

A buzz existed in football circles regarding the abundance of under-age talent in Donegal at the beginning of the 1980s. Signs were that these youngsters could compete with the best. In the late 1970s Jackie McDermott took charge of the first ever Donegal under-16 team. The side beat their Dublin counterparts in a curtain raiser to a national league game and many of the squad graduated to the minor and under-21 teams in due course. By 1980 the Donegal vocational schools side were contesting their fourth Ulster final in succession. The county minor teams of 1980 and 1981 both underachieved but between them had promising talent – Anthony Molloy, Tommy McDermott, Brian Tuohy, Matt Gallagher, Sean Bonner, Joyce McMullan, Paul Carr, Brian Murray, Declan Bonner and Sylvester Maguire all featured.

Donegal was very fortunate around this time to have one of the most progressive minor boards in Ulster. Headed by Naul McCole, Eugene Boyle and Liam Mullin, it presided over and guided youngsters and managers to new heights. Another big factor in developing young talent was the vocational schools and colleges sides. Men like Buncrana's Danny O'Brien and county star Michael Lafferty worked tirelessly with the vocational school sides and their impact on the careers of countless future county stars was considerable. Jackie McDermott of Ballyshannon, Sean O'Donnell and Eddie McDevitt and countless others – all performing trojan, sometimes unseen, work. These were all men who lived and breathed football. Between them they were nurturing talent that would in time deliver three All-Ireland titles.

By 1981 Joe Winston had assembled a very useful under-21 outfit, many of whom would benefit from Brian McEniff's senior team-building policy later that winter. Winston's side contested and lost an Ulster final to Monaghan that year but were rightly recognised as being one of the best sides in Ulster in an era of good under-21 teams. Incredibly, 13 of the starting 15 against Monaghan were available for selection the following year.

By the beginning of March 1982, two pieces of that year's under-21 football jigsaw had fallen into place. Aodh Ruadh had just been crowned under-21 champions of 1981 following that much delayed county final. A majestic Brian Tuohy captained Ballyshannon to victory – it would transpire to be a most fortunate time to captain the county champions.

There was something different about this under-21 squad. Reared on hard luck stories and near misses, previous Donegal teams often took the field hoping, rather than expecting, to win. Maybe there was a strange alchemy at work, but many of the squad had won titles either with club or school. Martin McHugh, a county championship winner with Kilcar commented on it, "That under-21 team feared nothing. We had some tremendous footballers on it." Winning titles wasn't foreign to this squad. The players knew they were good and they dared to dream. And a little known Four Masters club man, Tom Conaghan, had taken over the reins as manager at short notice following the departure of Joe Winston.

❈ ❈ ❈ ❈

Conaghan the manager was a straight-talking hard man who operated in facts. Absolutely no bullshit. Black and white – spades were spades. Like all managers he sought to influence his teams with regard to tactics, fitness, commitment and dedication to the cause. But above all else, Conaghan demanded absolute discipline. He was a hard taskmaster at Four Masters and he carried into the county scene the attitude which had reaped success for his club. Joyce McMullan had the opportunity to see Tom at first hand:

> He was successful at club level from the word go and took us to a different level. He brought a lot of organisation to the club. We were promoted the previous year and in 1981 we contested the county final, which we were beaten in. In 1982 we were back in the final again. Our success in it was unbelievable.

The training regime the under-21 squad undertook was like nothing the players had experienced before. Things were different before, remarked Anthony Molloy:

> It used to be that if you didn't want to train you didn't have to, any excuse would do. You would jog around the field once and then pull up. That all stopped under Tom. Things were done by the book and were done his way.

Conaghan often trained with the players or trained them himself, "I told them I wouldn't ask them to do what I couldn't do." Possessed of a steely will to win, he sought to instil this in his team:

> Before that we had a more reserved, laid-back, come-day go-day attitude in Donegal. I told the players that they were good enough to win and that they were better than their opponents. I tried to boost the players, give them confidence in themselves and get the 'second class citizen' attitude out of their heads. It was time to grow up and expect. If a player couldn't do that there was no place for him with me. I wasn't a loser and I didn't like losing; I didn't even like losing challenge matches.

Conaghan's Boys of '82

Matt Gallagher remembers Conaghan's style of management.

> It might not have been the first time we were exposed to that style of dis-
> cipline but it was the first time that we realised it was the only way to go
> and that skill without discipline was going nowhere – as has been proven
> time and again since. Tom brought in a huge amount of discipline and
> asked for a massive commitment. We trained on Tuesday and Thursday
> nights and Saturday mornings.

Conaghan pegged down a couple of challenge games at the end of March and
beginning of April against Armagh and Monaghan. Competition for every
position was a key tenet of the O'Dwyer doctrine and Conaghan set about introducing this in Donegal:

> If there's competition for places it means that no player can be sure that
> his place will always be there. O'Dwyer always told me to let the play-
> ers know that no-one's place was secure and the only certain thing was
> being in the panel.

As some players were later to discover, not even a place in the panel was a sure
thing with Conaghan as manager.

By the time Donegal made the trip to Breffni Park at the end of the month
for the Ulster first round match he had more or less settled on a team. Some
worries were voiced in the papers concerning a perceived lack of power at midfield and a lack of penetration up front.

A 1-10 to 1-7 victory was obtained with team work winning through on the
day. Trooping onto the field in the old style colours of Donegal – green and gold
hoops – Donegal's subsequent "dashing, never say die approach" prompted
the *Democrat* to link their attire and attitude to Donegal teams of yesteryear:

> Memories of great hearted Donegal teams of the 1940s, 1950s and 1960s
> were evoked by those traditional hooped jerseys and thereafter by the
> sheer courage of their present-day wearers. Like many of our former
> great sides this Donegal team made up in grit and guts what was lacking
> in overall class.

It was a decent start by Conaghan's boys. No Cavan team are ever easily
defeated in Breffni Park. Donegal had passed their first test without necessarily firing on all cylinders. The first team in what would be an historic six game
campaign was: Michael Kelly; Michael McBrearty, John McGowan, Matt
Gallagher; Eunan McIntyre, Tommy McDermott, Brian Tuohy; Sylvester
Maguire, Charlie Mulgrew; Martin McHugh, Seamus Meehan, Joyce McMullan;

Paul Carr, Pauric Gallagher, Patrick McGroarty.

Conaghan also had Sean Bonner, Corny Carr, Eamon Breslin, Joe O'Neill, Donie McCole, Eunan Doyle and Donal Reid available to him on the bench but their services weren't required on the day. Martin Shovlin, who had been a member of the panel under Joe Winston the previous year but had missed much of the action due to injury, had made Conaghan's first team at corner-back but once again injury forced his withdrawal following an accident at work. "The telegraph pole I was working on broke. I was belted to it and I was lucky not to be killed when it fell. I injured my ankle and my place went to Michael McBrearty. Winning teams aren't often changed and it's particularly difficult to get back into defence."

Next up was Down in the Ulster semi-final. It promised to be one of the clashes of the year in Ulster football. A neutral observer glancing through the match programme could be forgiven for thinking they had stumbled upon a senior match. Donegal were to field ten senior players while Down had seven senior stars in their starting 15. In addition, both teams had an abundance of senior fringe players on their respective panels. McEniff's decision to include under-21s in his winter league panel lent Conaghan's youngsters a mature confidence beyond their years. They had been blooded, had learned to take a knock or two and could give one in return. "Gaining the senior experience was fantastic," was how Matt Gallagher saw it. "We knew what it was like to play at senior inter-county level and it was great to be able to bring that to under-21 level."

Down didn't lack for senior experience either. After all, this was the Down of Greg Blaney, John 'Shorty' Trainor and Mickey Linden. If there was a buzz in Donegal with regard to the up-and-coming underage teams, the expectations in Down were higher still. The Ulster minor champions of 1979 had 20 members in the under-21 setup – and a point to prove. Donegal had entered the lion's den of Newry in 1981 and emerged with victory.

Conaghan picked his team still bereft of the services of the injury hit Shovlin and Reid. Marty Carlin, from Red Hughs, was the only change to the team that beat Cavan, coming in at corner-forward in place of the injured Paul Carr.

The pre-match hype was well justified. "MacCumhaill Park, Ballybofey, was certainly no place for the faint of heart," declared the *Democrat*. With seven minutes to go Donegal were defending a two-point lead which had its source in a good first half display. Donegal had goaled in the eighth minute when Martin McHugh found Pauric Gallagher who drilled the ball to the net.

Between then and the 23rd minute of the second half, Donegal held the lead although they were struggling for scores. They were two points ahead when a long-range effort from John Trainor dropped short and bounced in front of Michael Kelly in the Donegal goal. Somehow the ball eluded him and in the scramble that followed it was poked over the line. Mickey Linden added what seemed like an insurance point for Down on the 25th minute and that seemed to be that.

Up stepped Martin McHugh to rescue Donegal in their moment of need. It was a trait he would repeat again and again in the years ahead. Two minutes to go and a free won on the 50. McHugh pointed. One behind. With the clock ticking down a Down clearance was intercepted by the tenacious Eunan McIntyre. The incident sticks out in the mind of manager Conaghan, "Eunan went in for the ball. To this day, I don't know a fuck how he got it." McIntyre could be depended on to do the right thing. He ran straight at the Down defence who duly panicked and fouled him 35 yards from their own goal. Normal time was entirely up. The free would be the last kick of the game. McHugh was nerveless, "McIntyre won a ball he shouldn't have won and then won a free. I kicked the free over the bar." The scoreboard read 1-9 apiece when the referee blew the full-time whistle moments later.

In the event, while Donegal had fielded ten seniors, Down had only three on the field and star man Greg Blaney had gone to America. But there was no doubt who was the happier side facing into the replay in Newry. "We scored two late points," remembered Conaghan, "and people could see the character starting to come out in the team. People were starting to believe that we were going to do something."

Ardara midfielder Anthony Molloy had been in the stand watching the game. An under-21 player for the previous three years he had opted out of the 1982 squad. "I was fed up for some reason. I met Tom after the game and trained on Tuesday and Thursday nights. I then played in the replay in Newry. You could say it was a late call up."

Conaghan bared his managerial teeth several days ahead of the replay and caused ripples of shock across the county. He was not prepared to compromise on his basic principles – if you played on a Tom Conaghan side you committed yourself, no excuses. Anyone who didn't like it would know where they stood very quickly. Mid-fielder Sylvester Maguire, centre-half back Tommy McDermott and full back John McGowan found themselves relegated to the bench for "a lack of commitment to training." A worse fate befell Donal Reid and Eamon Breslin. They were dropped from the panel entirely, their crime – failure to attend training sessions. "I was working in the Great Northern Hotel in Bundoran at the time. Work held me back and I was dropped," was how Reid saw it. Despite late night telephone calls from senior GAA figures in the county Conaghan was not for bending. "If Charlie Mulgrew and Eunan McIntyre could thumb to training from Letterkenny, Reid could come down from Bundoran."

Joyce McMullan recalled the lengths players – in this instance Pauric Gallagher – would go to to avoid incurring the wrath of the manager:

Pauric was driving his mother's car to training in Ballybofey when the guards stopped us for speeding in the Gap. Pauric couldn't pay the fine and went to court instead. The judge asked him why he had been speeding. Pauric told him he was on his way to training and the manager was a strict disciplinarian. He made a whole story of it but I don't think he got off.

It was the Donegal football public's first exposure to the seemingly ruthless nature of Tom Conaghan's management system. Was he mad to drop McDermott and Maguire in particular, wondered football followers. For what – principles? Couldn't he cut the lads a little slack? There was much shaking of heads at his decision to face into an Ulster semi-final replay without two of his best players in the starting 15. Conaghan would drop his own mother, went the popular cry. Anyone who knew Conaghan knew it went much deeper than that. Conaghan was in the business of winning football matches. They understood that better than anywhere in Donegal Town. They trusted Conaghan there. He was involved with the senior side for a second year and in a short while their trust would be repaid completely when he delivered the Dr Maguire Cup to the town for the first time in 58 years.

Conaghan was a canny operator. His culling of Breslin and Reid at that point was of little consequence. Both were panelists and Reid was not match fit anyway after a lengthy lay off. They could be parachuted back in at a later date if need be. McGowan, the full back, had been replaced during the drawn match by Sean Bonner from Na Rossa who was Conaghan's preferred man for the position. As for McDermott and Maguire, both Martin Shovlin and Anthony Molloy were fit for the first time and were well capable of at least equalling the efforts of the Ballyshannon duo. Patrick McGroarty was also back in for Marty Carlin at corner forward. Conaghan liked McGroarty's style, "Patrick McGroarty did a lot of harm to different defences. If he got the ball he'd run at them. I told him to run with it at every opportunity."

Molloy had lots to offer too. His was a bustling power-house style of playing in the best traditions of the big mid-fielder. Conaghan had words for Molloy before he went on to the pitch. "You can prove a point today, it's no good only doing it in challenge matches." "I'll not let you down", Molloy replied. Conaghan was satisfied that the big Ardara man was going to give it everything. Going into the Down match Conaghan had succeeded in sending a strong signal to his entire squad of players without in the least weakening the chances of escaping Newry with a win:

Without falling out with the players I wanted to show them that things had changed and that nobody, whoever they were or wherever they were from, could walk on to the team. Molloy and Shovlin would have done anything for me and I knew this. I knew that they'd take a chance if they got it. Lots of people didn't see what I was doing.

He had made his mark and it would pay dividends.

The replay in Newry went Donegal's way, 0-9 to 1-4. The margin could have been greater, much greater. The *Democrat's* man bemoaned the fact that Donegal "simply will not rub it in when the going is good." Nonetheless, a second Ulster final beckoned and Conaghan had used his panel to good effect. The banished Ballyshannon duo of McDermott and Maguire had made an entrance with about ten minutes to go, just as Down had levelled matters 0-7 to 1-4. Two points were tagged on by the final whistle and Down were out.

Anthony Molloy turned midfield around from the Ballybofey match in favour of Donegal. When he ran out of steam towards the end the fresh legs of Maguire did the rest. Eunan McIntyre, who, with Tommy McDermott, would become one of the great lost Donegal footballers of the 1980s, was again magnificent with his ball winning, hard-hitting running game. He was Donegal's Mr Fix It. If an opposing forward was wreaking havoc McIntyre usually ended up on him. Mickey Linden and Martin Durkin both wilted under McIntyre's iron will that afternoon in Newry.

The full back trinity of McBrearty, Bonner and Gallagher were convincing and decisive. Matt, not the biggest man on the pitch, was catching ball in the clouds. That match remains his outstanding memory of the campaign:

> We had to go to the The Marshes to play Down and nobody had given us a chance. We put in a fantastic effort. There were two John Trainors on the team and one of them was 6' 4". Down got a sideline and Joyce McMullan climbed over this huge fella and pulled the ball out of the sky.

Some of the football was impressive, delighting the travelling support. One score saw Donegal handle the ball eight times without a single Down touch. The resulting point was tapped over by Pauric Gallagher, Matt's brother. Sadly, Pauric would tragically lose his life in a car crash in Boston some seven years later.

Derry awaited in the Ulster final. They too had come through a semi-final replay, dispatching Tyrone. The teams had a long wait before engaging in battle. Donegal had accounted for Down at the beginning of July yet it was two months later, in early September, before the final was played in Omagh. Indeed there was some talk that Croke Park intended to scrap the entire under-21 competition on completion of the 1982 series. Thankfully that didn't occur and the under-21 series is still going strong 21 years later.

The long delay caused problems. It was difficult for players and management to maintain focus with such an obvious break in momentum. Conaghan for one didn't waste his summer. On a wet day in MacCumhaill Park the Four Masters manager watched proudly as his captain, Donal Monaghan, received the Dr Maguire Cup on behalf of his team – the Donegal senior football champions of 1982. Conaghan was *some* operator. He'd developed a friendship with a man from Waterville in County Kerry. A man who was quite happy to impart regular advice on the 'phone as Conaghan steered the Donegal Town lads through the championship. A week before the county final the Kerry man landed in Donegal to give the Four Masters lads the benefit of his expertise. Conaghan's friend was Mick O'Dwyer, the greatest football manager Ireland had ever seen. A man with a quartet of All-Ireland medals himself and the manager of mighty Kerry who had by then five All-Irelands under his guidance. Certainly his friendship with Conaghan did Four Masters no harm whatsoever. It was the start of a hectic but productive period for the Four Masters players on the under-21 team. Joyce McMullan remembers it clearly:

> Michael Kelly, Seamus Meehan, Michael McBrearty and me were involved in both the club and county teams. It was a spectacular year for us. We won the club championship with Four Masters and then beat Derry in the under-21 final the following Sunday.

It was a seven-day double that surely even Conaghan hadn't dared dream about but greater glory was only weeks away.

One other positive occurrence over that summer was the showing by the county minors. Their league campaign in particular had caused a buzz among football followers. They had been surprisingly beaten by Antrim in the semi-final of the championship but had brought the Ulster Minor League title to the county – the first silverware for Donegal since 1974. Several names stood out. The captain, Brian Murray, a big midfielder from Ballyshannon. His club mate Gary Walsh, a shot-stopping goalkeeper. Declan Bonner, a lively red-haired forward from the Rosses. Martin McHugh's younger brother, James, who had tormented the best minor defenders in Ulster. And on the fringes of the team a lad by the name of Martin Gavigan from Ardara. Gavigan, a student at Thomond College in Limerick at the time, was concentrating on his studies first and foremost. There would be time for football later. The minors had beaten seven of Ulster's eight rival counties. They had pointed the way for their elders in the under-21 squad.

The Ulster under-21 final against Derry in Healy Park belonged to the Donegal captain. "Brian Tuohy led by example", wrote the *Democrat*, "with a display few folk could believe was really happening. No man ever merited the honour of winning captain any more than he did." Tuohy, the trainee garda from Ballyshannon, really came into his own in the second half.

Conaghan's starting 15 was: Michael Kelly; Michael McBrearty, Sean Bonner, Matt Gallagher; Eunan McIntyre, Tommy McDermott, Brian Tuohy; Anthony Molloy, Charlie Mulgrew; Martin McHugh, Seamus Meehan, Joyce McMullan; Paul Carr, Pauric Gallagher, Patrick McGroarty. The first half was a torrid one for the Donegal boys. Derry engaged in a game of endless switching to and fro, pulling Donegal markers all over the place and crowding out midfield. The tactic would eventually backfire but not before causing headaches for the boys in green and gold.

This was the Derry of Dermot McNicholl, Ronan McCusker, Terence McGuckian and Damien Barton. Their game plan was complex yet deviously simple. The smaller Donegal men were crowded out of midfield by the Derry giants Barton and Murphy and others, while the other Derry players roved all over the pitch. Sean Bonner and later Matt Gallagher took turns to follow Dermot McNicholl on his wanderings. McNicholl eventually ran himself into the ground. Donegal went in to the half time break behind – 0-3 to 1-2. Derry's goal was worryingly similar to one conceded earlier in the campaign. Dermot McNicholl launched a long high kick that ultimately found the net. "Michael Kelly and me let it into the net, " recalled Matt Gallagher. "He said I dropped it and I said he dropped it but we went on to win the game."

The to-ing and fro-ing of the Derry forwards was well illustrated when Donegal full-back, Sean Bonner, had an encounter with the Derry full-back, Fergal Moore! The move of the match saw Donegal string together eight passes before corner back Matt Gallagher shot narrowly wide.

Trailing by two points at half time, the Donegal management team knew that they'd have do something if the game was to be turned around. "We tried to open the midfield in the second half, we hadn't done it in the first half," remembers Tom Conaghan:

> Derry couldn't figure out how to deal with the long ball. They didn't know what was happening. McHugh was running into the half back line looking for the ball. Patrick McGroarty would carry it when he got it and then it was pumped into Molloy and he was laying it off. We had tried this in training and in challenge matches but it hadn't really worked.
>
> Years afterwards Jim McKeever told me it was the first time that he saw a running game, where players would carry the ball, being played.

Other changes were made in the second half which helped accentuate the difference between the teams. Donal Reid came back from the wilderness and appeared at midfield. It was Reid's first outing of 1982 and his had been a long way back. The talented Killygordon lad had been a revelation as a youthful under-21 back in 1980 but had then missed out entirely the following year due to injury. Reid, with Joyce McMullan, moved to midfield and proceeded to outfield the Derry duo of Barton and Murphy. Reid seized his chance aggressively and announced his arrival with a scintillating display of attacking football. According to the *Democrat* "[He] tore lanes through that hitherto solid Derry right flank."

Mulgrew moved to centre forward and as the *Democrat* noted, "is a different class player when prompting an attack." His midfield partner Molloy found himself switched into full-forward and he too revelled in his new position, electing to run at the Derry defenders and draw the frees which McHugh rewarded with points. The perfectionist in McHugh was unhappy though. Despite accounting for seven of Donegal's ten points he described the game as, "a bad day at the office. I must have kicked 13 wides and nearly lost the game single handedly." Donegal's most formidable line on the field was the half-back line of McIntyre, McDermott and Tuohy.

The final score was 0-10 to 1-5. And the inspiration behind Donegal's victory over Derry for their first Ulster under-21 championship since 1966 was the captain and man of the match – Brian Tuohy.

✳ ✳ ✳ ✳

It was a major breakthrough for Donegal football. And with the success of the minors in the Ulster league, commentators were already talking of a golden age for Donegal.

A bigger breakthrough was delivered at the end of September in Pearse Park, Longford, when Donegal slipped by Laois, 0-5 to 0-4, to book a place in the All-Ireland under-21 final. They were, reported the *Democrat*, "the first ever Donegal side to reach an All-Ireland final in any grade of inter-county football currently being played."

It was another gruelling outing and the match was played in atrocious conditions. Torrential rain from well before the throw-in until half-time left players, punters and pitch wringing wet. Goalkeeper Michael Kelly stood up to his ankles in mud and water in both goalmouths. Nonetheless, the Ulster champions emerged as winners by the narrowest of margins when the only thing shining in Pearse Park was the display of the Donegal defenders. Once again Donal Reid had made a second-half appearance around the middle with fellow sub Sylvester Maguire. Reid's contribution in particular was to prove the difference between the sides and it was the Killygordon man who slotted over the winning point. His display, coupled with an equally impressive 15 minutes against Derry, would eventually earn him a starting place in the All-Ireland final. It would be a long time before Donal Reid ever warmed a bench again as he went on to become one of the most consistent Donegal seniors of the decade.

The win wasn't without cost as Donegal had two players, McDermott and McIntyre, hospitalised suffering from concussion. Happily both made recoveries in the three weeks before the All-Ireland final. Tom Conaghan felt that while the game was physical, it would stand his charges in good stead:

It was really tight. You would have got hit in that game if you had been standing looking around you.

Afterwards the Laois manager told me that he thought the Donegal

Barry McGowan

players were more in command, more disciplined and the tight game wouldn't have done any harm for the final against Roscommon. He thought that the team was too open but that they'd learn a lot from that match. He made no apologies for the style of football his team played.

And none were expected.

The excitement in the county was palpable. Conaghan left little to chance as the countdown to the final began. To ensure players were not exposed to the risk of injury he imposed a sensible ban on club participation. He was given the week off by his employers to ensure maximum attention to detail. He had reason for worry and reason for cheer. A worry was the reliance on McHugh for scores. A subdued McHugh and Donegal would be in trouble. And Charlie Mulgrew had proved the only man capable of *really* taking on defenders. Conaghan had good reason for confidence in his defence and applauded his charges for their team spirit. "This Donegal team have certainly got the right attitude unlike a lot of Donegal teams in the past," he told the *Democrat*, "They are like a good club team – they are very close to one another."

Connacht champions and red hot favourites Roscommon stood between Conaghan and All-Ireland glory. They weren't exactly an unknown quantity as Donegal had played them twice in challenge matches earlier in the year. In the meantime Roscommon had accounted for the All-Ireland finalists of 1981, Galway, in the Connacht decider and had spectacularly decommissioned defending All-Ireland champions Cork in the semi-final. Donegal had never been as close to the holy grail of an All-Ireland title at any time in the history of the GAA. Never before had an hour's football stood between a Donegal team and an All-Ireland title[1]. Roscommon, on the other hand, knew all about winning. Their under-21 team of 1978 had lifted the All-Ireland crown, beating a Kerry team that contained Denis 'Ogie' Moran and Eoin 'The Bomber' Liston, both of whom would gain footballing immortality as Kerry's so-called 'Golden Years' rolled by. Roscommon came to Carrick-on-Shannon on Sunday, October 17, 1982, bigger in stature, bigger in reputation and expecting to win.

Conaghan fielded a team that had proved itself not only in that under-21 campaign but in many different grades at club, college and county. Michael Kelly; Michael McBrearty, Sean Bonner, Matt Gallagher; Eunan McIntyre, Tommy McDermott, Brian Tuohy; Anthony Molloy, Donal Reid; Martin McHugh, Charlie Mulgrew, Joyce McMullan; Seamus Meehan, Paul Carr, Patrick McGroarty. At eight minutes to three o'clock this was the team that emerged from the changing rooms and sprinted on to Pairc Sheán MhicDiarmada. No less than 15,000 Donegal people – men, women and children – were there in person to cheer these men-boys on. Carrick-on-Shannon had never seen its like.

None of the spectators knew it, but tension had simmered in the Donegal dressing room minutes before the team took the field. Pauric Gallagher had been dropped for playing soccer with Finn Harps and it was the hot topic of gossip within the squad. "Every player had been told to stay in line and knew what the penalty would be for stepping out of line," was the manager's view. Donal Monaghan heard Michael McBrearty making disparaging remarks about Conaghan and let Tom know. "Donal was very loyal. He was a great influence and was held in great respect" remembers Tom:

> Donal told the players that if they felt so bad about Pauric being dropped then maybe one of them would give Pauric his jersey. He told them that we'd change the team but one of the players would have to give up his place. The place went silent.

❄ ❄ ❄ ❄

Seán Gallagher was a priest born and reared in the parish of Gaoth Dobhair. He played a bit with Gaoth Dobhair in his time, won nothing, but over the years his proven credentials as a great Gael made him well known and much respected in and beyond his native county. An All-Ireland Scór winner and a writer of note, he knew his football inside out, and in time would become famed as Donegal's foremost football historian and statistician. Fitting then that one of the enduring memories of that 1982 All-Ireland was Fr Seán's hysterics in the commentary box as Donegal recorded an emotional and famous win over Roscommon, 0-8 to 0-5. "We've won it! We've won it! We've won it!" screamed Fr Seán as the game ended, any pretence at impartiality long-since abandoned. His unbridled joy was replicated all over the pitch as Donegal fans streamed on to greet their heroes and carry them off shoulder high. Donegal had looked the better side throughout but the fear of a late Roscommon comeback had kept the supporters in a state of high tension right until the final whistle. Only then did the supporters, led by Fr Seán, give vent to their almost disbelieving delight.

"The boys from the land of O'Donnell played like men possessed," raved the *Democrat*, grandly but aptly. Indeed they had and the winning margin of three points did not do justice to their superiority. "They swept at their opponents with a fury no Donegal team has ever displayed in the past," continued the *Democrat*. Lofty words written in the immediate euphoria of victory yet richly appropriate about a Donegal team that had delivered on the biggest stage and captured a first ever All-Ireland title at any grade.

The game was two minutes old when Donegal opened the scoring – a point from McHugh. The 'Kilcar wizard' was at his lethal best that day in Carrick-on-Shannon and went on to account for five of Donegal's eight points. Time and time again he sliced through the Roscommon ranks causing utter panic every time he touched the ball. And from the placed ball? Deadly accurate. Martin had prepared himself for the final with typical single-mindedness:

The Roscommon left-half back was supposed to be a fabulous player. He had marked Dave Barry out of it in the semi-final, scored two points from play and set up another score. I would always prefer to mark a player that has a reputation rather than one that hasn't. I would always focus myself. Mentally and physically, I was right going into that game. I knew that I was going to sort this boy out. That was the motivation that I had – I was going to prove that I was a better player than him.

Things began badly. The departure of Sean Bonner could have been the losing of the match. The Na Rossa man had built a huge reputation for himself at full-back in previous games but an injury picked up during the week revisited him in the early minutes and he had no choice but to leave the action. His misfortune was Pauric Gallagher's gain. His exclusion from the first 15 was short-lived – he hadn't even warmed his spot on the bench. Now he was on as Conaghan thought on his feet and reshuffled his pack, quickly and expertly. It was impressive. In a flash Conaghan sent Gallagher in at corner forward, moved Meehan back out to wing half-forward; McMullan back to midfield; Reid back to centre half-back and Tommy McDermott back to full-back. It worked. Flawlessly. In fairness, Conaghan had two great football brains to pick upon. From the outset his selectors had been Michael Lafferty and Donal Monaghan, two men who knew their football. Lafferty, a teacher in Donegal Town vocational school had many of the present under-21s under his wings for several years in his capacity as manager of the vocational schools county side. A footballer of note, he captained the senior team to Ulster success in 1983, and cut an impressive figure in the Donegal dressing room. "He had a great football brain," remarked Martin McHugh, "He had a big influence on us and his team talks were brilliant. He was ahead of his time."

Bonner had been geared up to mark Roscommon's star and danger man Paul Earley. Now Tommy McDermott found himself on the big Roscommon man. Earley didn't help his cause by playing a roaming game and travelling far from the Donegal square in search of possession – McDermott outplayed him.

It was 0-5 apiece at half-time. An in-form Donegal had played a clever short-passing game against the breeze and were actually unfortunate to go in level at the interval – McHugh (3), Donal Reid and Pauric Gallagher the scorers.

The second half took place largely in the Roscommon half of the pitch and belonged to Donegal. It was a low scoring half – Donegal added just three points but held Roscommon scoreless. It seemed as if Donegal had left their best performance of the entire campaign until the last match. In a team of heroes McHugh was exceptional. His legend was born that day in Carrick-on-Shannon. He added two points from frees but he was here and there everywhere, feinting between defenders like a ghost. Pauric Gallagher of Finn Harps and Donegal had the final say. Sidestepping his man smartly he struck over a beautiful point from an acute angle out on the right wing. That was 13 minutes into the half. It was also the final score of the game.

On a day when it was hard to find fault throughout the field, the only area of Donegal's game that could be faulted in any way was their scoretaking. As the second half wore on following Gallagher's point, their dominance wasn't reflected on the scoreboard. Donegal wides crept into double figures and, although Roscommon didn't look as if they could trouble a resolute Donegal defence, there was much nervous unrest both in the packed stands and along the line. Tension hung in the air like mist. A three-point lead would soon disappear if Roscommon sneaked in for a goal.

Tom Conaghan suffered terribly. He had played his hand. He'd thrown on Maguire for McGroarty and the Ballyshannon lad made his usual impact. But Roscommon were still technically in contention. The *Democrat* painted the picture:

> Tom is so wound up that a tumbler full of straight poitín wouldn't have relieved his tension. When he takes his team out onto the pitch he has a strained, anguished appearance like a stern teacher with a bad ulcer. Tom can inject confidence into his team but he seems to suffer for it.

Everyone sensed that Donegal were not going to be caught, that the county would shortly be All-Ireland champions but there were few people who dared put words to that thought. That changed in the 29th minute. From a long range free the Wee Man sought the insurance point. Somehow it went all the way to the back of the net. Pairc Sheán Mhic Diarmada erupted. Donegal voices let rip. All-Ireland Champions! As Seán Ó Baoill, the County Board PRO, later remarked, "That was the last many of us saw of the game – it was much later that we realised that the score had been disallowed for an adjudged square infringement." A minute or two later and it was all over, Donegal were All-Ireland under-21 champions of 1982! Only those who were present when *those* final whistles sounded in 1987 and again in 1992 could appreciate the depth of emotion that day in Carrick-on-Shannon. Tears were shed and looks were exchanged – this was a place and a feeling not one of the 15,000 Donegal souls present had ever experienced. Tom Conaghan tried to step back and let the enormity of the achievement wash over him:

> I felt that I had achieved something for Donegal. I had achieved what I set out to achieve. I met former players with tears tripping down their faces. I didn't want to do interviews, I wanted to be with the people of Donegal and to be with the team. Those things can pass you by at such a time. You can always be interviewed. I would always have preferred being with supporters and players to being on TV or radio.

It was, felt the experts, a team to go places. The powerful performances of

Molloy and Reid; McDermott's handling of Earley; the assurance of McIntyre and Tuohy; the tireless running of Mulgrew – all were applauded for weeks. People were already running out of superlatives to describe McHugh. Add McMullan, McBrearty and the Gallagher brothers and Donegal would claim their first All-Ireland senior title by the mid-1980s. Only time would prove the armchair experts right or wrong but the moment belonged to the under-21s of 1982. And to that man Tom Conaghan from Donegal Town – the manager of the first ever All-Ireland winning Donegal team. Many were the awards that came his way, all deserved. There were a few who expressed the view that Conaghan had inherited a ready-made team to win the All-Ireland. Theirs was a nonsensical view. That would be proved time and time again over the next decade as Donegal – with a ready-made team – would chase a senior All-Ireland that would prove so elusive. It was not a case of Conaghan being in the right place at the right time, rather the right man being in the right place. Donegal needed his forcefulness at the helm in 1982 and he delivered in spades.

Paul Carr, one of the stalwarts up front, reckons it was "as strong a Donegal panel as they come." The remainder of that panel got their deserved credit and most would feature in the green and gold of Donegal senior sides in the future: John O'Donnell, Maurice Carr, John McGowan, Donie McCole, Marty Carlin and Martin Shovlin. Shovlin, from Dunkineely, could rightly feel unfortunate. One of the best defenders in the county, Shovlin was practically guaranteed a starting place on any given Sunday but had a miserable year with injury. Time and again in 1981 and 1982 it relegated him to the bench. He would go on to become one of Donegal's most consistent and popular senior players of all time. But the spectre of injury would return to haunt him for the biggest game of all.

A week of bonfires, roadside stops and photographs with the Tadhg Ó Cleirigh Cup lay ahead. From Glenfin to Ballyliffen the heroes were acclaimed as football supporters and ordinary Donegal folk turned out to acknowledge the achievement. A seemingly unbreakable psychological barrier had been smashed. And for the first time, football folk dreamed.

1. Donegal junior footballers had contested two 'home' All-Ireland football finals in 1933 (against Mayo) and 1954 (against Kerry), losing both. The winners of 'home' finals in those days still had to advance to the All-Ireland Final 'proper' against the champions of Britain.

RESULTS	Ulster Championship	All-Ireland Series
	Donegal 1-10, Cavan 1-7	Donegal 0-5, Laois 0-4
	Donegal 1-9, Down 1-9	Donegal 0-8, Roscommon 0-5
	Donegal 0-9, Down 1-4	
	Donegal 0-10, Derry 1-5	

4

Eighty-Three
(1982 – 1983)

"Mcenifficent."

1983 Donegal GAA Yearbook

Michael Gillespie was the most senior GAA official in the county in the winter of 1982. Money, or the lack of it, was on his mind. It would, he reckoned, take the guts of £40,000 to run county teams properly in 1983. Just before the under-21 All-Ireland success Gillespie circulated a letter appealing for assistance in which he outlined his vision of potential future success – "An Ulster senior title in 1983-84, an All-Ireland semi-final in 1984-85, and an All-Ireland around 1985 onwards."

Many others around Donegal were having a similar vision. Success creates expectation. Commentators felt that Donegal football was entering a golden age. The county was expectant, success was demanded. What the summer of 1983 needed – what the county needed – and what Brian McEniff needed, was a good run in the championship.

McEniff could have taken precious little heart from the winter. Division Two remained as distant as ever. Donegal's league campaign was in reasonable shape by the time they played Clare in February. The county was celebrating its first All-Ireland win and did quite well in the pre-Christmas part of the league. In that period Donegal had lost to Louth but recorded wins over Monaghan and Longford either side of a draw with Laois. Clare then inflicted a surprise defeat but with two matches remaining Donegal still had the possibility of Division Two football within their grasp. For a second year they floundered against Wexford. "The promotion dream now regulation nightmare," read the stark headline in the *Donegal Democrat*. As it turned out Fermanagh were defeated in the final game and, as such, the league campaign was rescued as Donegal stayed 'up' in Division Three. Three wins, three defeats, one draw.

But by the time the summer came around everyone had forgotten the lacklustre winter football.

Not forgotten was criticism of Donegal's style of play during the national league. Nor the questions which surfaced about McEniff's apparent lack of ruthlessness. People are inclined to think that deeply analytical sports journalism is a recent phenomenon, not so; Brian McEniff and his players had it every Friday as far back as 1982 and before! Colm Murray, also known as 'Tine Sí', was relentless in his analysis of Donegal football. Murray was the man whom Donegal folk read in the local papers. In the *Democrat* and the *People's Press* Murray was not afraid to point out the negatives as well as the positives. A forerunner of "The Follower", he knew his football and put to press exactly what was occupying his mind. Sadly he did not live to report on the 1983 championship.

McEniff, Murray had written, had several "blatantly unfit players aboard." It was implied that McEniff was allowing a few mavericks to rule the roost:

> If Brian McEniff would only display that same ruthlessness off the field which he displayed on the field we might put an end to the recurring situation where players 'take the lend' of the manager regarding training or getting fit or being taken in trust for team places.

It was strong criticism of McEniff's man management, and of some of the older members of the squad. "Make your rules, Brian, and stand firmly by them," coaxed Murray. Rightly or wrongly, it would not be the last time it would be suggested that McEniff indulged the whims of his teams. McEniff, by now with a trio of hotels, might have wondered why he bothered. The summers were short on the streets of Bundoran and when he should have been concentrating on the tourists and the day trippers, he was thinking of football matches.

McEniff himself later conceded to journalist and football guru Eugene McGee that he might have a problem with disciplining players. "I must admit I'm not great at cracking whips, if there is a weakness in my capacity as a manager that might be it." He went on to point out that his approach was to try to relate to players and instil confidence into them. His methods were motivational rather than confrontational.

❄ ❄ ❄ ❄

Throughout the league Donegal had also come under the spotlight for their short-passing game. In defeat this style was always looked upon as a major contributing factor. The *Democrat* felt: "Overplaying the ball is a certain remedy for disaster . . . The Donegal gambit of delaying the pass when in possession led to their downfall . . . They pass and pass until evidently no man will risk a shot in case he spoils the movement."

The last word, perhaps fittingly, was left to Colm Murray, who described Donegal's short passing as a bad case of "ring-a-ring-of-roses".

Certainly Donegal's reliance on the short passing game was often a source of frustration for commentators and supporters alike. Two decades later and Donegal teams are still criticised for the short ball game. Pluses and minuses. There was some merit in the criticism around 1982-83 when Donegal had a core of big men in the team – Griffin, Lafferty, Bonner, Carr and Molloy – and could well afford to contest in the air. Yet short passing was also the aspect of their play which at its intricate best was a joy to behold.

Donegal were again pitted against Armagh in the first round in Ulster. It was a game that would define their year. By the time June came around Armagh and Donegal knew each other very well and the defending Ulster champions held no fears whatsoever for Donegal. The sides had met twice at the end of March in the Dr McKenna Cup with Donegal emerging victorious in a replay. People remember the drawn game for a number of reasons, including a protest by Armagh that extra time should be played while Donegal players pointedly headed for the showers and home. But the talking point of the day was once again Martin McHugh. Donegal had to start without him as he got lost en-route to Lurgan from Dublin. Yet it was his superb free kick deep into injury time that secured the draw and would stay long in the memory of those who witnessed it. The *Democrat* reported:

Armagh looked to have snatched a victory they didn't really deserve and referee Michael Greenan was casting numerous glances at his watch as the game was being played out in midfield. Then, two minutes into injury time, Greenan awarded a free-kick to Donegal in the middle of the field over 50 yards out from goal. Martin McHugh stepped up to take the kick which was into an extremely strong wind. The Wee Man struck the ball firmly, judging the distance and angle perfectly, and the ball sailed up the field and over the bar much to the disbelief of the Armagh crowd.

It was a classic McHugh point, displaying nerves of steel. His confidence was at a high having just picked up his first Railway Cup medal with Ulster. He had been nominated for an All-Star, and although he missed out on selection he would shortly find himself in New York with the All-Star team as one of the replacements.

Perhaps the one person never surprised by the accuracy of McHugh's place kicking was Martin McHugh himself. Autumn, spring, winter or summer, McHugh practised his kicking, hitting thousands of balls in Kilcar:

I would kick a hundred balls a day. I remember that my parents had a party in the house for my 21st birthday but I was down at the pitch kicking frees and wouldn't leave. When I left the field the thing in the house was over.

On the day of a club championship game I'd get up at six in the morning, have a cup of tea and go to our pitch and hit a hundred frees, come home, shower and go to Mass and then on to the game.

The replay was won by two points and although a shock defeat followed by a Nudie Hughes-inspired Monaghan, there were strong indications that Donegal were finding their groove.

At the age of 28, Big Martin Griffin from MacCumhaill's was already a Donegal football legend. At full-back or midfield he had a commanding presence and the ability to impose himself on a game. His easygoing and affable attitude made him a gentle giant off the pitch, but Donegal fans loved him for his take-no-prisoners approach to a match. As the summer approached Big Griffin was at the top of his game and Martin McHugh was impressed:

Griffin was the best Donegal player I ever played with. He never realised his full potential because he was never fit enough. A fit Martin Griffin would have been outstanding. I loved playing with him, for a big man he was very talented.

Following the under-21 success the previous October, expectations were unusually high in the county. Manager McEniff had married experience with youth and players like Noel McCole, Michael Carr, Anthony Molloy, Charlie Mulgrew, Paul McGettigan, Donal Reid, Eunan McIntyre and Brendan Dunleavy were first choice. And, of course, there was McHugh. "Things seem to be coming right at last," admitted McEniff. In retrospect, the odds were stacked heavily in Donegal's favour despite the fact this was the greatest Armagh team of recent times, with three Ulster titles – 1977, 1980 and 1982. It was an acknowledged football truth that Ulster was the toughest province in Ireland from which to emerge and claiming back-to-back Ulster titles was a rare occurrence indeed. Armagh and Donegal would have noted that defending Ulster champions had been dumped out in the first round six times in the previous 11 years. Donegal had already proved to themselves that they could beat Armagh and much had happened in the 12 months since Armagh had ambushed Donegal in Ballybofey in the previous championship. Nine of the team that McEniff would use throughout the 70 minutes against Armagh now had an All-Ireland medal. Everything had changed. "The younger players did not think we could win [last year]. There's no danger of that this year," commented veteran full-forward Seamus Bonner. The county awaited the visit of Armagh to MacCumhaill Park, and wondered if Ulster's first hurdle was about to be cleared for the first time since 1979.

Even before Donegal had kicked a ball in the championship, Down and

Derry were out. Sensing Donegal's lack of fear of Armagh, one astute football reporter had seen a tunnel of light opening up for Donegal: "The omens are good for Donegal's third Ulster Championship," prophesied Eoghan Corry in the *Sunday Tribune*.

Donegal delivered a devastating display of dashing skilful football and had six points to spare on Armagh by the end of the 70 minutes – 1-10 to 0-7 the score. It was as decisive as anyone in the crowd of more than 8,000 – the biggest attendance squeezed into MacCumhaill Park in a decade – could have wished for. Indeed Donegal curtailed the visitors to just one point from play. Twenty-eight minutes had ticked away before Armagh were allowed their first score of the second half. McCole, Griffin, McDermott, Gallagher, Dunleavy, Lafferty, McGettigan, McMullan and Bonner were all outstanding performers in a display that bore little resemblance to the lacklustre football the same team had produced in the league.

Charlie Mulgrew, at centre-half forward, pointed the way after only three minutes. Dunleavy and McMullan combined to prise open the Armagh defence and delivered to Mulgrew who scooted past defenders before brilliantly crashing the ball to the net. Donegal never looked back. McHugh was a doubtful starter but he played with the help of a pain-killing injection. Once again he stole the headlines. "His time on the field was curtailed to 43 minutes," recorded *The Irish Times*, "But in that time he landed five vital points, four from frees, and gave a class of display that makes one wonder just what he would have done to Armagh had he been fully fit." Indeed McHugh was stretchered off eight minutes into the second half, collapsing in pain having just converted a free. It was a tough time for the Kilcar man who was suffering shots of pain down his leg from a troublesome hip injury. He had been advised by one doctor to stop playing altogether. Not wanting to hear that, McHugh sought a second opinion. The prognosis was slightly better. "A doctor at Altnagalvin told me to take six months' rest from football but I didn't take a rest until I stopped playing."

The win caused a shock in the province and beyond. Yet Donegal football folk had expected no less. It was also the end of an era in Armagh football – that team of Joe Kernan, Mickey McDonald and Brian McAlinden would never again break out of Ulster.

The Donegal minors had exited the championship earlier that afternoon at the hands of Armagh but involvement wasn't over for captain Gary Walsh who returned to the pitch as sub goalkeeper with the seniors. While his arrival in the squad may have been a little fortuitous, the tall Aodh Ruadh club man would soon make the position his own and become one of the longest serving goalies in Donegal football history. "I was lucky to make the minor team in the summer of 1982," remembers Gary:

Andrew Faulkner from Donegal Town played in all the league games that year but picked up an injury. The minors played the seniors in a challenge in Ballybofey before the championship. It was only a trial game but there must have been 20 shots on me in 20 minutes and I might have saved 15 or so. McEniff saw this and took a bit of a gamble on me. He brought me into the panel and I remember travelling in a big nine seater with the likes of Donal Reid and Tommy McDermott. I was very quiet at the time and was hardly able to speak a word to fellas like this.

Gary became part of the senior squad for the league of 1982-83, as an understudy to the long-serving Noel McCole.

The Ulster semi-final against Monaghan in Irvinestown had far-reaching implications for Charlie Mulgrew. Midway through the second half he was felled off the ball. A broken jaw resulted and Charlie sat out not only the remainder of that match but also the subsequent Ulster final.

Donegal were simply too good for Monaghan and put on another fine exhibition of all-out attacking football. Monaghan, a team with a reputation as a tough side, turned ugly and the game was played with an air of vicious intent. Poor refereeing allowed many fouls and bad tackles to go largely unchecked and by the time the referee did take action and lined Eugene Sherry, it was too late for the game of football and for Charlie Mulgrew. "Donegal thus go into the Ulster final against either Cavan or Fermanagh aware at least that they can absorb lots of punishment and still record a respectable score," noted a caustic Sean Kilfeather in *The Irish Times*.

McEniff had lined out a team that included two forced changes from the Armagh game – Matt Gallagher had broken his hand in the championship opener and McHugh, suffering from a recurring hip problem declared himself unfit shortly before the throw in. The team that took the pitch was: Noel McCole; Des Newton, Martin Griffin, Tommy McDermott; Brendan Dunleavy, Michael Lafferty, Michael Carr; Paul McGettigan, Anthony Molloy; Donal Reid, Charlie Mulgrew, Joyce McMullan; Fintan Lynch, Seamus Bonner, Kieran Keeney.

New boy Des Newton came in at corner-back in place of Matt Gallagher and had a fine debut. An under-21 All-Ireland winner with Roscommon in 1978, Newton had recently arrived in Inishowen where he taught at Carndonagh Community School and played his club football with Urris. Gallagher's woe was to be his good fortune. Tommy McDermott was given the responsibility of stifling Monaghan talisman Nudie Hughes. He was not found wanting and as well as keeping Hughes scoreless he scored a fine point.

It was an admirable performance with Molloy and Reid much improved from the Armagh match. The entire defence, marshalled by Griffin and Michael Lafferty, were superb. And up front McMullan, Mulgrew and Bonner earned the major plaudits. Paul McGettigan stepped in for McHugh on the free-taking duties, scored three, and contributed a fine game from midfield. Donegal had been up for the game. An inspirational captain, Lafferty delivered one of his great motivating speeches before Donegal took the pitch. During the course of his speech it was said he drove his fist through a table while emphasising a point. An hour and a half later Donegal were through to their first Ulster final of the 1980s and only the sixth in the county's history.

The Ulster final of 1983 was a tough prospect for Donegal. Most onlookers had fancied either Armagh or Down to emerge from the province. Yet Armagh succumbed to Donegal while National Football League champions Down had crashed out unexpectedly to Fermanagh. Cavan, the sleeping giants of Ulster, accounted for Derry in the preliminary round, Tyrone in the first round and then culled Fermanagh. Cavan had once been Ulster's premier county, amassing 38 Ulster and five All-Ireland titles. But that had been a long time ago – their most recent Ulster title was 1969. Fate wasn't with Cavan either. An old Ulster piseog held that no team that competed in the preliminary round would win the Ulster title.

Matt Gallagher's services were lost on the Wednesday before the match. Appendicitis struck the unfortunate Naomh Brid defender. "It was a terrible, terrible disappointment," he recalls, "That I had been picked in the starting 15 made it even worse." One man's misfortune is another man's good luck and Padraig Carr was chosen to play in his stead. Martin McHugh had also been named, replacing Fintan Lynch. Mulgrew, obviously, was not available.

Donegal and Cavan had never met in an Ulster Final. It was, reckoned a football follower from the Six Counties, a "Free State final." "The most interesting and exciting Ulster football championship for many years reaches it apex in Clones tomorrow with a final that promises at least a lively and entertaining contest and possibly a first-class exhibition of the game," forecast the legendary Paddy Downey in *The Irish Times*.

He wasn't wrong. It was one of the best provincial finals in years – a fiercely competitive and enthralling game played out in front of a massive 30,000 crowd in Clones. And, in the strange way that football fate sometimes smiles delightfully on the right player on the right day, it was Seamus Bonner – the big veteran Donegal full-forward and the only playing link with both title-winning teams of 1972 and 1974 – who grabbed the headlines. Bonner was simply brilliant on the edge of the Cavan square, tormenting Cavan full-back McAweeney for the 70 minutes. The game was won for Donegal on the strength of a brace of Bonner penalty kicks. Twenty-nine minutes into the first half he blazed the first past Damien O'Reilly in the Cavan goal following a foul on Kieran Keeney by McAweeney. Four times in that first half the scores had been level, Bonner's penalty goal was Donegal's first time to hit the front.

Donegal were in sizzling form in the second half. "Their flair, skill, speed and tactical efficiency all dove-tailed to produce a performance which eventually subdued the lion-hearted efforts of the best Cavan team to represent the county since the 1960s," wrote Paddy Downey. Yet, Cavan stayed within striking distance. With two minutes remaining Jim McAweeney, under severe pressure, conceded his second penalty. Bonner, with the wisdom accumulated over 11 championship summers, sent the ball high and over the bar for the insurance point. A minute or so later and referee John Gough sounded the final whistle and Donegal were football champions of Ulster for the third time on a scoreline of 1-14 to 1-11.

Cavan had rocked Donegal to their foundations in the opening minutes. It took them a mere 16 seconds to register their opening point and worse was to follow when full-forward Derek McDonnell had the ball in the Donegal net on the fourth minute. While Bonner was lording things on the edge of the Cavan square, under-21 star Derek McDonnell gave Martin Griffin an equally torrid 70 minutes at the opposite end.

However, it was a day when Donegal had all the answers, both on and off the pitch. McEniff had a good game on the line and made a few decisive switches that paid huge dividends. Swapping Dunleavy and Carr was the managerial move of the match. Dunleavy curtailed Cavan danger man Donal Donohue – top scorer in the Ulster championship – and Michael Carr, despite a heavy blow to the face, gave a man-of-the-match performance. Newton meanwhile had settled into his corner back berth as if he'd always been there. The five under-21 stars of 1982 who had made McEniff's starting 15 stood out. McDermott was impeccable as ever, Reid was settling in and contributed two points, Molloy was splendid in the middle, Joyce McMullan wreaked havoc with his attacking runs while Martin McHugh was simply Martin McHugh. The Kilcar man had to leave the pitch gasping for breath with 15 minutes remaining. It transpired he had suffered a collapsed lung but not before contributing seven points, four from frees and three phenomenal scores from play.

"With about ten minutes to go I got an awful pain. I'd never felt pain like it in my life," remembered McHugh. He was taken off and initially it was thought he was suffering from a shoulder injury. Despite having played a leading role in setting his team up for victory, the pain was so severe he had no further interest in the game. Over a post-match pint McHugh bumped into Dr Jim McDaid and McDaid drove him back to Letterkenny. "I could feel every bump on the road back," recalled McHugh, "they discovered I had a collapsed lung at Letterkenny hospital." As he was being wheeled down the ward, highlights of the game were being shown on 'The Sunday Game' and patients and staff had gathered in the television room. "The nurse asked me if I wanted to join them but I was so far through that I couldn't even watch the game." Fortunately, the lung started to heal by itself the following day and by the time the squad arrived at the hospital the following night, Martin was able to partake in celebrations.

McEniff with his blend of youth and experience had delivered. The vision of an Ulster title had been realised well within the time parameters envisaged. Donegal football supporters were drunk on the vapours of success. All-Ireland

Matt Gallagher

was in the net. The whole place came down on top of us. I said to myself, 'That's it. End of story. Lights out.'" Charlie Mulgrew felt it was "as lucky as hell". Exit Donegal and sheer despair descended on disbelieving supporters ringed around the pitch. For Molloy the goal was, "an oul' fluke 50 that ended in the back of our net. It was a total freak. We had two men on the line when we should have had two fellas on either side of the 'keeper." It was an expensive lesson to learn.

More drama followed in the remaining seven minutes but there was to be no way back. Galway were now two points up and although they had to finish the game with 14 men when they lost centre half back Peter Lee through injury, Donegal simply could not penetrate the massed Galway defence. Stephen Joyce added a point from a free and although Donegal replied with two late points from the boots of Tommy McDermott and Martin McHugh it was too little too late and time simply ran out. The big breakthrough which had seemed on the cards hadn't materialised.

"They failed to do themselves justice and generally they can have few complaints about the outcome," reported the *Irish News*. While several Donegal players had undoubtedly suffered stage-fright and had offered only a glimpse of the talent that had shone in Ulster, nonetheless, disappointment was palpable regarding the manner of defeat. Most neutral observers shared Sean Kilfeather's view in *The Irish Times*, that "Donegal deserved a draw."

The Donegal full-back line of McDermott, Griffin and Newton emerged with their reputations enhanced as did Michael Carr – Griffin in particular was magnificent. At the game was a 17-year-old Manus Boyle. Nine summers later he would light up the stadium in Donegal's finest moment, but from his seat in the stand he was impressed by the figure Griffin cut, "He was immense, we couldn't believe that he was at full back instead of midfield." Matt Gallagher remembers a conversation with Tommy McDermott from a few weeks before the match. "We were out socialising a few weeks before the match and Tommy was determined that he was going to take Stephen Joyce. And he did, he had a superb match on Joyce." Elsewhere, things largely did not go to plan and most performances fell well below par. Even so, Donegal held their own in the first half and entered the interval leading by 1-6 to 0-6. Donal Reid, who had a good game, had opened Donegal's account after ten minutes while Kieran Keeney had picked his spot and sent a scorcher to the Galway net after 15 minutes. McHugh was having little joy from play but was hitting the dead ball as well as ever. The referee drew the ire of the Donegal crowd and caused neutrals to scratch heads in amazement by awarding a free against Des Newton just before half time which cut Donegal's lead.

The second half began well with McHugh causing Galway problems. He was fouled near the sideline and converted his free with a real gem of a point from the most acute of angles. In the ninth minute he repeated the feat and Donegal were four points up. Between then and the 27th minute another McHugh point was Donegal's only response to three Galway points. On the sideline McEniff knew his team were in trouble, "We played with lots of spirit and enthusiasm but were not combining the way we can do and even when we went four points up I knew we were struggling." Out on the pitch Joyce McMullan knew it too:

The performance was probably one of the worst Donegal performances I was ever involved in. We weren't well prepared for the semi-final. We would have been used to Ulster football and the All-Ireland semi-final was a big occasion for us. The day may have beaten us but the performance was cat.

Worryingly for Donegal, Galway were notching up close on a dozen wides while they had not recorded a single wide at the other end of the pitch. Then Val Daly struck and statistics were suddenly immaterial. Charlie Mulgrew felt the game had passed him by, "I didn't play well and should probably have been taken off – quite a few of us should have been taken off. I don't know what happened us."

McEniff was devastated. Although the general wisdom was that his team had exceeded all expectation and that they would have many Croke Park sojourns, McEniff found the defeat a bitter pill to swallow. Seven years later, on a better day, the tears welled in McEniff's eyes as he recounted the pain of that defeat to Vincent Hogan of the *Irish Independent*:

Something died in '83. It broke my heart. The team was so young, so vibrant. They could have taken on the world, but it just went flat on us. I couldn't even begin to describe the disappointment I felt that day. I knew we should have beaten Galway.

Hogan takes up the story:

The evening of that game, McEniff could not bring himself to return to the team hotel. Instead, he walked to a little park in Belgrave Square where – during his student days – he had lived in a tiny flat. There he sat alone for the entire evening, his mind wracked with unreasonable depression. It was almost six on Monday morning before he could rejoin his team.

McEniff himself came under some fire for his sideline performance. The players, perhaps feeling they had let their manager down, requested McEniff to stay on in the Donegal hot seat.

Molloy, disappointed with his own performance, spoke of putting things right the following year. So too did McMullan and Mulgrew. Matt Gallagher, still sidelined since his appendix operation, also indicated his yearning to run out onto the Croke Park sod the following year. Their enthusiasm augured well for 1984. A word of warning was sounded by an old hand, a man who knew a thing or two about the uncertainties of football. "We have a team that can come back," agreed Brian McEniff, "our biggest difficulty will be to get out of Ulster again."

Thousands turned out to greet the team in Bundoran and Donegal Town on the Monday night. For a county starved of football success it was to be expected, nevertheless, it was a slightly disquieting time for some of the players. The reception, while driven by the best of intentions, made Anthony Molloy and others a little uncomfortable "For Donegal, winning Ulster was like winning the All-Ireland because we never thought of going the extra mile. We had lost the match and didn't want to march behind a band."

Galway manager Mattie McDonagh asked Donegal for a challenge match as part of their preparations for the All-Ireland final. The squad that Brian McEniff brought to Tuam Stadium was largely made up of under-21s. "Someone put the ball down on the 70 yard line," remembered McEniff, "there was a light following breeze and McHugh put it over the black spot. It was as good a kick as I've ever seen. For a small man he was a great striker of the ball." Martin Shovlin was playing in defence, "We beat Galway off the field, so much so that the crowd booed them off the pitch." For Donegal it was a case of what might have been. For Galway, it was defeat to Dublin in a robust All-Ireland final.

Years later Martin McHugh would ruefully admit, "We all thought – well, we're a young team, we'll be back in 1984, '85 and '86." No-one, not even McEniff, could have possibly imagined that it would be seven long years before a Donegal team would again grace Croke Park on a championship Sunday. Donal Reid concurred:

> I joined the senior panel at the end of 1982 and won an Ulster title the following summer. There were six or seven of us who thought this would be the norm for the rest of our careers but we then had a seven-year lapse and learned it wouldn't be as simple as that.

Still, as 'Peigí Rose' – also known as Fr Seán Gallagher – later commented, "Didn't we have ourselves some kind of a summer?"

⁂

National League 1982-83	Ulster Championship 1983
Donegal 2-4, Louth 1-11	Donegal 1-10, Armagh 0-7
Donegal 1-7, Monaghan 1-5	Donegal 1-14, Monaghan 1-9
Donegal 0-7, Laois 0-7	Donegal 1-14, Cavan 1-11
Donegal 2-7, Longford 1-9	
Donegal 0-7, Clare 0-8	**All-Ireland Series**
Donegal 1-2, Wexford 1-8	Donegal 1-11, Galway 1-12
Donegal 3-12, Fermanagh 2-9	

RESULTS

5
Centenary Year
(1983 – 1984)

"We celebrated [promotion] over a good steak
in the Killeshin Hotel in Portlaoise that day."

BRIAN MCENIFF – ON GAINING PROMOTION TO DIVISION TWO

In the aftermath of the All-Ireland semi-final defeat by Galway, every single Donegal player was absolutely certain of one thing: escape from Division Three was crucial. They needed to get in among the big boys to gain the experience that would ensure the next visit to Croke Park wasn't part of their learning curve. Big match experience needed to be gained in pitches around Ireland in the national league against the likes of Dublin, Offaly and Cork and not in Croke Park on an all too rare championship visit.

As the county recovered from the trauma visited upon them by Val Daly, McEniff was already planning an all-out assault on Division Three. The county was awash with exciting under-age talent should McEniff decide to add to his panel. Some were ready, some were close.

The under-21s – despite the presence of Matt Gallagher, Tommy McDermott, Anthony Molloy, Paul Carr, Seamus Meehan, Joyce McMullan and Sylvester Maguire – had failed in the defence of their Ulster and All-Ireland crowns. A Derry team glittering with the talent of McGuckian, Scullion, Cassidy, Barton and McNicholl ran riot in the 1983 Ulster under-21 final.

Brian Murray, a former De La Salle star from Ballyshannon, was breaking onto the under-21 team. Gary Walsh, the minor and under-21 goalkeeper, was already on board McEniff's senior panel. Walsh, another product of De La Salle in Ballyshannon, had his Ulster senior medal and would take over from the long serving Noel McCole in less than a year.

Ardara had defeated an Aodh Ruadh side going for their third under-21 title in a row in the 1983 county final. Previously Aodh Ruadh had won four minor titles in a row, 1979–1982. Anthony Molloy reckons the two games against Ballyshannon were his best ever for his club:

> We played Ballyshannon in 1983 and they had ten county under-21 play-
> ers while we had one, me. We drew with them the first day and beat
> them by a point the second day. I got great satisfaction from that as they
> were the kingpins of underage football.

In addition to county star Molloy, Ardara had a powerfully strong full-back in
the form of Martin Gavigan. A student at NIHE Limerick, Gavigan's club form
saw him drafted into the county under-21 panel.

James McHugh, fast emerging from the shadow cast by elder brother
Martin, was another graduate from the excellent minor side that had won an
Ulster minor league in 1982. He too found himself in the under-21 side.

The stocky Declan Bonner from the Rosses, brother of under-21 All-Ireland
winner Sean, really caught McEniff's attention. Bonner came through the ranks
with Rosses Rovers – the amalgamated Rosses outfit that swept through under-
age football in the early 1980s. Three years a county minor, Bonner was a rising
star who had also been drafted into the under-21 panel. McEniff liked what he
saw. Bonner, still only 18, was handed a county senior jersey. He was in at corner forward in the opening National Football League game against Westmeath.
Bonner scored a point on his debut and seemed set for a long uninterrupted
career in the county jersey. As Bonner recalls, it didn't quite work out that way:

> I played my first match for Donegal in 1983 but didn't play in the cham-
> pionship until 1987. I wasn't giving full commitment to football. I would
> always play a couple of league games prior to Christmas and then go off
> and play with Finn Harps and I enjoyed playing in the League of Ireland.
> While I had been involved with Donegal since 1983, it wasn't until
> 1990 that my career took off. We played a league match against Cork in
> Ballincollig. The experiment with four quarters was going on at the time
> and I scored 2-2 in the first quarter. I had just come back into the squad
> under Brian McEniff and needed something to give me confidence. I
> never really looked back after that.

Donegal coasted to an easy 0-12 to 1-5 win over the midlanders at Mullingar at the
beginning of October. It was their first competitive match since Croke Park and
was played on a heavy mucky pitch with lashing rain being whipped down field
by a strong wind – a typical league encounter. Donegal emerged unscathed with
the team playing well. McHugh accounted for half of Donegal's scores and Molloy
was in at centre-half forward despite recent injury worries. The big Ardara man,
still only 21 years of age, was already being bothered by the knee problem that
would dog him throughout his career. McEniff didn't know it then, but he had put

a Donegal team onto the field featuring six – the biggest number so far – of the men who would bring Sam to the Hills nine years later. Reid, Gallagher, McHugh, Molloy, McMullan and Bonner all featured that day at Cusack Park, Mullingar.

The promotion hunt stayed on course a fortnight later when Wicklow visited MacCumhaill Park and Donegal cruised to a 0-13 to 0-4 victory. It was an impressive display against a Wicklow side with a reputation for being physical. They had spent a season in Division Two and had beaten Donegal at Aughrim in the 1981-82 league. The *Democrat* was there to record further good displays from Reid, Gallagher and Molloy, while the star of the show was new boy Bonner: "Particularly impressive was young Declan Bonner. The red-haired Rosses lad scored three magnificent points, two of them from acute angles, to cap a great display." In a playing career that stretched over a decade in the Donegal jersey, Declan Bonner seldom escaped reference to his distinctive mop of curly red hair!

A top of the table clash with Monaghan at Ballybay followed. Many expected a repeat of the violent championship encounter during the summer when Donegal had ran out winners. That didn't happen – on either account. Monaghan were deserving winners, 0-8 to 1-9.

Monaghan were in the driving seat. Donegal were now depending on someone else to beat them if they were to stand any chance of making the league quarter-finals. As it happened, Clare pipped Monaghan by a point in the next game while Donegal put themselves back in the hunt in Ballybofey, brushing past Laois by 1-10 to 0-8. McHugh, back in the side for the first time since the Westmeath match, was in fine form contributing three superb points from play and one converted free. With four games played, three teams now sat at the top of Division Three – Monaghan, Donegal and Wicklow.

Things looked good for Donegal by the time the players, management and supporters sat down to Christmas dinner. Clare, the team who had scuppered promotion hopes the previous year, had been accounted for at Ballybofey at the beginning of the month on a scoreline of 2-8 to 0-5. Donegal, with four wins out of five matches, seemed poised for promotion. But McEniff had some reason for discomfort. The final scoreline against Clare didn't really reflect the overall game – Clare had caused problems. And with Molloy out of the equation with injury, he had a serious quandary at midfield.

The Christmas break broke the momentum. Antrim and Carlow remained to be played and most supporters were confident that promotion was assured. In the meantime, McEniff pencilled in a number of challenge match in the New Year, beginning with All-Ireland champions Dublin at Dalkey. It promised to be a valuable indicator of how far Donegal had come. McEniff's assessment of the subsequent 1-6 to 2-8 defeat was blunt. "We played third division football against a first division side," he told the *Democrat*.

It was the first time that Donegal played Dublin in the 1980s. John O'Leary, Gerry Hargan and Mick Kennedy were the Dublin players who would go on to survive the decade in the sky blue and a date with destiny in 1992, while Gallagher, Reid, McHugh, McMullan, Bonner and substitute Gary Walsh all opposed them that day in Dalkey; and it was the day Matt Gallagher scored the most spectacular goal of his career. The ball was dribbling harmlessly wide of the Donegal goal following a shot by Dublin half forward Maurice O'Callaghan when Matt came tearing into the picture. In a dramatic attempt to clear the ball Matt succeeded in blasting it to the roof of the Donegal net, much to the delight of the Dubs. For once he hadn't much to say for himself!

At the beginning of February Donegal made the trip to Casement Park for the penultimate round of the national league and, by indulging in a short passing game in the worst of conditions, contributed hugely to a surprise 0-8 to 1-6 defeat by Antrim. It was a huge setback for the county. McEniff was never more disappointed as his team trudged off the field like broken men. "I think the boys took Antrim for granted," he recalled. Once again Donegal seemed to have shot themselves in the foot. Certainly progression to the quarter-finals was almost certainly gone and the best it seemed they could now hope for was a play-off with Wicklow to decide who would join Monaghan in Division Two. Donegal were away to lowly Carlow in their final game while Wicklow faced bottom of the table Westmeath – games both Donegal and Wicklow were expected to win as they chased the second promotion spot.

Despite the Antrim defeat there was some positive news in the camp, Molloy was back after his knee problems and McHugh was on song up front. Indeed McHugh was about to receive national recognition for his brilliance in the green and gold jersey. When the All-Star team was announced later that month, McHugh found himself in illustrious company named at right corner forward in an All-Star team that contained Paudie O'Shea, Tommy Drumm, Jack O'Shea, Barney Rock, Matt Connor and Colm O'Rourke.

McHugh was the only Donegal man to get an All-Star although Des Newton, Tommy McDermott, Martin Griffin, Michael Carr and Seamus Bonner were also nominated. Big Griffin in particular was most unfortunate not to join McHugh on the All-Star selection as many neutral observers felt he was the best full-back of the championship. All-Star politics had cost him his place and the full-back position was filled by Stephen Kinneavy of Connacht champions Galway.

McHugh's All-Star quality was very much to the fore as he notched up a personal tally of 1-6 in Donegal's emphatic but expected 2-11 to 0-3 win over Carlow at a wet Dr Cullen Park. It was the day Sylvester Maguire made his full senior debut for Donegal and an impressive one at that. As the players started off on the long journey home the talk on the bus centred on the expected playoff against Wicklow. McEniff recalled the moment they realised they were promoted to Division Two without having to kick another ball:

Just as we pulled into Portlaoise the result of the Westmeath-Wicklow game came through and it was a draw which gave us promotion to Division Two. We celebrated our victory over a good steak in the Killeshin Hotel in Portlaoise that day.

It was a good day for McEniff and Donegal football. Promotion to Division Two had been his goal, even more so than championship success. As the *Democrat* pointed out, everything would change because of the higher standard of football Donegal would now enjoy, "Better players, better opposition, better grounds, better referees." At the fourth attempt since taking over as manager, McEniff had finally broken the status quo and moved Donegal into new territory with some of the country's top teams. It had been achieved quietly and without fuss. "It was a special journey home for us all right," recalls Sylvester Maguire.

❄ ❄ ❄ ❄

One hundred years after the founding of the Gaelic Athletic Association, the Gaelic footballers of Ireland's most northerly county were certainly to the fore in March 1984. The vocational schools team – the proverbial bridesmaids for several years – finally delivered an Ulster title at the beginning of March. Five Donegal men were involved in Ulster's successful defence of the Railway Cup title – Michael Carr, Michael Lafferty, Martin McHugh and Tommy McDermott all played while Des Newton was on the panel. McEniff was manager and, often in partnership with Tyrone's Art McRory, would go on to become Ulster's most successful Railway Cup manager of all time.

Once again, Armagh lay in wait for Donegal in the championship. Donegal got one up on the Orchard County at the end of March when they beat them by 1-8 to 0-8 in a scrappy opening game in the Dr McKenna Cup. McEniff gave Brian Murray a call just before the game and the Aodh Ruadh youngster got his first run out in a senior jersey that day, contributing a solid 20 minutes near the end and scoring a fine point. Another huge piece of the jigsaw had just fallen into place.

There was other football to be played before Armagh would be faced at the Athletic Grounds on a championship Sunday in June. A much decorated Kerry team that would go on to lift Sam in centenary year came to MacCumhaill Park for the first round of the Centenary Cup. It would be another of those progress indicators for Donegal. Kerry had come through Division One of the National League unbeaten. This was the team that had been on course two years previously to claim an unprecedented fifth consecutive All-Ireland title. That dream came undone thanks to a late, late Seamus Darby goal for Offaly, a goal not unlike Val Daly's effort that felled Donegal the following year.

MacCumhaill Park was jammed as young and old flocked to glimpse the greatest footballing machine of all time. Practically every single Kerry player who lined out that day was already regarded as a football legend across the land. For Donegal players, it was an all too rare chance to play the mighty Kingdom competitively. Matt Gallagher, who marked the peerless Mikey Sheehy, remembers the occasion:

> We stayed with Kerry for a while and then they just blew us away. They never panicked. We played at the top of our game but when we made a couple of mistakes they punished us. They were so good and just knew what to do. The Bomber was such a huge player for them and was just impossible to mark. We played well and Kerry were gracious enough to say that but lots of teams played well against Kerry without beating them. It was great to play them competitively. The only other way we would have done that was in an All-Ireland semi-final or final.

It was a credible effort by Donegal and although they fell by 0-8 to 0-11, Kerry were made to fight very hard for their three-point victory. For 50 minutes Donegal stood toe-to-toe with the Kingdom with the Donegal defence more than holding their own with a forward line that boasted the services of Timmy O'Dowd, Denis 'Ogie' Moran, Pat Spillane, Dermot O'Donoghue, Eoin 'Bomber' Liston and Mikey Sheehy. McEniff had much reason to be happy with his defence of late. In particular Matt Gallagher, Des Newton, Big Griffin, Tommy McDermott, Michael Carr and Brendan Dunleavy had jelled incredibly well as a unit and seldom under-performed.

Up front, as always, was where Donegal's problems lay. When they were really needed scores weren't always forthcoming. This was a Donegal team which relied too heavily on the magic boots of Martin McHugh. McHugh had to come off for much of the second half against Kerry when he took a heavy knock to the face but as usual he was Donegal's top scorer with four points. Indeed McHugh seemed intent on adding to his ever growing legend within the county. His club, Kilcar, had not been beaten at their home pitch in Towney in a league game in almost four years. While Kilcar had many fine footballers, this record owed much to McHugh. When Na Rossa rolled into Towney at the beginning of April 1984 the Bonner brothers set about the task of demolishing that record – and very nearly succeeded. Three points behind, Kilcar desperately pegged them back to one as time ran out. McHugh, who had been quite brilliant throughout, collected the ball well out from the Na Rossa posts and rode several heavy tackles to land a famous point and maintain an incredible record. It was, noted the *Democrat*, a score worthy of an All-Star.

❄ ❄ ❄ ❄

Indeed one of the Bonner brothers, Donal, swapped Towney for Croke Park just a couple of weeks later as Donegal romped to a spectacular 3-9 to 2-3 win over

Longford in the All-Ireland Vocational Schools final. It was another famous day. Former county player and McEniff's senior team trainer, PJ McGowan, was in charge of a fine Donegal side that included a few players who would go on to achieve great things in a Donegal jersey.

On the panel was a young lad from Carrick Vocational School by the name of John Joe Doherty. Killybegs Vocational School provided a corner forward who was described in *Democrat* pen pictures as being an "accurate, dangerous forward with great fielding ability." His name was Manus Boyle. Boyle was one of a deadly full-forward line that included match winners Luke Gavigan and the aforementioned Donal Bonner. "Unreal footballers," commented Martin Gavigan years later. Injury would shortly destroy the playing careers of two of those three players and their loss to Donegal football would be immense. Twenty years later, Manus Boyle, John Cunningham and Tommy Ryan would describe Donal Bonner as simply the best footballer they ever played with at any grade. High praise from a trio of All-Ireland winning senior footballers who had played with some of the best footballers the county had ever seen.

The vocational schools side of 1984 was the first Donegal team to win an inter-county football title at Croke Park. There were huge performances throughout the pitch. The most dangerous full-forward line on a Donegal team for many years accounted for 2-6 between them. Manus Boyle's first outing in Croke Park was a memorable one. In addition to an earlier point, he scored Donegal's third goal by taking the ball around the goalkeeper before blasting it to the net: "It was great to play in Croke Park and get on a pitch where there were stands. My main memory though, was how good Donal Bonner was."

The Donegal team who claimed Donegal's second All-Ireland title at any grade were: David Meehan; Jimmy Brennan, Denis Carbery, Cornelius McFadden; Rory O'Neill, Niall Campbell, Cormac McGarvey; Patrick Gallagher (captain), Brian Mor Gallagher; Owen Bonner, Eamon McNiallais, Eamon Cunningham; Manus Boyle, Luke Gavigan, Donal Bonner. Subs: Brian Coyle, Roger McShane, Paul Carr, John McConnell, Conor White and John Joe Doherty.

The youngsters weren't yet done. There was another title to come from a young Donegal side. The minors had fought their way through to the final of the Ulster league against Down – a title Donegal had also claimed in 1982. This team had new names. Manus Boyle, the vocational schools star. John Cunningham, a name the whole county would soon come to know, was a centre-half back with a long senior career stretching ahead of him. And the star of the team was a big attacking midfielder by the name of Barry Cunningham. All three were products of Jimmy White's invigoration of under-age football in Killybegs. In 1984 Killybegs won the county under-18 title for the first time. They defended it in 1985 and won two Ulster minor titles in those years just for good measure.

Donegal had five points to spare over Down in the league decider at Irvinestown. Unfortunately they later failed to add an Ulster championship title and fell to Armagh at a windswept Athletic Grounds. A speedy little black youngster by the name of Joey Cunningham scored the winning point in Donegal's 0-7 to 2-2 defeat. It wasn't to be the last time that Joey Cunningham would destroy Donegal hopes.

❋ ❋ ❋ ❋

The seniors scraped past Antrim – a team that had begun to make a nuisance of themselves – and reached the final of the McKenna Cup against Tyrone who had just made the leap to Division One. Tyrone and Donegal hadn't met competitively in four years but Donegal had much to fear from their Six County neighbours. The subsequent nine-point thrashing inflicted by Tyrone was not ideal mental preparation for the championship which was by now just three weeks away. Tyrone simply walked through a listless Donegal. Eugene McKenna, Plunkett Donaghy and Damian O'Hagan proved too hot to handle while John Lynch earned the wrath of the Donegal supporters for his brand of man-marking on McHugh. That Tyrone defeated Donegal so easily without the services of their ace forward, Big Frank McGuigan (who would score 11 famous points from play in that summer's Ulster final), was of even more concern to despondent Donegal supporters. It didn't augur well for the championship. Question marks were forming.

McEniff's team seemed to have the whip hand over Armagh but statistical anoraks in Ulster would have been aware that only Down and Derry had successfully defended their Ulster titles in the previous 20 years. History was against the Ulster champions too. When Donegal won the title in 1972 and 1974 they were dumped out of the following year's championship in the first round on both occasions.

Preparation for the Armagh game was thrown into disarray the week before the match. Martin McHugh, who by his own admission was playing the best football of his life, was injured in a challenge match in Sligo. "I must have scored seven or eight points in the first half," remembers McHugh:

> I was going through with the ball in the second half and a fella pushed me in the back. I ripped my hamstring from top to bottom. Mickey Lafferty got hurt in the match too and we both missed the Armagh match. I was worth more than two points and I think we could have gone on to defend the Ulster title.

To compound the predicament that McEniff found himself in, McIntyre and Mulgrew had both emigrated to the States and Sean Bonner was also gone. All would be missed sorely as Armagh's old hand, Joe Kernan, and a speedy newcomer by the name of Gerard Houlihan were about to prove that Armagh still had a sting in their tail.

The first round game in 1984 was Ulster football at its most typical. An action-packed yet foul-ridden game which contained a well-taken goal, some quality points from play and frees, a missed penalty, hard tackling and two send-ings off. But it was Donegal who finished on the wrong side of a 0-12 to 1-10 scoreline. There was plenty of talking points for the visiting supporters. Seamus Bonner uncharacteristically hit a weak penalty which Brian McAlinden easily toe-poked wide. Tommy McDermott got sent off 15 minutes into the second half. Gerry Curran from Ballyshannon, who had not even been in the panel up to then, was parachuted in by McEniff and went on to hit five good points from frees.

Years later, Martin Gavigan would marvel at the way McEniff would pull players out of thin air:

> At the end of the day McEniff would have done anything to win, it did-n't matter if you trained or not, if he thought he could get something out of you, it would be for the winning of the game that McEniff would do it, not favouritism or anything.

Big Griffin, recovered from injury, was back at his best. Sylvester Maguire made his championship debut and was Donegal's best forward with three points:

> Tommy McDermott was the referee that day and I asked him how long there was to go. He said there was one minute left and I knew we were going to be caught that wee bit short, and we were caught.

Gary Walsh also made his championship debut when Noel McCole had to come off injured mid-way through the second half. It was to be his last appearance in the Ulster championship. McEniff moved Donal Reid back into defence follow-ing McDermott's dismissal and he looked very impressive attacking from deep.

In the absence of Martin McHugh, Donal Reid had slotted into the centre half-forward position and was involved in one of the sendings off – his man was sent to the line for putting him through a hoarding at the side of the field! Reid the for-ward had been guilty of several notable misses in front of goal in games stretch-ing back as far as the national league. McDermott's misfortune had forced McEniff to pull him back. To those who hadn't seen Reid in defence before it must have seemed a strange switch to make. As always, McEniff knew what he was doing as Reid had been playing club football with the Bundoran side.

> McEniff got to know me well as a player at centre half-back. I suppose he thought I was better facing the ball than getting the ball and turning. I found that I could read the game well from there. I didn't have the accu-racy to be a forward, nor the incisive pace that was needed. He started to play me in the back line and I enjoyed it. I knew then that I should have

probably played in the back line long before that.

Reid, a hotel manager in Bundoran with McEniff, would only line out as a forward once more in a championship career that stretched almost a decade ahead. Reid the defender had just been born. The move to defence didn't completely dull his attacking instincts. As the years rolled by, Reid became known as an attacking half-back. It gave Donegal a hitherto undiscovered attacking dimension. Reid's method of defending was, for the time, unorthodox but highly effective. He explained it thus: "Half-forwards are usually very quick. I felt that if I could get a score he would spend more time watching me than me having to watch him."

The decision to play a challenge match so close to the championship vexes McHugh yet. He missed the most important part of the club season too. His club had defeated eventual county champions Four Masters in the first round, first leg match in Donegal Town:

We went out after two replays and I wasn't fit to play in either of them over the head of that challenge match. That's the most disappointing thing. I wasn't bold enough to stand up and ask why we needed a challenge game so close to the championship.

Already one of the leading figures on the pitch, McHugh would soon become a leader in the dressing room. Chastened by the crushing disappointment of centenary year, he'd never again sit quietly when he felt something needed to be said.

After the heady excitement of the previous year it was going to be a long inter-county free summer for Donegal supporters. Not having taken part in the championship and then seeing his team eliminated was a source of great regret for Martin McHugh, "I felt we could have gone on to greater things. We could have gone on to win Ulster in 1984. Things went completely downhill after that."

McEniff, with some justification, claimed that his team were tired. It had been a long road and many of the players had been in almost constant action for their county since the under-21 campaign of 1981. A rest, however forced, could do no harm.

❀

RESULTS

National League 1983-84

Donegal 0-12, Westmeath 1-5	Donegal 0-8, Antrim 1-6
Donegal 0-13, Wicklow 0-4	Donegal 2-11, Carlow 0-3
Donegal 0-8, Monaghan 1-9	
Donegal 1-10, Laois 0-8	**Ulster Championship 1984**
Donegal 2-8, Clare 0-5	Donegal 0-12, Armagh 1-10

6

No More Steak Dinners

(October 1984 – August 1986)

"It was not Brian McEniff's fault."

MARTIN McHUGH – NEWCASTLE, MAY 1986

Donegal made its acquaintance with Division Two of the National Football League at Dr Hyde Park, Roscommon, in the second weekend of October 1984. It was a meeting that lived in the memory not because Donegal claimed a valuable league point, but rather for the dubious timekeeping of Offaly referee Jody Gunning.

With the final minute ticking down Donegal led by two points. There had been little or no stoppages. Danger loomed as Roscommon won a free within shooting range of the Donegal goals. As the Donegal defence lined the goalmouth expecting Dermot Earley to blast for goal in an effort to save the game, they were amazed when he tapped it over the bar. Time was up. Big Griffin, who'd had a great game at full-back, took his sweet time with the kick out. As his punt sailed into midfield the expected whistle blast did not materialise. Roscommon won another free, far out on the right wing. All Dermot Earley's great experience was now brought to bear on proceedings. He played a quick one-two with Eamon McManus, charged straight at the Donegal defence and won a soft free. Job done, he tapped it over the bar himself for the equaliser. Finally, three minutes over time, Jody Gunning blew the whistle.

Welcome to Division Two and craftier, more physical football. Donegal's defence, as always, had a fine outing and only McHugh really really shone up front. It had been a bit of an eye-opener.

By the time Donegal faced their second match against Mayo, the county side had been through the wars. Des Newton was out with a broken foot but even the loss of the ever-consistent Roscommon man paled compared to a controversy that had its source in Gaelic Park, New York, at the beginning of November.

The New York junior and senior championship finals were being staged. The County Board had issued a warning that Donegal inter-county players – who were in demand to play for the Donegal New York team – should stay at home and concentrate on the national league. It was, as Brian McEniff commented, "a ticklish problem" as Donegal inter-county footballers had a long association with the game in the city, stretching back to his own playing days.

McEniff however was anxious that his players wouldn't travel. "I wish Donegal [New York] all the best in the final but I would hope the players would make the proper decision and make the commitment to their county at home," he told Sean McGoldrick, the County Board PRO, in the week before the New York finals (the interview was published after the incident). Five senior players ignored the warning noises and played in New York. Michael Lafferty, Brendan Dunleavy, Martin McHugh, Joyce McMullan and Anthony Molloy all starred in Gaelic Park. Indeed McHugh and Molloy had also featured the previous Sunday when the senior final had ended in a draw. The County Executive was furious and lashed out at the entire senior panel.

Michael Lafferty, arguably the county's most successful senior captain, was stripped of the captaincy. Travel expenses to training were cancelled until Christmas. A written commitment to Donegal would be required from every single player. And, there would be no more steak dinners after training sessions. McEniff, confirmed the County Board chairman, Michael Gillespie, was fully supportive of the County Executive's stance. A full meeting of the County Board later fully endorsed the decision. The players were stung. A strike was threatened.

In the end the Mayo match went ahead and the unfortunate Connacht men suffered at Fr Tierney Park, Ballyshannon, as the Donegal players answered the critics who questioned their commitment. Eight points separated the sides at the end. The Donegal defence that day had a new man in the line up, one Martin Shovlin from Dunkineely. It was as impressive a full debut in the Donegal senior jersey as they came. Shovlin, the under-21 man who was dogged by injury in 1981 and 1982, had finally caught the eye of the county selectors again. Playing at wing half back, he was pitted against a rising star in Mayo, Padraig Brogan, who would have a part to play in the footballing futures of both Mayo and Donegal.

Early in 1984 his club, Naomh Ultan, made the wise decision of asking Shovlin, with his bit of county experience, to devise a club training programme. His subsequent training regime nearly killed some of the Dunkineely lads but it paid off and by summer's end Naomh Ultan were intermediate champions. Shovlin himself impressed along the way and got the call from McEniff. The man described by Naomh Ultan as "that most ruthless of trainers" was a county man again.

In the end the New York controversy was buried. A marathon four-hour meeting between players, team management and County Executive sorted the problem. According to Joyce McMullan, "It went away just as quick as it

Noel Hegarty

arrived." Despite a sealing of lips by both sides, it seemed that everything had been restored, including Michael Lafferty's captaincy. Gone though, went the rumour around the county, was the big feed after training – there would be no more steak dinners!

Anthony Molloy made no apologies for travelling to New York:

> It was great to get to the States in those years. I went out in 1983 for a couple of weeks and for a couple of weeks again in 1984. It was the only thing we were getting out of football at the time. Some people probably weren't happy with us leaving our clubs to go out and play in the States. I think we might have been cut down to tea and sandwiches, but the steak dinners were reinstated some time afterwards!

Donegal had three matches remaining before Christmas against Offaly, Monaghan and Dublin. All three resulted in defeats. They left themselves with too much to do thanks to a terrible first half display against Offaly. Despite holding Offaly scoreless for the last 21 minutes of the game they couldn't peg them back and lost by 0-9 to 1-8. Monaghan were simply the better side at MacCumhaill Park and when Dublin visited the same venue at the beginning of December Donegal were edged out in a thriller. It was a day when the referee took centre stage, making some questionable decisions around goals and becoming the epicentre of an after-match scuffle.

Donegal showed no respect for the mighty Dubs who had earlier lost their All-Ireland crown to Kerry. It was a real edge-of-the-seat contest that ended in disaster when Dublin hit the front for the first time two minutes from the end – Barney Rock punching home a goal. Square ball, was the opinion of every Donegal supporter in MacCumhaill Park but not the referee, Padraig Gorman of Sligo. It was an unfortunate end to the match for Martin Shovlin as he had a blinder on Rock throughout. It was one of those maddening matches. McHugh had the ball in the net as early as the 13th minute. Penalty, indicated the referee, hauling back play. McHugh's subsequent kick was deflected out by O'Leary. A big opportunity had been missed.

Later, Ciaran Duff had a goal disallowed for Dublin for a square infringement. And later still, in injury time, Donegal forwards were adjudged to have fouled John O'Leary as they helped a last-gasp punt into the Dublin square to the back of the net. McEniff was so incensed by some of the decisions that he raced onto the field afterwards to remonstrate with the referee. Things got out of hand when he was joined by an even more aggrieved supporter who grabbed the official. McEniff pushed the spectator away and a confusing melee ensued. Martin Shovlin recalled Dublin midfielder Brian Mullins being escorted from the field. The Donegal manager later escaped with a caution for his conduct from the Games Administration Committee at Croke Park.

No More Steak Dinners

Donegal were now in big trouble. Only two games remained and both needed to be won. However, by the time Donegal fans drove out of Dundalk at the beginning of February, everyone had resigned themselves to another stint in Division Three. Louth, described by Matt Gallagher as "as durable team" had just sneaked a win in injury time following an ugly battle in St Bridget's Park.

Redemption followed at Ballyshannon. Wexford, who were chasing promotion, were decisively outclassed by a Donegal team that had found its rhythm again. McHugh was outstanding from the dead ball, knocking over eight glorious points. McMullan was back in form and Reid was relishing running from deep.

Clones was chosen as the battlefield for the subsequent play-off with Louth. Many expected the game to be another rough-house affair but that didn't materialise as Donegal scraped through by 2-7 to 2-5 in a poor game. Seamus Bonner, in the twilight of a great career, was the saviour and his two goals – one just seven minutes from the end – proved the difference. Another Donegal stalwart was nearing the end of his career. Goalkeeper Noel McCole injured his elbow and his deputy, Gary Walsh, stepped in to make his competitive debut:

> I came on with about ten minutes to go. We were losing when I came on and I hardly touched the ball other than for a couple of kick outs. Martin Griffin was full-back that day and to have someone like that in front of you was brilliant. He was a great big fella, always full of conversation. If there was a high ball coming in you didn't jump with Griffin – you stood back and let him jump.

Division Two status had been maintained but only just. McEniff took his fair share of flack following the game and experienced a difficult time from some delegates at the next County Board meeting. For the first time since he took on the job in the autumn of 1980, the wolves were at the door.

❄ ❄ ❄ ❄

The Open Draw and the McKenna Cup provided breathing space. Laois, Wicklow, Waterford, Derry and Fermanagh were all defeated – some with a struggle, some impressively – allowing Donegal gain some much-needed momentum. A young Cork side ended the Open Draw adventure at Croke Park towards the end of April with a win that was more convincing than the 1-6 to 0-10 scoreline would suggest. It was another unhappy outing at GAA headquarters – would Donegal ever win a competitive senior match there? – but some consolation was gained by the red hot form of Donal Reid and Joyce McMullan. And the old warrior himself, Seamus Bonner, got his goal at Croke Park. "We didn't play well. Maybe the hoodoo was working then," mused Matt Gallagher.

A five-point victory over Cavan at the end of July brought a fifth McKenna

Cup title to the county, the first since 1975. But by then the seniors had another disastrous championship to their name and the McKenna Cup was no longer the kind of silverware Donegal supporters would settle for.

✴ ✴ ✴ ✴

It had all begun so well in Ballybofey on the third Sunday in May 1985. Down, national league semi-finalists, were hot favourites to emerge victorious. McEniff had no problems with his team being underdogs. "We'll give them hell," he promised the *Democrat*. And his side did just that.

"The followers of football in Ulster have a rich season in store if the rest of the provincial championship equals the marvellous quality of this game," was the enthusiastic opinion of Paddy Downey in the next morning's *Irish Times*. He wasn't wrong and 7,400 supporters, the vast majority of them roaring on the home side, witnessed an intoxicating game of football which saw Donegal withstand everything Down had to throw at them in a super-charged, top quality second half.

Donegal had a good opening 35 minutes yet it was the Mourne men who went in at half time the happier team. With 20 minutes on the clock Donegal were 1-4 to 0-2 ahead. The whole team was contributing to the *blitzkrieg* being inflicted on Down and Martin McHugh was tormentor-in-chief. Down had no answer to him despite the presence of Paddy O'Rourke at centre-half back. It was McHugh who collected the ball at midfield in the 18th minute and waltzed past several defenders before unleashing a great goalbound shot. Pat Donnan, in the Down goals, managed to parry the ball out but only as far as Kieran Keeney and the Ardara man duly hammered it to the net.

Then disaster struck. Mason had just tagged on a Down point but worse was to follow in the shape of two Down goals in just four minutes – scores which caused shock waves to ripple around MacCumhaill Park. Mickey Linden didn't endear himself to Donegal players or supporters when he seemed to take a dive in the parallelogram. Goal number one was a converted penalty from John McCartan. Goal number two came courtesy of a glorious volley by Liam Heaney following a defence splitting pass from Ambrose Rodgers. Rodgers, who had a fine game in the red and black jersey, struck over a great point just before John Gough's half-time whistle sounded. In scarcely five minutes an impressive five-point lead had been obliterated and Donegal now faced a three-point deficit.

There was much reason for the concern on Donegal faces around the ground during the break. Midfield was being lost and Down were actually creating more scoring chances. However, over in the dressing rooms, McEniff was ahead of the game and making the changes that would produce a grandstand second half and ultimately a Donegal victory. The most important of the changes was the transfer of Anthony Molloy to midfield. The big Ardara man, noted the *Irish Independent*, "provided the platform from which the victory effort was finally launched". Molloy's presence around the middle also helped Big Griffin, who had been struggling a little, to up his performance. Gallagher, Keeney, Maguire, Dunleavy and Newton were also about to stand up and be counted.

Gary Walsh was making his full senior championship debut in the white heat of Ballybofey. Noel McCole's career, which had stretched back to the Ulster Final replay of 1974, was over bar the shouting. Ever present between Donegal's championship posts from 1974, the injury he picked up in the national league play-off didn't heal and he handed his mantle to Gary Walsh. Walsh marked his arrival with a breathtaking display of goalkeeping. Three times, early in the second half, he denied Down at a time when a Down goal would have spelled the end. The saves, reckoned the *Independent*'s man, were of "near miracle quality". Fiercely competitive, Walsh hated conceding goals. "While I played well in my first championship match, I was disappointed to let in two goals."

A ding-dong battle ensued which raged throughout the second half. Donegal played like men possessed yet Down just about clung on to the lead. All that changed in the 64th minute when Kieran Keeney was pulled down in the square. Penalty for Donegal – all eyes turned to Martin McHugh. McHugh had been plagued all day by Down's gamesmanship when he was taking frees. Big Liam Austin constantly stood with his arms raised less than the required 14 yards away and would rush at McHugh as he struck the ball. John Treanor and Mickey Linden had got in on the act too by running alongside McHugh in an effort to distract him.

McHugh knew what to expect as he placed the ball on the penalty spot. An All-Star, Railway Cup winner and experienced championship campaigner, he was oblivious to Down's antics. His mind was flashing back to the penalty John O'Leary had saved in the same goals in the national league:

> I looked at the line but nobody was telling me anything so I had to make up my own mind. Willie Lafferty, who has died since, was a great supporter and he shouted out, "Don't let McHugh take that penalty," because he remembered me missing the one against Dublin. I changed my style for that kick. I would normally have hit it with the inside of my boot but this time I hammered it with the outside of my boot.

The *Democrat* takes up the story:

> There was an extraordinary scene as McHugh stepped back to take the penalty with Down players trying to get as close as possible to him to distract him and Donegal players getting between them and McHugh. Despite all the pushing and shoving around him, however, McHugh remained ice cool and fairly rattled the net with a blockbuster of a shot.

Three points up but McHugh wasn't finished yet. Two minutes later he added a supreme insurance point. Matt Gallagher hoofed a mighty clearance up the right wing which McHugh duly collected and kicked between the posts from long range while scarcely glancing in that general direction. He had contributed 1-7 in scores but his brilliance on the day could not be measured merely on scores alone. By the time the 1984-85 season statistics were added up, McHugh was the top inter-county scorer in the country with 6-89, ahead of Barney Rock, Eamon McEneaney and Dermot Earley. Seamus Bonner added a point and Matt Gallagher had the final say when he deflected a late Ambrose Rodgers goal effort over the bar for a famous 2-12 to 2-8 victory.

It was a good day for Donegal football. But the euphoria was short-lived – Monaghan would see to that. Less than a month later they completely crushed Donegal in Castleblaney. Ten points separated the sides at the end of a dark day for Donegal. Donegal scored 0-7 against Monaghan's 1-14. That McHugh scored six of those points from frees was a good indicator of a Donegal attack that suffered a complete breakdown. Midfield had crashed. Mulgrew was in the midst of a three-month suspension which didn't help matters. Only Maguire, Newton and Gallagher emerged with any credit. While he had played well, Matt Gallagher recalls the game in stark terms:

> It was like a nightmare, and it was one we repeated in 1995. It was prob-ably the dirtiest game I ever played in. They brought us to Castleblaney and just battered us. We kept battering back at them but it didn't work and we didn't play well. We don't play well when we get involved in that. Monaghan were a very good side and they blew us away.

The concession of a goal in the second half shattered the confidence of right-half back Donal Reid:

> Our heads weren't in it. I was blocked while coming out with the ball – we weren't sharp enough – and when I turned around the ball was in the roof of the net. I don't think we younger lads realised how serious this football was and we weren't putting in the effort we should have been.

In fairness Monaghan had a good team which had earlier won the national league at Armagh's expense and they would go on to win the Ulster title that year. It was a team that never really got the recognition it deserved. That was of little consolation to a bitterly disappointed McEniff, who acknowledged the display as "pathetic". Rumour was that he'd had enough and was about to quit. As usual, he had his fair share of critics that day as thousands of Donegal fans streamed out of Castleblaney with ten minutes to go.

It was difficult to explain what had happened. Years later McEniff was still none the wiser: "the only game I could never quite explain." Some 12,000 people had just witnessed one of the worst Donegal performances of all time. McEniff, as ever, was frank when he spoke to the press. "I have to find out what is wrong. If I find it is myself, I will go. No one will have to tell me to go. I will want to do what I think is right for the county."

It was the end of the road for some old hands. Seamus Bonner pulled the curtain down on a great career that stretched back to 1972, included 27 championship appearances, numerous thundering goals and three Ulster senior championship medals. As the big Dublin-based Garda left Castleblaney that day he was not to know that seven years into the future he would still be involved, albeit in a different capacity, when Donegal football had its most famous day. Lafferty, Keeney and Griffin would have other days in the Donegal shirt but their tenure too was coming to an end. A new team would have to be built. Conaghan's boys from 1982 would have to form the backbone as the old hands stepped aside. And fresh blood would have to be found to inject new life into a jaded team that was plainly going nowhere.

As it happened, the youngsters who would one day provide Donegal football with new life and new hope were on view that very summer as they dazzled the county with their undoubted footballing ability.

❊ ❊ ❊ ❊

In 1979 a young fellow by the name of Jimmy White managed a Killybegs under-12 side to a county title. Two years later the same bunch of lads captured the under-14 county title as they cut through an unfortunate Ardara by 5-14 to 0-3. The scoreline was typical of their winning margins. It wasn't that the opposition was poor, Killybegs really were *that* good.

There was one notable addition to the Killybegs side in 1981. John Cunningham, a Killybegs man born in London, had made quite an impact since arriving in the fishing town and was now team captain. Razda had landed. Cunningham really was some player. In August 1982 Jimmy White took his protegees to Dublin to compete in the Óg Sport Gael competition. Seven games later they were undefeated and had reached the quarter-final where they were just squeezed out by Kildare. Player of the tournament, as judged by Brian Mullins, Mickey Whelan and Jack O'Shea, was the youngster who less than two years previously had never played Gaelic football – John Cunningham.

Killybegs first ever county minor championship was realised in Centenary Year, as was the minor league title. The side was captained by Manus Boyle. Three of his team mates that day were John Cunningham, his cousin Barry Cunningham and Barry McGowan. In 1985, all three had a year's football they would never forget in the company of a lad from Carrick and another from Termon.

❊ ❊ ❊ ❊

John Joe Doherty was a sub on the All-Ireland winning vocational schools team of 1984. He was marked as one for the future by neutrals attending the Naomh Columba versus Aodh Ruadh under-16 county final of 1984 – a game he totally dominated. When Donegal subsequently fielded an under-16 county team for the first time in a number of years, John Joe was captain. By the time Doherty prepared to line out with the Killybegs trio for the Donegal minors in the 1985 Ulster Minor Championship in May, he had a second Vocational Schools All-Ireland medal in his pocket – this time as a player. Cork had been outclassed in the All-Ireland Vocational Schools final at Croke Park at the beginning of April as the Donegal lads romped to a ten-point win with Doherty contributing a fine game from wing half back.

It was a busy April for the 17 year old. Less than a fortnight later he was instrumental in Carrick Vocational School's seven-point win over Newry Technical College in the Ulster Senior Vocational Schools final, the first time a Donegal school had won the title. Doherty scored two goals that day from full-forward. Incidentally, at wing half forward on the Carrick team was a goalscorer by the name of Noel Hegarty. It was a tremendous achievement for such a small school. "One cannot talk about that year without talking about the school in Carrick," said John Joe Doherty:

> We did something that year that has not been done since; we won the Ulster vocational schools championship. I think there were only 16 boys doing their leaving certificate that year and 14 of them were playing. Considering the number we had from which to pick a team, it was a great achievement.

❅ ❅ ❅ ❅

Barry Cunningham was already a Gaelic footballer of renown at club, school and county level. When Cloughaneely Community School, Falcarragh, captured the McLarnon Cup for the second time in three years in March 1985, it was Cunningham – the captain and man of the match – who got the winner with the last kick of the game, a famous free 30 yards out near the sideline. It remains one of his fondest memories:

> We went into the game as no-hopers. St Eunan's had a more talented team than us but we had the determination to win it. I wouldn't be a noted free taker but the free was on the right and I'm left footed so there was no one else to take it. I hit it as hard as I could and it went over. Me, John and Barry McGowan would have had a bit of craic about it at county training years later. We'd hit a few frees from the same spot to see if we could put it over. One out of 20 might have gone over.

As Falcarragh went wild, St Eunan's, who had made it an all-Donegal Ulster final, were devastated. Included in their ranks was a youngster from Termon by the name of Tommy Ryan who'd spent the hour marking John Cunningham. Brian McEniff had already spotted Barry Cunningham and he'd had a brief call up to the senior panel during the Open Draw series. But for now, Cunningham had a busy summer ahead with the county minors.

❄ ❄ ❄ ❄

Fittingly enough, it was Jimmy White who was at the reins of the county minor side in 1985. Barry McGowan enjoyed the experience and, with so many club mates around him, felt there was a "home-like atmosphere on the team". By the end of April Donegal had wrapped up the Ulster minor league for a second year in a row when defeating Cavan at Irvinestown – achieved without the services of the Cunninghams and Barry McGowan, who were on colleges duty. By the time May and the championship came along, the Cunninghams, McGowan, Ryan and Doherty were key players in a formidable line-up.

A Down team that boasted the services of Barry Breen were dispatched at Ballybofey. John Cunningham, the captain in his third year with the minors, blasted home a Tommy Ryan-won penalty as Donegal won by 1-7 to 0-6. John Joe Doherty felt the game was the hardest they played all year. On the infamous afternoon that the seniors were crushed by Monaghan at Castleblaney the minors walloped Monaghan's minors by 14 points, although with 15 minutes to go they were only leading by a point. Enter super-sub Conor White, brother of Jimmy, and his two goals in the space of three minutes saw Donegal through to an Ulster final.

The Ulster final against Cavan at Clones saw an awesome display of football which resulted in a 2-11 to 1-3 victory and a first Ulster Minor Football Championship since 1956. For a team that gave some truly outstanding performances throughout the year, especially in the minor league, this match saw them reach new heights. They were quite simply the most exciting minor team Donegal had ever seen. Barry McGowan was fully aware of the way in which the gods of footballing fortune had smiled on him:

> It is a great honour to play as a minor for your county, to win an Ulster title and then play in Croke Park. Unfortunately on that day in Croke Park we seemed to stall very badly and just couldn't make it count.

Cork emerged narrow two-point winners on a wet day when the Donegal forwards could not convert possession into scores. The afternoon yielded fine performances from Barry Cunningham, John Joe Doherty and John Cunningham in particular yet the latter two were particularly disappointed leaving Croke Park. "We had a serious amount of possession," remembered John Cunningham. "I don't know how we lost. A ball came across the square, John Joe Doherty slipped and the ball hit him in the chest and a Cork forward ran in and kicked it to the net." John Cunningham had a well-struck penalty pushed over the bar near the end. On leaving the pitch that day his cousin Barry made a promise to himself, "After the game I said to myself that things would be different if I ever got back to Croke Park."

Preparation for the match had been a wee bit problematic. Barry McGowan remembered there was a bit of naivete in the Donegal camp:

> Both the players and the management were very naive. It was under-standable because no-one in our camp had ever been in that position. We sought every kind of advice but nothing really prepares you for it.
>
> The night before the game we stayed in the Ardboyne Hotel in Navan. I didn't get much sleep that night with all of the excitement. We were 17 and 18 year olds and for some of us it was probably our first time to stay in a hotel. We were waking each other up in the middle of the night. It wasn't great preparation for the game but that couldn't be blamed on the management, it was young lads being themselves. There was the hotel atmosphere and the rooms were very hot. It was just unnatural for us. It was poor preparation for us and then we had to endure a trip to Dublin the next day. I remember it was a wet and miserable day. Things just didn't seem to be adding up for us.
>
> Things didn't go well for us on the pitch. We had enough chances. Cork made three or four attacks in the second half and got a goal and two points out of it. At the final whistle it felt like the world had ended.

Defeated by 0-9 to 2-5, the conquerors went on to win the All-Ireland title. As Fr Seán commented afterwards, "There is no tomorrow for a minor team."

Nonetheless the whole county was impressed. It was no longer premature to say that the golden age of Donegal football had arrived. The future of Donegal football was there for everyone to see. Sadly, that future would not see Donal Bonner displaying his talents on the biggest stage. An outstanding prospect, he was in his third year on the minor team, had two All-Ireland voca-tional schools medals and was already a member of the county under-21 team. "I rate Donal Bonner as the best footballer I ever played with," said Tommy Ryan some 18 years later. "He was two-footed, supremely skilful and, from a standing position, could outfield men much taller than him." An injury picked up while playing for the Donegal junior team that summer would all but end his career. It was a cruel blow to the youngster and a huge loss to Donegal. Tommy Ryan put it into perspective. "It was bad enough losing the chance to win a minor All-Ireland title but losing Donal Bonner was a bigger blow. He was head and shoulders above everyone else on that team."

No More Steak Dinners

Going into the winter of 1985, McEniff knew that a successful national league campaign was expected. While promotion to Division One was an objective, a repeat of the previous season's regulation battle would raise serious questions. And he knew, more than anyone, that his future as manager would depend on his fortunes in Ulster. He had about eight months and a national league campaign in which to rebuild his team.

McEniff had used the successful McKenna Cup campaign to look at some old and some new faces. Charlie Mulgrew, back from suspension, was flying and illustrating what a loss he had been to Donegal during the summer. Marty Carlin from Killygordon was something of a sharp-shooter. Brian Murray was slowly establishing himself around the middle. Declan Bonner was back – still juggling both football codes. Sean Bonner was back in at full-back and looking in shape. McHugh was in good form having managed Kilcar to their first senior championship since 1980. Indeed, as he faced into the 1985-86 season, McHugh would be the new Donegal captain.

Things got off to a good start in Wexford in early October despite a late scare in the final two minutes which saw a ten-point winning margin reduced to three. Fr Tierney Park, Ballyshannon, then witnessed a magnificent drawn encounter with Mayo at the end of the month. It was a day when Donegal played with great spirit to come from behind and earn a draw with the Connacht champions and it was also the day that John Cunningham made his senior debut. It was a good start and it got better a fortnight later when Cork were accounted for at Fermoy by 2-4 to 1-6. Joyce McMullan was the hero of the hour with a terrific goal strike coming literally seconds before the final whistle. It was a fortunate win for Donegal but nonetheless it maintained an impressive unbeaten record and it saw them share the top spot in Division Two with Mayo.

Dublin ended that status with an emphatic seven-point win at Croke Park. It was another of those games which emphasised just how far Donegal had to go. Dublin, beaten All-Ireland finalists, were never bothered by Donegal's best efforts and the county's ability to win a senior game at Croke Park seemed as remote as ever.

The final game before Christmas saw Donegal back on target for promotion. Longford came to MacCumhaill Park and were decisively defeated by nine points. McHugh was back after injury, Bosco Gallagher was in for Walsh in goals, Des Newton had yet another magnificent match, and Big Griffin made his first appearance in some time much to the delight of the home crowd. With Christmas beckoning Donegal were sitting pretty. Five games played: three wins, a draw and one defeat. Dublin had defeated Mayo so Donegal found themselves sitting second in the Division Two league table, two points adrift of Mayo but a point ahead of Dublin. It was simple really. All Donegal had to do after Christmas was beat Cavan and then Galway. That achieved, they would secure promotion and a place in the national league quarter-finals.

McEniff was busy over the Christmas break. In the early New Year he announced a ban on alcohol as he promised a tough new attitude towards discipline. He was also examining his possibilities. By the second week of January 1986, McEniff was looking at some 40 footballers, old and new faces, that he considered the best talent the county had to offer. He took them on a trip to Monaghan for a trial game to have a further look. Some of the names that travelled that day would go on to achieve great things, some would simply fade into inter-county oblivion. McEniff named an A team that selected from: Bosco Gallagher, Tommy McDermott, Sean Bonner, Des Newton, Martin Gavigan, Brendan Dunleavy, Paul Carr, Joyce McMullan, Barry Cunningham, Martin McHugh, Donal Reid, Marty Carlin, Pauric Gallagher, Manus Boyle, Declan Bonner, John Kerrs, Brendan McGready, Eunan Gallagher, Kieran Keeney and Seamus Meehan. His B team consisted of: Gary Walsh, Eamon Breslin, Seamus Ward, John Joe Travers, Eunan McIntyre, John Cunningham, Martin Shovlin, Martin Griffin, Michael Gallagher, Leslie McGettigan, Paschal Brogan, Paddy Hegarty, Luke Gavigan, John Murray and Tommy Ryan. Michael Lafferty and Michael Carr were also in the mind of McEniff although both were unavailable through injury. Matt Gallagher had left for London after the championship defeat the previous summer but would be back in time for that year's championship. McEniff didn't know it, but that day in Monaghan he observed 13 footballers who would share a glorious day in Croke Park with him less than seven years later.

Any thoughts of future glory were far from the minds of McEniff or his charges when they slumped to a disastrous 0-7 to 2-7 defeat at the hands of Cavan in Breffni Park in their penultimate league game. A Cavan goal after 90 seconds set the tone for a miserable Donegal display. It was, Brian McEniff told the *Democrat,* "a disgrace to the county". Any thoughts of promotion were dead.

A major reason why Donegal were not firing on all cylinders against Cavan was revealed later. According to Pauric McShea, there was no finance available and thus the team did not train over the winter. "It was one factor that didn't help in the below par performance against Cavan," he told the *Democrat* later.

Donegal needed a victory over Galway in their final game and a plethora of other results to go right for them to even win a play-off. They'd had their chance and had failed to take it. As it happened, they did get a victory over Galway in Ballyshannon. It was a tough day for their tormentors of 1983 as Leslie McGettigan blasted to the net in the very last attack of the game to earn a barely-deserved one-point victory. Val Daly and Galway headed for Division Three for the first time. On paper, Donegal's four wins, one draw and two defeats looked promising. The reality was different. The reality would be there for all to see just two months later in Newcastle and it would cost Brian McEniff his job.

County Board finances were running low and officials came to the dressing room after the Galway game to tell the squad that there was no money to train the team. "I was captain at the time," remembers Martin McHugh, "I stood up and said we'd train ourselves." Training was moved to Inver beach. McEniff, Charlie Mulgrew and a couple of others ferried the lads to training where car headlights and the moon illuminated the session and, as Atlantic surf cascaded on the shore, Donegal's finest set about preparing for the championship. Kilcar, with Martin McHugh as trainer, had won the county championship the previous year. McHugh now took on the task of training the county side:

> I trained the team at the time. We trained really hard. I had Griffin in better shape than he ever was. I remember giving out to Griffin at the training and telling him that I wanted more from him. Griffin fucked me out of it and fucked the jersey at me. I told him he could go if he wanted. He came back and apologised; we had him in the right frame of mind.

Joyce McMullan remembers the training as being "really savage stuff". The heavy sand sucked the strength out of the players' legs as McHugh concentrated on stamina training. "We were running, running and running harder," recalled McHugh:

> The team was in good shape but we moved the training back to Ballybofey too early. We moved it back about seven weeks before the championship but we should have stayed there for at least another three weeks.

It was a poor manner in which to prepare for the Ulster championship. McHugh was disappointed:

> I was disappointed with the County Board's attitude to the whole thing. It seemed to me that the county team was seen as a hindrance and it was only a matter of fielding in the championship and then playing the club championship.

Before the championship date with Down in the summer, Donegal had their McKenna Cup title to defend. They saw off Derry in Ballyshannon on an atrocious day for football. McEniff gave Manus Boyle his county debut and played John Cunningham at centre-half back for the first time. Manus had been Donegal's only scorer in the 2-1 to 0-5 defeat of Armagh in the under-21 championship on St Patrick's Day a week or two earlier. He remembers his call up to the county panel:

> McEniff rang on the Tuesday and called me to training. I went up and trained with the team and he didn't say much. We all left together but he rang me on the Saturday to tell me that I'd be collected and was going to

the match. I played wing half back and McEniff told me that he'd never play me there again because I wouldn't stay back.

Defeat followed at the Athletic Grounds when Armagh had a point to spare in the semi-final. Problems were there for all to see. With Big Griffin in the twilight of his inter-county career and no longer considered for the first 15, the full-back position had been causing problems – Dunleavy had been the latest attempt to fill the gap. McMullan and Molloy weren't working out in the middle, while the forwards – bar Donal Reid who had struck a rich vein of form – were struggling.

Although Anthony Molloy was struggling to find his form, both he and his manager could see the funny side of things when he ballooned a good chance late in the second half:

> It was a tight match and there was a fair bit of sledging going on in it. I got a great pass from somebody and was about 30 yards out. The whole place opened up and I went through to the 21 and thought I was going to bury it. I hit the corner flag. An Armagh fan called to McEniff, "Where did you get that boy from?" "We picked him up coming up the road," was McEniff's reply.

As mid-May rolled in, the *Democrat* put it very simply when it ran the headline "McEniff's job on the line in Newcastle". McEniff himself had no illusions. His tenure would be over as soon as Donegal lost their next championship match. Sure, he would like to keep the job and continue down the road he had started but defeat meant he would have to take his chances and run the gauntlet of an election. He was happy that he had named his best team: Gary Walsh; Tommy McDermott, Des Newton, Matt Gallagher; Michael Carr, Brendan Dunleavy, Eunan McIntyre; Anthony Molloy, Michael Lafferty; Sylvester Maguire, Donal Reid, Joyce McMullan; Martin McHugh, Charlie Mulgrew, Leslie McGettigan. On the bench he had Noel McCole, John Cunningham, Martin Griffin, Eunan Gallagher, Marty Carlin, Brian Murray and Martin Gavigan.

In hindsight McEniff had precious little fresh talent on board. Ten of the side that had lost to Galway three years previously were still there, only McCole, Griffin, Paul McGettigan, Bonner and Keeney had departed the first 15. There was new young blood in the shape of Leslie McGettigan, who was a member of the under-21 team that would go on to lose an Ulster final later that year. Gary Walsh and John Cunningham were the other under-21s in the squad. It was a far cry from 1983 when McEniff had a host of under-21s scattered throughout his team. As they made their way to the Down seaside resort of Newcastle, Donegal knew they had a tough assignment on their hands. McEniff, with his encyclopedic knowledge of football, was aware that Donegal had never won a senior championship game at a Down venue.

It was a poor game and a poor result for Donegal. "As an example of championship football the first-round Ulster match between Down and Donegal at Newcastle yesterday will hardly command a chapter to itself in the annals of Gaelic games," wrote Paddy Downey in *The Irish Times*. Down used all their formidable craft and no small amount of luck to hold on to a one-point lead and emerge winners on a scoreline of 1-10 to 2-8 but the match did go into the annals in that it marked the end of Brian McEniff's six-year reign as Donegal manager.

It was, wrote Peadar O'Brien in the *Irish Press*, "an eminently forgettable game of squandered chances, poor passes and some inordinately bad football." In fairness to both sides, the game was ruined by a gusting crossfield breeze which made ball control particularly difficult. Donegal were in deep trouble after just nine minutes. Marty Carlin had opened Donegal's account with a point. That was cancelled out by a Brendan Mason point and then, in the space of a few minutes, Down found the Donegal net twice in rapid succession, one had taken a wicked deflection off a Donegal defender and left Walsh stranded. It smacked of déjà vu as in Ballybofey 12 months earlier when Down had stunned the home support with a similar double strike just before half-time. This time however, in the swirling winds of Newcastle, there was to be no way back. If Donegal were looking for culprits they most definitely could be found in the forward line. It was an inept performance. Peadar O'Brien hit the nail on the head with his analysis:

> They were often caught out of position and had a sinful determination to make that one pass too many. It all resulted that they only scored one goal and two points from play. The other eight points came from frees. In contrast, Down scored all but one point from play and this was the major difference between the sides.

In fairness, Down contributed to Donegal's lack of scores from play by indulging in cynical fouling. With the wind factor negating against freetakers, Donegal found it difficult to convert the fouls into scores. There were several off-the-ball incidents and Paddy O'Rourke in particular was lucky to remain on the pitch following a foul on McHugh.

Donegal had problems all over the field. Molloy and Lafferty were in trouble around the middle with Liam Austin and John McCartan. This in turn forced the Donegal forwards to travel far from the Down goals in pursuit of the ball. Paddy Kennedy and Paddy O'Rourke had the centre of the Donegal attack well marshalled while the half forward line of Greg Blaney, Mickey Linden and Brendan Mason had a profitable outing in the red and black. Down led 2-3 to 0-4 by half time. Indeed, were it not for the defensive heroics of Newton, McDermott and Michael Carr, the game may well have been wrapped up after

35 minutes. Matt Gallagher, who had played so well the previous year, was having a miserable time. Having returned from London only two months earlier, he was off the pace of championship football, "I played badly, caused a goal and was taken off. It was the right thing to do. I was the wrong choice as I probably hadn't played enough football."

Martin Gavigan, on the fringes of the team, would agree. He thought he should have been on, "I was a bit disappointed that I hadn't got a place on the team because I had been training, I was very fit and had put in a big effort."

McEniff made good substitutions during the second half, bringing on Griffin for Matt and Brian Murray for Brendan Dunleavy. Fourteen minutes after the restart Letterkenny's Leslie McGettigan netted impressively to leave just two points separating the sides. Big Griffin, who lifted Donegal when he came on ten minutes into the half, was then most unfortunate to have a piledriver booted off the line by Paddy O'Rourke. When McHugh added a point minutes later Donegal were still in the hunt. McHugh however saw the Griffin shot as the turning point, "If we had got that goal and gone ahead we would have won the match". Nonetheless, the forwards suddenly sparked to life and Down had a real challenge on their hands.

Entering the final moments Down clung grimly to a two-point lead as Donegal surged forward. Down were seen at their most cynical in injury time when McHugh was blatantly pulled down by Paddy Kennedy just outside the parallelogram when he appeared to have the winning goal in his sights. McGettigan pointed from the free but time was running out and, as Paddy Downey observed, it was "poor recompense for the loss of a golden opportunity". Molloy, operating in the unfamiliar confines of corner-forward, had one final chance to level proceedings but, from an acute angle, his shot strayed wide. Another empty summer beckoned.

The wolves, howling for McEniff for some time, now came to collect. Questions were posed about hesitant positional switches and the number of players who shared, and missed, frees. No one was more disappointed than McEniff. Despite a poor overall performance Donegal had been at their bravest in the second half and had come close to snatching victory. Few were the teams that visited Down in their own backyard and emerged with a win. At the end of the 70 minutes McEniff's team had failed by a single point. Players were quick to weigh in behind their manager. "It was not Brian McEniff's fault we lost the match. I don't care what anybody says, the players lost the match," asserted McHugh immediately afterwards. Joyce McMullan agreed, "I was disappointed for McEniff. He put a lot into it and he's going to get a kick in the teeth again. The whole team is behind him but still the guns are going to be out for him."

Joyce was quite correct, McEniff was in trouble. He eventually made the decision to stand for the job again and addressed delegates accordingly at the July County Board meeting. "The future for Donegal football is bright and I

Donal Reid

would like to be around for it," he stated. McEniff had allies on the County Executive. Michael Gillespie, the chairman, complimented McEniff for not drawing down travelling expenses. He also stated that under McEniff's guidance Donegal had come from being ranked 20th in Ireland to around 11th or 12th. It was not enough.

McEniff had only one competitor for the post but a formidable one. Tom Conaghan, the man who had delivered that historic under-21 All-Ireland in 1982, was ready and waiting. He had been on stand-by for the position as far back as August 1983. At the August County Board meeting, his hour finally came.

As the rain battered against the windows of the MacCumhaill Social Centre, Brian McEniff's watch over the fortunes of Donegal football came to an end. Fifty-two votes were cast – 36 by the clubs and 16 by the Executive. The decision was emphatic. Conaghan collected 33 votes, McEniff trailed behind with 19. It was over. McEniff had certainly lost the support of the northern – mostly junior – clubs and, in the days before the vote, some of the senior clubs also drifted away from him. It seemed to be the end of the road for the man who had given most of his adult life to Donegal football. It was the third time in 12 years that McEniff had lost the reins. "I don't think I will be back," he told the *Democrat* in the immediate aftermath.

As he made his way home through the Gap in the rain, Brian McEniff faced his first winter in many years bereft of a football team to guide, coax and inspire. There would be other days – other impossibly glorious days – but for now all that lay ahead was a long winter in Bundoran.

❄

RESULTS

National League 1984-85
Donegal 0-8, Roscommon 0-8
Donegal 1-13, Mayo 1-5
Donegal 0-9, Offaly 1-8
Donegal 0-7, Monaghan 0-11
Donegal 1-4, Dublin 1-6
Donegal 0-8, Louth 0-10
Donegal 1-12, Wexford 0-6
Donegal 2-7, Louth 2-5 (playoff)

Ulster Championship 1985
Donegal 2-12, Down 2-8
Donegal 0-7, Monaghan 1-14

National League 1985-86
Donegal 3-6, Wexford 3-3
Donegal 0-14, Mayo 1-11
Donegal 2-4, Cork 1-6
Donegal 0-8, Dublin 0-15
Donegal 1-11, Longford 0-5
Donegal 0-7, Cavan 2-7
Donegal 2-8, Galway 1-10

Ulster Championship 1986
Donegal 1-10, Down 2-8

7

Return of the Hard Man
(August 1986 – July 1987)

"Nothing will make me change my ways."
TOM CONAGHAN, AUGUST 1986

Four years had passed since the Donegal footballing public had last been exposed to Tom Conaghan. Much had happened in the interim – the seniors were in Division Two and an All-Ireland semi-final had been contested and lost. The golden promise of 1983 had faded fast and for a year or more the team had drifted in the doldrums. Over in Donegal Town they had added another club title – the senior championship in Centenary Year – under the guidance of Conaghan.

There had been tough times too for Tom Conaghan and his family. He had buried his son Kevin on Christmas Day, 1984. The youngster, who had travelled all over Ireland with the under-21s back in 1982, had been killed in a car accident. "He was a lovely cub and went everywhere with us that year," remembers Martin McHugh. For a long time after football was trivial and alien in the mind of Tom Conaghan.

Friends and admirers of the All-Ireland winning manager rallied around and by the summer of 1986 he had been persuaded to immerse himself in football again. By the time Donegal fell in Newcastle, Conaghan was ready. As it came down to a straight contest between himself and McEniff for the job, Conaghan spelt out his plans and vision for the future. It was abundantly clear that Conaghan the manager had changed not one iota. The disciplinarian approach that had yielded an All-Ireland four years previously was unashamedly intact. "Nothing will make me change my ways," he told the *Democrat*. The county liked what it heard and, by a sensational margin, Conaghan got the senior job.

Almost immediately he was making the headlines. As he outlined his ideas to the County Board in his acceptance speech it was the sound bites on discipline which delighted the journalists. Tom the man was back. But with his eyes wide open and a sting in the tail:

> Although quite a few of the team and panel members would have pre-
> ferred Brian as team manager to me, I will not hold that against any play-
> er. I will be fair to each and every player but I would like it to go out
> from here and now, any player who steps out of line only does it once.

Conaghan was under no illusions that he might not be welcomed with open arms
into the Donegal dressing room. Veterans of 1982 remembered the various she-
mozzles when Conaghan had laid down the rules with an iron fist. "It was not a
popularity contest. As far as I was concerned I would not be doing my job right
if everybody loved me," Conaghan remarked years later:

> I told the players that I wouldn't be giving up and that unless I was
> removed by the County Board, I'd see out the three-year term. I told
> them I wouldn't walk away from it and that they would have to give an
> even bigger commitment than they had at under-21 level.

Many supporters saw a Donegal team that was weak on discipline and now
floundering. A team that had promised so much was all washed out. What
they needed was some tough love, and the man for that job was undoubtedly
Tom Conaghan. In the opinion of Martin Shovlin, "Tom was fair but you had
to give him a bit of leeway too."

Six weeks ahead of the national league the new manager launched an inter-
divisional senior championship – eventually won by the South-West – which he
used to look at the talent available to him in the county. His first panel numbered 32, and included Martin Shovlin, Manus Boyle, John and Barry
Cunningham, Martin McHugh, Declan Bonner, Joyce McMullan, Matt Gallagher,
Donal Reid and Charlie Mulgrew. Gone, it seemed were Brian Murray, Gary
Walsh, Anthony Molloy and Martin Gavigan.

There was a bit of annoyance a few miles up the road in Ballyshannon. Aodh
Ruadh were county champions of 1986. They would win it again in 1987 and
would feel they were getting scant recognition from the county manager. In addition, a couple of Ballyshannon men, now operating outside the county, also had
reason for grievance. Brian Murray recalls the time:

> Different managers have different views and different plans. Tom want-
> ed to have all his players in the county. Me and Gary lost out. I wasn't
> playing county football through no fault of my own. It was annoying
> because I had done nothing wrong.

While disappointed with his exclusion it benefited Gary Walsh professionally:

It actually suited me as I was doing my accountancy finals that year. I went to Athlone in October 1986 and studied hard for the year. While it was disappointing at the time, he probably did me a big favour. I only went home on three or four weekends during the year whereas if I had been on the county team I would have been expected home for training.

A week later and things had changed drastically. McHugh, the biggest name in Donegal football, had opted out of the panel for the winter. Gone too was possibly Donegal's most reliable defender, Des Newton. Among others, Martin Gavigan was named again. Gavigan had been a member of McEniff's last panel in Newcastle and had played a game or two at the end of the summer under caretaker Donegal manager PJ McGowan. In time, under Tom Conaghan, Gavigan would be transformed into one of the best centre half-backs in the country. But not quite yet. In that week Martin Gavigan had made other plans:

I wasn't in the panel so I booked a flight to America to go away for the summer. A few days later Tom called into the school asking would I rejoin the panel. I told him that I had given it my best shot and I wasn't included so I was off to America and that was it. When I did come back I got on grand with Tom.

As football supporters and the local press analysed every inclusion and exclusion, Conaghan continued to fire from the hip. Following a team meeting in Donegal Town he commented: "I made it clear to them, it was going to be my way or no way." While unwavering discipline was an elementary part of Conaghan's approach to football management, there was something deeper at work. Conaghan felt that the county had underachieved in recent years. Lack of discipline, as far as he was concerned, had been a major factor. In particular he was adamant that the attitude to training and attendance would have to change. "I couldn't believe that the players could have changed as much in five years. It was the same old thing and it was worse than being back at square one."

In fairness, he had a point. "There were times when we used to do a couple of laps of the pitch," laughed Martin McHugh, "and afterwards the boys would be saying to McEniff, 'Phew, that was tough' and next thing we'd be playing a wee match." That was all about to change.

The *Democrat* sent a man along to the first training session at Townawilly. An under-13 match was in full swing on the main pitch but through a gap in the hedge he spotted the seniors in the next field going through their paces. His subsequent report brilliantly captured the new regime:

Twenty-three turned up for the first session and all were on time. Tom Conaghan looked in command with his patriotic green tracksuit. He directed operations from midfield with whistle at the ready. He praised, he criticised, he advised. He stopped play for a moment or two to emphasise a point and then continued again.

Passing, moving, catching, kicking, turning, shooting; all aspects worked on, improved and brought into action. It was a tough session. Apart from few calls from free men or the team 'characters', there was little talk. There was far too much work to be done. The players, wearing an assortment of jerseys, move back onto the main pitch after the youngsters left.

One might be forgiven for thinking they had offended the new manager. He makes them run up and down the field ... jog ... sprint and so on. The steep incline of the road end of the Townawilly pitch had yet to be climbed. The whistle blows and the stampede conquers the slopes several times. Team physio, John Cassidy laughs at the panting players and recalls how Conaghan forced Four Masters up the same slopes on their way to winning the senior championship. He adds: "Wait until he has them going up 30 or 40 times!"

A clear message rang around the county – Conaghan was going to be his own man. Breaking with tradition, he would train the team himself. Anyone who couldn't attend training needed to have a good excuse, those who didn't show up simply "dropped themselves". The day of the excuse was gone. Players who were injured would have to prove the fact, "whether he tripped on a carpet or slipped at a disco" and there would be no more "running around the country to horse-doctors". The van driver from Donegal Town, the toast of the smaller clubs, had something of a different approach then to the hotelier from Bundoran. Some would say it was just what Donegal football needed.

Kildare at Newbridge was not an easy league opener. Although regarded as a team in decline they had a good record on their home turf. Noel McCole, the veteran 'keeper whose Donegal career seemed to have ended in Clones 18 months earlier, was back between the posts. Big Griffin was in at full-back and captained the side. Barry Cunningham and Declan Bonner were in at midfield and, at top of the left, Conaghan named Manus Boyle. The full team was: Noel McCole; Sean Bonner, Martin Griffin, Tommy McDermott; Donal Reid, Corney Carr, Myles Sweeney; Declan Bonner and Barry Cunningham; Marty Carlin, Charlie Mulgrew, Joyce McMullan; Leslie McGettigan, Michael Lafferty, Manus Boyle.

A four-point win flattered Kildare. Donegal conceded a goal in the final minute and might well have shared the spoils. Conaghan's first team had lost but optimism reigned. Conaghan was confident that his stated aim of retaining Division Two status in his first year was still on track. Charlie Mulgrew was seeking a move to defence. A good display at centre half-forward in the league opener put paid to any chance of that, "The centre-half back had been a Kildare stalwart but was past his best. I happened to have a good game at centre-half forward and Tom told me that he wasn't going to let me move into defence."

By the time Donegal faced Cork in Ballyshannon, Conaghan had switched his team around. Martin Shovlin entered the picture again. Shovlin, despite a few outstanding performances in the county jersey in McEniff's time, had never managed to make the big breakthrough. In his second game in charge, Conaghan handed the Dunkineely man a lifeline. The *Democrat* predicted that Shovlin's return to the inter-county scene "will raise a few eyebrows". It did, but not in the manner the *Democrat* inferred. "Tom had great belief in the 1982 under-21 squad and always said that he would liked to have worked with the squad," recalled Martin Shovlin, "When he did get in he called the bulk of the team back."

Matt Gallagher was in for the first time since being substituted in Newcastle and had a point to prove. Naomh Bríd would avail of Matt's services again after his Bundoran sojourn and the following summer he would help them to the Intermediate Championship title. Big Griffin was back in midfield where he really belonged. The result was a convincing and emphatic win over a Cork team that would claim the following year's Munster championship. A disciplined Donegal defence held a Cork forward line that included John O'Driscoll to just five points. For the first time in many years the Donegal forward line ignited as a unit with Marty Carlin and Manus Boyle between them contributing six of Donegal's eight points. It was also the first time in many years that Donegal were described as being "fitter, faster and keener" than their opponents. Shovlin and Gallagher seized the day and were superb as was Leslie McGettigan.

But the day belonged to the new captain. Big Griffin had one of his best days in the green and gold jersey and was easily man of the match. Fitter than ever and now in the twilight of a career that should have delivered more, Griffin was majestic that day in Ballyshannon.

Ulster champions and defeated All-Ireland finalists, Tyrone, were next up. Donegal earned a draw, 1-6 to 0-9 when perhaps two league points were on offer. The key moment occurred nine minutes into the second half and involved two-thirds of the full forward line that would wreak havoc against Dublin on a Sunday in September six years later. Declan Bonner, at full speed, chased a high ball that seemed to be going harmlessly wide some ten yards to the right of the Tyrone goals. Aidan Skelton, the Tyrone goalkeeper, was on hand to shepherd the ball wide. By the time Bonner got there Skelton was convinced the ball was over the line. Not so, claimed Bonner later, "It was at least a half foot from the line when I knocked it back". Bonner's pass found Manus Boyle who duly hammered it into the empty net.

Conaghan was disappointed to have dropped a league point but happy that a new team spirit was already resonating from his charges. He had further reason for cheer when a good win was recorded in Longford in mid-December by 2-7 to 1-4. Again Manus Boyle featured prominently and notched up 1-2 for himself in a man of the match display. The Killybegs lad was proving to be very effective around the opposition square and it was his goal that had insured the points for Donegal in the 26th minute of the second half. Sylvester Maguire had kicked for a point and when it unexpectedly rebounded off the upright it was Manus who reacted fastest to blast to the net from a narrow angle. Manus was happy to be involved in the league games:

> I did reasonably well for the first couple of years under Tom. We were play-
> ing with people who protected us. Mickey Lafferty was full-forward at that
> time and if someone lifted his hand to you, Lafferty looked after you.

The Division Two league table was particularly tight as the teams took their Christmas break. Cork and Derry were sitting joint top with six points, Donegal sat second with five points, while Kildare and Laois were sitting on four points each. Although he acknowledged that tough matches lay ahead, Conaghan was happy that his team had put in the effort and were seeing the reward. The consensus around the county was that Conaghan had succeeded in a very short time in altering the attitude of Donegal players for the better. Results, it was said, proved that point.

Little did Conaghan know that the five-month period between August and December of 1986 was his honeymoon period. Difficult times lay ahead. Controversy would soon engulf the Donegal Town man and in time it would serve to overshadow his proven abilities as a manager. Some players, officials and supporters would turn against him. And it would mark the beginning of a turbulent relationship with the local press.

McHugh was in the news too. It seemed that half the county had their say on McHugh's absence from the county side via the letters pages of the *Democrat*. Former Donegal captain Pauric McShea, McEniff's right-hand man from 1983 to 1986, upped the ante over Christmas when he suggested that with McHugh and Newton back in the team Donegal could win an Ulster title.

Conaghan fired his first salvo of the New Year by imposing a ban on all non-GAA sporting activity. It hit the headlines. The ban had immediate repercussions for Manus Boyle, a soccer star with St Catherine's in Killybegs, who had to sit out a local cup final. Charlie Mulgrew and Marty Carlin, both playing members of Letterkenny Rugby Club, would miss the Forster Cup semi-final against Malone if they were to follow Conaghan's directive. Conaghan denied that he had imposed a ban, but remarked ominously that his panel were free to play whatever sport they chose but they would pay the price if they did. It was vintage Conaghan. Full and total commitment was required and nothing else would do.

Donegal's chances of promotion had been boosted by the return of McHugh, Dunleavy, Molloy and John Cunningham to the panel. Des Newton came back in the fold too, enduring the long trips from north Inishowen to

Townawilly for training.

Cavan had sunk Donegal's promotion hopes some 12 months earlier and now they had to be faced down again in Ballybofey. Straight into the action came Newton, Dunleavy and McHugh. Big news on any other day but the county was still talking about Mulgrew, Carlin and Griffin. Charlie and Marty were gone – dropped from the panel entirely following their decision to play rugby for Letterkenny in the Forster Cup semi-final. When they had turned up for training with the Donegal squad a few nights later they were sent home. Speaking years later Charlie Mulgrew does not want to rake over old and troubled ground:

> I had my notion about it and he had his notion about it. I still feel he was 100% wrong in what he did because of the carry on that was going on elsewhere. Still, he was the boss and I wasn't supposed to play but I did.

Big Griffin was also in trouble. A breach of discipline saw him relegated to the subs bench. Conaghan hadn't blinked.

The Cavan game was unremarkable as a spectacle. In fact it was a poor game, typical of many national league matches being played out across the country, devoid of the passion and spectacle of championship football. Matt Gallagher had raised a cheer by wandering far from corner-back to raise the umpire's flag with a well-taken point. McHugh had a decent second half, scoring three good points. And Manus had struck the net yet again. Donegal held a one-point lead until two minutes from time when John Brady hit the equaliser. However, the game was to mark a watershed in Donegal football and the career of Tom Conaghan.

The *Donegal Democrat*'s subsequent report on the game triggered an eventual stand-off between the Donegal manager and the newspaper that would span the remainder of Conaghan's reign in charge. Connie Duffy, one of the most affable reporters covering Gaelic games in the county, had been disappointed by Donegal's performance. His report was critical of both the team and the manager:

> The team played dour dreary football devoid of imagination, tactics and the usual fighting qualities we have come to take for granted. Further examination of the facts might suggest otherwise but many supporters blamed the team manager's unorthodox line out for the poor performance.

Donegal, suggested Duffy, "seemed to have no match plan or suitable positional switches" to counter Cavan. He expected "corrective measures" at half-time but none were forthcoming. Disappointed that promotion had slipped away for a second year, Duffy concluded:

> If they play as badly in their final two games they should count their

lucky stars they will still be in Division Two next season because if Sunday's performance is any indication, there's still a lot of work to be done in many departments on and off the field.

It was a stinging critique of the performance. To make matters worse, it was also reported that players were unhappy. A few of the players had taken the opportunity to speak to the *Democrat*. It was clear that all was not well in the camp, a chasm appeared to be opening up between management and players. It all came down to the question of respect – respect that was demanded and respect that was accorded. The discipline required and the punishment handed out by the manager was questioned. Some of the punishment was said to be selective and over trivial matters. And, revealed the *Democrat*, player-power had been to the fore when players on the county panel refused to train a few days before the Cavan game, seeking a guarantee that Mulgrew and Carlin would be restored to the panel. It all made for fascinating if disturbing reading for GAA followers.

Conaghan was incensed. Sixteen years later he is still incensed. In his world, loyalty and respect ruled supreme. A very clear line had just been crossed by the *Democrat* and by certain players. It was the opening shots of war – all out war.

Had McEniff been manager one would be inclined to think he would have dealt with the issue differently. McEniff's media savvy was well known and perhaps had its source in his capacity as a businessman. John Cunnigham knew where McEniff's strengths as a man-manager lay:

He was a real politician. He had great organisational skills but his nose for trouble was the best. He could smell it coming a mile away. He could dampen a potential disaster in a couple of minutes. He had a knack of knowing when things were going to boil over and he could defuse it.

Conaghan, on the other hand, would argue that McEniff had never endured such sharp criticism. The controversy was set to run and run.

A stiff challenge awaited in Greenlough as a battle-weary Donegal prepared to meet Derry. Conaghan extracted full support from his squad at training in Ballybofey a week ahead of the game. Against all the odds an unexpected but highly welcome 1-9 to 0-7 victory was obtained. Donegal got well and truly stuck in – Danny Quinn of Derry picked up a booking but so too did McDermott, McHugh, Maguire, Dunleavy and Boyle. It was a hard-hitting and robust affair but it seemed that Donegal had put a difficult few weeks well behind them.

Promotion was still on the cards leading into the final game against Laois. Conaghan went into the game aware that he had the support of the vast majority of the County Board following the March board meeting. Laois, with eight players in their squad from the All-Ireland under-21 semi-final in 1982, came to Ballyshannon at the beginning of March needing a win to avoid relegation. A

Donegal win on the other hand would result in a promotion play off with Derry. Few could have predicted the drubbing Donegal would receive at the hands of the national league champions of 1986. Ten points separated the sides by the time the final whistle sounded. It was a robust ugly game with dangerous tackles flying throughout. Off the ball there was just as much action. The game yielded a classic Martin Griffin story. Manus laughs as he remembers the incident:

I was in the dugout along with Martin Griffin and Paddy Carr. Kieran McCready, who was well on in age, was the sponge-man. McHugh went down in the corner furthest from us and McEniff shouted to Kieran to go over and help the Wee Man. McCready was halfway across the pitch when Griffin shouted: "The Wee Man will be blue moulded before that man gets to him." The Laois subs in the dug out next to us were laughing as hard as us.

Kieran himself enjoyed the yarn too. Donegal were no match for the visitors and by half time were trailing 0-1 to 1-6. The second half was no better despite a bright opening few minutes, and as the *Democrat* noted, Donegal accepted defeat easily: "Donegal's ever-present inferiority complex syndrome surfaced again and forced them to abandon the notion of winning this game." It was, acknowledged Conaghan, the worst performance of the league. To make matters worse, Cork and Derry, two teams defeated by Donegal, were promoted.

It had been a remarkable few months. Donegal had played seven league games, had won three, drew two and lost two. Yet the drama and controversy that had accompanied the latter stages of the league masked the fact that Conaghan's stated initial aim of retaining Division Two status had been comfortably achieved. Conaghan had spent the seven games experimenting, few players had enjoyed two games running in the same position.

Amidst all the controversy supporters had been impressed with the new corner-forward Manus Boyle. Boyle, who had been hitting the headlines with the under-21s in 1986, had been called into the senior team for the McKenna Cup back in March that year by McEniff. However, it was Conaghan who give him his chance and the Killybegs youngster had grabbed it with both hands finishing the league as Donegal's top scorer with 4-11.

Another forward who had contributed 0-15 to Donegal's league campaign, making him Donegal's second highest scorer, was Marty Carlin. As Donegal flopped against Laois in Ballyshannon Carlin was standing in the crowd looking on. If Donegal were to advance their footballing fortunes it was clear that men of the calibre of Carlin and Mulgrew would need to be on the other side of the wire. It was a story that had a long way to go.

Conaghan used the McKenna Cup to experiment further with a few untried players. Martin Gavigan got a much needed run out at left half back against Tyrone in Omagh but had a quiet game by his later standards.

Connie Duffy pushed his luck in the aftermath by posing a few searching questions. "Is the best county team fielding? Is the team handled properly? Do the players possess the true spirit of the team? Are they in top physical condition or have they peaked? Have some of them the physique for inter-county football?" A hot summer lay in store.

Conaghan settled on a panel at the beginning of April that would carry Donegal's bid in the championship. As always it had its talking points. Mulgrew and Carlin were again banished and it seemed there was no way back this time. They had briefly rejoined the squad after the McKenna Cup but the rugby issue had reared its head again and *that* was most definitely that. Michael Lafferty was gone. Galway-based student Barry Cunningham, who was writing his name in stars with the under-21s, was also dropped. A handful of newcomers were introduced, among them Tommy Ryan from Termon and John Joe Doherty of Naomh Columba. John Joe's stay was brief:

> I only trained for two nights and pulled out again. I do not know why but I just didn't think it was for me at that point in time. I do not know if I was too shy, but I just did not think I was ready for it. At the time I probably felt I was too young to play. Tom took it well in fairness. People will say that Conaghan wasn't the kind of man to take things well but he had no problem with me.

Conaghan talked of "keeping things tight" in the weeks leading up to the championship meeting with Armagh. 'Tight' meant, among other things, players coming along to training on time. Molloy remembers the time well:

> If training was fixed for seven o'clock the training would start at that time, you couldn't come along at quarter past. Tom closed the gate and once it was closed no one else could come on to the field. It was a good enough thing, because in the past boys had always arrived late to training. That went on in this county for years. Tom instilled that kind of professionalism. If that professional attitude had been adopted after we won in 1982, we might not have been beaten by odd points in first round championship matches.

One player who kept his head down in the new regime and got on with playing football was Donal Reid. Reid was arguably the most consistent player in the Donegal team and had gone 56 consecutive games for the county when he picked up a bad knock while playing with Donegal in the National Hurling League at the beginning of April. Reid's attitude was simple:

> My view on managers, regardless of who they are or what they're like, is that you play for him. It's about the jersey you put on – it's not about the

manager. A lot of people had disagreements with Tom and didn't like him. I wasn't going to worry about players that had decided to watch from the stand. I was going to play for my county regardless of who was manager.

Conaghan demanded total loyalty and, in the main, the squad he assembled gave him that. Donal Reid outlined the lengths players would go to:

> When my first child was born, I collected my wife Maura at the hospital and brought her and the child back to the house. I didn't even have time for a cup of tea and took my boots and went to training on Murvagh beach. At the start of the year Tom Conaghan had told us that, barring death, we were to be at training. That is how serious it was. I wouldn't do that nowadays. I put football before everything; I put it before family and work.

Reid, despite the hardships, was a character. He contented himself to play his football within the parameters laid down by Conaghan. His dry humour never wavered though. Not for a moment. Once Conaghan informed them at half-time that they needn't come back into the dressing-toom again if they lost. As the others grimly considered the task that lay ahead, Reid – deadpan as ever – had a question for the manager. "What about our clothes Tom?" He may not always have agreed with the manager's decisions but few were the games he missed during Conaghan's three years in charge. And the boys appreciated his sense of humour.

In the midst of a series of challenge games against the likes of Derry and London, Martin Griffin became the latest name to be dropped from the panel when he opted to play soccer instead of turning up in Letterkenny to play Derry.

Conaghan talked his old friend and mentor, Mick O'Dwyer, into a challenge game against The Kingdom at MacCumhaill Park. It was a useful exercise, and although the reigning All-Ireland champions didn't field at full strength, the 1-20 to 4-8 Donegal victory was football at its most encouraging. It was the latest in a series of good wins from challenge games. Lost in the small print of Connie Duffy's match report following the Kerry game was a timely and astute warning – "Donegal must now be more wary than ever for it is the norm for them to flatter and then deceive."

Conaghan had much to prove and much to lose as June drew closer and that date with Armagh at MacCumhaill Park. Gerry McDermott, writing in the *Democrat*, put words to the unspoken thoughts of half the county:

> Conaghan has proved himself to be his own man and for that quality alone he must be admired. However, looking at the cards that have been dealt and watching his hand closely one must confess to having a lack of confidence in Donegal's ability to beat Armagh without players of the calibre of Michael Lafferty, Marty Carlin, Brian Tuohy, Charlie Mulgrew,

Return of the Hard Man

Barry Cunningham, Paul Carr (Letterkenny), Gary Walsh and Martin Griffin (who went to the USA on Monday).

As the seniors ran onto the pitch at MacCumhaill Park, Donegal supporters had already been having themselves some summer. The under-21s had delivered an Ulster title in fine style in May and had drawn with mighty Kerry in the All-Ireland final a week before the senior championship opener. The county was buzzing with excitement and expectation at the prospect of another All-Ireland title. The same air of expectation was not prevalent with regard to the seniors. Most Donegal supporters were "already resigned to the fact that Donegal were on their way out of the Ulster Championship before the ball was even kicked" reckoned Gerry McDermott in the *Democrat*.

Conaghan's team contained nine players from his under-21 side of 1982. Only Manus Boyle, from the 1987 under-21 squad, was on the team. Indeed Manus was making his senior championship debut as was Declan Bonner. Martin Shovlin had also been selected but had to bow out due to an ankle injury. John Cunningham and Tommy Ryan were on the bench.

As it happened, things were about to hit rock bottom for Conaghan's men. Sean Kilfeather, as ever, was there for *The Irish Times*:

Taking their cue from the weather, the footballers from Armagh and Donegal served up a miserable match at Ballybofey yesterday and hordes of disappointed supporters in the crowd of about 8,000 were voting with their feet and leaving in droves long before the end.

It was indeed a dark day for Donegal. Ger Houlihan had slotted home a goal after 29 minutes and a struggling Donegal entered the dressing room at half time trailing by seven points. Des Newton got himself sent off nine minutes after the restart and with him went any hope of Donegal staging a comeback. The final score was 0-6 to 1-8, but as the *Irish Independent* reported, "at no stage did Donegal look like making a late match-winning surge."

It seemed that Conaghan's critics had been proved correct. Donegal were truly woeful. The *Irish Press* picked up on the fact that Conaghan had Lafferty, Griffin and Mulgrew, to name but three, available to him but had opted not to play them for disciplinary reasons. Watching from the terrace was Gary Walsh who had been excluded from the panel the previous August, "I passed my finals that June and remember going to watch the match at Ballybofey, it was a shambles. It was disappointing to see a Donegal team with so little heart."

Those who knew their game saw much that day in Ballybofey. Conaghan couldn't be blamed for some of the poor performances throughout the field – including that of a very much off-form Martin McHugh – but he had paid a high price for fielding at least two players who were just not good enough for inter-county football. Eyebrows had also been raised at his persistence in playing Dunleavy, who struggled throughout, at full forward while Donegal were crying out for his formidable presence in defence. And Kieran Keeney, a man many considered to be an out and out forward, found himself switched to corner back.

Conaghan found himself under some pressure. Gerry McDermott was under no illusions as to where the blame lay when the *Democrat* hit the shelves the following Friday:

> Tom Conaghan has the most important job in the whole of Donegal. All that is asked of him is to produce a successful team. The supporters want success, the county needs success and if Tom Conaghan can't provide it, or even show signs of being able to provide it, then the County Board must look elsewhere. We cannot spend the next two years watching football like this!

By the time Conaghan made his report to the County Board at the beginning of July, the whole county was awash with excitement in the aftermath of the under-21 All-Ireland success. Serious drama had been expected at the meeting but it didn't materialise as Conaghan reflected on the seniors performance and the problems that had arisen during the year.

It had been a roller-coaster year for the senior manager. The county seemed split on the merits of his management style. No other manager in Donegal GAA history had generated such debate. Brian McEniff had presided over many a dark day for Donegal football but had never drawn such pointed criticism.

The whole county almost needed the summer to recover. A remark Conaghan had made in the immediate aftermath of the Armagh match had been lost in the hullabaloo but showed there was reason for hope. "The only thing I would say to the supporters is to be patient, Donegal will get success," he had promised. When the winter rolled in again he would deliver on that promise. The most uncompromising of managers had many many tough days ahead and would field much flak but despite it all his proudest day yet lay ahead.

❊

RESULTS

National League 1986-87	Donegal 1-9, Derry 0-7
Donegal 1-10, Kildare 2-11	Donegal 1-12, Wexford 0-6
Donegal 0-8, Cork 0-5	Donegal 0-5, Laois 2-9
Donegal 1-6, Tyrone 0-9	
Donegal 2-7, Longford 1-4	**Ulster Championship 1987**
Donegal 1-8, Cavan 1-8	Donegal 0-6, Armagh 1-8

8

McGowan's Men of '87
(1987)

"The future of Donegal football is secured."

JOHN CUNNINGHAM – JUNE 28, 1987

Alittle to the left and about 15 metres out from the Donegal posts, Fermanagh corner-forward Paul Coyle kicked for a point. His effort was to become the major talking point of the game. The scoreboard operators moved immediately to register a score. Standing at the foot of the post however was Sean Ward from Dungloe, a well-known and much respected figure in Donegal GAA circles. The referee, Jim Curran, had neglected to bring neutral umpires along and so Ward had found himself nominated as one of the four officials. The Dungloe man was quite sure that the kick was wide and signalled accordingly. The referee consulted both umpires and agreed, much to the outrage of the Fermanagh contingent. "It was a bit dubious, anyone in the stands could see it was a point," remembered left-half forward Barry McGowan.

The first round of the 1987 Ulster under-21 championship at Ballyshannon was a mere 14 minutes old when the incident occurred but less than an hour later the significance of Coyle's disputed kick became apparent. Donegal had struggled to a 2-7 to 2-6 victory. "We won by a dubious point," mused manager PJ McGowan. "It was," agreed Barry Cunningham, "one we should have lost." Fermanagh appealed the result to the Ulster Council but never got a hearing. Donegal had just about cleared the first hurdle.

An inauspicious start then to the campaign. Hopes were high around the county that the under-21s were the team to watch in 1987. The previous year's side had been annihilated by defending champions Derry in the Ulster final. Some small consolation was gleaned that day from the fact that many of the key Donegal players would still be eligible for the grade in 1987, among them Seamus Ward, John Joe Doherty, John Cunningham, Brian Mór Gallagher, Barry Cunningham, Manus Boyle, Joey McDermott and Luke Gavigan. Gary Walsh,

Martin Gavigan

and Declan Bonner, to name two, were gone, but the backbone of a very good team was in place.

While the Fermanagh game was dominated by talk of the point that was or wasn't, there had been little cheer in the quality of football produced by PJ McGowan's men. It had been a stuttering start and offered only the occasional glimpse of the sheer class that had dazzled the county back in 1985 when many of the same boys had dominated minor football in the province.

Luke Gavigan was was sent off in the second half, having got into an altercation with Fermanagh's Damien McKenna, but not before leaving his usual mark on the game. Luke – whom older brother Martin rated a much better player than himself – found the Fermanagh net twice in the 19th and 21st minutes of the first half.

A super-fit Tommy Ryan was in flying form at centre half-forward and had linked well with senior star Manus Boyle. Ryan was a student at Sligo RTC who were enjoying great success in the Trench Cup and it showed. Ryan had, in the opinion of Barry Cunningham, "improved beyond all recognition from minor to under-21". Barry McGowan and Dermot Ward also clicked well while John Cunningham, the captain, had a modest game at centre half-back. Nonetheless, Cunningham was on hand to ensure that Fermanagh were held in the closing minutes as they pressed desperately to level the match. It was the only really mediocre display Donegal would produce in a truly outstanding campaign of glorious football that, seven games later, would result in an All-Ireland title.

The sheer class of the team was abundantly evident at Bellaghy just one week later when Derry were comprehensively dethroned of their Ulster title. In the space of a week PJ McGowan had dusted off the cobwebs and his side kicked into a rhythm that was simply a class apart. Like the Fermanagh encounter it had its moments. One occurred far from the pitch when Naomh Mhuire's Cormac McGarvey was involved in a car accident en-route to the game. McGarvey was uninjured but unable to make the pitch in time to line out in the half-back line. His fellow club man Kevin Sharkey and Seamus Doohan of Cloughaneely were slightly hurt in the crash and were taken to Magherafelt hospital.

The game had been originally fixed for Magherafelt but the Ulster Council, with its often questionable wisdom, switched the game to Bellaghy unbeknownst to Donegal. As the Donegal players, supporters and officials began arriving at Magherafelt they discovered at the last minute that they had another seven miles to travel to Bellaghy. Brian Mór Gallagher almost became Donegal's second casualty before a ball was kicked when, having hitched across from Coleraine, he too arrived at Magherafelt.

Showing two changes – the Glen men, Doherty and Hegarty, were in – from the Fermanagh game, the team was: David Meehan; Thomas Maguire, Seamus Ward, John Joe Doherty; John Connors, John Cunningham, Diarmaid Keon; Barry Cunningham, Brian Mór Gallagher; Paddy Hegarty, Tommy Ryan, Barry McGowan; Dermot Ward, Manus Boyle, John Sweeney.

It was evident from the throw in that Donegal were on song. Barry Cunningham and Brian Mór started as they meant to continue by lording things at midfield. It was impressive to watch – Donegal had the advantage of a fierce breeze in their backs and set about exploiting it fully. Three minutes in and Manus had the ball in the back of the Derry net. Barry Cunningham had lofted a kick high into the Derry full-back line, Manus caught brilliantly, side-stepped the 'keeper and lashed it to the net. Boyle had scored four good points against Fermanagh, two from play and two from frees, but it was that simply executed yet cheeky goal against Derry which signalled the beginning of a remarkable campaign by the talented Killybegs man.

Six minutes later and Derry were in real trouble when they lost their influential centre half-back, Henry Downey, who had to be stretchered off with a badly broken leg following an accidental clash with Manus Boyle. Centre half-forward Tommy Ryan had a clear view of the clash:

It was freakish and inexplicable. A ball went high over my head and Downey, who was three or four yards behind me, back-pedalled. Manus and him went for the ball in the air and Henry's leg was broken while he was in the air. Manus had fallen to one side and although Downey tried to get up he couldn't, it was a bad leg break.

It was a great personal tragedy for the talented dual-star from Lavey who would be out of action for the best part of a year. PJ McGowan remembers it well. "I remember going to the hospital to collect one of our boys who had the accident on the way to the match, and talking to Henry, and he had an important exam a couple of days later." It was testament to Downey's character that he made a complete recovery and six years later would win an All-Star and be named the Texaco Footballer of the Year as he captained Derry to their first All-Ireland victory. Donegal would see much of Henry Downey in the years ahead.

Barry Cunningham stepped up to tap over a 14-yard free with 20 minutes gone. Somehow it ended up in the back of the net and Donegal were well and truly on their way. A third goal was toe-poked in by Tommy Ryan almost on the half-time whistle. Three points had also been registered – one by Manus, one by Barry Cunningham, not unlike his famous McLarnon Cup score, and one real beauty from 50 metres by Brian Mór. Derry, for their part, had managed just one point.

In the second half – against the wind – Donegal players all over the field stood up and were counted. Tommy Ryan was the star performer of the second half. John Cunningham was, according to Michael Daly in the *Democrat*, "an inspiration". "We played exceptionally well all over the pitch that day," remembered John. Although Derry inevitably clocked up the scores in the second half with the aid of the elements, it was spine of the Donegal team – the Cunninghams, Brian Mór and particularly Tommy Ryan – who doggedly won and then held on to possession to frustrate the Derry men; 3-5 to 1-7 was the score at the final whistle. The Derry goal came from a penalty late in the second half and Donegal were very good value for their comfortable four-point victory. That man Manus had added both Donegal's second half scores.

It was, in a footballing sense, ample revenge for the culling that had occurred in Omagh in the Ulster Final seven months earlier. Joe Winston, no stranger to under-21 campaigns, was back on board as a selector with PJ McGowan. He liked what he saw. "I think now this is as good a team as the 1982 team," was his after-match comment. He wasn't far wrong.

Two victories behind them, the spirit of the team was building nicely. Many of the boys had been together on minor teams and hadn't been together since they'd turned 18. Manus Boyle remembers the carefree outlook of the squad:

> The team had worked hard as minors but hadn't seen one another for a couple of years. Suddenly, we were all brought back together at an age where we could have a drink and have the craic. Paddy Hegarty and Dermot Ward kept the whole thing going. They'd say if we won we'd have a great night out. We'd get slaughtered in the Abbey Hotel and have a great night out. We never thought much further ahead than that.

The campaign would see Donegal having to face down the best sides the country had to offer. Armagh was not one of those but nonetheless promised an interesting Easter Sunday contest in Lurgan. Not unlike the game in Bellaghy, Donegal overcame both their opponents and the elements. Armagh had the advantage of a strong breeze in the first half and looked to be in control as they entered the interval enjoying a six point lead, 0-2 to 1-5. However, Donegal had played a shrewd first half of damage limitation and it was evident to everyone in Davitt Park that it was Armagh who were in big trouble at the break. Indeed, it took a mere nine minutes for Donegal to haul Armagh back to level terms. Two minutes later it was Manus Boyle's point that saw Donegal take a lead they would never relinquish. It finished 1-9 to 1-6. It was hard to find fault. Armagh, with Jarlath Burns, Benny Tierney and John Rafferty, but not the brilliant Joey Cunningham, had been slayed.

PJ McGowan not only had a decent team on his hands but a hell of a panel. Tommy Ryan, the hero of the Derry match, was out for the Armagh game having been sent off and suspended while playing for Sligo RTC. In came an unfit but highly effective Joey McDermott from Glenfin. Danny Gallagher replaced a most unfortunate David Meehan in goals – Meehan had broken his arm in a club game. Luke Gavigan was back from suspension at the expense of Dermot Ward. McGowan's switches were to prove flawless.

Danny Gallagher had a baptism of fire in the Donegal goals. In the very first minute the Dungloe lad was extracting the ball out the back of his own net following a mix up between himself and full-back Seamus Ward. Not the best of starts and a further Armagh point with the aid of the wind threatened a half hour of pure havoc for the Donegal defence.

The Killybegs duo of Boyle and McGowan registered Donegal's only scores of the half on the sixth and ninth minute respectively. For the next 21 minutes Donegal stood firm against Armagh and the wind. Ward, Keon, Connors and the Cunninghams simply pulled down the shutters. It was impressive. There was no panic. Possession was won deep in defence and moved, from man to man, up the field. Manus Boyle came out to centre-half forward and foraged effectively around the middle. Barry McGowan, not for the last time that year, had his marker changed in an attempt to curb his surging runs and clever linkage play. Armagh had scoring opportunities but added only four points to the 1-1 pilfered in the opening minutes.

The second half was as academic as most onlookers had expected. Manus took the breath from Armagh and the crowd by starting and finishing a truly exceptional move after just three minutes. Boyle jumped highest to knock an Armagh kick out into the hands of Joey McDermott and dashed goalwards. The Glenfin man had found Luke Gavigan. Gavigan's delightful inch perfect volley was collected by Boyle and it was goodbye Armagh.

Cormac McGarvey got a run in the final 15 minutes but the unfortunate Naomh Mhuire lad was destined never to regain his place in the aftermath of his accident in Derry. The gods of football were not smiling on McGarvey. He had heroically dashed to Bellaghy following the crash but by the time he arrived John Connors was in at right half back. Connors was outstanding against both Derry and Armagh and for McGarvey, there would be no way back in 1987.

❄ ❄ ❄ ❄

Monaghan football was enjoying something of a renascence. Their seniors had claimed a national league title in 1985. That same year they added an Ulster title. Some of the biggest football names ever to come out of Monaghan became household names – McEneaney, McCarville and the legendary Nudie Hughes. In 1987 their under-21 team had reached an Ulster final against Donegal and contained within its ranks one of the best prospects in a Monaghan jersey for many a year – a Louth man called Stefan White – son of Louth 1957 All-Ireland winner Stephen White.

With a minute remaining at Irvinestown Donegal were sitting on a three-point lead and seemingly on their way to the presentation area. It had been a frustrating afternoon however. Possession had not been a problem but conversion into scores certainly had for Donegal. Any number of scoring chances that would have seen Monaghan left high and dry had been squandered. Payback came when a high ball was pumped into Stefan White's corner. John Joe had been having an outstanding afternoon on the Monaghan danger man but for once was beaten to the ball. White's thundering left foot shot had goal written all over it but Danny Gallagher somehow managed to parry it. Unfortunately his deflection came off the post and was subsequently bundled over the goal line by an in-rushing Monaghan forward. Level. Manus Boyle had a last gasp opportunity to secure the title with a difficult long range-free but it fell short. It ended 0-7 to 1-4. Replay – it was all to do again. Disappointment hung in the air as the huge Donegal support trooped out of the grounds. "It is close to unforgivable that a team who dominated for 50 out of 60 minutes play could only get a draw," commented Michael Daly in the *Democrat*. It was an accurate summation of Donegal's day.

Despite the doom and gloom, there had been much to shout about. Donegal had given a fine exhibit of classy football. When they moved the ball as only they could, this Donegal team was breathtaking to watch. And they were a tough outfit all over the field, never found wanting if a rugged tackle needed to be landed.

PJ McGowan had found himself rejigging his side before they took the pitch. Seamus Ward was under doctor's orders not to play and John Connors was moved to full-back. John Bán Gallagher had been due to make his first appearance at midfield but now found himself wearing Connors' number five jersey. Brian Mór Gallagher had had a close call. He'd been dropped but Ward's tonsillitis proved to be his redemption and he was back partnering Barry Cunningham at midfield. And another Naomh Columba man, Paul Carr, was in at corner back as the injured Thomas Maguire lost out. As with the Armagh game, the changes in personnel in no way affected Donegal's rhythm. It was another very good call by PJ McGowan.

McGowan had been canny in his selection of team mentors. The aforementioned Dodo Winston had a great track record with Donegal underage football and was a natural choice. McGowan also had Jimmy White on board. The young Killybegs man was regarded as something of a football messiah in his home town and indeed throughout the county. Not alone did Jimmy White know his football, he had provided a third of the team as five Killybegs men were on the first 15! And he was the manager of the 1985 Ulster title winning minor team.

As ever, the game suffered due to the windy conditions. Even so, Donegal – playing against it in the first half – were quite happy entering the interval at 0-3 apiece. As the second-half progressed it was painfully apparent that it was not to be Donegal's day in front of goal as chance after chance went a-begging. All would be rued when Stefan White finally caught a ball ahead of John Joe and bore down on the Donegal goal.

Donegal's defence though had been phenomenal throughout. John Connors was a revelation at full-back, the Dungloe lad was almost unbeatable at the heart of the Donegal defence. Paul Carr had seized his chance with admirable vigour. Just 18 years old, Carr's challenge looked to be enormous as he faced 60 minutes on Monaghan captain and senior player Michael Conlon. It was grist to Carr's mill, he totally outplayed his man and his performance received the ultimate tribute when Conlon was substituted. John Joe, Diarmaid Keon, John Bán and Barry Cunningham all stood out, as did Paddy Hegarty and Manus Boyle up front, but it was Razda who had led from the front. Cunningham was simply awesome. The *Democrat* noted:

> Centre half-back, John Cunningham, had a great game; his marking was tight, his clearances strong and accurate and as always his physical presence and the manner in which he motivates others around him did much to get and keep Donegal going.

Cunningham was the out and out leader on the field. His contribution to the team was immeasurable. There seemed little doubt that he had a long illustrious career ahead of him in the senior jersey of Donegal. A week later, at St Molaise Park in Irvinestown, Cunningham joyfully raised the Irish News Cup over his head as exuberant Donegal supporters saluted the Ulster under-21 champions of 1987.

❋ ❋ ❋ ❋

Barry Cunningham, a student at University College Galway, had left himself lots of time to get to the replay at Irvinestown.

> I got a taxi from Galway and was having a cup of coffee in Sligo at one o'clock. I had been told that the game was at three o'clock. I got a paper to get a preview of the game and saw the game was at two o'clock. I only arrived at the pitch just before the throw in. Nobody had thought to call me and tell me the game had been moved forward an hour. In a strange way it took the pressure off me. I was rushing to get to the game and wasn't thinking about what was going to happen during the game.

Preparation like this may have flustered lesser men, but Cunningham gave an outstanding display in the middle of the park.

There was no mistake second time around. Donegal repeated their dominance but unlike the drawn match their superior possession was also reflected on the scoreboard. Nonetheless, Monaghan proved to be sticky opponents and it wasn't until the final quarter that Donegal's accurate kicking put six points between themselves and the men in white and blue. In fairness to Monaghan they were a decent team who had accounted for a much talked about Down team on their way to the final.

Donegal started at lightning pace and for 20 minutes it seemed certain that a stunned Monaghan were about to be swamped. Manus and Barry McGowan had early points before John Cunningham thundered up the field on a 40-yard solo run and had a great shot well parried by Monaghan's 'keeper Dermot Murphy. Indeed Murphy recovered well to also save the rebound from the inrushing Dermot Ward. The inevitable Donegal goal came in the 16th minute. An ultra-fluent five-man move ended with a spectacular goal strike by the impressive Paddy Hegarty. Donegal were out of the traps and flying. Manus added a further point following a foul on a ring-rusty Tommy Ryan who was back from a month's suspension. The scoreboard read 1-3 to 0-1 and a rout threatened. Michael Conlon and Stefan White had other ideas and in the ten minutes before half time struck four unanswered Monaghan points. On the very stroke of half time Dermot Ward pointed when he might have added another goal.

Barry Cunningham was displaying the form at midfield that would characterise his entire campaign. He simply caught everything in the air and when his feet touched the ground panic broke out in the opposing ranks. Monaghan tried to counter his effectiveness in the second half by crowding midfield but although they reduced the deficit to a single point in the opening moments the half belonged to Donegal. The scores stacked up as the Donegal attack clicked into gear – all six forwards on the day registered scores.

Stefan White and Michael Conlon had good reason to never again want to see the Glen duo of John Joe and Paul Carr as the two lads repeated the shackling of the previous game. "Carr was a horrible man to have marking you," remarked Tommy Ryan, "he would follow you to the toilet." For the second Sunday in succession Carr saw Conlon replaced. Behind them Danny Gallagher had settled in well, he pulled off a magnificent save in the closing minutes and was rewarded with his first clean sheet. Carr was a great prospect but he emigrated to England soon after the under-21 campaign and missed out on future Donegal successes.

Michael Daly was on hand for the *Democrat* and had high praise indeed for the displays of the two Johns, Connors and Cunningham, they were "close to faultless". Few at Irvinestown that Sunday, May 10, 1987 would have disagreed. It was an exhilarating time to be a Donegal Gaelic football supporter. There was simply so much talent on view. Barry McGowan, at left half-forward, was becoming more devastating with every game he played. His pace was phenomenal and he had a style of playing Gaelic football that was almost regal. Over on the other wing Paddy Hegarty played football with the conviction of a man from Glen who knew what he was at. Young Gavigan had been quiet since his two-goal blitz against Fermanagh but his hour would come.

Five matches gone – Ulster champions. Unbelievably, their best football lay ahead before summer's end. Another All-Ireland was very much to the forefront of supporters' minds. The general consensus was that PJ McGowan's boys had an All-Ireland in them. If they had then they would have to beat Laois. In an ironic throwback to 1982, Laois had again come through in Leinster. Back then a Donal Reid point had earned Donegal an 0-5 to 0-4 win. Five years later it would prove to be every bit as close.

Sam's for the Hills

* * * *

Hugh Daly, from Ballyshannon, had been one of the best known names in Gaelic games in Donegal. He held the position of secretary of the Donegal County Board for a remarkable 23 years in a tenure bridging three decades. When his son Michael joined the staff of the *Donegal Democrat* in the late 1980s the important role of bearing witness to the fortunes of Donegal football fell into good hands. Like all the Dalys, Michael knew his football. As Donegal reached only their second All-Ireland at under-21 level on May 17, 1987, Michael Daly was on hand to capture a classic match.

What was an exceptional game of football, not only because of the closeness of the scores throughout, but because of the way both sides chose to play their football – fast, clean, clever and classy – ended with a memorable one-point win for Donegal, crafted and executed by full-forward Manus Boyle, who, since Sunday has been the toast of the county.

Donegal 1-7, Laois 1-6. Although no silverware was on offer that day, seldom had a Donegal side emerged with more credit from a game of football. Laois were a first-rate football team, by far the best Donegal would meet, yet this remarkable bunch of Donegal footballers delivered. Already, their legend was secure. Six of them – a lad from Glencolmcille, one from Termon and four from Killybegs – had their most famous hour five years later, but seldom was their football more celebrated than that day in Carrick-on-Shannon.

Donegal knew they had a game on their hands within seconds of the throw-in. Laois ripped into them with several frenetic attacks that chilled the hearts of the Donegal defence. John Cunningham, and behind him, John Connors, had the toughest of afternoons although both would emerge with credit. The Turleys, Leo and Michael respectively, proved the sternest of challenges for the centre of the Donegal defence. Razda, in a senior career that took in eight championship campaigns and countless league matches across the land, reckoned he never met a more difficult adversary than his opponent that day, Leo Turley. "I didn't know who Leo Turley was at the time but as the game progressed I realised he was a really good footballer," remembered Cunningham. Later that summer the Cunninghams and Michael Turley swapped adversary for common purpose as they played together with Donegal New York.

With five minutes gone Laois had spurned not one but two goal chances. John Connors and John Cunningham were in for an afternoon of aerial combat with the Turleys as Laois pumped high ball after high ball into their key men. Dermot Ward then proved his incalculable worth to Donegal by settling the ship with a fine individual point at the other end. The Glenfin lad was a real livewire around the small square, always hunting for scraps when others would have given up. It was those predatory instincts that saw him in the right place at the right time to volley Donegal's goal on the 11th minute.

From there until half time the football produced by both sides came from the very top drawer. By the time Mickey Kearins of Sligo signalled that 30 minutes had elapsed the teams were level at 1-3 apiece. During the famous 1977 All-Ireland semi-final between Kerry and Dublin the great GAA commentator Micheal O'Hehir memorably remarked, "29 minutes still remaining in this game, hallelujah." Neutrals lucky enough to be in Carrick-on-Shannon at half time as Donegal and Laois ran for the dressing rooms had similar emotions. The Laois goal had come two minutes from the break, quite a superb strike from all of 20 metres which fairly shook the back of the Donegal net. The second half held great promise.

And so it transpired. As the defence coped with everything Laois threw at them, Donegal had real heroes in attack – Manus Boyle was sizzling, Tommy Ryan was at his industrious best while Barry McGowan and Paddy Hegarty were wreaking havoc out on the wings. Yet Laois could not be shaken off and midway through the half the teams were level for the third time. For once it was not a case of a Donegal team lacking the killer instinct and reneging the opportunity of putting away their opponents, as the *Democrat* noted it was a case of Laois being "superb". But Donegal had the winning of the game and his name was Manus Boyle.

PJ McGowan sprung into action on the sideline. Brian Mór Gallagher was struggling at midfield and was moved in to full-forward. Ryan and Boyle pulled back into midfield and centre half-forward respectively. Barry Cunningham revelled in the company of Ryan and turned it on. It was a mesmerising finish to a game of football. Donegal went a point up. Laois equalised. As neither side seemed capable of breaching the other's defence and play ranged from 40 to 40 a draw appeared inevitable. A draw would have done justice to Laois. And a replay between these two teams would most definitely have been greeted by cries of "hallelujah" from neutrals.

Manus Boyle had other ideas. Stung that he had missed a scoreable free some time earlier, Boyle struck despair into the hearts of Laois supporters with barely two minutes left on the clock. John Cunningham, who had held Leo Turley to a meagre two points, lashed a free towards Manus on the Laois 40. Boyle sailed high and caught the ball. By the time he hit the ground he had nothing on his mind but the winner. Away back when Donegal had defeated Derry at Bellaghy, Boyle had been chastised in the press and up in the stands for not spreading the ball more to those around him. It seemed that he had learned nothing in the interim – this was a job he was going to complete himself! Tom Conroy, the Laois full-back, had moved out with Manus but he was cannon fodder to the Killybegs man as he soloed goalwards. Manus recalls:

All I can remember is soloing the ball and bearing down on goal with John Cunningham beside me. John was making sure a Laois defender wasn't getting near me and was elbowing him. He was shouting at me to go on. I kicked the ball and it dropped over the bar.

Manus had made it to the 21 yard line and hit the most glorious of winning points off his left boot. 1-7 to 1-6. Goodnight Laois. Hello All-Ireland final.

It was a celebrated day for Donegal football, a day that warmed the hearts of Donegal supporters who witnessed it. This was a Donegal team that knew how to win. Determination and utter conviction oozed from their every step. On a day when heroes could be found all over the place, Michael Daly famously described Manus as supplying the "gloss" while Tommy Ryan provided the "undercoat".

❅ ❅ ❅ ❅

Tuam Stadium was to be the setting for Donegal's All-Ireland bid on June 7. Donegal folk departed for Galway in droves. Further along the western seaboard in the Kingdom of Kerry, a much smaller exodus headed north. If Donegal were to capture an All-Ireland they would do so at the expense of the most successful footballing county in the land. "If you're in an All-Ireland final who better to be up against than Kerry. They're the team to beat at any grade in this country," said PJ McGowan in the days before the game.

McGowan knew all about Kerry. They had caused him heartache enough in 1987. McGowan had steered Donegal to the All-Ireland Vocational Schools final just six weeks previously. His team hit an impressive 3-9 in Croke Park that day but were still to lose by a point to the defending All-Ireland champions – Kerry. McGowan had been around for a long time and although he gave the impression of being a gentleman to the tips of his toes, he knew all the tricks. And that included pulling the wool over the eyes of the Kingdom – on and off the pitch!

Sometimes you have to be up very early in the mornings for these Kerry fellows! Both teams had the same team colours. I took the MacCumhaill jerseys with me. But we discovered on the Saturday night that Kerry had only one set with them – the green and gold. I got my wife to bring up the green and gold jerseys. I remember the match was the curtain raiser for the national league final. Both teams were ten minutes late going out because of the jerseys. The way it was resolved was; we had to give Kerry the MacCumhaill jerseys and we played in the green and gold, but we had to get the Kerry jerseys into our dressing rooms for safe-keeping for the return of our jerseys. Kerry was playing Dublin in the national league that day, and for the first half we had great support, because all the Kerry folk thought we were Kerry!

Statistics from the under-21 series in recent years pointed to a Kerry win. The champions of Munster had not lost a single game nationally in the grade since Kerry had lost to Mayo in 1983. In the three years since 1983, Cork had been kingpins of the under-21 grade. Mayo, Derry and Offaly had tried and failed and the under-21 crown had taken up residence in Ireland's southernmost county. It was all to do as PJ McGowan and his entourage headed for the N17.

PJ McGowan was something of an enigma. He had never really hit the big time as a Donegal player. Yet he was there in 1974, on the fringes of the team, as Donegal claimed an Ulster senior title for the second time. He made an appearance as a sub in both the drawn Ulster final and again against Galway in the All-Ireland semi-final. McGowan didn't get to realise his full county potential as he was studying in England. In 1973 he won a Lancashire Championship playing for De La Salle College in Manchester. When the Lancashire provincial team won the British championship in 1977 it was with McGowan as player-manager. He knew a thing or two about football and his career as a physical education teacher gave him an extra edge. McGowan returned home in 1979 and plunged straight into the Donegal football scene. He was soon associated with the senior set up again and became team trainer. But it was with the students that his managerial talent really came to the fore.

McGowan soon had two vocational schools All-Irelands under his belt – the back-to-back titles of 1984 and 1985. He went back a long way then with a handful of his key players – Manus, Luke, John Joe and John Bán had all enjoyed glory in Croke Park with the quietly spoken McGowan. In 1986 he managed the vocational schools to Ulster success and the under-21s to the Ulster final where they fell to Derry. He was accustomed to success and would shortly be lauded as Donegal's most successful manager ever. By summer's end he would have managed a third Donegal team to an All-Ireland.

❆ ❆ ❆ ❆

Tommy Ryan had a rare dilemma. Sligo RTC had qualified for the Trench Cup final, a remarkable achievement for such a small college. The final was fixed for the Friday before the All-Ireland under-21 final. Captain of the college team, Tommy was torn between loyalty to his Sligo teammates, with whom he trained four mornings a week, and to his county. "The two managers came to an arrangement," he remembers:

> I wasn't involved in the discussion but at that time I would have thought nothing of playing on Friday, resting on Saturday and playing again on Sunday. I don't know what the decision was and while I didn't start for Sligo, I was told to tog out.
> I was brought on and midway through the second half I caught a ball

under our bar and was shouldered in the chest as I came out with it. I didn't feel anything at the time but I wasn't fit to get out of bed the following morning. I had three cracked ribs and it later transpired that I shouldn't have been playing at all.

Ryan said nothing and fervently hoped that he'd be able to play in Tuam.

※ ※ ※ ※

An hour's football from an All-Ireland title. As it happened, Donegal were three weeks away from that title. Kerry trooped from Tuam Stadium leaving behind an All-Ireland that seemed to be theirs for the taking. Two minutes before referee Mickey Kearins sounded the final whistle Manus Boyle had ensured that Donegal would survive to fight another day. Boyle had chipped over a 30-metre free and the relief gushing from Donegal folk could be felt in Salthill! Donegal 1-7, Kerry 0-10. It was the afternoon that Donegal nearly lost their All-Ireland.

It was also, noted the *Democrat*, the day Donegal played "their worst football of the entire competition". Few of the estimated 4,500 Donegal supporters present disagreed with that analysis. Only the sheer never-say-die attitude that bound this particular Donegal unit together saw them grimly hang on to secure a draw against a Kerry team that threatened to utterly swamp them.

The first 20 minutes belonged to Donegal. Back was the team that had mesmerised Laois. Donegal were clinical as they played into a strong wind. Dermot Ward and Manus Boyle traded early points with McEvoy and Gaire and then, with five minutes gone, Donegal hit Kerry with everything they had. The pace Donegal played at had to be seen to be believed.

Manus picked the All-Ireland final to have his best game of the campaign and began cutting swathes through the Kerry defence with impunity. One such run saw him evade a brace of Kerry defenders before blazing a shot over the bar. Another resulted in a sideline ball but stayed long in the memory of onlookers. Manus, at full speed, ran onto a ball some 90 yards out. With defenders in close attendance he elected not to pick the ball from the ground but bore down on the Kerry goals with a dazzling soccer-style dribble before unleashing an explosive shot that crashed off the Kerry crossbar. Such was the power of the shot that the ball crossed the sideline, in front of this writer, without a player from either side getting a hand to it. Manus remembers it well:

There was a fella closing in behind me and it seemed better to keep it on the ground. When I watched it on video afterwards I found myself shouting at me to pick it up! I didn't know what I was going to do, my head was down and I just kept on going. It would have made for a great goal or point but it went out for a sideline. It would have been easier to score than hit the crossbar. The keeper didn't move, I'd say he didn't know what I was going to do next. Paddy Hegarty asked me to do it the following Tuesday night at training but I couldn't.

Magnificent. Had it gone in – and the Kerry goalkeeper had been well beaten – Donegal may well have proceeded to take Kerry apart.

However, Donegal's purple patch yielded just four points and despite peerless defensive displays from John Connors and John Joe Doherty in particular, Kerry tagged on the points late in the half and went into the interval leading by two points, 0-4 to 0-6. There was already much to worry about. Ominously, Donegal were not playing to form around the centre. John Cunningham, Barry Cunningham and Tommy Ryan had left their previous match-winning form at home. Michael Daly described it thus: "Donegal suffered a major coronary in the pivotal midfield, centre back and centre forward positions." Kerry were a big strong side and it was certainly no picnic around the middle of the park. At midfield Kerry boasted the services of Mick Galwey who dominated his sector through sheer size and physical strength. Galwey had won an All-Ireland senior medal with the Kingdom in 1986 but it was with an oval ball that he would earn fame as a Munster and Ireland rugby forward. In Tuam that day he tortured Donegal.

Donegal got what should have been the perfect start to the second half. The winning of the game was handed to them on a plate. Hardly a minute had elapsed when Mickey Kearins showed no hesitation in pointing to the penalty spot following a foul on Dermot Ward. All heads turned to John Cunningham. Razda, having an off day by his own high standards, remembered all too well the last time he had hit a penalty of such magnitude:

It was like revisiting old ghosts. I had taken a penalty in the 1985 All-Ireland minor semi-final in Croke Park. I struck it fairly well but didn't place it. The goalie, Jerome O'Mahoney, stuck out his hand and the fucking ball hit his hand and went over the bar. I was thinking to myself, 'Here we go again'.

The pressure was on but the inspirational captain was not found wanting:

I was well up for it. I just placed the ball and bang, all I can remember is it hitting the back of the net. It was like a fierce release of emotion that I had been building up since the miss in Croke Park. There was such relief at getting rid of it.

Donegal were a point up – surely this psychological boost would lift them from the alarming mediocrity displayed in the closing ten minutes of the first half. "I must have run 60 or 70 yards to get back to centre-half back and by the time I got back I was fucked," remembered John. He was barely back in position before Kerry had hoisted the ball high over the Donegal bar for the equaliser. A couple of minutes later they hit the front with a point from Gerald Murphy. "I had visions of losing two All-Irelands to Kerry in the one year. That would've been a bitter pill to swallow," recalls PJ McGowan. Donal McEvoy, who had been held by Paul Carr in the first half, came into his own and was creating havoc with his direct runs at goal. The time for heroes was now.

John Connors, a colossus at the heart of the Donegal defence since the drawn Monaghan game, had his finest hour in a Donegal jersey. He wasn't even supposed to be there. Before the game PJ McGowan had intended to move Connors out to his original position at wing half back and play Seamus Ward at full-back. Ward had been lost to McGowan in the Ulster final replay at Irvinestown. He had replaced Brian Mór with ten minutes left in that game as Monaghan succumbed but lasted only nine minutes. Following an incident with the Monaghan full-forward Declan Brennan, Ward got his marching orders. Brennan wasn't so fortunate and he had to be carried from the pitch. As it turned out Ward couldn't play against Kerry so Connors was again patrolling the Donegal square.

Connors was simply magnificent. Time and time again he kept his team in the game. Pierce Hoare was in at full forward for Kerry. At 6'3" Hoare had several inches to spare on Connors and should have lorded proceedings on the edge of the Donegal square. Connors utterly outplayed him. Not only did the Dungloe lad get in the tackles and blocks but he also outfielded his much feared opponent. Eight minutes into the second half the Kerry selectors admitted defeat and moved their danger man away from Connors.

With 13 minutes gone and Kerry now two points ahead, PJ McGowan made a tactical switch that would pay dividends. Donal McEvoy, Kerry's out and out play-maker, was causing all kinds of trouble over on Paul Carr's side of the field. McGowan switched Diarmaid Keon onto McEvoy and Keon, who had been having a difficult afternoon on PJ Gaire, closed down the threat from McEvoy. Kerry's period of dominance, just like Donegal's opening 20 minutes of the first half, was over. The game opened up. Barry Cunningham and Manus both struck long range points to bring Donegal level with 15 minutes on the clock. There was only two scores left in the match. With seven minutes to go Gerald Murphy gave Kerry a lead they looked like holding. John Joe Doherty was irritated that Murphy had got the score, "I had been having a good match until Murphy came on. It was only afterward when I read the paper that I discovered this sub had scored three points." Unperturbed, Donegal battled for every ball and displayed admirable character in never giving up. It paid off and with two minutes remaining Tommy Ryan was fouled 30 metres out. "I had done nothing in the game because the cracked ribs had left me very weak," remembered Ryan:

I don't think PJ McGowan ever forgave me, he was fuming. He moved me into full-forward and I was marked by Mike Brosnan. A high ball came in. I backed into him and he came out over the top of me. Kearins, who had played football with my father in his playing days, gave us a free that shouldn't have been given.

And up stepped Manus Boyle.

❄ ❄ ❄ ❄

Donegal and Kerry renewed acquaintances three Sundays later in Dr Hyde Park, Roscommon. Tom Conaghan's seniors had meekly bitten the dust in Ballybofey two weeks earlier so all Donegal eyes were now firmly focused on the under-21s. If there were lessons to be soaked up from Tuam they most definitely included keeping quiet the Kerry quartet of McEvoy, Galwey, Murphy and Hoare. A tall order, literally. McGowan wisely handed the marking of McEvoy to Diarmaid Keon. He could but hope that the Cunninghams, Gallagher, Ryan, McGowan and Hegarty had their bad game over them. Donegal knew that they would have to improve dramatically from the drawn game. Anything less than the form that characterised their previous games would result in painful defeat.

McGowan had thrown his team in against the Tyrone seniors a week before the final. Tyrone were still in the Ulster championship and had places up for grabs as they prepared to defend their Ulster title against Armagh. Thus the Tyrone 15 played at championship pace. So did the Donegal youngsters. It was just the robust highly competitive fare Donegal required to get the drawn match out of their systems. A much more direct Donegal led a stunned Tyrone by 2-3 to 0-1 on the half hour. McGowan gave members of his panel a run out in the second half. "With five minutes to go," grins PJ McGowan, "We were well on top. Then Tyrone got stuck into us!" Tyrone eventually overcame the Donegal youngsters but only by six points and not before Donegal had notched up 2-10.

McGowan's team for the final picked itself – Danny Gallagher; John Joe Doherty, John Connors, Thomas Maguire; Diarmaid Keon, John Cunningham, Paul Carr; Barry Cunningham, John Bán Gallagher; Paddy Hegarty, Tommy Ryan, Barry McGowan; Dermot Ward, Manus Boyle, Luke Gavigan. He had Seamus Ward, Brian Mór Gallagher, Cormac McGarvey, Conor White, Joey McDermott, Peter McIntyre, Seamus Doohan and Emmet Golden in reserve. "We will not miss them this time," predicted PJ McGowan, as the Kerry match loomed.

❄ ❄ ❄ ❄

"Manus Boyle will do well to repeat his previous display," argued Michael Daly

John Joe Doherty

in the *Democrat*. Following the drawn game Manus had attracted the attention of a former Galway star and respected GAA author who was lavish in his praise. "Boyle," declared Jack Mahon, "is one of the best under-21 footballers I have ever seen". It seemed unlikely however that the Killybegs man could hope to reproduce in Roscommon the dizzy heights of his Tuam exploits. By the time Donegal exited Dr Hyde Park on a sunny Sunday, June 28, 1987, Manus Boyle was a Donegal football legend.

"We probably respected Kerry too much the first day," felt Barry McGowan. John Cunningham concurred:

> Deep down we all knew that we were good enough. We got the whole thing about playing Kerry in an All-Ireland out of our system in the drawn match. We realised then that we were the better team and we did not seem to be under as much pressure on the second day. We went out and performed.

Before taking the pitch John Cunningham addressed his team. Manus Boyle recalls it vividly:

> It was when he really came to the fore as being a good captain and leader. In Killybegs we don't believe in making just anybody captain. John was starting to impose his attitude, strength and belief on that team. He gave a brilliant team talk and we didn't go out on to the pitch for a while, we took half a minute to think about what he said. I don't know if there was a door on the dressing room, but if there was, it wasn't fucking there when we went out! We would have went through a wall.

Right from Mickey Kearins' throw-in the tension was palpable, but it was emanating mostly from the stands. The players were quite relaxed and fully confident of victory. The few opportunities presented in the opening minutes were spurned. Fully 15 minutes of play would pass before the scoreboard operators were troubled for the first time. Yet it was Donegal who had much the better of the opening exchanges.

Barely 90 seconds had passed when Barry McGowan tested the Kerry goals. His effort was poked to safety and some five minutes later Luke Gavigan forced Moran, the Kerry goalkeeper, to produce a fantastic save from a sizzling goalward drive. Despite the distinct lack of scores, Donegal were settling into their groove. So much so that, with nine minutes gone, Kerry had still to pass the half-way line.

It was perhaps inevitable that it was Manus Boyle who broke the deadlock. Not for the last time that afternoon Luke Gavigan outpaced his man in the dash for the ball and off-loaded it to Manus who pointed in full flight. Impressive. Luke Gavigan, a footballer who had it all, had not delivered anything like his true potential since demolishing Fermanagh with his two goals back in March. PJ McGowan however had bravely stuck with the Ardara forward, mindful of his awesome potential. Gavigan would repay McGowan's faith in full that day in Roscommon.

Then Kerry got a goal totally against the run of play. A sideline kick swung into the Donegal goalmouth. As the ball broke Mick Galwey pounced first and slammed it to the net. Game on. Out at centre half-back John Cunningham was in a formidable frame of mind. The *Democrat* captured his opening 15 minutes with panache: "His intensity radiated out like a beacon to his colleagues," wrote Michael Daly. It was to be John Cunningham's greatest day in a Donegal jersey. It would take his county five long years to reach a senior All-Ireland final and when that Sunday in September came around, John Cunningham would experience bitter personal disappointment. That was all in the future. With barely a quarter of the game gone in Roscommon, Cunningham's burning intensity forced the Kerry mentors to switch their game plan. Hoare came out to centre half-forward to curb Razda's forward runs. He was wasting his time. So too was Martin Dennehy who facilitated Hoare by moving into full-forward. John Connors was just too good. Hoare had been held scoreless, Dennehy would suffer the same fate.

Spurred on by the efforts of their defence, the forwards hit a purple patch. In the closing eight minutes of the half Donegal struck five times. Three pointed frees from Manus Boyle were interspersed with fine individual scores from Dermot Ward and Barry McGowan. Kerry's only other reply came from Gerard Looney, the third Kerry player to fill the full-forward position. Looney beat Connors to the ball and struck a sweet point off his left boot. That was his and Kerry's only score from full-forward as John Connors proceeded to shut him out of the game. Kerry had recorded another point to leave it 0-6 to 1-2 at the break. John Cunningham had reason to be pleased:

> We were very fortunate in the first ten or 15 minutes in that everything just clicked into position. This settled everybody down and gave us a launching pad. In some of the other games it was a dogfight at the beginning and we never really got into a rhythm. I got a few balls at centre back, gave them to Manus and he tipped them over. That happened two or three times and Kerry were scunnered.

Players had their say in the dressing room at half time. The scene was relaxed remembers Barry McGowan, "I told the other players that we knew we were the better team and we just had to go out and prove it. We did just that. We played tremendous football in the second half."

Manus was relaxed and enjoying himself. He and Tommy Ryan had built up a great partnership in the Donegal attack. "He knew which way I was going to run and I knew which way he was going to run," remembered Manus:

I gave Tommy two dropped kick passes. PJ McGowan didn't like me hitting drop kicks and when I made those passes I grinned over at him. I got a point from one of those passes when the ball came back out to me. A Kerry defender thumped me in the back, this pushed me past another player and I scored.

The three-week break had given Tommy Ryan's cracked ribs ample time to heal and Kerry were about to see the real Tommy Ryan. As the second half resumed in Dr Hyde Park the Termon lad suddenly sparked to life. A minute hadn't elapsed on the clock before Ryan sailed over a point from out on the left wing. A couple of minutes later he had a big hand in Donegal's only goal of the game.

There seemed to be little threat to the Kerry goal as Luke Gavigan soloed out near the corner flag. The corner forward slipped the ball back out to Ryan who swung over a cross in the direction of Paddy Hegarty. Hegarty was quick off the mark to claim possession above the heads of two Kerry defenders before rifling a shot for goal. Half blocked, Hegarty's shot was pounced upon by Manus Boyle who fired it to the corner of the Kerry net. His captain was impressed, "You need players that are prepared to stand up on the big day. Some people freeze on the big day. With others, it brings out the best in them and Manus seems to be one of those." Donegal were on their way to an All-Ireland title.

Unfortunately for Kerry, Manus Boyle was now unstoppable. Confidence oozed from him. Nine year later, Tom Humphries wrote of Manus in his acclaimed book, *Green Fields*, "Manus is confident, and quick, and a winner. A boy who goes well when he has the roar of the crowd at his back and something worthwhile to play for." Humphries was mainly referring to Boyle's contribution in the Donegal shirt in September 1992. The description was equally apt back in June 1987. Boyle revelled in the white heat of an All-Ireland final. He added another point from play and Kerry were suddenly six points adrift and in trouble. Hoare was back in on John Connors again while Looney was trying his luck on John Cunningham. No change was forthcoming from either defender.

Kerry weren't going to go down without a fight. Gerald Murphy halved the scoring difference with a goal after eight minutes. John Joe was livid, "I'd promised myself he wouldn't get three points off me again but he sneaked that goal". A converted free six minutes later silenced the Donegal supporters who had been celebrating a trifle prematurely. Fifteen minutes remained on the clock. A two-point lead could be wiped out in a single kick. Donegal hearts ticked a little faster as their boys spurned a brace of goal chances to put the game dead. Kerry tried everything. Mick Galwey was roaming all over the place, eventually opting to loiter with ominous intent on the edge of the Donegal square. Up close and shadowing was Barry Cunningham who would have followed Galwey home to Kerry. Cunningham had gone into the game with a clear plan in his mind:

John Bán marked him in the drawn game and tried to catch the ball with him. That just wasn't possible. I stood in front of him the next day to spoil him. I sacrificed my own performance to negate his.

The final ten minutes belonged to Donegal. Five scores were recorded, four of them from the feet of Donegal players. Dermot Ward, who had been as consistent as ever, had been racing out from the corner all afternoon winning ball ahead of his marker. Manus gratefully hooked over a 30-metre free following a foul on the Glenfin man after 20 minutes. A minute later Kerry had their final say, a pointed free from Hoare.

Gavigan was on hand to provide Boyle with a clever crossfield ball for the Killybegs man to solo goalwards and fire over yet another point to complete his scoring for the day. One goal and seven points was his quite remarkable final tally. It was a peerless display that would be officially acknowledged with the man of the match award. Afterwards, Barry Cunningham paid a famous tribute to his Killybegs clubmate, "You need a Manus Boyle if you are going to win All-Irelands." It was both a tribute and a prophecy as Manus Boyle would contribute a man of the match performance on that famous Sunday in September in 1992. When that quote was put to an ever modest Manus in an interview in 2003, his response was, "You need boys like Barry Cunningham to win All-Irelands."

John Joe Doherty had a knowledge of Manus that few others have had:

Manus was a brilliant player. Nobody in Donegal has marked him more times than me. I played at full back for Glencolmcille and he played at full-forward for Killybegs. It was very frustrating trying to mark him, he only had to see the posts to score. I would be able to play Manus fairly well from play but when I sat down to read the *Democrat* the following Thursday, I'd see eight or nine points after his name without fail.

The final scores of the day fell to the Wards of Glenfin. On the stroke of full time Dermot Ward capped a fine display with the final point of the game. A couple of minutes earlier the Donegal supporters were on their feet to salute his brother Seamus who had driven a spectacular point over from all of 40 metres. Ward, a hero of the hour against Armagh, had a much deserved run out on the big day, coming in for John Bán with 12 minutes to go. It was fitting that the big Glenfin man was to contribute 12 incisive minutes to his team's greatest hour.

The scenes when Mickey Kearins blew the full-time whistle reside fondly in the minds of all those that were there. Some 5,000 Donegal voices, maybe more, give vent to their triumph. The pitch gates were swung open and Hyde Park became a sea of green and gold. Players were back-slapped, mauled and hugged as a county celebrated. Some supporters celebrated in person their second All-Ireland in five years, while others were witnessing it for the first time.

Here and there, as the sea of people heaved to and fro, a Donegal player would be raised high on the shoulders of the faithful and thrust into the clouds. Sometime just before five o'clock on a famous Sunday in June, 1987, John Cunningham raised the Tadhg Ó Cléirigh Cup high above his head.

❄ ❄ ❄ ❄

"It was a fabulous performance, great talent and a subs bench that would have graced many a county team," said PJ McGowan, the man who could now right-fully claim to be Donegal's most succesful under age manager of all time. And if ever there was a Donegal man not begrudged his success it was the genial McGowan.

It was the most glorious of days. Back in the mid-1980s Donegal supporters had appreciated that they were seeing the future of Donegal football tumbling all before them at minor level in Ulster. Two years later these youngsters had taken the ultimate giant leap that had delivered to Donegal an All-Ireland of colossal importance. "There is a special magic about beating Kerry in an All-Ireland final and although the result of this contest was long in doubt, victory ultimately rested where it richly deserved," wrote Sean McGoldrick in the *Irish Press*.

Correct, but there was more to Donegal's win than *merely* an All-Ireland title. Michael Daly and half of Donegal realised that. "In 1982 Donegal created history winning their first ever All-Ireland under-21 crown," wrote Daly, "On Sunday a new team repeated that feat and the general feeling is that a mixture of both would indeed be a potent concoction." He wasn't wrong. In time, six of the players from the All-Ireland side of 1987 would join seven of those who triumphed in 1982, and between them they would provide the backbone of a truly great team that would create GAA history.

There had been false dawns before. The dawn that rose with the under-21s of 1987 would prove to be no false dawn.

❄

RESULTS	Ulster Championship	All-Ireland Series
	Donegal 2-7, Fermanagh 2-6.	Donegal 1-7, Laois 1-6.
	Donegal 3-5, Derry 1-7.	Donegal 1-7, Kerry 0-10.
	Donegal 1-9, Armagh 1-6.	Donegal 1-12, Kerry 2-4. (R)
	Donegal 0-7, Monaghan 1-4.	
	Donegal 1-11, Monaghan 0-8. (R)	

9

The Top Rung

(November 1987 – March 1988)

"They shall be spoken of amongst their people."

THE FOLLOWER – MARCH 4TH, 1988

The embers were still hot from the bonfires that had greeted the under-21 heroes when, almost morbidly, speculation returned to Tom Conaghan and the team he would pick to elevate Donegal out of Division Two.

Autumn beckoned, and after the magical journey with the under-21s, Donegal football turned back in on itself. Doom and gloom reigned supreme. According to the scribes and the insiders, all was not healthy in Donegal football. "Even the dogs can bark this on the street," claimed the man known as 'the Follower' who had begun contributing a weekly column in the *Democrat*. His identity was a poorly kept secret for many years. Cormac McGill, originally from Convoy but exiled in Leitrim, had been watching Donegal football since the 1930s. Green and gold blood ran through his veins and he simply lived and breathed Donegal football. His column quickly became *de rigeur* reading for everyone associated with the GAA in the county. His unique style of writing seamlessly combined English, Irish and Latin. If, as has been widely claimed, Con Houlihan educated the masses from his pulpit on the back page of the *Evening Press*, then the Follower evangelised the gospel of Donegal football. Blindly optimistic where Donegal was concerned, the finest chapter of the county's footballing tale would soon be told by the county's finest scribe.

Few would have disagreed that the national league of 1987-88 was a crucial campaign for the seniors. Some argued that it was even a make or break season. If anything, the success of the under-21s only intensified the pressure on Conaghan to deliver something – *anything*. Every would-be manager from Malin Head to Bundoran were merging the best of the 1982 and 1987 All-Ireland sides and conjuring up instant senior All-Ireland success. It was never going to be that easy. Nonetheless, away back in 1981 and 1982, Brian McEniff had bitten the bullet and parachuted several under-21 players into his, admittedly ageing, squad.

The county waited to see if Conaghan would follow the signpost left by his predecessor. Would Conaghan pick the team the whole county wanted him to pick? True to form and without really saying or doing anything, Conaghan had punters beside themselves with barely concealed rage with not a ball yet kicked.

By the time he named his panel midway through October he had most definitely acquired another notable if sporting adversary in the guise of the Follower:

> I could not even in the wildest flights of imagination agree with the panel he has chosen. I will vouch for his honesty, his integrity, his commitment to do what he thinks is best for Donegal football but still I will not agree with the panel chosen.

Opinions varied on Conaghan's panel. Gary Walsh was included by Conaghan for the first time. Dropped from the panel 12 months earlier, Walsh was happy to let bygones be bygones, "I was working and living in Leitrim. I got a message that I was to ring Tom. I didn't ask him why I had been left out of the panel, I just came back and started training again." The usual suspects that needed little introduction were there: Sean Bonner, Brendan Dunleavy, Joyce McMullan, Donal Reid, Matt Gallagher, Anthony Molloy, Martin McHugh, Sylvester Maguire and Declan Bonner. In there too were Martin Shovlin and Martin Gavigan, both of whom would fully establish themselves in the months ahead. Brian Murray still floated on the fringe of the team. Brian Tuohy, Conaghan's captain back in 1982, was also there. Not withstanding his under-21 form, Manus Boyle had earned his place on the strength of his scoring prowess over the previous season. He was joined by four of his under-21 colleagues, John Connors, John Joe Doherty, Diarmaid Keon and Tommy Ryan, the latter had only recently returned from the States. The remainder of the panel consisted of James Carr from Kilcar, Cathal Campbell and Eamon Breslin from St Naul's, Pól MacCumhaill from Gaoth Dobhair, Eugene McMenamin and Seamus Devine from Robert Emmets, Willie Scales and Michael McGeehan from St Eunan's, Michael Kelly and Corny Carr from Four Masters, Ted Breslin from Ardara, Myles Sweeney from Dungloe, and Joe McGarvey and Denis Doohan from Cloughaneely.

The Follower voiced the concerns of many across the county, "I do not like your panel, Tom. However, upon your shoulders be it and as you are the manager we will back you all the way, reserving the right to express opinion." Where, it was asked, was the likes of Barry Cunningham who was on his way back from the States and presumably available? Where were Mulgrew and Carlin, Newton, McGettigan, McDermott and Lafferty? It seemed as if the whole county was on standby for Conaghan to fall very hard indeed from his delicate state of grace.

Conaghan was quite unperturbed. Criticism had run off his back before and it was still running off it now. His infamous ban, which had grabbed the headlines at the beginning of the year, was back in full swing. Conaghan confirmed to the *Democrat* that indeed nothing had changed. All or nothing. Same as always.

As he faced into his first game at Ballybofey at the beginning of November, Conaghan – despite what his detractors might say – was not too far off the mark. He had on his panel 14 of the key players that would be involved with Brian McEniff less than five years later in the successful quest for Sam. Conaghan was seven matches away from hitting the big time and in the process could rightfully claim to be fully vindicated in both his choice of players and his approach. The tragedy was that the weekly theorising about who was in the team and who was out almost overshadowed a football campaign that was both historic and ground-breaking.

❄ ❄ ❄ ❄

Kildare fell heavily at MacCumhaill Park – Donegal destroyed them 1-10 to 1-3. McHugh with 1-5 and McMullan with 0-3 led the way with Kildare finally managing their first score a full 16 minutes into the second half. Shovlin was flying while Matt Gallagher was solid if unspectacular in the corner-back berth. However, Matt was about to fall out of favour.

Manus had just picked up a month's suspension at club level so Conaghan had to proceed without the Killybegs ace. Already weary of criticism, it was just the opener the team needed. "There was a lot of question marks over the team and we had a point to prove," Joyce McMullan told the *Democrat* afterwards. Brendan Dunleavy, in at full back, agreed, "We had been getting a lot of stick from the press and the public. People had been dubious and doubtful."

They still were. Kildare had been disappointingly inept for a side that had shown such promise in the Leinster championship. They were the side that had beaten Donegal by four points just 12 months previously but had seemingly faded in the interim. The jury on Donegal was still very much out.

A difficult proposition lay ahead – Roscommon in Hyde Park. The Follower was generous with his opening paragraph several days later:

> The wry smile that etched itself across the Conaghan countenance in MacCumhaill Park widened ever so little as referee Conlon signalled the end of a dour bitter, struggle at cold, wet and windswept Hyde Park on Sunday last.

Trailing the home side by 0-2 to 0-8 at half time, Donegal had fought bravely to snatch all the league points on offer on a scoreline of 1-6 to 0-8.

The diehard Donegal supporters who braved the elements witnessed a tough game of winter Gaelic football. Roscommon hit hard, exceedingly hard, but Donegal had men in their ranks who were not found wanting. Gary Walsh, in only his second game under Conaghan, was laying down the foundations that would see him retain the Donegal number one jersey for nine successive seasons. Shovlin, Tuohy, Reid – as ever – and McMullan were motoring well. John Joe Doherty's debut in the senior jersey was every bit as impressive as his under-21 form had promised.

McHugh, worryingly, was still the man Donegal relied upon for the scores. He finished the game with 1-4. The old nagging unease remained. An out-of-form or immobilised McHugh and Donegal would always be in trouble. He was a one-man scoring machine. It was a McHugh goal on the 13th minute of the second half that give Donegal the breakthrough they deserved. McHugh had tested Gay Sheerin in the Roscommon goals twice in quick succession just after the restart but bizarrely his goal, when it came, was struck from all of 50 metres and somehow skidded all the way to the net. For the travelling support it reawakened memories of the joyous October Sunday five years earlier when, against the same opposition, a long range McHugh free made it to the net in the dying moments of the All-Ireland under-21 final. That goal didn't stand but this 50-metre strike did. Joyce had earlier converted and, after 15 minutes another McHugh free levelled matters.

Tommy Ryan was making his senior debut. He'd been impressive through-out the hour and completed a highly satisfying debut by kicking the winner 11 minutes from time. The simple fact was that with two matches gone, Donegal were sitting joint top of Division Two with Down. By no means could it be described as anything but an admirable start.

A big test, the biggest so far, came in the third game. Galway, in Tuam, would either silence the critics or open the floodgates. Back in March 1986, in McEniff's last national league game as Donegal boss, Donegal had dispatched Galway to the wilderness of Division Three. Galway had breezed through Division Three unbeaten and were back hoping to avenge relegation by knock-ing Donegal off the top perch. Conaghan created consternation by sticking with the team that beat Roscommon, despite the availability of Manus Boyle. The team was Walsh; Bonner, Dunleavy, Campbell; Doherty, Tuohy, Shovlin; James Carr, Gavigan; McHugh, Reid, McMullan; Ryan, Molloy, Bonner.

For the first time, as Donegal supporters and scribes made their way home along the N17 following the Galway game, there was scarcely a hint of castigation. An impressive display of never-say-die football had been witnessed as Donegal showed remarkable guts and determination to earn a draw despite the setback of conceding a brace of goals within a minute midway through the second half.

It ended 0-11 to 2-5. Tom Conaghan's men were now all alone at the top of Division Two, a point clear of Down and Galway. Indeed Donegal were most unfortunate not to have taken the full complement of points from Galway but no-one was complaining, certainly not Conaghan whose demeanour was that of a happy man.

Conaghan had unearthed a real gem in Cathal Campbell. The St Naul's man had made the number four jersey a prisoner with only three county games under his belt. As the *Democrat* observed, he was already a firm favourite with the crowd. Campbell, Doherty and Shovlin were instrumental in the early stages against Galway as their aggressive running onto the ball opened paths ahead for the forwards.

Despite good passages up front Donegal trailed by 0-1 to 0-3 with 12 minutes gone. Conaghan signalled Molloy to go out to the middle in a direct swap with Carr and it was the move that changed the game. "Tuam," wrote the Follower, "belonged to Molloy." "Molloy owns Tuam," agreed the headline in the *Tuam Herald*. The big Ardara man had his best game in a very long time and his spectacular fielding handed Donegal the edge around the middle of the park. Gavigan, his clubmate, revelled in his company.

Donegal were 0-4 to 0-3 ahead by the time Manus made his appearance some 18 minutes into the first half. Donegal voices lifted the roof off the stand with their welcome for the new hero of Donegal football. Manus would have a quiet game by his immeasurably high standards but would have the final say before the hour was up.

McHugh was lost four minutes later. Despite his size, 50-50 balls held no fear for the Wee Man. He came off the worst when he met Mattie Coleman at full speed and shipped a heavy knock to his left shoulder. He looked to be in serious trouble as Conaghan and physiotherapist John Cassidy helped him over the sideline. It was the last Donegal would see of McHugh for a while.

Despite a good start to the second half, Donegal only managed to fashion a two-point gap ahead of the Tribesmen and a price would be paid. Two Galway goals in rapid succession rocked Donegal on to their heels. Four points down with 15 minutes remaining, the game had 'home win' stamped all over it. The away team kept its cool though. Mentally they were not beaten, and shrugging off the shock of the double-strike, Donegal played on.

McMullan pointed with 11 minutes remaining. Tommy Ryan then grazed the crossbar with a piledriver. Two in it. Gay McManus converted a free, the deficit was back to three with eight minutes remaining. Bonner, who broke the hearts of many a Donegal club side with his accurate frees in Lettermacaward, hit a glorious dead-ball from all of 45 metres. Time seemed to be running out though. Pól MacCumhaill had replaced McHugh and the Gaoth Dobhair man was on hand to swivel around three Galway defenders to send over another Donegal score with three minutes left on the clock. The last thing Galway needed was to concede a free with Manus Boyle on the pitch. Concede it they did and Boyle ever so sweetly hit the equaliser.

It was a performance that oozed character. The Follower was most gracious: "Stand up Tom Conaghan and take a bow as you accept our thanks. You have got the attitude right. You seemingly have instilled a requisite never-say-die spirit into this dedicated bunch of players."

John Connors had been the cornerstone of the Donegal defence in the under-21 campaign earlier in the year. Barry Cunningham remembered Connors' debut for the soon-to-be All-Ireland under-21 champions:

> John Connors hadn't played with us at minor level and you mightn't have given much for him when you saw him. He came into the team against Derry, played a stormer and held his position for the year.

The call up to the senior squad inevitably followed and Connors made his senior debut against Clare in Ballyshannon in the last game before Christmas. With less than two minutes left, Connors struck the point that secured a 1-7 to 0-9 win. The defender had turned poacher, having replaced an injured Joyce McMullan. Rooted to the bottom of the table, Clare had shown the Donegal table toppers scant respect and had given the usually uncompromising home defence an afternoon most would want to forget. Clare had five points on the scoreboard to Donegal's three with 15 minutes gone and, although they wouldn't score for the remainder of the half, also accumulated six wides. Donegal were all at sea until Declan Bonner – having his best game of the pre-Christmas period – rattled the Clare net. Reid and Ryan were involved in the early stages before a shot from Manus came off the post. Bonner latched onto the ball quickest and sent it thundering to the net nine minutes before the break.

The second half was equally torrid for Donegal. This was a Clare outfit who were not for lying down and with four minutes to go they hit the front. For the second Sunday in succession Donegal had the greater mental reserve. Manus hit the equaliser with three minutes left and was there again to flick the ball to Connors for the winner. Happy Christmas Donegal! Walsh had been magnificent. Sean Bonner at corner back was as solid as a rock. John Joe was John Joe. Gavigan, already known as Rambo, was there to stay. His importance to the team was quickly becoming apparent. Martin McHugh was coming up against Gavigan in every training session:

> Conaghan gave new players a chance. He unearthed Gavigan and that was the big one – we wouldn't have won an All-Ireland without Gavigan. He was a tremendous footballer. One of the reasons my game improved was that I marked him in training. His physical presence was immense and he was very, very quick.

Gavigan meanwhile, was enjoying himself, and was grateful to Conaghan. "He gave me a fair chance once I got started. He played me at midfield. I didn't really like playing at midfield but I would have played anywhere just to get on!"

Bonner, Boyle and Ryan had between them produced some sumptuous football. And Molloy had once again been outstanding. Conaghan, said all the lads, had a soft spot for Molloy. In the eyes of Conaghan the big man from Ardara could do little wrong. In the eyes of onlookers his last couple of games had been flawless. Molloy was a huge favourite with the crowd and had his own theory on why this might be the case:

> I would have been a favourite with the crowd. Brian Murray might have played better than me some days but would have got stick if he did some-thing wrong. I could have a mediocre game but people, including the press, would say that I had a great game. We had a massive following at that time. After games, no matter where we went, 50 to 100 people would come troop-ing into the bar after us. We socialised as a group and 15 or 20 of us would have gone everywhere together. It was a great thing because it instilled a great spirit between ourselves. We had the craic and knew everybody. That would have carried on support-wise the following Sunday.

Donegal were poised. It was hard to see what all the fuss had been about. Four games played and unbeaten. Conaghan shrewdly talked hopes down. "Forget all this talk about promotion," he told the *Democrat*, "We'll accept it if it comes but we will still be taking things one game at a time and that's not going to change." Conaghan was being coy. Promotion was his priority. On taking over the manager's job, Conaghan had sought advice from Kerry's O'Dwyer. "Mick O'Dwyer told me that Donegal would have to get out of Division Two and play against the bigger teams. He told me to gear the team up for promotion and be prepared to do unpopular things."

Supporters of the manager around the county – and there were many – enjoyed the festive season happy in the knowledge that the much needed kick in the rear that Donegal football had been calling out for had been delivered by the formidable boot of Tom Conaghan.

Connie Duffy acknowledged the new-found character being displayed by Donegal. "For the first time in many years Donegal senior footballers have shown a little fight-back. Too often they lay down when the going got rough and this cost them important games and titles." Connie probably didn't know it then, but he had just captured a large chunk of the legacy that Tom Conaghan would leave to Donegal football.

❄ ❄ ❄ ❄

There was still meat on the turkey when the next instalment of the Conaghan management saga broke. Des Newton, who'd always had an uneasy relation-ship with the manager, announced his transfer back to his native Roscommon. In going he fired a fierce salvo of criticism in the direction of Conaghan. "Mr Conaghan's ego-trip since last September 12 months has left the career of many good players in tatters. I am lucky and fortunate to have an alternative," he told the *Democrat*. Newton had not been selected for any of Donegal's four pre-Christmas national league games. He had been and still was a fine defender and his departure was greeted with dismay by football people. Newton would go on to win Connacht titles with Roscommon in 1990 and 1991, but, sadly for him, All-Ireland success would prove elusive.

Conaghan spent January whipping his team into shape. A series of challenge games were held and the squad was comprehensively strengthened by the return of Carlin, Mulgrew, McGettigan and the Cunninghams. When Conaghan played an A selection against a B selection at Townawilly a week into the New Year, scattered among the teams were 16 players who would win All-Ireland senior medals.

Naomh Bríd, Matt Gallagher's club – operating a stone's throw from Conaghan's home turf – seemed to strike a blow for the anti-Conaghan brigade when they submitted a proposal to County Convention proposing an end to a second three-year term for an outgoing manager. Reappointment for an outgoing manager would then be decided on an annual basis. The motion was defeated and although Naomh Bríd insisted that it was not in any way aimed at Tom Conaghan, some doubt lingered.

Conaghan was firmly focussed on three Sundays in February, the consequences of which were immense for Donegal football. Division One status, if it could be obtained, would be a giant leap towards serious contention for Sam Maguire. Cavan, never an easy option, were first up. In Breffni Park.

Connie Duffy, as ever, was on hand to comment on a famous 2-6 to 0-11 win.

Donegal are now closer to Division One than they have ever been following their magnificent victory over Cavan at Breffni Park. They overcame the dreadful muddy conditions and a tough home team to record perhaps their most important win since Tom Conaghan took over the reins as manager.

Four thousand hardy souls, half of them from Donegal, braved the elements and witnessed a fiercely competitive game of uncompromising football. It was, someone said, no place for the faint of heart.

Conaghan went with Walsh; Sean Bonner, Dunleavy, Campbell; Doherty, Tuohy, Shovlin; Molloy, Gavigan; Reid, Mulgrew, Declan Bonner; McHugh, Boyle and Ryan. Before the 60 minutes were out he threw in McGettigan and Barry Cunningham. By Seamus Aldridge's full-time whistle the Follower would describe them as "the grittiest, most courageous, toughest set of warriors as ever wore our beloved green and gold."

Half time score: 1-3 to 0-6. There were talking points aplenty up in the stand. Molloy and Gavigan were getting the better of King and Reilly. The half-back line was something to behold. Shovlin was well on his way to his best game so far in

Sam's for the Hills

a Donegal jersey. For a light man he was utterly fearless. It was good to see Mulgrew back and as industrious as ever. "McHugh," noted the Follower, "was devastating." Yet Donegal should have trailed at the break – Phil Smith, the big Cavan full-back, had spectacularly contributed the Donegal goal himself under pressure in his own goalmouth. Donegal got a little rub of the green in the middle of the quagmire. "Chronic conditions," remembers Martin Gavigan, sympathising with Smith's plight, "The weather conditions seemed to be brutal around those years. We played in mudbaths. Nearly every league game we'd be up to our eyes in muck, particularly in Breffni." Yet it was all to do in the 30 minutes ahead.

Leslie McGettigan made a welcome return and came in after the interval for Tuohy who'd picked up an injury. Reid slotted back to centre half-back to allow McGettigan up front. Conaghan had fallen into the same trap as McEniff by playing Reid in the forwards. In fairness to Conaghan he already had *some* half-back line. Nonetheless, as Reid's second half against Cavan would show, he was born for the half-back line. McHugh and Ronan Carolan traded points as Barry Cunningham replaced Declan Bonner. Cunningham made an immediate impact and not for the last time when Donegal needed inspiration, he provided it. Cavan tagged on two further points but their efforts were doomed to failure. Molloy broke Cavan hearts by totally dominating proceedings both in the air and on the ground around midfield. The supply of ball going into the Cavan forwards was reduced to a trickle.

The final quarter belonged to Donegal. Two points adrift, Cunningham was fouled. McHugh floated the free into the Cavan square where it was lashed to the net by the right fist of Manus Boyle. Opportunist, cheeky and deadly as ever. Now Donegal turned up the heat. Despite Cavan's best efforts – which would still yield a pair of points – Donegal sensed victory and hit Cavan with everything. McHugh – who had tormented the entire Cavan defence – and then Boyle completed the Donegal scoring with a point apiece with nine minutes still on the clock. Donegal defended en-masse but it still fell to Walsh to hold the Donegal line. Seconds remained and Donegal were two ahead when Ronan Carolan swung a leg at a ball deep in the Donegal danger area. Walsh had the ball well covered as it came skidding along the ground towards him. Corner forward John Brady then got a leg to it and to the horror of the Donegal defence the ball looped high over Walsh's head. Somehow Walsh got there, pushing the ball over the bar, to secure a famous win.

There would be many good days in the years ahead but Breffni Park that Sunday at the beginning of February 1988 was special. True, Donegal's promotion was not yet assured but as the travelling supporters awarded their heroes a sustained standing ovation after the game, they were saluting their side's new-found raw courage as much as their win. This was a different Donegal. A Donegal who eked results that weren't theirs for the taking. Eugene McGee, the Cavan manager, had been around a bit. His words in the Donegal dressing room rang true: "Over the years I have seen Donegal teams in similar situations, to put it bluntly, lying down. I can tell you one thing, you guys didn't lie down today." McGee had managed Offaly to an All-Ireland in 1982 at the expense of the mighty Kerry and his words were confirmation that under Tom Conaghan, Donegal were a new force to be reckoned with.

A week later the inevitable occurred. Down came to MacCumhaill Park and destroyed Donegal with the bones of the team that would waltz to an All-Ireland less than four years later. Only four points separated the sides after 60 minutes but the gulf in footballing terms was immense. In trouble all over the field, only Manus Boyle emerged with his reputation intact. Level at half time but drowning, Donegal's five points had come solely from the boots of Boyle. A further 30 minutes of aimless football would net a meagre two points – Manus got a sixth and two minutes from time Shovlin would venture up field for a rare score.

Conaghan was chided for not taking corrective measures from the sideline but the result seemed inevitable from the opening minutes. Players were chided too. Elements of the crowd were vocal in their criticism. "Public opinion is indeed fickle," noted the Follower, "People who cheered on the brave effort in Breffni on Sunday last decried the very same players." It fell to another wise old head to put the whole thing into perspective. Dunleavy, who'd been having a vintage campaign at full-back, had 14 years of experience in the county jersey to call upon, "Maybe defeat was a good lesson for us and something we hadn't experienced so far. It will be a cheap lesson if we can go out and beat Laois in two weeks time."

❋ ❋ ❋ ❋

It had been a long tough road from the depths of Division Three. A road littered with the debris of failure and modest achievement. Careers had been made and discarded along that road. When Brian McEniff was appointed Donegal manager on August 31, 1980, Division One football was but a dream. A fantasy. Fifty seven league games later, Tom Conaghan was about to trade fantasy for fact.

O'Moore Park, Portlaoise, would go into the annals of Donegal GAA history as the venue where the county struck gold and finally joined the cream of the land in Division One. It was somehow fitting that Donegal lined out against Laois in a game that would have so much bearing on the future of Donegal football. The two counties had a unique bond stretching back to the under-21 All-Ireland semi-final of 1982 and again in 1987. Laois and Donegal had slogged together for three seasons in Division Three before the midlanders broke free in 1986. Now they were on their way back down. One last handful of pride could be salvaged with Donegal's scalp.

It was a day when, at best, Donegal broke even in the first half but made the second their own. The fare was far from classic in the opening quarter but executed at a frenetic pace. Conaghan had stuck with the team that lost to Down – Sean Bonner was the only man to lose out while his brother Declan came in from

Anthony Molloy

the start. The manager made no less than seven positional changes. It seemed to work. The team that would win promotion were: Walsh; Doherty, Dunleavy, Campbell; Reid, Tuohy, Shovlin; Molloy, Gavigan; Declan Bonner, Mulgrew, McHugh; Ryan, Cunningham, Boyle.

Molloy had last played the football he produced that winter for Tom Conaghan's Donegal back in the heady days of the under-21s in 1982. In the muck and mire of the seven games that took Donegal out of Division Two, Molloy was awesome in the true sense of the word. Apart from his unquestionable skill, Molloy had presence. He was Griffin-like and more in his importance to Donegal. When he turned it on he was a colossus. On the field Anthony Molloy was Tom Conaghan's idea of what a footballer should be.

Donegal and Laois both scored two points in the opening 30 minutes. Molloy accounted for both scores. Midfield was his. It was a day when half a dozen Donegal heads rose above the parapet. Walsh, yet again, was unbeatable. In the eight national league campaigns Donegal had contested since the winter of 1980, the promotion campaign of 1987-88 had the greatest number of clean sheets – in five out of the seven games Walsh hadn't been beaten. Donegal folk were just getting to know a goalkeeper who would one day keep a clean sheet in a match that would bestow an All-Ireland.

Dunleavy had his proudest day in the green and gold, captaining his county into the top flight. As the sun sunk on a career that stretched back to the winter of 1974, Dunleavy had found himself in the very heart of the Donegal defence. He wore the position and responsibility well and had yet another outstanding hour.

Conaghan had seen the light with Reid and pushed the Killygordon man back to wing half-back. Result. Reid tore strips out of Laois. In time, Reid would be left there at half-back and the dividends would be rich. Tuohy, who had promised so very much but never got to deliver, was at his discerning best. When Tuohy played football he played it with his head.

McHugh was as sharp as ever. Forever developing his game, McHugh's role in the Donegal attack was slowly changing at his own instigation. Joined at last by the likes of Manus, Tommy Ryan and Declan Bonner, the pressure on McHugh to get the scores was slowly waning. While he would still finish Donegal's top score-taker of the league campaign, he was taking on the role of playmaker more and more. It was a role in which he was devastating. McHugh became the channel.

Having kicked eight first-half wides Donegal picked up where they left off in the opening minutes of the second half. Scores went a-begging. Eventually – inevitably – Donegal changed gears. Gavigan began playing football that lifted Donegal; Laois would have cause to remember Rambo. McHugh collected from John Joe and flicked the ball to Gavigan. Gavigan found Boyle and Manus put it between the posts. McHugh followed up with a converted free and with ten minutes left Donegal were home and dry. Leslie McGettigan came on for Ryan and had hardy drew breath before he created the only goal of the game.

Reid, McHugh, McGettigan – decisively – and Gavigan were all involved in the build up but it fell to the well-known rugby player, Charlie Mulgrew, to fire the ball to the net. Game over. Hello Division One!

Bonner traded scores with Lawlor but it was all over. It finished 1-5 to 0-3. Although level on points at the top of the table it was Down who won Division Two thanks to a better scoring average. That was immaterial, Donegal were up. It was a day of days for Donegal football. "They shall be spoken of amongst their people," wrote the Follower with his usual verve. There was much celebration in O'Moore Park as the team and manager were warmly saluted by the large travelling support. A proud moment for the team, none was prouder than their manager.

Tom Conaghan had been utterly unshakeable in his belief that his way was best. That belief had courted criticism and conflict along the way but could not now be denied. Conaghan had defied his critics and the top flight football he brought Donegal to would serve as a critical bridge to future success. Donegal would not relinquish Division One football as delivered by Conaghan's team for 15 years. There is no denying that without Division One football Donegal would never have had its glorious Sunday in September. In Martin McHugh's opinion:

Promotion was very, very important. In fairness to Conaghan, we trained very hard for the league, it was the first year we did that. It was important for us to start playing against better teams in Division One.

Joyce McMullan was of the same view:

When I first started playing we were playing teams like Tipperary, Sligo and Leitrim and, no disrespect to them, it was rubbish. From 1988 on we were playing only the best teams. That certainly made it more attractive for both the players and the supporters. There's no doubt our performances improved dramatically afterwards.

Martin Gavigan agreed that it was a special moment.

I have an old photograph from after that match. The joy of it all. A bit of success at last. The old characters – Bart Whelan, Charlie Faulkner – the people who had put so much time and effort into the game were all there. And happy.

Promotion brought with it additional pressures. Training, already stiff under Conaghan, had been increased that season. Donal Reid shook his head in disbelief years later as he recalled the rigours of the training regime:

Many's the night that we trained on snow at Murvagh or Inver beach. We used to run for five or six miles on the beach. We would go around a corner and find Conaghan waiting on us with his hands deep in his coat pockets and roaring us on. We were up to our knees in sand and the froth was hanging from our mouths. We had to run around him and run back up the beach. That was tough. I had a friend from South Africa staying with me at that time. He was watching from the dunes and could not believe the training amateur footballers were doing.

That Monaghan beat Donegal in the quarter final of the national league was largely irrelevant but as a game it surely had its talking points. Monaghan came to Healy Park in Omagh with a reputation as a big hard-hitting team. They left Omagh with a semi-final spot under their arms and the wrath of an entire county on their backs.

The first half was bursting with incident. McHugh, usually lethal from the dead ball, struck the post with his first attempt of the game from 45 metres. It was to be indicative of his day. The ball would largely refuse go over the bar for the Wee Man.

With barely 15 minutes gone, Gary Walsh made the most uncharacteristic of errors and, against the run of play, Monaghan had the ball in the Donegal net. Even so, Donegal hauled them back and by the 29th minute McHugh had levelled proceedings.

McHugh, like a lot of the Donegal players, was still enraged from events that had occurred just five minutes earlier. That Manus Boyle had the beating of Gerry McCarville was not in doubt. The Killybegs lad had far too much pace for the veteran Monaghan full-back, he was always out in front of the defender and threatened to run riot. "I was playing well on McCarville. He was punching and kicking me," recalled Manus.

On the 24th minute things came to a head, apparently off the ball. McCarville could be seen lying prone on the ground. All eyes turned to Manus, including those of Antrim referee John Gough. A consultation with an umpire duly saw an accusatory finger pointed at Boyle and the Killybegs man got his marching orders. Manus was furious:

> I had the beating of McCarville. I was walking out the pitch when, without any contact from me, he collapsed. He threw himself down. Donegal players were always honest but what McCarville did really pisses me off.

Donegal players were livid. As was Conaghan. Afterwards, with tempers running high, he would accuse McCarville of "lying down" to get the Donegal number 14 sent off. McCarville made a miraculous recovery for someone apparently out cold. Manus had scarcely crossed the line when McCarville was up and running about again. The price Manus would pay was high – three months' suspension. The incident still rankles the Killybegs man although he now diffuses it with humour, "There are a good few Monaghan people in Killybegs. When I walk by them I always look over my shoulder to make sure they haven't fallen."

Suffice to say the numerical disadvantage Donegal had to bear for the remainder of the game had a huge bearing on Monaghan's two-point win, 0-6 to 1-5. Donegal never lay down and – led by Molloy – battled courageously to the bitter end. That Donegal had 13 wides compared to Monaghan's five over the hour spoke volumes about their afternoon of defective kicking. Donegal had lost but there had been much to admire in their struggle with adversity. "Defeat with honour" was how Michael Daly summed it up in the *Democrat*.

❊ ❊ ❊ ❊

It had been some winter. Whatever lay in store as the summer approached, the winter had been special. Donegal had arrived.

Nowadays, managers, players and supporters play down the importance of the league. It wasn't always so. It certainly wasn't so in the days of Tom Conaghan. That Donegal went on to become part of the All Ireland winning club made it even easier to play down the league. The players, management and supporters that trekked around the country on dark, wet and windy winter days to see Donegal play in the Division Three basement did not play down the importance of the league.

Division One football, as with winning the Sam Maguire, was always thought to be beyond Donegal. It took single-mindedness, determination, immeasurable effort on the training fields and a little luck to bring Donegal to the national league summit. And it took Tom Conaghan. Not intending disrespect to any county, Mick O'Dwyer had once put it in the crudest of terms to Conaghan – "If Donegal continue to play with shite they'll be shite." Conaghan took that to heart and his Donegal hauled themselves out of the mire and took their place on the league's top rung.

❊

RESULTS	
National Football League	
Donegal 1-10, Kildare 1-3	Donegal 2-6, Cavan 0-11
Donegal 1-6, Roscommon 0-8	Donegal 0-7, Down 0-11
Donegal 0-11, Galway 2-5	Donegal 1-5, Laois 0-3
Donegal 1-7, Clare 0-9	Donegal 0-4, Monaghan 1-5 (q/f)

10

The Men Behind The Wire

(March 1988 – September 1989)

"Even though I wasn't playing, I wanted the boys to win."

MATT GALLAGHER

The writing was on the wall for Donegal as far back as late March in Belfast. Antrim became the third Ulster team to account for them in recent months and in the process dumped Conaghan's men out of the McKenna Cup. For a while attention naturally turned to the under-21s. The county was utterly convinced that they could and would defend their title. Of the players who featured in Donegal's famous 1987 campaign, only a handful – Manus Boyle, Seamus Ward, Paddy Hegarty, Paul Carr and Thomas Maguire – were over the bar in 1988. Donegal sought to repeat a summer of dizzy heights. It began well. Fermanagh were felled in Enniskillen. Derry were scalped in Ballybofey. Donegal followers got a first real glimpse of Noel Hegarty from Glencolmcille who came on in both games and impressed. A lad with a future it seemed.

The dream ended in the long grass of Cootehill, thanks to the accurate score-taking of Fintan Cahill and Ronan Carolan. An All-Ireland title was relinquished and another waylaid that April afternoon in the Cavan border town. Noel Hegarty, who came on as a sub remembers, "feeling as though I was being sucked into the grass. The condition of the pitch was a major factor in our defeat. Our team was far too good to lose to Cavan." "We had as good an under-21 team as the year before," agrees PJ McGowan.

It was a huge disappointment to Barry Cunningham:

> The game was switched from Breffni Park to Cootehill and the pitch must have been left uncut for about six weeks before the game. There was eight inches of grass and four inches of mud. It was a pure mudbath. We lost the game by a point or two and that was a big disappointment. The further on we would have gone the better we would have got.

The Men behind the Wire

✻ ✻ ✻ ✻

The McKenna Cup had shown that Ulster football was still as unpredictable as ever. A series of challenge games allowed Conaghan to experiment. Matt was back, but wouldn't be around for long. Murray was on the fringes but about to drop off the panel. John Cunningham seemed certain to make the starting 15. Molloy, inspirational all winter, seemed weary to the bone. Both Molloy and Gavigan were carrying injuries. Manus hadn't kicked a ball for three months thanks to Gerry McCarville. The forwards just didn't look right. And Joey Cunningham, Jim McConville, Ger Houlihan and company lay in wait.

Nonetheless, the team that went into battle against Armagh looked good on paper. No less than 11 of them would win an All-Ireland medal as a player four summers later. For once there was little real criticism of Conaghan's selection: Walsh; Doherty, Dunleavy, Gallagher; John Cunninghan, Reid, Shovlin; Molloy, Gavigan; Martin McHugh, Mulgrew, Ryan; Declan Bonner, McMullan, Boyle. In the aftermath of the bruising defeat that lay ahead other questions would surface.

✻ ✻ ✻ ✻

Donegal endured their fair share of dark days but Sunday, June 12, 1988, in the scorching heat of Armagh city would take some beating. The worst point of Conaghan's managerial career had been reached. The previous year had been bad, this was worse. Donegal made the trip to Orchard County headquarters and produced one of the worst performances in living memory. Peadar O'Brien of the *Irish Press* was thoroughly disgusted at the football he witnessed. "Dull, uninteresting, unexciting and extremely poor," recorded O'Brien. It was an accurate call. Donegal had a nightmare that afternoon.

It began in the opening moments and never let up. Joey Cunningham tested Walsh immediately with a piledriver which the Donegal 'keeper barely managed to push onto the crossbar and wide. Ninety seconds later Ger Houlihan made no mistake, wrong-footing half the Donegal defence before rifling the ball past Walsh from close range. Game over with the guts of 70 minutes left on the clock. There was no way back. Tommy Ryan was making his championship debut but had an unhappy outing. "I was marking Peter Rafferty and don't think I got more than four or five touches of the ball," he remembered. "Joey Cunningham wrecked us in the first half and the game was over by half-time."

A decent individual performance from someone in a green and gold jersey was hard to find. It truly was one of those days. With their team trailing 0-1 to 1-4 and only 16 minutes gone, Donegal supporters steeled themselves for a massacre. Making his championship debut was Naomh Columba corner back John Joe Doherty. "The biggest cheer came when the crowd heard that the Republic of Ireland had scored in Stuggart," he recalls. "I was marking Jim McConville, a player that I still have great time for. He was very fast and we had a great battle in the corner." McConville was held scoreless. As Donal Keenan noted in the *Irish Independent*, Armagh were nothing special either: "Relaxation and uncertainty up front allowed Donegal get back into the game when they should have been dead and buried." In fairness, Reid and Razda had upped things considerably and were succeeding in stemming the flow a little. Cunningham collided with Armagh wing half-forward Niall Smyth and ruptured cartilage in his knee. He played on with Killybegs for the rest of the season but eventually the injury caught up with him and he missed part of the 1990 season when he had it operated on.

At half-time it stood at 0-4 to 1-4. Five minutes after the restart Armagh buried Donegal. Houlihan, raiding in the Donegal square, was pulled down and a penalty conceded. McGurk converted and that really was that. Any hope Donegal had faded as the ball struck the net. "They looked like a team which had been thrown together hours early," opined Keenan. "The entire game was riddled with errors, Donegal being the main culprits. Passes were sprayed awfully astray, players in possession simply lost control of the ball and gave it away to the opposition." What little quality football that was played came from the home side; 0-8 to 2-10 it finished.

It was the day the Republic Ireland beat England in Stuttgart in the European Championships. When news of the Republic's goal came through from Germany it provided the only animation of the afternoon as the Athletic Grounds erupted in celebration. Paul Callaghan, who would later win an All-Ireland medal as Gary Walsh's understudy, was with the Burt contingent in the crowd. Mischievously, Callaghan started a rumour to the effect that England had secured a draw. It swept around the Athletic Grounds. Leaving Armagh, large sections of the crowd didn't know what to believe.

Things weren't so light-hearted in the Donegal dressing room as the post-mortem began. Conaghan, however, was in no mood to take responsibility. He pointed the finger firmly in the direction of the players. "The players have to carry this one, that's the way I would see it," Conaghan told reporters afterwards. The *Democrat* rating system, where the performances of players were marked out of ten, made for horrific reading; four was the highest rating awarded.

The Follower had his thoughts too – a few of the players weren't up to the "requisite standard". In fairness to the Follower, whose musings often found agreement among the Donegal football public, there appeared little light at the end of the tunnel that day in Armagh. John Joe was amused by some of the criticism:

> The funny thing about that game was that people were saying that we were probably the worst Donegal team that ever played. Thirteen of the team were involved when we won the Ulster championship in 1990.

Furthermore, of the 18 players Conaghan used that day, 15 would lift Sam.

The Men behind the Wire

Conaghan had little time for armchair and bar stool critics and less for those in the local press. Back in March, just after Donegal had secured promotion, Conaghan let rip at the County Board meeting in Ballybofey. "I think now that we're in first division football maybe it's time we got press that would cover first division. Maybe they can step up their game a little bit seeing we have stepped up ours." It was a heavyweight punch fired from the hip. Several rounds remained to be fought.

"Let's face it, we got a result this year already, we got promotion into the first division. You have to be patient," Conaghan observed testily in Armagh. Not for the first time it fell to the level head of Brendan Dunleavy, the old warrior, to put it into a footballer's perspective. "We all went out to do our best. When that happens and things don't go right you just have to accept it, carry on and look for better days."

✻ ✻ ✻

July brought talk of the men behind the wire. It had arisen before and was back to haunt Conaghan. John Travers of Aodh Ruadh was first out of the blocks at the County Board meeting: "We have a limited supply of talent but we lost talent needlessly. There are half a dozen players not playing county football who should be."

Delegates knew well those Travers referred to – among them McDermott, Murray, Curran and Maguire from his own club. Lafferty was motoring well at club level, where was he? Was Griffin really finished? Newton's departure was much lamented. And there were others. Earlier, John McConnell from Ardara – who would become chairman of the County Board 11 years later – expressed the opinion that Donegal were now "bottom of the pile".

Conaghan's term had 12 months to run. At worst, between league, McKenna Cup and championship he had nine games left holding the reins. For some, those 12 months and nine games couldn't pass quickly enough. And that most definitely included some players. As September rolled in it was obvious that a crisis loomed large in Donegal football. The Follower bit the bullet and put words on it, "The nub of the crisis is that many players do not want to play under the present set-up". Conaghan, opined the Follower, "must leave his entrenched position, must meet the players at least half way".

Yet again, without a ball being kicked, football was hitting the headlines. For the wrong reasons. County Board secretary, Bart Whelan, was about to have his say. "The County Board are not too happy at the moment because there seems to be a vendetta being carried out by one newspaper in particular within the county against Tom," Whelan told Charlie Collins, then in his pre-Highland Radio days with Donegal Community Radio. The war between the *Donegal Democrat* and Conaghan that had its first skirmishes early in 1987 was now raging out of control. Whelan went on to say that because Conaghan and some journalists didn't see eye to eye, the result was negative publicity for the Donegal manager. "They have a peculiar way of expressing their opinions about the team and his style of management."

Whelan, it was clear, wasn't impressed by the Follower either. Nor was Conaghan, labelling the columnist a "mouthpiece for players who weren't prepared to come out in the open themselves". In an interview with Connie Duffy at the beginning of October, Conaghan put it on the line:

> From the day I took over there was an anti-Tom Conaghan thing in the camp, at least with a few of the players. I know quite well there were players speaking behind my back trying to stir things up. I knew there would be a certain amount of this, I suppose it was only natural with new management. They had been around a while and weren't going to be pushed around.

The manager wasn't finished:

> It was a known fact that there was a certain element of player-power within the county and maybe that was one of the reasons I was given the role to get Donegal football the way it should be so that players would have pride wearing the county jersey.

Conaghan found it hard to equate the level of criticism with the success he and the team had delivered. There was, he told Duffy, "24 other counties in Ireland who are below us". As far as he was concerned, much of the criticism was personal. And, quite clearly from his earlier comments, he was weary of players sniping at his managerial style. He would face them down. As always.

The panel, when it came, merely added fuel to the fire. Talk wasn't so much of those included but those missing. Sean Bonner, it was said, had no intention of lining out under Conaghan again. His brother Declan had just returned from America and was for playing soccer over the winter. According to Conaghan, Matt wasn't interested. The Killybegs lads, newly crowned Donegal senior champions, weren't there. Manus had a dodgy knee that would require surgery but was playing a bit of soccer. A couple of others were fishing. The Cunninghams were emigrating as was Paddy Hegarty and Leslie McGettigan. Sylvester wasn't there either. And so it went.

Tucked away in the list of those included in the new panel was James McHugh. An outstanding club footballer with Kilcar for years – many would say the best club footballer in the county – McHugh couldn't be described as a find. Now 24 years of age, he had been an outstanding county minor and had concentrated his significant talents on club football. Nonetheless, it was under Conaghan that he got his run in the senior jersey. The last few places of the 1992 jigsaw were most definitely falling into place. James McHugh's introduction was short-lived and took in only a couple of appearances in the league and McKenna Cup. His career until then had been blighted by serious leg and ankle injuries and an ankle injury kept him out of contention for a starting place in the winter of 1988-89:

> I went up and down to Donegal the whole winter and was only watching the training. I got fed up and decided to pull out of the squad. I wouldn't have been fit enough for championship football anyway. It wasn't a big issue for me as the club was going well.

Division One was dominated by Ulster teams. Armagh, Down, Derry and Monaghan were there too, while Meath, Kerry and Dublin filled the rest of the roster. It was truly a different league. A league that half the county seemed convinced Donegal would exit on their first visit. One thing was certain, all camps of opinion in Donegal were anxious for the talking to cease and the football to begin.

Killybegs won their first county senior title in 36 years at the end of August. Tragedy had befallen the team earlier in the season when Eamon Byrne died on the pitch in Ballyshannon. "I was centre half-back and Eamon was wing half-back," recalled John Cunningham, "I noticed that he was struggling but we came off the field together at half-time. He was standing right beside me when he had a heart attack and died." The Killybegs team decided to put a big effort into the Ulster club championship and the players stayed with the club side as the national league commenced. Success was not forthcoming in the Ulster club championship – Killybegs would be runners-up in the competition in 1991, an all too rare feat for a Donegal team – but no representative of the club would feature in the Donegal team in the following championship. Manus Boyle was at a loss to explain it:

> We'd told Tom Conaghan that we were going to concentrate on the Ulster club championship. He told us to 'have a go'. I had an operation on a knee injury and, with Joyce McMullan, used the swimming pool to rehabilitate. I went training one night and my knee flared up so I went back to the pool for a couple of weeks. When I went to rejoin the panel I found the door was shut. Tom and me never had harsh words. I met him at a couple of club games. He would come over to me and tell me that I had played well but he never said 'See you at training on Tuesday night'.

Barry McGowan was playing a bit of soccer with Fanad United at the time. He attended a panel meeting called by Conaghan but opted out.

> I felt that I was jaded and would benefit from a rest. I was only 21 but had played a lot of football. In hindsight what I was doing was crazy. I'd

often play for Fanad in the morning and then rush off to play with Killybegs later. Later that year I began to pick up injuries. I asked Tom if he minded me taking a few weeks off and he told me that I should and we'd see how I got on. We left it at that.

Donegal's sojourn in Division One began in Armagh's Athletic Grounds in late October, but didn't provide the winning start the county yearned for. Four months and more had passed since the championship farce but despite enjoying the lion's share of possession the final outcome was the same for Donegal; 0-9 to 0-10. The age-old problem of failure to convert possession into scores came back to haunt Conaghan's men as it had haunted Donegal teams for years.

Dunleavy had been lost in the first half to injury, John Connors replacing the captain. Walsh, yet again, proved his worth. Midfield – Molloy and Gavigan – were in top form, Gavigan had his best game to date. Murray and Carlin were on board while Pat Ward of Naomh Conaill and Seamus Carr from Naomh Columba were the two new faces. Yet, it slipped away as the forwards over elaborated and shot wide from close range. A brace of league points had been presented, wrapped in orange ribbons, to a grateful Armagh. For the record, the first Donegal team to play Division One football was: Gary Walsh; John Joe Doherty, Brendan Dunleavy, Cathal Campbell; Donal Reid, Brian Tuohy, Martin Shovlin; Martin Gavigan, Anthony Molloy; Marty Carlin, Brian Murray, Pat Ward; Seamus Carr, Charlie Mulgrew, Martin McHugh. Subs: John Connors for Dunleavy and Tommy Ryan for Ward.

As opening games go there was good and bad. Valuable points had been spurned. With Meath and Kerry both to follow, the road to relegation pointed straight ahead. Yet, it had to be said, Donegal actually performed well against Armagh. Good football had been played, only the forwards hadn't clicked.

Brendan Dunleavy was injured and Conaghan appointed a new captain, Anthony Molloy. Molloy had been the heartbeat of the team for some time and remembers the moment he found out that he was to become captain of his county:

It was thrown on me one night at training and I'll never forget it as long as I live. While I would have had expected it at some time, I wasn't expecting it just then. Conaghan said to me, 'Molloy, you're captain from here on in'. I was a proud man on my way home that night and was thinking 'Christ, here I am, captain of the Donegal senior team'.

Molloy was made for the job and had no trouble in filling the position. Martin McHugh was happy that a good decision had been made:

Making Molloy captain was a good decision. It even changed the outlook on captains, before that the county champions nominated the captain.

Some players can't carry a captaincy but Molloy could carry it. Molloy might not always play well but he'd give you everything on the field.

Meath came to MacCumhaill Park at the beginning of November with a lot of baggage: double All-Ireland champions; national league champions; the dirtiest team in Ireland. In fairness, Meath were simply a tough team but, like a bad smell, a reputation for dirt followed them relentlessly everywhere they went. They had creamed Dublin for three years on the trot in Leinster – that didn't sit well in the capital. Hence the tag 'dirty'. In footballing terms in Ballybofey they found their match in Donegal. Connie Duffy was impressed:

> In what must surely rank as one of the most impressive results ever to come out of MacCumhaill Park, Ballybofey, in recent times, Donegal out-played, outclassed and outwitted national league and All-Ireland champions, Meath in a thoroughly absorbing and dramatic encounter.

Meath had rolled into Ballybofey short a handful of their full team and despite having McQuillan, O'Connell, O'Malley, Ferguson, Coyle, Harnan, O'Reilly, Hayes, Beggy and Stafford in the starting 15 they had no answer to a fired-up Donegal who hit Division One form for the first time. It was impressive to behold. Teamwork and the early ball reigned supreme. Duffy in the *Democrat* captured it well:

> It was an unusual Donegal performance in many respects. The forwards looked much more comfortable playing together as they attempted a more direct approach. They weren't afraid to take chances from far out while at the same time making space available for their colleagues if they wished to push an attack even further into the opponent's goalmouth.

It was as if Donegal had finally pushed open the door that led to the merging of possession with scores. Fifteen points were hit that day to Meath's 1-6. On a day when below-par performances were non existent, Connors was magnificent at full back, Molloy gave a captain's performance at midfield and McHugh struck a rich vein of form up front. McHugh's performance was reminiscent of a county final that stretched back eight summers. It was, noted the *Democrat*, "his best game in years". Meath had no answer to the Wee Man and when he moved out to centre half-forward he destroyed them.

Liam Hayes, soon to be an All-Star, met Anthony Molloy for the first time in a competitive match. He was a shaken man as he departed Ballybofey. Molloy had comprehensively outplayed him. Gavigan, Carlin and Ryan ran amok while Murray marked his cards with an absolute stormer. Gavigan was relishing the challenge against the absolute cream of Gaelic football.

We were getting good matches. Derry, Down, Kerry, Meath – a good variety of teams. We didn't come out on top in every game and we got roastings too. But we were learning all the time. You had to either stand up to the likes of Mick Lyons or get walked over.

Donegal had the better of exchanges throughout the first half but entered the dressing rooms sharing the spoils as a cracking David Beggy goal had levelled matters just before the half-time whistle. On the restart, Donegal moved quickly to stamp their authority all over proceedings. Murray, operating at half forward, hit three glorious points. Carlin added a fourth and that was that. McHugh was in exhibition form and by the time Seamus Prior blew the full-time whistle he had nine points accumulated. He had not scored more in eight years of inter-county football. McHugh had few who doubted him. Nine points against the best team in the country illustrated his unquestionable status as one of the best forwards in the land. "Life without the Wee Man would be intolerable," mused the Follower.

Reid, who'd been as solid as ever in the half-back line, was well impressed – "This was one of the better games I've seen Donegal playing and I've been involved in a lot of games." Even better lay ahead.

Some 200 miles separated Donegal from Kerry but the distance in football terms was immeasurable. This Kerry team, now an ageing proposition, had been the best football team the country had ever seen. Five All-Ireland titles had been annexed in the 1980s alone. Nelligan, O'Donovan, Lynch, Doyle, the Spillanes – Pat and Tom, O'Shea and Liston were still there as Donegal ran onto Austin Stack Park in Tralee. Football legends stood everywhere Donegal looked. John Joe Doherty was on Pat Spillane. John Connors had the 'Bomber' Liston for the afternoon. Molloy was on Jacko. Big Murray was on O'Donovan. Gavigan ended up facing a rising star of Kerry football, Maurice Fitzgerald. And Tom Conaghan was up against his old friend and mentor, the legendary Mick O'Dwyer.

A self-confessed acolyte of O'Dwyer, Conaghan engaged in mind games with the high-priest of Gaelic football before the match. Donegal had travelled all the way to Tralee and had carelessly overlooked the fact that they wore a similar jersey to that of Kerry. When it came to a clash of jerseys, tradition held the both sides would wear provincial colours. Kerry had access to the blue of Munster. There wasn't a set of Ulster yellow to be found in Tralee. A stand-off ensued. O'Dwyer offered the blue jerseys to Donegal thinking that the man he had done so many favours would feel obliged to accept. They were politely refused. And so, in the heart of the Kingdom, Donegal took to the field wearing the green and gold jerseys they had adopted from Kerry and Kerry took the field in blue. At one stage during the game, a confused Pat Spillane made a great pass to an unmarked man in green and gold.

That man was Martin Gavigan. Years earlier, back in the days when there was no television in the Gavigan household, the young Martin used to watch the great Kerry versus Dublin clashes in a neighbour's house. Now he was playing against those very players he had admired down the years. And about to get one up on the biggest name of all.

> Pat Spillane was tearing along one time on one of his solo runs and I called for the ball. "Here Pat!" I was in a green and gold jersey and he passed the ball to me! It was a vital ball, I went up the field and we got a score out of it. I rememer him complaining bitterly afterwards about the jersey clash.

Although thankful for the advice O'Dwyer had so freely given, Conaghan pulled the jerseys stunt to show his mentor that he was his own man. Nothing new there then. Team colours would count for nothing as Donegal again delivered an hour's worth of Division One football. It was an exquisite afternoon. After the hour it stood at 1-10 to 0-11. Quite simply, Donegal were the better team. Michael Daly had this to say:

> At all times [Donegal] showed a refreshing positiveness, the passing from defence to attack had an invariably pinpoint accuracy, the ball-winners, Tuohy, Gavigan, Molloy spoiled their forwards with an abundance of possession that was sprayed out with imagination and intelligence and had a muddled Kerry defence in complete disarray.
>
> The victory, put back-to-back with the hammering of All-Ireland champions, Meath, dispels any doubts about the ability of this Donegal side.

Donegal had heroes all over the place. None more so than around the middle of the park. Molloy was magnificent. He had taken over Griffin's mantle as the doyen of the crowd. Molloy and Gavigan lorded over all-comers. Jack O'Shea and Maurice Fitzgerald attempted to stem the Ardara men's dominance of the sector by moving there but suffered a similar fate to Hannafin and Brosnan. Murray produced yet another flawless display up front. Some 3,000 members of the Kerry footballing public got an opportunity to watch a true master at work as McHugh yet again seized the day with an awesome display of kicking and general play.

The best player on the pitch though was from Dunkineely. Shovlin had a heart the size of a continent. He epitomised the spirit of Donegal that day in Tralee and in the closing minutes as Kerry pressed dangerously it was Shovlin who repelled them again and again.

Donegal could have been home and dry by half-time but entered the break level, 0-5 apiece. Brian Murray sealed it for Donegal 11 minutes into the second half. On the receiving end of a great pass from Marty Carlin – who himself had an outstanding afternoon – Murray skipped past Charlie Nelligan and fairly blasted the ball to the net. Although Kerry inevitably added scores so too did

Donegal and Seamus Carr had the final say two minutes before the end. Donegal had been red-hot. At one point during the second half they held possession for a breathtaking two minutes. This was a team on its game.

That Sunday in Tralee in November 1988 was Tom Conaghan's finest hour. Fifteen years later his eyes well up as he recalls the day his team came of age:

> Going to Tralee and beating Kerry proved that even though I was a student of Mick O'Dwyer, I had more in me for Donegal than for Kerry. Mick O'Dwyer took the defeat like a man. Whether I would get back for a further three years or not, I had proven myself and established Donegal in Division One.

Three played, two wins. Four tough games still lay ahead. Last up before Christmas was the team who had won Division Two outright at the end of February – Down. The Mourne men needed the points having lost two of their three outings. They got them in Ballyshannon three weeks before Christmas. At one stage Donegal enjoyed a seven-point lead but it was Down who would emerge victorious by four points. Three goals dominated the game. Murray's lightning strike in the first half was no more than Donegal deserved. However, Down had a pair of goals at vital intervals during the second half which signposted their way to victory. Greg Blaney had the first, cutting Donegal's lead to one point while inspiring Down to add to their tally and hit the front.

With five minutes remaining, Donegal were still very much in contention and trailing by just one point when Blaney triggered a move which ended in the Donegal net – Mark McCartan getting the goal. Game over. Another one had been allowed slip away.

Up in the press box the Follower was greatly concerned that the Donegal bench wasn't what it could be. He was tired of lads not willing to play under Tom Conaghan, "'mickey mousing in another code" when they should be playing for Donegal. He would have found little argument from a tired Tom Conaghan. A tough year was over. A tougher one lay ahead.

❄ ❄ ❄ ❄

Derry saw to it that Donegal's opener of the New Year did not realise league points. The two-point defeat in Drumsurn left Donegal in serious difficulty. Drowning in fact. It would now be an all-out struggle just to stay up. Division Two seemed relentless in its reeling back of Donegal.

Donegal were bereft of Martin McHugh's services in Drumsurn and it showed. Molloy was flu-stricken as the opening acts of a great rivalry with Brian McGilligan began. James McHugh was in and Joyce was back, coming on for the second half and drawing Donegal level within five minutes of the restart.

Brian Murray

Both sides squandered scoring chances in the 25 minutes that remained but it was always Derry's game and so it proved.

The Follower again voiced the concerns of many when he opined that Donegal had on board a few players not of county standard: "There is a gaping chasm between the good club man and the good county man. It is not the fault of the lads. We simply are sending boys on men's errands." The Follower desisted from offering suitable replacements but the names tripped easily from the tongues of supporters.

Tom Conaghan was fed up with the talk of the men behind the wire. "There's far too much emphasis on players who are not playing for Donegal and players who should be in for Donegal. It's time this was dropped," he told the press in the immediate aftermath of the Derry game. He had spent the previous 60 minutes doing a bit of straight talking with his charges in the dressing room.

Donegal had two games remaining. Monaghan and Dublin. At least one had to end in victory. It was a tall order. Dublin were surely unbeatable in Croke Park. Everything then was on the line when Monaghan visited Ballyshannon. Donegal had last defeated Monaghan in the national league in November of 1982. Seven years later almost 4,000 people crammed into Fr Tierney Park to witness Donegal's do-or-die bid to retain Division One status.

It finished 1-6 to 0-5 in favour of Donegal. It was not the prettiest of football but produced the requisite result. Monaghan landed in Ballyshannon short several regulars. It would tell. Molloy had yet another blinder – superb in the air, devastating on the ground. He had the decisive hand in Donegal's goal ten minutes from half-time, picking the ball clean off the ground to set up McHugh and Murray in an effort that Seamus Carr eventually finished to the net.

McHugh had another fine outing. The Follower was lavish in his praise:

If Martin McHugh ever goes for the Dáil every man and woman who profess to love our national game must give him a number one. The debt we owe this man in footballing terms can never be compiled. He led by example. His footballing brain is honed to a very fine edge. As a procurer, carrier and finisher he has no equal.

Donegal held out well in the second half and were quite deserving of their four-point win. The victory did not impress everyone. Connie Duffy in the *Democrat* was quite critical of Donegal's play and the impasse between paper and management continued as neither Conaghan nor his assistant, Donal Monaghan, would comment on the game when contacted.

A rare trip to Croke Park lay ahead in the final game of the league. Division One had its pitfalls but one of them certainly wasn't the exotic trips to the capital that would continue throughout the 1990s. Some 3,000 Donegal supporters – many of them exiles in the city – flocked to headquarters despite the icy cold.

Donegal were to emerge with credit but on the wrong side of a 0-9 to 1-10 score-line. As Kerry defeated Monaghan that same day, Division One status was retained without any further ado.

The whole game hinged on a Dublin goal midway through the first half. Involved in the goal move were a handful of Dublin names that would face Donegal on a Sunday in the future when an All-Ireland was the prize: Paul Bealin, Charlie Redmond and Mick Galvin. Redmond tore past John Connors and blasted a goalbound shot to Gary Walsh's left. Walsh, having another stormer, somehow denied him with a breathtaking save but the rebound was met by Mick Galvin who fisted to the net. Leading by a point prior to the goal, Donegal spent the remainder of the game playing catch-up. It never came but defeat was borne with honour intact.

McHugh enjoyed his day in Croke Park. Truly on top of his game he was rel-ishing pitting his wits against the big guns that Division One threw up. Peerless against Meath and Kerry before Christmas, McHugh was astonishing against Dublin. In a performance that he would repeat less than four years later, McHugh collected the ball time and time again around the middle and cut swathes straight down the middle of the Dublin defence. Tommy Carr moved onto McHugh in the second half but had precious little joy on the Kilcar man. McHugh, with 0-31, would easily finish Donegal's top scorer of the league campaign.

Nine of the Dublin players – John O'Leary, Gerry Hargan, Tommy Carr, Mick Deegan, Paul Bealin, Vinnie Murphy, Charlie Redmond, Mick Galvin and Eamon Heery – would still be there in September 1992. Eight Donegal players would make it to the 1992 Final – Walsh, Doherty, Reid, Molloy, Gavigan, Martin McHugh, Murray and McMullan. The sides had encountered each other in Division Two during the 1984-85 and 1985-86 seasons but 1989 was the real beginning of an epic league rivalry. First blood had been drawn and it had gone to Dublin. Many battles lay ahead, culminating in the replayed national league final in 1993.

❋ ❋ ❋ ❋

As March arrived, so too did the countdown to the Ulster championship. Donegal had been drawn against Cavan. Tom Conaghan's summer and his future would be defined by 70 minutes in the cauldron of Breffni, the graveyard of many a visiting championship team. Conaghan's reign as Donegal manager was entering the final straight.

Conaghan was now the epicentre of controversy. There was no escaping – the onslaught was weekly. Coming up to St Patrick's Day, Donegal narrowly pipped Cavan, 1-9 to 1-8, in the first round of the McKenna Cup. Donegal had surren-dered a huge ten-point lead in the second half and just about held out for the win. Despite this psychological boost ahead of the championship, Conaghan was again taken to task in the *Democrat* for his sideline performance. The Follower had questions too, mostly centring on the absence from the panel of Matt Gallagher, Manus Boyle, Barry Cunningham, Barry McGowan and Sylvester Maguire.

"Tom was very big into discipline at the time and you had to take him the right way," remembered Martin Shovlin. "The way I looked at it was if a manager was appointed, I would do what he said. I mightn't always like what I was told to do but I would have done it." Anthony Molloy felt that:

Tom's mistake was that he over-elaborated on discipline and some of the boys that should have been playing didn't play because of it. That was Tom's way of handling things. If you didn't do it Tom's way you could stay away.

It seemed Conaghan couldn't win. It was reported that plans to bring in new players for the championship campaign – namely Manus Boyle and Barry McGowan – had been objected to by the majority of the panel. It was said that only a small number of players were in favour of the move.

Down ended Donegal's interest in the McKenna Cup with a 1-14 to 5-7 defeat at Rostrevor. Yet again Conaghan took a hammering in the *Democrat:*

The mentors on the line gave a most unconvincing performance. Their tactics were unproductive. Not once throughout the entire game did they seem to act on the obvious and to be perfectly honest it cost the side the game.

Gary Walsh conceded more goals that day than in any other match with the county.

I don't know what attitude we brought up with us on the bus but we got an awful tanking. Even though I didn't make many mistakes that day I let in five goals – that's my worst record – and Mickey Linden got three of them. The conditions were very bad. The goals were pure bog and you could hardly lift your feet out of it.

Work commitments resulted in Gary transferring from Aodh Ruadh to Burren in the early 1990s. Between that and county duty with Donegal, he got to see a lot more of Mickey Linden.

Even in club matches, Mickey was my bogey man. Mickey would never have taken a shot, he would always get in close to the goals and would try to go around you. He was so fast, even with the ball in his hands. I would always have seen one-on-one as one of my strengths but he would take a solo or shimmy and go either side of you. He was a great finisher.

When May arrived Tom Conaghan had a point to prove. Every game from here in was potentially and most likely his last in charge. He knew it well and was tired of the speculation about the men behind the wire. The question was, had he the players to do it and did those players want to do it? The answer to both questions was a resounding yes.

❄ ❄ ❄ ❄

Fifteen thousand flocked to the hallowed turf of Breffni Park to witness the battle being joined. Cavan, red-hot favourites and fancied in Ulster, had no answer as a superior Donegal cut through them with remarkable impunity. The final scoreboard read 3-12 to 0-14. Suddenly the summer looked a whole lot rosier.

It was Conaghan's first championship win. It was well celebrated that May Sunday in the town of Cavan and elsewhere. It was simply impossible to find fault anywhere with the Donegal display. Cavan had just been slayed by a team who had seemingly kept their best wine until last.

Not 30 seconds had passed before McHugh had Donegal on the scoreboard. Fouled himself, McHugh punished Cavan with a point – the first of six he would score. As Donegal playmaker, operating from the pivotal centre half-forward position, McHugh tormented Cavan that day in Breffni.

With scarcely five minutes on the clock and the score sitting at two points apiece onlookers knew they had some game on their hands. And so it proved as play raged from end to end. Prisoners were an option neither side considered. Slaps were being traded off the ball here, there and everywhere. Donegal were not found wanting in the football stakes. Connie Duffy was wholesome in his praise, singling out the "super fitness, utter dedication and total commitment" on display by the team. It was breathtaking to watch. "They matched Cavan in the air, beat them to the pass, out-thought them on the field and showed them how scores should be taken," marvelled Duffy. It was no exaggeration, Donegal really were that good. Cavan were by no means a push-over in the early stages and hit a ten-minute purple patch that resulted in a four-point lead with something over 20 minutes gone. Indeed, had it not been for a superb Walsh save from Michael Faulkner, the gap would have been greater.

Despite the early pressure, Donegal were showing encouraging signs of finding top drawer form. McHugh was lethal. McMullan and Ryan were flying. Molloy was having another towering game in the middle, outplaying first King and then Faulkner. He was joined in the centre by Michael Gallagher of Glenties, who had a fine championship debut. He remembers it well:

> There was great excitement for me because I was 27 years of age and I came onto the scene late. It was a big step but once the game started everything was fine. Twenty-seven was a late age to come and play

inter-county football so I cherish that memory.

Conaghan had slotted Gavigan into the centre half-back spot. Gavigan had just found his optimum position in the green and gold – the number six jersey was to become his prisoner.

Ten minutes remained of the first half when Tommy Ryan kicked off the Donegal onslaught. His first effort could have been a three-pointer but was a little on the high side. A couple of minutes later he added another point. Carolan converted a free but McHugh and McMullan seemed to be involved in everything. Anthony Molloy felt, "it was Joyce's best ever game for Donegal". McHugh did the spadework for the inevitable Donegal goal but it was Tommy Ryan who gleefully rifled it to the net. Level pegging.

In only his second championship game, 22-year-old Ryan was giving Cavan veteran Gerry Sheridan his fill of it. Sheridan was wilting under the hot Breffni sun but gave the Termon man an introduction to some of the niceties of the Ulster championship. "Gerry Sheridan and Pat Faulkner in the Cavan full-back line were coming towards the end of their playing days," grinned Ryan:

> They would have kicked your picture if they could. I got a score from along the sideline, lost my boot and Sheridan threw it into the crowd. I didn't look for it and I told him that I'd manage without it – but he was about five yards away from me when I said this. His fists were clenched and I could see the rage in him. His look said that if he got his hands on me he'd give me the greatest hoke I'd ever get. Somebody threw my boot back and I made sure I was a good distance away from him before I bent down to put it on!

It was no picnic at the other end but Reid (who held Carolan well), Gavigan and a ferocious Shovlin had the game sussed. Cavan were getting nothing easy. Even so, the frantic pace continued unabated and the sides made for the dressing rooms under the Breffni stand locked together at 1-8 to 0-11.

The second 35 minutes belonged to Donegal. Cavan would add only three points during that period, two of those from frees, as Donegal brought the shutters down and hit 2-4. Tommy Ryan started where he had left off and opened the scoring with a point after two minutes. It was a lead Donegal would never relinquish. Joyce put the game beyond doubt with a goal shortly after. It was all over bar the shouting. McMullan was sizzling, playing as good a football as he'd ever played for Donegal, and added a second scorching goal in the closing minutes. Donegal had just won their first championship match since 1985. Goalkeeper Gary Walsh was proud of the manner of victory. "People expected us to get a tanking," he recalled, "but to me it was as good a performance as Donegal had ever put on in the championship."

Perhaps unwisely, Brian McEniff added his name to the chorus of opinion regarding players who should be included in Conaghan's panel. The *Democrat* picked up on an interview McEniff gave to the *Anglo Celt* in the aftermath of the Cavan match in which he indicated that there were several players he would include in the panel, including Barry McGowan, Manus Boyle, Matt Gallagher and Michael Lafferty. It seemed unusual that McEniff would have contributed to the controversy. In hindsight, McEniff – as shrewd as ever – had just fired the opening salvo of the managerial election campaign he knew would follow whenever Donegal exited the championship.

✻ ✻ ✻ ✻

It had been the summer of 1983 since Donegal folk last had cause to visit Clones in pursuit of their senior footballers. It made a refreshing change therefore to ascend the famous hill in the Monaghan border town and exchange banter with the supporters of Derry as the two counties prepared to battle for an Ulster final spot. The image of Ulster football had been bruised and battered following a torrid game in Omagh between Tyrone and Armagh. Ulster football needed a redeeming match. It got it. Sean McGoldrick in the *Irish Press* was satisfied with the fare served:

> The belief that this would be one of the better football contests in the Ulster championship was fully vindicated with the two teams concentrating totally on their football to ensure that the estimated attendance of 10,000 saw an enthralling contest despite the near-oppressive heat.

Clones was boiling, the temperature gauge was fixed at more than 80° Farenheit. Below on the pitch Donegal and Derry traded the opening blows of an epic championship rivalry that would burn fiercely into the 1990s. The ball was barely thrown in before Donegal swept at Derry with intent and purpose. For ten minutes Donegal crashed on to Derry in waves: Carlin shot wide. McMullan pointed. Murray missed a sitter. McHugh pointed. Damien Barton pointed and finally got Derry off the mark. It was frenzied stuff. Then Donegal won the match.

Brian McGilligan, in his head, had Gary Walsh's kick out already in his hands. Michael Gallagher committed daylight robbery and in a flash Donegal were on the attack. Gallagher struck a sweet through ball to McMullan. Joyce's gift was to run with the ball before sending McHugh clear with a perfectly weighted fist pass. McHugh glided around his man and sent a piledriver beyond Colin McKenna in the Derry goal. Game over. Derry always seemed to be chasing after that. Donegal had the game won in their heads.

Donegal's shooting left lots to be desired with the wides already in double figures. Not for the first time a scoreboard was not reflecting Donegal's undoubted superiority in a game. Had the scorekeepers been counting wides Donegal would have notched up 17. It was, noted the Follower, "nothing short of prolific". A month later it would cost Donegal an Ulster title.

Gormley eventually hit the net for Derry but Donegal were still good value for their 1-5 to 1-3 half-time lead. Press men were all in agreement about one thing: Conaghan had Donegal in fantastic shape. They were flying. Good performances abounded – Reid, Tuohy, Gavigan, Shovlin, Molloy, Gallagher and Carlin. John Joe, the youngest man on the Donegal team, was on his way to man-of-the-match award.

The second half had a similar feel. The *Irish Independent* marvelled at the good and bad in the Donegal performance:

> At times they moved like a well-tuned sports car, cutting the Derry defence to shreds with their accurate, short-passing game. But, on other occasions, they lost their way, over-doing the passing approach.

Donegal sealed matters early in the half. Molloy won possession around the middle and sent a huge kick deep into the Derry danger area. McHugh beat Brian Murray to it but goalkeeper McKenna thwarted his goalbound effort with an admirable parry. Tommy Ryan was proving a real handful – usually of jersey – for Tony Scullion and as the ball broke across the goalmouth Scullion fouled the Termon man. Penalty. McHugh did even better second time around and sent McKenna the wrong way. It was the *coup de grace*. Even though the game had almost 25 minutes left to run it was all up for Derry. Still the wides continued. Even McHugh was accumulating them! Kieran Rooney noted in the *Independent*:

> McHugh's own performance epitomised the contradictions in the teams overall display. The brace of goals was brilliantly taken, yet the centre forward accounted for five of Donegal's second-half wides.

What Rooney might not have realised was that McHugh was a brave man to be playing at all. A sign fell on him in Killybegs the Tuesday before the game, aggravating an old injury, and necessitating an x-ray in Letterkenny hospital.

Derry did peg back to within a goal but the biggest cheer of the day came 12 minutes from full-time when Martin Shovlin hit the insurance point on the run. Derry cut the deficit by two points before the end but it was too little too late. For the first time since 1983, six long summers, Donegal were in an Ulster final.

❋ ❋ ❋ ❋

The Tyrone team of the late-1980s had something of a reputation. Scattered throughout the side were several hard men. Any team who ran up against Tyrone knew they would be hit and hit hard. Their path to the Ulster final of 1989 was littered with incident – the game with Armagh in Omagh had been a free for all and by the time they had defeated Down in a torrid Castleblaney confrontation an unsavoury reputation preceded them.

The meeting of Donegal and Tyrone in the Ulster final was the first championship encounter between the neighbouring counties since Sean O'Donnell's last game in charge of Donegal back in the summer of 1980. Strangely the two sides seemed destined not to meet in the Ulster championship. Donegal were embarking on an Ulster odyssey that would see them contest five provincial finals in succession. After the Ulster Final of 1989 they wouldn't encounter Tyrone again until 1994. Even so, the rivalry that was born in Clones that July was immense and dark, particularly among the supporters. A dislike, perhaps mutual, swept Clones. Thirty thousand people with opposing views. Two tribes went to war and a ceasefire has still to be declared.

❊ ❊ ❊ ❊

The whole game swung on a refereeing decision that is questioned to this day. Donegal were a point up and only seconds remained. Referee Michael Greenan gave a debatable free against John Connors. Martin Shovlin had a good view of it. "It was a charge if anything. The Tyrone player put down his head and bored on. I can still see the free dropping over the back stanchion." It seemed harsh at the time and Donegal supporters were quick to howl their anger at the Cavan official. From the dead ball Stephen Conway struck the equaliser for Tyrone with the assistance of the post. It was the last action of the game; 0-11 apiece, the teams would have to do it all again.

As Donegal supporters watched the game on television that evening it seemed their initial reaction had been correct, John Connors had indeed been done an injustice. Had Donegal just lost an Ulster Final due to a poor refereeing decision? Team captain Anthony Molloy thought so, "The referee made his call but we felt hard done by". Martin Gavigan was also extremely annoyed at the referee. "I never forgave Greenan for that. We had earned our win." The truth was Donegal had played poorly and had yet again rebuffed countless opportunities to put the game well beyond Tyrone. Brian Murray was disappointed, "We had loads of chances. Maybe we lacked belief. We still had good players and I thought we were good enough to win. It was one we should have won."

It was by no means a classic as it was riddled with fouls but it surely was a thriller. For Martin Shovlin it was, "a physical game, the Tyrone boys wouldn't hide behind the fence when it came to the physical side of football". At no time did more than two points separate the sides. Mulgrew and McHugh opened the scoring with points for Donegal. McCabe hit two in reply and so it went. Tyrone went two ahead, Donegal pulled them back through two McHugh frees. There was nothing between them, except that Donegal were stacking up wides

– wides that would cost them victory. Both teams threatened the other's goal on a number of occasions but failed to find the net – Tommy Ryan perhaps spurning the clearest opportunity. At the interval Donegal led 0-7 to 0-6.

The second half was a carbon copy of the first. Donegal added four points, Tyrone five. Donegal had their moments. Mulgrew, Molloy, Shovlin, Gallagher and Gavigan were going well. Reid was covering every blade of grass. It was frustrating to watch however as Donegal squandered their possession up front. Yet when Tommy Ryan hit a late point to leave the score 0-11 to 0-10 in favour of Donegal it was looking good and, naively, the Donegal players started to celebrate. Tom Conaghan was two minutes away from an Ulster title. To hell with the begrudgers, this would be sweet. It was not to be. Stephen Conway would have the final say.

Anthony Molloy remembers it as a hard lesson learnt, "When Tommy scored the point near the end we started to celebrate. Tyrone took a quick kick out and the next thing the ball was over the bar at the far end of the field." The limited nature of the panel was evident to Martin McHugh. "The problem was that we had good players standing on the terraces," he recalled:

> All we needed was one other player and we would have beaten Tyrone. Conaghan's ideas were right but he fell out with too many players. If we had the whole squad training in 1989 we could have won the All-Ireland. We weren't far away that year.

Watching from the terrace, Matt Gallagher was experiencing mixed emotions, "Even though I wasn't playing I was hoping the boys would win. Conway's free was a great score but the result was terrible as Donegal had played well."

✳ ✳ ✳ ✳

One week later it all fell asunder. Tyrone utterly destroyed Donegal. The final score was 0-7 to 2-13 – a 12-point hammering – as Tyrone claimed their third Ulster title of the decade. It was an eminently forgettable Sunday. Nothing went right. Donegal simply drowned as Tyrone hit score after score. In the space of a week Donegal had lost all their vigour and sparkle. They were a team out on their feet. There was few redeeming features to be found anywhere on the pitch in a Donegal jersey. Connie Duffy couldn't understand it:

> It was as if Donegal fielded two teams of widely contrasting qualities for the final and for the replay. On Sunday week they had fire in their bellies, they were realistic contenders for a crack at the Connacht champions in the All-Ireland semi-final. Last Sunday they played like a muddling junior team that had been hurriedly gathered together about half an hour before the match.

The talking points from a Donegal perspective were mostly negative. McHugh had popped up inside 30 seconds for the games opening score. It was the one and only time Donegal folk had reason for optimism. Shortly after, McHugh sustained a shot to the shoulder he injured in the drawn game and was the quieter for it. "I played on but wasn't really fit too," he remembered. Five minutes later and Donegal were in real trouble. Walsh, totally exposed at the back, hauled down Eugene McKenna. Penalty. Conway duly blasted to the net and Donegal were dead men walking.

Twenty minutes later Tyrone wrapped things up. Plunkett Donaghy, having a majestic afternoon, lofted a huge kick towards the Donegal goal. Brendan Dunleavy, in for the injured John Joe Doherty, raced for the ball. So did Martin Gavigan. Both ended up sprawled on the ground as Damian O'Hagan and Eugene McKenna played a one-two beyond John Connors before O'Hagan palmed the ball past Walsh. It was all over. Donegal's dream of an Ulster title had been fading, it was now dead. Gavigan was shook by the clash with Dunleavy where Dunleavy's head met Gavigan's cheekbone. Years later the man they call Rambo was able to laugh about it: "In all the years I played football that was the hardest shot I ever got. From my own man too!"

Martin Carlin wanted to change things around and said as much during the half-time break. He suggested that he'd be better off roaming out the field than lying in at corner forward. Conaghan was having none of it. "You can roam all you want, Marty," he responded, "but when the ball goes into the corner you'd better be in it!"

The second half was a long drawn-out affair for Donegal and their supporters. The diehards who followed their county through thick and thin stuck it out to the bitter end while the more watery supporters started filing out of St Tiernach's Park midway through the half. It was torture for the Donegal fans that remained as the Red Hand supporters gleefully celebrated victory long in advance of the full-time whistle taking every opportunity to rub it in. Relief that the humiliation was over was the overwhelming feeling when referee Michael Greenan finally called an end to it. "We never really got into that game," remembered Gary Walsh, "they got a goal when two of our players collided. We never really recovered from that and got a spanking."

Nothing needed to be said. As the countless Donegal buses and cars snaked slowly out of Clones, a simple shake of the head sufficed as GAA men and women exchanged silent but knowing glances. It was unfathomable what had just happened. Or was it? "Sure half the team was behind the wire," said one of the players who lined out for Donegal that day. The recriminations quickly got under way. "We hadn't the men or the method for the occasion," was the opinion of Connie Duffy in the *Democrat*. Many agreed. The game was "sacrificed for want of some basic ideas on tactics, imagination and know-how," continued the hard-hitting Duffy. Tyrone appeared to have learned most from the drawn game and changed their team and game plan accordingly. Donegal hadn't. And lost. Donal Reid is clear on the reasons for Donegal's replay defeat:

We lost that final between the drawn match and the replay. While we did talk a bit, we trained when we should have done some more talking although it's easy to be wise in hindsight. I've spoken to Tyrone players since and asked them what they did between the matches. They didn't train at all. They had a couple of meetings and talked about our weaknesses and strengths. Kieran McGarvey [Tyrone's full-back] told me that one of the things they wanted to do was stop me from making runs down the right wing, which they did. We didn't really talk about those things. We went ahead into the next game without having given much consideration to what happened in the previous game.

But still the talk came back to the men behind the wire and those Conaghan had sent into battle. "It is easy to say now," wrote the Follower, "had we but Manus Boyle, Matt Gallagher, Sylvester Maguire, Barry McGowan, Declan Bonner, etc., etc., in the panel things would not be as they now are." Tommy Ryan agreed. "No more than Mick McCarthy could do without Roy Keane in the World Cup, you don't head to Clones with half your team looking down at you from the hill". In an earlier appraisal of the panel someone had speculated that it was impossible to put square pegs into round holes. Martin Gavigan agreed, but saw both sides:

You can blame the manager but you can also blame players for not being there. I was there because I wanted to be there. It's so easy to fall out and not get on with people but I think players have to take a bit of responsibility for not being there. If rules are there you have to abide by them. The rest of us were there and went along with the rules.

It seemed unlikely to Gavigan though that McEniff would have found himself in a similar stand-off with key players.

Tom was on the right track except that he fell out with a few people when we needed to build up a strong panel. You have to field your best team and that was one thing McEniff had - the negotiating skills to get the best players out on the field on any particular day. He would do *anything* to get the best players out. Tom had some good ideas but when you are dealing with grown men you have to be fairly sensible about it too – you can't have your rules carved in stone without having a wee bit of leeway. Tom wanted discipline but you have to have a bit of leniency too. Enforce it in a nice way if you like! I suppose that is McEniff's greatest attribute. I remember I fell out with McEniff once. Next night he was over at the gate

shaking my hand. The last person I wanted to see was him but that's
Brian! It didn't matter who fell out with him he had a way around them.

Yet the team Tom Conaghan had put onto the field had been seconds from
Ulster glory only a week before. Seconds from an All-Ireland semi-final. In the
run-up to the drawn game, even Conaghan's harshest critics across the county
had to concede that, like it or otherwise, Donegal under Tom Conaghan were
capable of getting results. His managerial approach had worked in terms of
achievement. Division One status had been achieved and retained. An Ulster
final had been reached for the first time in six years. Back in June, the Follower
had offered the opinion that Tom Conaghan's Donegal "is as fit and perhaps fitter than any Donegal side I have seen in almost 50 years. There is a doggedness,
a determination, a resolute streak coming into their play that is most welcome."
Conaghan's methods and image were that of a hard man but his unshakeable
belief that he would fashion a team in his own mould had borne fruit. It hadn't
been pretty but the results were real. Now his critics would bemoan the success
Donegal might have enjoyed had he stayed on side with the men behind the
wire. It was all conjecture.

   Conaghan did not suffer fools gladly. Journalists – some of them anyway –
he most certainly considered fools. Unlike McEniff, Conaghan wasn't one to
explain his football philosophy over a cup of tea. It just wasn't his way.   His
three years at the helm had been colourful. Controversy had dogged him. His
poor relationship with the *Donegal Democrat*, the county's main GAA paper, had
been unfortunate. Perhaps Conaghan had been brash, perhaps he had been
misunderstood. It was immaterial now. Anthony Molloy saw the breakdown
in the relationship between Conaghan and the press at first hand:

> Tom Conaghan had his own way of doing things and didn't get on too well
> with the press. It was the first time journalists would have been banned
> from certain places or banned from talking to players. You always have to
> keep the media on your side. Tom adopted strong arm tactics with the
> press but he was always going to lose that argument. That's the way he
> did things. He didn't care about anybody, he was his own man.

Manus Boyle, notable by his absence from the Donegal first 15, wondered if the
media was part of the problem:

> It was a time when the media was starting to have an increased input in
> GAA affairs. It was putting a huge emphasis on certain players, particular-
> ly those who weren't playing. Whether it is right or wrong, the press can
> report whatever side of a story it wants. If there was less media attention
> on Barry McGowan and me, Tom Conaghan would probably have brought

us back. The media attention was embarrassing for me. I didn't want it and the players on panel wouldn't have wanted it – they would have had to put up with enough as it was. I wanted the team to do the best it could.

Loyalty had been one of the fundamentals of the Conaghan era. He expected no less and had never compromised. His belief had always been that success would not be achieved without complete dedication. Manus could see a side that perhaps the media didn't:

> Tom stuck with the players he had and brought the team within a kick of winning an Ulster title. To this day, I still rate Tom Conaghan as an exceptional person to manage a football team. As a motivator and some-one who gave a commitment, you couldn't get better.

Conaghan's days as manager were numbered and he knew it. He was up against Brian McEniff, PJ McGowan and Hugh McClafferty. "Judge me on what I have done," said Conaghan, urging clubs to look at his record. McEniff mean-time was promising to merge the core of the senior team with the under-21 side of 1987. McEniff had canvassed fiercely for the job in the run-up to the election in September. There was only going to be one winner and by 31 votes to 23, McEniff was the man.

Tom Conaghan was gone. He knew he had made enemies along the way but was happy to live with the consequences. As far as he was concerned it had to be done. He left behind a tougher Donegal set-up. One that McEniff was glad to inherit and build upon. A foundation that only a man like Tom Conaghan could have poured was left behind. Things would never slip back to pre-1986 days. Discipline had been injected. Donegal football had been kicked up the backside by Tom Conaghan. It would never look back.

RESULTS

Ulster Championship 1988	Donegal 1-6, Monaghan 0-5
Donegal 0-8, Armagh 2-10	Donegal 0-9, Dublin 0-10
National League 1988-89	**Ulster Championhip 1989**
Donegal 0-9, Armagh 0-10	Donegal 3-12, Cavan 0-14
Donegal 0-15, Meath 1-6	Donegal 2-8, Derry 1-9
Donegal 1-10, Kerry 0-11	Donegal 0-11, Tyrone 0-11 (f)
Donegal 1-11, Down 2-12	Donegal 0-7, Tyrone 2-13
Donegal 1-5, Derry 0-10	

11

Return of the Mac

(September 1989 – August 1990)

"It's all about the championship."

BRIAN MCENIFF, SEPTEMBER 1989

McEniff was back. And with him the men behind the wire. It had been a long three years watching from the sidelines for the Bundoran hotelier. He wanted his old job back and he wanted it badly. With defeat in the Ulster final replay, Conaghan, despite his obvious success, was finishing his term on a low.

Even though PJ McGowan (who would eventually take the reins in neighbouring Fermanagh) and Hugh McClafferty declared an interest, it was only ever going to be a two-horse race for the job of Donegal manager. Conaghan, the uncompromising disciplinarian and doyen of the grassroots versus McEniff, the GAA politician and football aristocrat. Few were the stones that McEniff left unturned in the lead up to the election. He was meticulous in his approach. Calls were made. Favours pulled in. It would be his last effort at the helm. He would, he said, take Donegal to the national league quarter-final in the spring and would deliver an Ulster title the following summer. And he did.

✳ ✳ ✳ ✳

The election, when it came, saw McEniff emerge with eight votes to spare over Conaghan. He was back in business. Anthony Harkin from Ardara, Naul McCole from Dungloe and Seamus Bonner in Dublin came in with McEniff as his selectors. Mickey Lafferty would join in the New Year as a fourth selector. It was an appointment the players would have no reason to regret. Lafferty would have a big say in the monumental days that lay ahead.

All talk in the county revolved around the panel. Who would come back and who would make way? It was evident from listening to McEniff that while he was determined to maintain Division One status, his main aim would be focussed on the championship. Players all over the county were fielding phone calls at all hours of the day and night as McEniff played his hand.

The panel, when it came, held few surprises. The prodigal sons, those available anyway, had returned. Declan Bonner, Sylvester Maguire, Manus Boyle, Barry McGowan and Matt Gallagher were all back in the fold. Tommy Ryan was in the United States, so too was Michael Gallagher and John Connors. The Cunninghams were in England, as was Leslie McGettigan. John Joe was in the panel but injured. Sean Bonner was also injured but on his way back. The new men in included Diarmaid Keon, Gerry Curran, Paul Carr, Luke Gavigan and Dermot Ward. Gone were Michael Kelly, Cathal Campbell, Corny Carr, Seamus Carr and Paddy Gavigan.

McEniff had 16 of his future All-Ireland men on board. With the Cunninghams and Ryan unavailable but obviously prominent in his plans should they return, McEniff was getting close to lift-off. He also mentioned in passing that he intended to take a look at the Dungloe lad, Tony Boyle, when he returned from the States.

Boyle's reputation as one of the best young footballers on the scene was well known throughout the county. At club level he dominated games. The only way to get by Dungloe at under-age level was to keep Boyle quiet. His name first cropped up with Rosses Rovers almost a decade earlier. Fr Seán Gallagher had refereed the county under-12 final of 1980 as Rosses Rovers – who would win the under-12, 14 and 16 county finals that year – faced MacCumhaills. It was a delightful match despite the grass in Glenties being much too long for the youngsters. At right half-forward for the Rovers side was a little fellow who knew how to play football. His name was Tony Boyle and he had just won his first county title.

His rise was meteoric. Vocational schools, minor and under-21. He'd played centre half-forward when the vocational schools side lost the 1987 All-Ireland final by a point to Kerry in Croke Park. As a minor he was lethal. It seemed certain that he would join the senior panel when he made it back from America.

If McEniff wasn't already aware of what was expected from him the Follower was about to put him in the picture – "Sam, within the period of office," instructed the man from Dromod. The Follower also voiced the concerns of many with regard to the number of players unavailable to McEniff due to emigration. The Celtic Tiger was several summers away and would never roar in Donegal anyway. Donegal people were still catching planes out of Ireland in their hundreds. John Cunningham was just one of the Donegal footballers forced to emigrate:

I didn't play in many national league games. I wasn't earning much

James McHugh

money working here and I would to go to London after the football finished in September. I would usually stay there until around Christmas time or a month or two afterwards. I would come home then and train for the football. I had good contacts in the construction game and I used to earn good money over there.

Some of the biggest names of recent years were on the other side of the Irish Sea and the Atlantic Ocean. Tommy McDermott and Eunan McIntyre, two fabulously gifted footballers from 1982, had been lost to Donegal for years as they made their living across the water. In time, McEniff would consider flying the talented McDermott back from London for league games. Now the big names of 1987 were to be found working on building sites and bars in Boston, Queens and London. John Connors, Tommy Ryan, the two Cunninghams, Leslie McGettigan and Paddy Hegarty all toiled far from home. It was something McEniff would have to address.

❄ ❄ ❄ ❄

It was no longer a game of two halves but four quarters as the GAA experimented with the infamous new rules. It all took some getting used to. The game speeded up massively – goalkeepers could now kick the ball from their hands which meant the game restarted much quicker following a score or wide. Speed suited Donegal.

The Royal Liver National Football League Division One of 1989-90 got under way at the end of October. The build-up was noticeably quiet. The weekly clamour that had dogged Conaghan's term was absent. McEniff, always two steps ahead on the public relations front, was far too media-friendly for that. And for now anyway, it seemed that peace had come dropping slow in the Donegal camp.

In league and championship, where it counted, Donegal's record against Armagh was dismal. Apart from sporadic McKenna Cup victories, Donegal had to go back to the 1983 Ulster championship for their last big win over the Orchard County. McEniff's charges put that right in Ballybofey in October hitting an impressive 3-12 to Armagh's 0-13. McEniff was on his way to fulfilling a promise.

Donegal were back into the groove that had carried them past Cavan and Derry in the championship. It was, commented Connie Duffy, "delightful to see" as short-passing was fused with unerring accuracy from play. "Their determination to establish control was evident from the start and they achieved it with flair, style and intelligent use of teamwork which bewildered their opponents," wrote Connie.

Three goals in three quarters put Donegal firmly in the driving seat. Rambo careered through for the first and his shot practically ripped the net from its stanchion. Joyce snapped up the second while Marty Carlin knocked in a clever third. Armagh had no answers to a Donegal forward line firing on all cylinders. Suddenly, accumulating the scores wasn't a problem with Gerry Curran (0-1), Charlie Mulgrew (0-1), Joyce McMullan (1-1), Manus Boyle (0-2), Marty Carlin (1-1) and Martin McHugh (0-3) all hitting the scoresheet. Add Molloy (0-1), Reid (0-1), Gavigan (1-0) and sub Maguire (0-1) and you had the unusual spectacle of a Donegal side scoring freely from all over the pitch. It had been a long time coming but was worth the wait.

Donegal travelled the well-worn route to Cavan town and Breffni Park at the beginning of November. They had expected it to be tough – Cavan would seek retribution for the whipping they'd received the previous summer and would lay down a marker for the one to come. No one expected the warfare which lay ahead. It was a day when Cavan abandoned all sporting principles and, as Mickey Kearins lost control, laid into Donegal with gusto.

It was a difficult outing for Donegal. It was impossible to build any momentum as skirmishes raged all over the pitch, on – but mostly off – the ball. McHugh came in for dog's abuse, as did Mulgrew. For 60 minutes the boys boxed with the occasional burst of football. They came through it and managed an admirable 1-12 to 0-13 win in the most trying of circumstances. Fittingly, considering he had been singled out as a human punch-bag, it was McHugh who struck the Donegal goal. Two weeks later McHugh would receive the prestigious Ulster Player of the Year award as voted by the Ulster GAA Writers Association.

Still, Donegal had to work for the full complement of points. Leading 1-3 to 0-3 after the first quarter, Cavan hit a purple patch in the second to lead by three points, 1-4 to 0-10 it stood at half-time. Murray replaced Molloy in the middle and swung things Donegal's way. Indeed Donegal could have had a decisive penalty in the third quarter had it been anyone but Rambo who shipped the tackle inside the parallelogram. The slap, which would have felled an ox, tumbled Gavigan but where others would have lain down, Gavigan bounced to his feet and played on. It took a good man – or Brendan Dunleavy – to hit Gavigan hard enough to keep him down.

The final 20 minutes belonged to Donegal. McHugh, Manus and Joyce had the final say as referee Kearins earned the wrath of the Cavan players and crowd by penalising their goalkeeper with a 14-yard free at a crucial juncture. Kearins would require an escort off the field on the final whistle as all hell broke loose around him.

Two matches played and Donegal had availed of all the league points on offer. For a second game in succession, the forwards had shared the scoring responsibilities – McMullan (0-1), Mulgrew (0-1), McHugh (1-3), Carlin (0-1) and Manus Boyle (0-6). The potential was tremendous. Better was to follow.

Kerry came to Ballyshannon a fortnight later and with seconds left in hugely entertaining game a share of the spoils seemed certain. Not for the first time

Manus Boyle was the man to undo a Kerry side. It all started with Martin Shovlin. With the scores level and possession vital, there was no better man than Shov. Fielding bravely, he was hauled to the ground 50 yards out as Kerry decided to break up any possible attack far out the field. With Manus Boyle in the opposing 15 this was a mistake. Last kick of the game, indicated Mickey Kearins. Despite the obvious distractions of the Kerry players and the wind, Manus connected sweetly and the ball carried all the way over the bar for a memorable victory. Barry McGowan made his senior debut at corner-forward that day. "Charlie Nelligan and Jack O'Shea were playing," he remembers, "I was star-struck and spent most of the game watching them play."

The forwards hadn't been as exuberant as before yet Manus and Gerry Curran had been on song. Curran was quite something and McEniff always fancied having him on board. Out of nowhere, he'd parachuted Curran into the Ulster championship against Armagh back in June 1984. He hadn't played since. Immensely talented, Curran gave the impression that he could take the county scene or leave it. He would never realise his potential in a Donegal jersey but his contribution over that winter was worth the admission prices alone.

Sean Bonner was back in the scene at full back under McEniff. His falling out with Conaghan, his old boss from 1982, had been bitter. Matt had slotted into the right corner like he'd never been away. Paul Carr was proving his worth while James McHugh also got a run out. Martin was happy to see his brother come into the squad:

> It was a bit unfair on James at that time because he was nearly always classed as Martin's brother. James was a better footballer than me because he could play anywhere from corner-back to corner-forward. He played midfield and centre half-back for the club. We were used to playing together at club level and it was great to play with a player where you'd know every move he'd make.

The league table made for impressive viewing. Donegal were clear on six points with three games played, Cork followed with five points while Dublin sat on four.

As ever, Down proved to be a difficult proposition. The defining moments of the game occurred within three minutes of each other. Joyce McMullan had the beating of Eamon Burns all day. A Down defender had earlier taken an off-the-ball swipe at Joyce and when Burns repeated the offence in the third quarter he was given his marching orders. At the time Donegal were a point ahead. McEniff was immediately edgy on the sideline: "The sending off was actually counter-productive and we lost our shape. It is always very difficult to play against 14 men and takes time to adjust." (Three summers later and his team would prove the wisdom of those words at the expense of Derry). Burns had scarcely reached the bench when Ambrose Rodgers had the ball in the Donegal net. It ended at 0-14 to 1-15 – Donegal never managed to recover and reverted to old lacklustre ways.

The decade had ended on a losing note. Yet the distance that Donegal football had travelled since 1980 was truly remarkable. From the bottom rung at the beginning of the decade Donegal were now considered to be one of the top seven or eight teams in the land. The groundwork that would permit the Sam Maguire travel to the North West was in place. Glory was just around the corner.

❋ ❋ ❋ ❋

McEniff had long carried a reputation for being soft on players. Back in the early 1980s it was said that he allowed certain players call the shots and that discipline wasn't always what it should be in his squad. McEniff inherited from Conaghan the core of a team that had been fed a strict diet of no-nonsense discipline for three years. It was relatively simple to maintain those principles, albeit in a less confrontational manner, yet there were signs early in the New Year of 1990 that McEniff still didn't relish the tough decisions.

Trial games and a series of challenges afforded McEniff the opportunity to examine the options open to him. Standard procedure really. He liked much of what he saw. It was clear that Declan Bonner, who had featured sparingly before Christmas, was about to secure a regular spot in the first 15. Bonner had never really fully committed to Gaelic football despite the fact that he seemed to have been around forever. Soccer was in his system. Talented above the ordinary he very nearly made the big time. Celtic had noticed him in the early 1980s but his expected two-year contract failed to materialise when Celtic manager Billy McNeill left the club for Manchester City. In the end it was Finn Harps that got his services most winters. Now, in the depths of winter 1990, he was ready to commit to Gaelic football. In the trials and challenge games in the early New Year he ran riot. Bonner was most definitely in. John Joe too was up and running well after his injury lay-off. Tommy McDermott was home, temporarily, and the old assured touch was still there. John Duffy from Ballyshannon rattled in two goals in a challenge game. Tony Boyle was back from the States but working in Galway. Keen to be involved, Boyle thought nothing of travelling to Ballyshannon for county training and then driving back to Galway to work a night shift. The trial game was a personal tragedy for Sylvester Maguire. The Ballyshannon man had sustained a broken leg on his home pitch.

McEniff, it seemed, was loath to drop anyone from a large and cumbersome panel. Michael Daly had advice in the *Democrat*: "There comes a time to bite the bullet and stop being nice to people. Have a bite, Brian." Donal Reid had been around for some time and played under both Conaghan and McEniff. It was his opinion that the players had hardened mentally and McEniff the manager in 1990 wasn't much changed from the 1986 vintage:

In my opinion Brian didn't change. If you could have married Tom Conaghan and Brian McEniff you'd probably have the perfect manager. Tom was a disciplinarian while Brian was very good at handling players. I always felt that Brian was lenient towards certain players. That was just his way; that's the way a businessman deals with situations. Sometimes Brian didn't have the necessary discipline.

Joyce McMullan, another loyal servant to Donegal football, noted subtle differences in the support the team got:

McEniff maintained the discipline from then on and put a bit more pressure on people to make sure they were at training and putting in the effort. He would also ensure that injuries were tidied up and the things that should be looked after were looked after.

Matt Gallagher, like Reid, could detect a change in the players' mindsets:

Tom had brought in a certain discipline and Brian realised when he came back that he'd need more discipline. The boys had got used to greater discipline. We took a more scientific approach to the game. There was less tolerance for boys missing training or doing the things that fellas would sometimes do. Players weren't snitching on each other, but we were watching out for each other and pushing one another on. Everybody knew we had a good side and had a chance of doing something special.

❆ ❆ ❆ ❆

It was back to Fr Tierney Park in February as the football resumed. Derry made the trip across to Ballyshannon and returned home in Division Two. Donegal rifled through a Derry side that had surrendered to their fate long before the final whistle. The final score was 0-11 to 0-3 as a gale-force wind whipped 1,500 hardy souls that witnessed Donegal provisionally book a spot in the quarter-finals. It was not a day for dazzling football but for hard grafting. That was how Donegal played it with McHugh, not Martin but James, the star of the show.

Donegal had never played at Ballincollig, seven or eight miles west of Cork city. Neither had Cork. With Páirc Uí Chaoimh once again deemed unplayable, Donegal finally met the All-Ireland champions at the second time of asking. Hundreds of supporters and the team had made the journey in vain one week earlier with the match being called off at the very last minute.

For 56 minutes the game was in the bag for Donegal. Bonner, with a couple of goals in the first half, had Cork on the back foot. By the end of the third quarter Donegal seemed to be in the driving seat, leading 2-9 to 1-8. Shovlin was marking Dave Barry out of it. Gavigan, Molloy, Bonner and the McHugh's were dangerously sharp. Victory was not to be. Four minutes from time the Kildare-born Cork duo of Tompkins and Fahy combined and goaled. A mesmerising three minutes followed. Tompkins thumped the ball over the Donegal bar three times on the trot and McCarthy added a fourth. Donegal 2-10, Cork 2-14. Donegal hats came off to the reigning All-Ireland and national league champions. Robbery it might have been, but robbery committed with panache.

Dublin rolled into MacCumhaill Park at the beginning of March with all the customary arrogance that surrounded the metropolitans. They had yet to fall at the hands of this Donegal team. Their boat was about to be called ashore as Donegal overturned tradition and romped to a 1-10 to 0-9 victory. In hindsight, it was a landmark Sunday in Donegal GAA history. It was another big scalp, one of the few that had remained to be taken. More importantly, it sparked a confidence among the boys who now always believed themselves capable of taking Dublin. Nine of the 1992 starting 15 took the field that day in Ballybofey. By full-time a further three joined in battle against the Dubs.

It was a complete Donegal performance. Perhaps stung by the manner of the Cork defeat there was a resolute determination about Donegal that suggested they wouldn't be caught this time. Gary Walsh was called upon early and often as play swung from end to end. In one of the best games of his career he won the man of the match award, "Those awards don't often come the way of 'keepers," he remarked wistfully. Joe McNally might have expected a penalty but it was not forthcoming. Matt Gallagher, his marker, was having his typical game and was two or three steps ahead of McNally at all times. Using his head. It was Matt who intercepted a Dublin attack to set the wheels in motion for the Donegal goal coming up to half-time. Matt slipped the ball through to his old friend Reid who characteristically went on the offensive from half-back. Bonner was by now making tracks and when the ball came his way he flicked it cleverly to Luke Gavigan who sent a searing shot past John O'Leary. It was the winning of the match.

Donegal carried a four-point lead into the interval and matched Dublin score for score in the second half. The display warmed the hearts of the Donegal faithful huddled around the ground. Donegal were stretching themselves as a team, pushing out the boundaries. There was the time when the mental capacity to withstand the type of sustained pressure Dublin threw at them would not have been there. It was now. John Joe, back after injury, was taking no prisoners. Gavigan and Molloy, apart from playing well, laid down a marker with the Dubs around midfield – slaps would be taken, expected even, but by God they would be returned. "We were very strong in the league," remembered Gary Walsh, "teams didn't like coming to Ballybofey."

Shov spent the afternoon in the company of Vinnie Murphy. Vinnie had come across many different breeds of defenders in his time but had never met anyone quite like Martin Shovlin. In the end Murphy was taken off. Shovlin has a clear recollection of his struggle with the Dublin legend:

> He was something else at that time. There was big talk of Vinnie. I had
> a couple of great tussles with him. He was a great man to play against but
> he was as strong as a bull – twice the strength of me. You could hit
> Vinnie and he would fucking hit you back and that was it. He was play-
> ing at wing half-forward that day. It never suited him at wing half-for-
> ward and it was a position I played him well. He shook hands with me
> as he left the pitch – I thought it was decent.

Gerry McCaul, the Dublin manager, wasn't best pleased with the result. The
referee got a blasting. It appeared also that the Dublin boss begrudged Donegal
their win. "We'll find out how good they really are in the championship, that's
the real test," he added icily. The day was coming when Dublin would find that
out for themselves although Gerry would be out of a job by then.

Donegal met Meath in the quarter-final of the national league at Clones on
April Fools' Day. For three-quarters of the game Donegal had them on the ropes
and then, inexplicably, let them off the hook in the closing minutes; 0-13 to 2-12 it
finished. Donegal had six points to spare with 45 minutes gone. In stepped David
Beggy with two killer goals and Meath were in the semi-final. It was not a good
day for Donegal. Their cause was not helped by the absence of Matt while
Shovlin had to come off injured at half-time – another blow, as he had kept Beggy
very quiet for the opening 30 minutes.

Naturally enough, goalkeeper Gary Walsh remembers the goals:

> Anthony Harkin always preached about how Meath got goals. When
> they attacked down one side of the field, defenders naturally got sucked
> to that side. Then they would switch the ball across the field to someone
> coming in on the blind side. We talked about that before the game. I
> don't know whether fellas went to sleep or just lost focus. Beggy was
> such a fit and fast fella that he didn't have to make his run until late.
> They'd just throw the ball in from 30 yards out and he'd come racing on
> to it. He was a very good finisher.

Liam Hayes was in at midfield for Meath. He was at a loss to explain why Donegal
"inexplicably froze". A journalist with the *Sunday Press*, Hayes later wrote:

> We never smelled victory, there wasn't even the slightest whiff, and then
> suddenly we were handed the game. The Meath dressing room wasn't
> dripping with satisfaction after that victory. We hadn't earned it.

Colm O'Rourke, a Meath legend who would go on to become one of Gaelic football's best-known analysts, agreed. Meath had played "like losers". O'Rourke described Beggy's first strike:

> I got the ball about 40 yards out. When I looked across the field, two Meath players were sprinting in behind the Donegal defence. Kevin Foley was closest to me but for obvious reasons I ignored him and kicked cross-field and there was 'Jinxie' [David Beggy] taking it, and without breaking stride, burying the ball in the corner of the net. I'll never forget that goal. It was one of the best I have ever seen and the crowd knew it too.

Little other than McHugh impressed Connie Duffy of the *Democrat*:

> Martin McHugh's performance, which at time verged on genius, was in total contrast to the rest of his colleagues. It was satisfying to see his pure instinctive skills inspiring and influencing the game. Sadly it takes more than one player to make a team.

As ever, McHugh's sheer presence was remarkable. Not alone did he have an acute sense of where he was on the pitch but he seemed to know by instinct where everyone else was as well. He was a supreme playmaker. "It was one of my best ever games for Donegal but I regretted it six months later," grinned Martin ruefully:

> I got a ball and Mick Lyons came out to get me. I was wide open but I saw him coming at the last minute and just got the ball away. He thumped me and we both went to ground. The ball was dropping over the bar when I was getting up. I just looked at him and laughed. He had missed me, but if he had got me he would have killed me.

Sean Boylan was sick of the sight of McHugh. As well as being man of the match in the quarter-final, McHugh had been man of the match in a league encounter in Ballybofey 16 months previously. Martin O'Connell had an unhappy afternoon marking McHugh in Ballybofey while Liam Harnan was equally ineffective in Clones. When the teams met later in the summer, Boylan nominated Kevin Foley to police McHugh.

Connie Duffy had further worries. There was, he mused, a few players on board who had reached their 'sell-by' date. It was true that the backbone of the Donegal team were no kids. "Face it," maintained Connie, "for most of the squad this year could be make or break." The Follower was also lamenting Donegal's ability to hold on to their six-point lead. In fairness to Donegal, late comebacks by Sean Boylan's Meath teams was their forte. Teams like Dublin and Kildare, among others, could and would bear testimony to that. Meath hadn't won back-to-back All-Irelands in 1987 and 1988 without being that little bit special.

Yet Connie Duffy had merit in his argument. A few of the players were thinking the same thing. Many of the older lads had been on board the Donegal train since 1981, a lot of miles were on the clock. They weren't getting any younger. Deliverance day, if ever it was to come, had a year or two at best to make an appearance.

❊ ❊ ❊ ❊

McHugh and Reid were in the United States as preparations for the 1990 Ulster championship opener with Cavan were in full swing back home. The two boys had been named as replacement All-Stars and spent a fortnight in New York and San Francisco, touching down in Ireland just a week before the much awaited Cavan clash in Ballybofey. Always seeking that certain edge, Reid voraciously swallowed up what knowledge he could to improve his game:

> I really enjoyed the trip and found it to be a great learning experience. It was a great experience to meet other players and Mick O'Dwyer. I learned an awful lot from Mick O'Dwyer in those ten days and I still use some of his words and training methods to this day.

Three or four weeks earlier, although still in the country, neither had lined out as McEniff indulged in a bit of experimenting at a pitch re-dedication in Aghyaran, County Tyrone. As Donegal took on Tyrone with nothing at stake, McEniff grasped the final pieces of the jigsaw and give runs to the final two or three players who would complete his All-Ireland winning team. Tommy Ryan was back from America and was clearly going to win a place in the squad if his form in Aghyaran was anything to go by. Tony Boyle exhibited his frightening pace and skill and seemed on the verge of a place. John Cunningham was back from London and flying. Another cert for the squad. Noel Hegarty from Naomh Columba made a brief appearance but would have to wait for another day. Nonetheless he had been spotted and his wait would be short. All the pieces of the jigsaw were now on the table – it was just a matter of putting it all together.

McHugh returned with a groin injury from the All-Star trip. Cavan would have to be faced without him. Tuohy, so sound in the corner back position, was another injury casualty. Sean Bonner became the third high-profile casualty with Matt moving over to take his place at number three. McEniff's first championship 15 since 1986 was: Gary Walsh; John Cunningham, Matt Gallagher, John Joe Doherty; Donal Reid, Paul Carr, Martin Shovlin; Anthony Molloy, Martin Gavigan; James McHugh, Brian Murray, Joyce McMullan; Declan Bonner, Charlie Mulgrew, Manus Boyle. Donegal and Cavan supporters steeled themselves for a repeat of the national league fireworks. Those expecting trouble weren't disappointed. Paddy Downey of the *Irish Times* was not impressed – either by the fisticuffs or Donegal:

> There are strong grounds for suspicion that the Donegal football team dislike their supporters. That was the impression we got at MacCumhaill Park, Ballybofey, yesterday when they seemed hell bent on giving them all heart attacks. They left it until the last six minutes to come from behind and beat Cavan in this foul-ridden, ill-tempered and, at times, disgracefully dirty first round Ulster championship game.

There had been modest matches in MacCumhaill Park down the years, but seldom one as scrappy or poor. Any notion of a flowing game was shattered by 57 frees with nine players booked. In addition Pat Faulkner of Cavan and Donegal's Declan Bonner were sent to the line. The referee, Seamus Murray, "rarely had a more difficult assignment' noted Downey.

Peadar O'Brien was in full agreement in the *Irish Press*, suggesting that the boxing commentator Harry Carpenter would have had plenty to report on had he been in the 15,000-strong attendance. Yet the result went Donegal's way, 0-13 to 0-9, although the waste of possession by the home team was painful to behold. In the *Irish Independent* Donal Keenan could hardly believe his eyes: "Favourites Donegal seemed afraid to win. Cavan just did not know how. If they did Donegal were at their most vulnerable."

The teams were level no less that eight times over the 70 minutes and it was only six minutes from the end that Donegal turned on the style and hit Cavan with five scores without reply. It had been a tough tension-filled outing, a day when defences largely held out and were helped by erratic forward shooting. Donegal's defence held Cavan forwards scoreless from play with Ronan Carolan accounting for seven of Cavan's nine points. John Joe, John Cunningham and Paul Carr had solid games in the green and gold jersey. John Joe was taking his third Ulster championship campaign in his stride. "The older players were quite keen that season," he remembered:

> The younger lads on the panel probably figured our day would come, but it was mostly the likes of Anthony Molloy and Martin McHugh that drove on the team in 1990. Looking back on it, it didn't seem to be a hard championship to win. I saw my involvement in that team as something of a bonus because few of the under-21s of 1987 had made it to senior level by that stage.

Declan Bonner had been going well up front until his sending off in the 29th minute. As Bonner and Faulkner were being talked to by referee Murray, all hell broke out at midfield with up to a dozen players becoming embroiled in an ugly skirmish. Anthony Molloy, who went on to turn the game in Donegal's favour in the second half, was in the thick of it but escaped with a booking following a clash with Seamus Gannon, the Cavan centre half-forward. Bonner, much more sinned against than sinning, was sent to the line along with Pat Faulkner.

Unfortunately for Molloy, his altercation with Gannon was caught on video. For the first time, the Ulster Council used video evidence in disciplinary proceedings:

> I know it might have been stupid on my behalf but a lot of different things happened that day at midfield. If I didn't look after my own then who would? I got involved with Seamus Gannon who, funnily enough, I've been very friendly with since. Several players were called to the kangaroo court in the Four Seasons Hotel in Monaghan. Big Stephen King, Mickey Faulkner, Gannon, Declan Bonner and me were all there and we had great craic. We knew our fate before we arrived and when we got to the hotel an hour and a half before the meeting, we went to the bar and had a heap of pints. Bonner and me got a month each. We had a great year afterwards but I lost out on an All-Star award over it.

So too did Bonner. At that time, players sent off at any stage during the year were ineligible for the All-Star team. The only silver lining from that dark cloud was that both suspensions ended at midnight on the day before the semi-final.

A second successive Ulster semi-final beckoned. The closer it came the longer McEniff's injury list grew. John Joe and Gerry Curran both broke bones in club games. Paul Carr, who had a fine outing against Cavan, was injured in training. Sean Bonner was still unavailable as was McHugh and Tuohy. McEniff added Michael Lafferty to the playing squad. Back too, after a long absence, came Martin Griffin. For the old hands it would prove to be a timely call.

As it transpired there had been nothing to worry about as Donegal demolished Derry by 1-15 to 0-8 – ten points the winning margin. Connie Duffy, as ever, was there for the *Democrat*:

> This 70-minute saga had as good a script as any and the game's storyline twisted and turned as the contest unfolded. The sub-plots included a dream start, an injury crisis, opportunities lost, above-average performances and the most implausible of all, the spectacle of the wounded Martin McHugh scoring two points – a miracle of almost religious proportions.

Pat Roche in the *Irish Times* would describe McHugh's recovery as "Lazarus-like" and lauded him for a spectacular contribution following his appearance after 50 minutes. Yet, it was a game largely won without the influence of the Wee Man. One of the main contributors to the victory was Brian McEniff who improvised cleverly in rejigging his injury-torn side before the throw-in. Murray was originally destined for full back, John Connors for corner back, John Cunningham for centre half-back, Gavigan for midfield, Mulgrew for centre half-forward and Tommy Ryan was in at full forward. McEniff ripped that one up and started afresh: Matt moved to full back, Connors to corner back, Gavigan to centre half-back, John Cunningham outside him, Murray to midfield. It worked. The link play between Murray, in particular, and his forwards was exceptional. Connie Duffy noted the birth of a new order, "Midfield was a powerhouse with Murray and Molloy probably establishing a new partnership."

Anthony Molloy was pleased with his new midfield partner:

I would have partnered at least ten midfielders during my career. Murray and me became the settled partnership after that. As regards understanding, Murray was the best player I ever played with. We had a great understanding of each other and complimented each other in every way. Big Murray was a great player to play with and never got the credit he was due.

Having played at full-forward, centre half-forward and wing forward, Murray was glad to move to his favourite position of midfield:

It meant a little more freedom. I had the height and strength to play there and was good at distributing the ball. Molloy had immense physical strength and presence, great football ability and tremendous aerial power. We had a good balance. A lot of the players would also have felt that we were the best partnership.

Gary Walsh was impressed with the new partnership and saw it grow over the years that followed:

Brian Murray and Anthony Molloy deserve an awful lot of credit. They played to their strengths and knew their limitations. They didn't do anything too fancy. They got the ball and used it, often giving it to James or Martin. Some midfielders try to do too much. Molloy and Murray knew what they were there for and stuck to it.

Manus scored the quickest point of the championship with mere seconds on the clock. It was a blistering opening period which saw Donegal move three points up with just four minutes gone. Gormley replied from a free but when Damien Barton sliced a penalty wide after seven minutes it felt like Donegal's day and so it transpired. Donegal's goal came after 12 minutes, Murray unselfishly put

Manus through. Mulgrew added another point – Donegal's last score for some 32 minutes! Despite the scoring drought Donegal were in control. As Tom O'Riordan noted in the *Irish Independent*, "When it counted Donegal had the clout and the better players through the field."

"When McEniff came back in 1990 he wanted the players to be continually on the move," remembered Manus Boyle:

> If you're on the move, you're giving and receiving the ball and playing in support – that is where the short passing game came from. It's based on players always being on the move. If you're stuck at corner-forward it is better that the ball is played in to you, but if you're on the move all the time it is natural to keep possession of the ball. Martin McHugh was a great believer in holding possession. He didn't like giving away cheap ball. He would rather see the ball being kicked wide than see a player being caught in possession.

Donegal would be heavily criticised for this style of football in many quarters but it ultimately landed the biggest prize of all. "We got a bit of stick about it," said Joyce McMullan, "but I don't give a damn. The short-passing game is better than hoofing the ball into small, light forwards."

Reid, Gavigan and Shovlin were manning the half-back line and, with unshakeable authority, ensuring little chance of a Derry revival during the fallow period in Donegal's scoring. James McHugh kick-started the Donegal scoring machine again and the final quarter was a rout.

McEniff's injury woes continued apace. John Connors had to come ashore with an ankle injury while the unfortunate Charlie Mulgrew seemed championship jinxed yet again, suffering a dislocated collarbone this time. Barry McGowan made his championship debut, coming in for Connors and simply "oozed class". On for Mulgrew came Lazarus himself – McHugh. Yet it was a day when the other Donegal forwards had flourished. Manus and Declan Bonner between them had accounted for 1-8 of Donegal's score. James McHugh and Charlie Mulgrew had contributed points, Joyce had scored two. The Follower was a happy man at last, announcing to his public, "I have seen a Donegal forward line no longer dependent on Mairtín Beag to get the scores".

A small crowd of just under 5,000 had made the trip to Clones. "The atmosphere was so bad that neither team could raise a gallop," remembered Gary Walsh. World Cup fever had the country firmly in its grip and the Ulster semi-final had clashed with the Republic of Ireland versus Egypt match in Italy. Large numbers of both Derry and Donegal supporters exited St Tiernach's Park with ten minutes play remaining to catch some of the soccer game on television in the Clones pubs. It was certainly no more exciting than the fare on the Gaelic pitch as Jack Charlton's men were held to a scoreless draw by the mighty Egyptians.

Less than a month later one of Irish soccer's heroes was in MacCumhaill Park, playing football there for the first time since lining out for Donegal against Fermanagh in the national league in the late 1970s. Packie Bonner was in Ballybofey to join in a practice match with the Donegal team as the countdown to the Ulster final continued. MacCumhaill Park soon became engulfed with dozens of fans as the news spread that the big Rosses man was in town. Packie's legend had been secured when he saved a penalty in a penalty shoot-out with Romania.

❄ ❄ ❄ ❄

McEniff's team selection for the 1990 Ulster final in July was, personnel-wise, very close to the side that contested the Ulster series in 1992: Walsh; Doherty, Gavigan, Gallagher; Reid, John Cunningham, Shovlin; Murray, Molloy; James McHugh, Martin McHugh, McMullan; Declan Bonner, Ryan and Manus Boyle all started. Connors and Mulgrew were the omissions from the semi-final with Martin McHugh and John Joe starting in their place. There was no first 15 jersey for Paul Carr, back from injury, or Barry McGowan.

McEniff had succeeded in seemingly fashioning a forward sextet that possessed flair and proven scoring ability. Without doubt this Donegal team were now one of the province's most experienced sides. The Donegal boss was convinced he had picked the team to capture his county's fourth Ulster title. Back in September when McEniff had the job in the bag, almost his first words had been, "It's all about the championship." An expectant Donegal football public held its breath.

On the Friday morning before the game, Gary Walsh had only one thing on his mind – the Ulster final. Based in Newry and working with the Goodman group, Walsh got a phone call at noon telling him one of the group's English customers had gone bankrupt. Instead of heading for Bundoran for the usual pre-match gathering on the Friday before a big game, Walsh found himself in Wigan. When he arrived home on the Saturday afternoon, Walsh went to Bundoran and spent a couple of hours training with McEniff at the Bundoran pitch. Although the preparations hadn't been ideal, Walsh would go on to record his third consecutive clean sheet in the championship.

On Sunday, July 15, 1990, McEniff and his men duly delivered that precious fourth Ulster title. Clones was not a place for the faint of heart. The final whistle after 70 minutes of end-to-end attacking football was greeted with sweet relief – Donegal emerging champions by a kick of the ball having just weathered massive Armagh pressure in the closing minutes; 0-15 to 0-14 it finished. As Paddy Hickey noted in the *Irish Independent*, it was a close call, "Donegal's habit of sitting on a lead almost deprived them of capturing their first Ulster Senior Football title since 1983."

It had been a stressful finish. Painful for Donegal folk who had been bay-ing – not unreasonably – for the final whistle for what seemed like an eternity. There had been no getting rid of Armagh. Some, like the *Independent*'s man, would say that Donegal lacked the killer punch but this was an Armagh side – anchored by the Grimley twins, Ger Houlihan, Kieran McGurk and Jim McConville – that had come to Clones not in search of a greasy burger or a warm bottle of beer, but an Ulster title. Unfancied and written off, Armagh were playing with pride. That was always going to be a difficult proposition. Yet, despite wasted possession, much of the football played by Donegal caught the eye. "Their play," noted Paddy Hickey, "was regularly punctuated with sparkling multi-man movements, often beginning in the last line of defence."

The brothers Grimley had come into the Ulster final with hard-men reputations. "They were animals of men but they wouldn't touch you," recalled Tommy Ryan, "and if you were ever going to hit a man you'd do it in the Ulster final. They had altercations with Tyrone men but they must have been talking when they should have been listening." Barry McGowan agreed with Tommy's assessment, "The Grimleys were mountains of men and they'd put the fear of God in you. You could hear the ground shaking as they approached. I wasn't sorry to see the back of them."

The scoreline stood at 0-7 to 0-5 in favour of Donegal at half-time. Ten minutes before the break Tommy Ryan had the ball in the Armagh net but Fermanagh referee, Damien Campbell, bizarrely hauled back play and awarded a free, "There was nothing wrong with the goal, the referee should never have disallowed it," remembered Tommy Ryan. Declan Bonner pointed the free but a possible match-winner had been wiped from existence. The turning point never came. Sean Kilfeather of the *Irish Times* sensed a suitable moment for Donegal to deliver:

> Twelve minutes into the second half Donegal moved into a four-point lead (0-11 to 0-7). What they needed at that stage to turn screw with finality was a goal but instead they appeared to relax their grip on the game.

Tony Boyle was in the dugout and chomping at the bit. Although new to the panel, the Dungloe man wanted to be involved, "To me, sitting on the bench wasn't good enough," he recalled:

> I could see Tommy Ryan was tiring and knew a change was going to be made. I was nearly jumping out of the dugout. Brian gave me the shout and I started warming up. I kept asking him for the slip of paper but he was too engrossed in the game to heed me. There was a break in the play, I grabbed the slip and didn't wait for him to tell me where to go or what to do. I only knew that I was coming on for Tommy.

Martin McHugh

Although only 19, Boyle had a strapping physique that seemed almost at odds with his God-given footballing ability. He perfected a new style of forward play that was often copied but never bettered. Boyle would slide out in front of a defender and win the ball:

> I wasn't the most agile forward and didn't fancy bending down to get a low incoming ball. I knew that if I slid and got it in my hand there would be very few defenders that would wrestle it from me. It was very hard to defend against once I got my body in front of a low ball. If I could time it right, the full-back would fall over me as I went down and I'd get up and be gone.

Full-backs would struggle with Boyle for the rest of the 1990s, but with nine minutes remaining in the 1990 Ulster decider, Armagh clawed back Donegal and drew level at 0-12 apiece. It was the sixth and last time the sides would be on level terms. Then, in a five-minute period, Donegal proceeded to win the match. Manus heaved over a point. McHugh pointed a 45. Two up, then Tony Boyle introduced himself properly to Donegal senior football fans. Boyle takes up the story, "Molloy sent one of his famous passes out near the corner flag. I managed to retrieve it with a sliding tackle, gave it to Barry McGowan who slipped it to Manus and he scored the winning point."

Then the waiting game began as Armagh tagged on a further point and an entire county willed the Fermanagh official to sound the whistle. Barry McGowan collected a ball in the Donegal defence, "Players can be most critical of themselves and can remember the bad times. I nearly cost us the game. I tried to fist the ball out of defence and it was intercepted." Armagh substitute Shane Skelton pointed to leave the minimum between the teams. Then referee Campbell sounded the full-time whistle and the closest final in four decades was over. Donegal folk in the 20,000-strong attendance let rip with seven long years' worth of suppressed angst. Back in an All-Ireland semi-final at last – it wasn't supposed to have taken this long. That summer evening away back in August 1983, stunned by Val Daly's Galway, few Donegal people would have believed it would take seven years to come out of Ulster again. Those had been innocent days. This was a famous day.

It was a day when solid Donegal performances could be found throughout the field. Martin McHugh and Manus Boyle – enjoying his first championship victory over Armagh – caught the eye of the national press, as did Matt Gallagher, Martin Gavigan and, as ever, that man from Dunkineely, Martin Shovlin, who would collect the Ulster GAA Writers Footballer of the Year award before the year was out. Following in the footsteps of Frankie McFeeley in 1972, Pauric McShea in 1974 and Michael Lafferty in 1983, Molloy raised the Anglo-Celt Cup high over his head. The common link between these victories was Brian McEniff; player-manager in 1972 and 1974, manager in 1983 and now again in 1990. McEniff had the Midas touch. The man had brought his county more footballing glory than it had dared hope for. The Follower, as might be expected, had the word for it – "McEniffricent".

※ ※ ※ ※

The month that had to be passed between the Ulster final and All-Ireland semi-final was willed into submission by a county high on excitement and wracked with anticipation. McEniff had plotted feverishly in the interim. Cork and Kerry provided top-quality opposition at the end of July as McEniff took the boys on a long weekend trip down south. It was all about football and all about bonding. The craic was mighty. Castlehaven officially opened their grounds on the Saturday evening – Cork and Donegal providing the football entertainment. That was the evening that Tony Boyle – emphatically – clinched the Donegal number 14 jersey as his alone.

Colman Corrigan was an All-Star full-back in 1987 and 1988. Recently back from injury he would go on to win a second All-Ireland medal with Cork later that year. Tony Boyle ran riot that evening in Moneyvoulihane, so much so that Corrigan was replaced at half-time. Donegal had just found a full-forward capable of striking real fear into the hearts and minds of defenders everywhere.

Tony Boyle has happy memories of the trip south which cemented his place on the first 15:

> I remember that weekend more for the couple of pints we had on the Saturday night. At that time, I knew the boys by name only. I was very shy when I joined the squad. Only for Declan Bonner I might not have lasted in the squad at all. Declan took me under his wing and was in with everyone so I just hung on to him. We had a bit of a session that weekend and I got to know the Shov and the others.

As Declan recalls it, Tony's shyness, "lasted all of ten minutes".

The Sam Maguire Cup was resting in Casltlehaven that weekend. A handful of the lads – the two McHughs, Joyce, Molloy and Reid – had their pictures taken as they posed with the fabled piece of silverware. Little did Molloy know but he would have that cup all to himself a couple of years down the road.

As the semi-final approached excitement reached fever pitch. The air of expectation peaked above anything previously witnessed in 1972, 1974 or 1983. The time was ripe for the breakthrough. Donegal was awash with green and gold. The best wishes of an entire county lay with McEniff's boys. It was not going to be easy. The team that stood between Donegal and an All-Ireland final was Meath. Opponents didn't come any tougher.

The build up was terrifying in its intensity. Donegal folk had never seen anything like it. Copious column inches were now dedicated to Donegal in the sports pages of the land. Journalists who had only ever made the odd trip north to Ballybofey to cover a championship opener were now camped in the county. The flavour was being sampled. Their articles had two recurring themes: Donegal was a breathtakingly beautiful county and their footballers hadn't a hope against Meath.

McEniff was besieged. He attracted journalists like moths to a flame. The boys up from Dublin were impressed. Coffee in the Hollyrood with the boss. Articulate, quotable, likable. They marvelled at his business success, wondered at his gentility. The tape recorders were rolling. Séan Moran of the *Sunday Tribune* went to Bundoran. In a couple of sentences he astutely captured the essence of McEniff: "Fit looking, tanned, trim, dressed in a suit or a tracksuit, he looks about ten years younger than his age. He talks quietly, listens quite a bit and everyone else listens when he talks."

Five nights before the match the cameras and press were in Ballybofey at training. The big news was that the youngster Tony Boyle was most definitely in the side despite the dodgy knee that even then was causing bother. Losing out was Tommy Ryan, suffering from a knee injury he had picked up while playing in Chicago the previous summer. It would not be the last time Tommy would miss out in Croke Park. "A calculated gamble," said McEniff. A full championship debut in, of all places, Croke Park. Cannon-fodder for Mick Lyons jotted the hacks.

Although only 19, Tony Boyle had long-standing problems with the cartilage in his knee. He tore cartilage in it on the Sunday before the semi-final while playing that most sedate of games, snooker:

> Out of pure boredom, my brother and me went to play a game of snooker at the local pub. Whatever way I leaned on my knee, I tore another bit of cartilage. I nearly had to be carried out of the snooker hall and when I got back home I couldn't sleep. I was physically sick with worry that I was going to miss the match. I iced my knee all night but I couldn't bend it when I got up on Monday morning. I went to a German physiotherapist in Portsalon. He worked on me for 45 minutes and I was able to train that night. Only for that I was gone.
>
> I always remember that when running out of the tunnel for the Meath match, I thought my two knees were going to collapse; the cartilage was going mad in them. Once I got moving and warmed up I was grand.

The team was scribbled into a dozen notebooks – Gary Walsh; John Joe Doherty, Matt Gallagher, John Cunningham; Donal Reid, Martin Gavigan, Martin Shovlin; Brian Murray, Anthony Molloy; James McHugh, Martin McHugh, Joyce

McMullan; Declan Bonner, Tony Boyle, Manus Boyle. John Joe lost his place when he got injured at training on the Thursday before the match. Just over two years later Martin Shovlin would get injured at training on the Thursday before the All-Ireland and his place would be filled by John Joe. That was for the future, McEniff had to reshuffle his defence for the game at hand. Paul Carr came in at full-back, Matt moved over to the right corner.

One by one the journalists reached the same conclusion. Donegal would experience the pain of defeat. "A one-way ticket into darkness," wrote Vincent Hogan in the *Irish Independent*. "Football form suggests Meath; football experience suggests Meath and football facts suggest Meath," agreed Peadar O'Brien in the *Irish Press*. There was little doubt that the odds were stacked high against Donegal. Meath were contesting their fourth semi-final in five years. During that period they had accumulated two All-Irelands and two national leagues. Yet, that visit up north had made an impression. "A Donegal win would be the most popular result in Gaelic games since Down won the All-Ireland in 1960," admitted Paddy Downey in the *Irish Times*.

Closer to home Connie Duffy perfectly captured the task which lay ahead. The whole county knew it, Connie wrote it. To win, Donegal "must reach previously unscaled heights". It really was as simple, and as difficult, as that. Nothing else would do. Not for the first time the focus shifted on to the Donegal forwards. If they converted the possession that Donegal would surely win, then an All-Ireland final was the prize. Matt Gallagher knew what was needed, "Instead of going to Croke Park and shivering, we needed to go to Croke Park and say 'this is where I want to be and this is where I should be playing'". The pressure was on. McEniff himself acknowledged that the time had come. "It's now or never," said the man from Bundoran as all of Donegal headed for Dublin.

❄ ❄ ❄ ❄

Donegal had Meath at full stretch for an hour on August 19, 1990. And then for ten minutes, when it mattered most, Meath caught fire and booked themselves into an All-Ireland final. Another dream dead. Another false dawn.

At 3:35pm it had all looked so different. Five minutes old, the game was already erupting in front of just over 40,000 spectators. Donegal were hitting Meath extremely hard. According to Joyce McMullan, Donegal had no choice, "Once we were drawn against Meath, we knew we would get slaughtered if we went out there in any way half-hearted". According to Manus Boyle, concentrating on the physical side of the game came at a cost, "We were so hyped up about the physical end of it that we forgot to play football and forgot all the things we had trained for."

Peadar O'Brien, in the *Irish Press*, watched as the Donegal half-back line tore lumps out of Meath: "The Meath attack did not appear to relish the no-nonsense tackling by men like Martin Shovlin, John Cunningham and Donal Reid who hit first and asked questions afterwards."

As might be expected, a certain defender from Dunkineely was having a ball and delighting in the fierce intensity of the tackling. His would be a man-of-the-match performance:

> It was really enjoyable, it was hell for leather for the first five minutes. I remember Gavigan meeting Beggy one time just as I was coming into the picture as well. Beggy was just straightening himself up from the Gavigan slap when I met him. I tossed him good and proper. Fuck me, I didn't think he was that weak but in fairness he was already well shook by Gavigan.

Beggy and Shovlin would later become friendly on an All-Star tour in Toronto. Shovlin came in for a bit of abuse himself. No matter how many times Meath would knock him down, he'd just get up and play on – Cool Hand Luke hadn't a patch on Shovlin. "That would have been one of the most physical games we ever played in," winced Anthony Molloy, "I saw Shovlin's shin bone, but he just got up and played on." Barry McGowan was to come on in place of an injured Shovlin:

> I warmed up for Martin Shovlin two or three times after tackles that would have killed any ordinary man. He had treatment and was taken off on a stretcher on each occasion. Being the man that he was he hopped up again and played on. He gave an unbelievable performance.

But in Croke Park that Sunday war had just been declared on every Meath man on the field. Donegal stayed within the rules but were merciless in their approach. A clear message rang out, Donegal would not be intimidated by Meath. This was going to be no repeat of 1972, 1974 or 1983. Irrespective of the final result, Donegal weren't going to be over-awed.

Conditions were difficult but didn't hinder either side in serving up a splendid game of football. It was a tense, rough and physically punishing first 35 minutes, played in the most humid of conditions and a heavy downpour. Both sides had recorded 1-4 by half-time. Declan Bonner was under no illusions about the nature of the Meath defence. "Tony and me went for the first high ball that came in," he recalled. "As I went for it, Mick Lyons came across me and took me out of it. I remember thinking that if I wanted to play at this level I would have to start learning very quickly."

Preparations for the semi-final had gone badly for Gary Walsh:

> I bought a new pair of gloves for the match but couldn't find the brand that I normally wore. I wore them in the semi-final and never wore them

again. Because of the clash of jerseys we had to wear the Ulster strip and a red jersey was produced for me. It had pads in the elbows and a really tight collar. I hated this jersey – I blamed the gloves and the jersey!

Conditions weren't favourable either.

It had been a wet morning. Croke Park always had a good covering of grass and once a ball hit it, it would fly. For the first goal the ball just whizzed past my fingers. What came next happened so fast I can barely remember it. The ball hit the post, came out and hit me on the back of the neck and went into the net. It was a disaster.

The scores had been sporadic and reflected the titanic struggle raging between the 40s. Bernard Flynn and Manus Boyle traded the goals. Flynn's goal had fluke written all over it while Manus had converted a penalty just before the interval. It was the first time Donegal had drawn level.

The second half settled into a similar pattern. Beggy and Stafford both had points before Declan Bonner struck twice to pull Donegal level again – and for the last time; 1-6 apiece it stood with 43 minutes gone. Donegal drawing level was the football equivalent of a long-distance runner pulling up beside his adversary on the final bend. Now was the time to sprint for the line. That sprint never came.

Murray had a bad wide when a point was desperately needed – in fairness to Murray he had an excellent game in the middle. Murray was due to get married to a Meath woman the following week. There was much banter in the lead-up to the match and in its aftermath. Revelling in the midfield role he favoured, Murray matched Meath with his physical presence:

I tore into them. If I got a slap, they got a slap. We got stuck into them because if we didn't, Meath would have walked all over us and destroyed us. They were physical and played right at the edge. Of course they could play football too and had some exceptional players. We were a bit over-zealous in that game. If we had played the style of football we played in 1992 it would have been a different story – I don't think that Meath team would have been able to stick with us.

Donegal were still making all the play and still hitting Meath harder than they had ever been hit. Yet the scores wouldn't come. Martin Breheny watched for the *Irish Press* as Donegal's chance came and went:

When Donegal drew level [Meath] fears grew into real demons. Donegal looked like men released after years of paying homage to so-called superior forces. Enter the doubt factor. Galloping in Meath's shadow,

Donegal were compact and concrete. But once they drew alongside, they became clumsy and uncertain. Responsibility was off-loaded like a ticking parcel and the transfer was rarely tidy.

For the next 17 minutes only one score was registered – a point by Flynn. It was during those 17 minutes that Donegal missed the All-Ireland final boat. In Donegal's greatest hour of need the forward line utterly collapsed. Confidence died. The half-forward line was simply wiped out. Ball wasn't getting into the full forward line. Silly mistakes abounded. It was painful to watch as Donegal kicked themselves out of contention. Outfield Donegal were motoring nicely. The defence were holding out, a magnificent Molloy and Murray at midfield had the upper hand. Up front it was simply breaking down. Declan Bonner was the only forward on form and had an outstanding game in the right corner. "I had the beating of Terry Ferguson that day," remembered Bonner. "I kicked three points but we lost the match. I would have preferred to play badly and win than play well and lose." Donegal added seven second-half wides to their first-half tally of six, Meath recorded three in total. Eight of the wides came from the half-forward line. "Donegal have no-one but themselves to blame," noted Peadar O'Brien, "When it came to taking scores some of their forwards were at loggerheads with their shooting boots". Donegal had so much possession that Meath were living off crumbs.

Martin McHugh had been truly majestic when the sides last met. However, the All-Ireland semi-final of 1990 was a game the Wee Man would wish to erase from memory forever. The experience has stayed with him:

> It was the hardest game I ever played in. I usually prepared well for big matches and I prepared well for that match too. The whole game bypassed me. Kevin Foley marked me and didn't get two kicks of the ball but I didn't get three kicks.

James, Joyce and Martin would receive much personal criticism – largely borne out of sheer footballing ignorance – in the aftermath of the match. McHugh would be stung badly by it. The adulation of the masses is indeed a fickle thing, many of those pointing the finger at the half-forward line seemed to forget the immeasurable contribution they had made, not only en-route to the semi-final but year in, year out in the Donegal jersey. Martin McHugh recalls:

> I had a good Ulster campaign and was man of the match in the Ulster final. A lot was expected of me and I was disappointed. I was really in bad form and didn't leave the house on Monday, Tuesday or Wednesday. I didn't want to go back to playing football. My son Mark was born on the Wednesday and only for that I don't know what would have happened.

There was a really hateful letter in the paper the following Thursday. It was hateful about the half-forward line but I got the brunt of it. I was able take the criticism but I didn't think my mother and father deserved to read it. I didn't go out to play badly. I don't know where the letter was coming from.

I was disappointed because I always prepared well. I was disappointed in myself and I was disappointed for James. The half-forward line got a lot of stick about that game but it wasn't that the Meath half-back line played well either, it was just that the game passed us by.

McHugh's old comrade Anthony Molloy could see the hurt in the Wee Man, "There was no man as disappointed coming down the road in 1990 as Martin McHugh". Joyce McMullan was annoyed at the criticisms, "I thought it was cowardly of people to snipe and write cowardly articles in the press. That was disappointing. The boys had given everything that year."

Donal Reid holds his own strong opinions on the demands the public make on amateur sportsmen:

I remember an incident in Heaney's Bar when I was having a drink with my wife. A man came over and told me I was a bollocks and good for nothing and that he'd buy me a ball for Christmas. We could never go into a bar without getting hassle, some of it was banter and we didn't mind but some of it was bad. There were times when you just wanted to have a drink and chat about anything other than football. Another woman in my company asked the man who he thought I was. 'That's Joyce McMullan,' he replied. When it was pointed out to him that I was Donal Reid he made no apology and walked away. He came back 15 minutes later and said, 'Now Reid …' That's what we sometimes had to listen to. We were amateur players that were getting no money out of the game.

The so-called glamorous life of an inter-county footballer wasn't all that it was cracked up to be. In the lonely days after a defeat, the players would discover who their real friends were.

Fourteen minutes left and trailing by a point against Meath, a goal chance fell to Martin McHugh. His shot beat the keeper but not Kevin Foley who got a vital stop. A goal would have put Donegal two points ahead and possibly kick-started their sprint for the line. Two minutes later, Donegal's world caved in as all Meath's experience kicked-in.

Back in April, in the national league quarter-final at Clones, Meath had buried Donegal in the final 15 minutes with two killer goals. Five months later in Croke Park they repeated the feat. John Cunningham was playing at left full-back, "I heard a call from Matt Gallagher and tried to pass it to him. I put it too high and

David Beggy stole it." The ball broke to Brian Stafford who volleyed it, skimming it low past Walsh. "It went to my weaker side, hit the ground and flew past me," recalled the big goalkeeper, "It had gone into the net before I even had a chance to get down." "Psychologically, it was a terrible blow," felt McEniff.

One minute later O'Rourke found the brilliant Flynn who added a screaming goal and it was all over. Walsh was most disappointed with this third goal, "It went across me. I should have done better with it and would have saved it on a good day." "Déjà vu," thought Brian Murray, "Clones all over again." Donegal heads dropped. There was nothing remotely fluky about Meath's double-strike. The art of soaking up pressure on the ropes and then launching a fierce counter-attack when the opponent was spent, was Meath all over. Muhammad Ali would have been proud.

The pre-match predictions were coming home to roost. Colm O'Rourke had acknowledged beforehand that the media were expecting "a difficult game for a while, but that Donegal would assume their respectful role and collapse." O'Rourke had lots of opinions on football – not all of them finding agreement in the North West. Nonetheless, he called the Donegal game correctly: "New teams generally don't win big games from behind, their best chance of victory generally lies in building up a decent lead before half-time."

O'Rourke had a tough 70 minutes as John Cunningham shadowed his every move around Croke Park. McEniff had done his homework and decided Cunningham was the man to do a job on O'Rourke:

> O'Rourke was was one of the best footballers of the era but I knew that, deep down, he wouldn't be as brave as people might think. He played under Eugene McGee in Australia and I saw then that he wouldn't go into the fire to get the ball.

Having detailed Cunningham to mark O'Rourke, McEniff then set about winding him up. Cunningham remembers how McEniff and Lafferty went about this:

> It was presented to me as a damage limitation operation. They weren't telling me that I could mark him out of it, they were telling me to do the best I could. That really wound me up. To be honest I out fought O'Rourke both physically and mentally. Every time I meet him he talks about me battering him around Croke Park.

O'Rourke was held scoreless but his full-forward colleagues Flynn and Stafford did the damage. Matt Gallagher rates Bernard Flynn as his toughest opponent, "He was strong but slippery and could kick with two feet. He gave me a torrid time in the semi-final," he grimaced. "I learned many lessons from him that day and put them to good use."

Meath completed their scoring with two further points. Donal Reid conceded a penalty by slide-tackling Stafford. Walsh was pleased to make a good save from Stafford's penalty kick and Manus had a goal effort pushed over the bar but it was all academic. The final scoreline was harsh but didn't lie. It read 1-7 to 3-9. "Meath will be the first to admit that their opponents did not deserve to be beaten by an eight-point margin, or anything near it," commented Paddy Downey in the *Irish Times*. Martin Breheny agreed, "This sporting life can be so cruel". "Our defenders were reasonable, our midfielders average and our forwards terrible," was the bleak assessment of Tommy Ryan. "It was a case of Donegal going to Croke Park again, playing well and coming down the road beaten," said team captain Anthony Molloy.

Martin Gavigan was disappointed with his day:

My man scored four points that day. Four shots, four points. We were so concerned about keeping out goals. I was covering the route towards goal at all times even if the play was coming up the wings. I got caught out a few times because they cleared the ball back out to the 50 and my man just slotted it over the bar.

John Cunningham, Donal Reid, Martin Shovlin and Paul Carr all played well in the Donegal defence. "Rarely has the Meath attack found it so difficult to operate smoothly," wrote Donal Keenan. Matt also had a good game despite Flynn's 2-2 and had provided sterling cover for the other defenders. Molloy had a magnificent outing in midfield and once again outplayed Liam Hayes. Hayes, thanks to an article he had penned, came in for special attention all afternoon from Donegal supporters. Apart from Declan Bonner, the forwards had a miserable afternoon. In fairness to the two Boyles, Tony and Manus, they had their moments but were starved of possession. Tony Boyle wasn't happy with his display, "While I felt that I had done reasonably well for my first start, I knew that I could do better. My only regret is that I never got to play against Mick Lyons again." The most feared full-back of his generation, there were few forwards who would regret avoiding a meeting with him. Tony Boyle truly was one of a kind.

Manus Boyle met Mick Lyons some time later:

He told me that he couldn't believe Tony Boyle was so tough for someone so young. He hit Tony the first and second times the ball came in. I signalled Bonner, the three of us met in the middle and I hit Lyons. Lyons was shocked. He told me that we were only young fellas and that we shouldn't have been doing things like that to someone like him.

Coming out with credit in the physical stakes was one thing but the Donegal dressing room was downcast. "A lot of players didn't perform," remembered James McHugh:

> I don't know if we approached the game with the right attitude. I think we were happy enough to have won the Ulster title. The majority of that team had not been to Croke Park before. Still, the Meath game stood to us in 1992. As individuals, it helped us in the long run.

The bitter taste of defeat was mixed with the realisation that this chance may well have been *it*. An All-Ireland final might never again be a mere 70 minutes away. Colm O'Rourke paid a visit to the losing dressing room in his capacity as Meath captain. A quiet Donegal dressing room listened as the man from Skryne spoke:

> In the 1986 All-Ireland semi-final against Kerry we sustained the type of defeat you sustained today. We learned from that experience and came back to win an All-Ireland the next year. You lads are good enough to win an All-Ireland. If you take a decision here and now that you are not going to allow this setback to be the end of your effort, you *can* win an All-Ireland. You must stick together to do so.

Meath also paid tribute to Donegal's fighting spirit. David Beggy, Liam Hayes and Bernard Flynn agreed that it was the toughest game they had ever played in. There was little consolation to be taken from that fact for either side. Some of the Donegal players felt that perhaps they were too physical in their approach to the detriment of playing good football. And a few of the Meath players would later reflect that had still not recovered from the bruising Donegal encounter by the time they met Cork in the final and lost. Brian Murray met Terry Ferguson at a tournament in Cavan after the final:

> He told me that the semi-final cost them the All-Ireland. He told me they were never hit as hard or had such a tough game. But that was never Donegal's way of playing, we were always a footballing side. Who knows what would have happened if we had played football?

Manus Boyle was friendly with Larry Tompkins. Tompkins told him that Cork couldn't believe how dead the Meath team was. Cork secured the elusive football-hurling All-Ireland double with an 0-11 to 0-9 victory over Meath.

✳ ✳ ✳ ✳

No one could deny that Donegal had arrived on the big stage. Their problem, as ever, would be getting out of Ulster the following year. The national media had been hugely impressed and were anxious to see them back in Croke Park. Vincent Hogan noted that almost 30 years had passed since an Ulster side had last captured Sam Maguire. "Worse than that," he concluded, "no team has retained the Ulster crown in 14 summers. We may not see these men again. If not, the loss is ours." Colm O'Rourke had alluded to the Ulster jinx before the game:

> Donegal are tarred with the Ulster brush, which means they have no chance in Croke Park. At this stage many Northern teams are probably beginning to believe this themselves. When there is a good enough team in Ulster they will win an All-Ireland.

He would be proved correct. That team would be Down and they would pave the way for Donegal and Derry. Ulster football was about to start believing.

Brian McEniff was down. But he was most certainly not out. Before the semi-final, McEniff had told a journalist, "I may be a dreamer but dreamers sometimes get it right". It wasn't the first time a McEniff dream had ended badly but he was clearly prepared to go away and dream it up all over again. "The one thing we have to take out of this is that we have to get back as soon as possible to gain the experience it takes to win at this level," he told Michael Daly afterwards.

An old saying, perhaps Chinese in origin, goes, "The glory is not in never falling, but in rising every time you fall". Donegal had fallen, yet again, but the promise that they would rise to fight again seemed somehow believable.

⁂

RESULTS

National League 1989-90
Donegal 3-12, Armagh 0-13
Donegal 1-12, Cavan 0-13
Donegal 0-11, Kerry 0-10
Donegal 0-14, Down 1-15
Donegal 0-11, Derry 0-3
Donegal 2-10, Cork 2-14
Donegal 1-10, Dublin 0-9
Donegal 0-13, Meath 2-12 (q/f)

Ulster Championship 1990
Donegal 0-13, Cavan 0-9
Donegal 1-15, Derry 0-8
Donegal 0-15, Armagh 0-14

All-Ireland Series
Donegal 1-7, Meath 3-9

12

A False Dawn

(October 1990 – September 1991)

"Coming away from Clones, I asked myself if Donegal
was ever going to achieve anything."

BRIAN MURRAY

Paddy Cullen was six days in the job. His feet had barely touched the ground yet here he was, 150 miles north-west of the capital, in Ballybofey of all places. One of the best known faces of the legendary Dublin team of the 1970s, Cullen was the new Dublin manager. Ironically, his first assignment would pit him against Donegal – Cullen's footballing fortunes over the next three years would be inextricably linked to the men in green and gold.

By the time the Dubs rumbled into the Twin Towns at the beginning of October, McEniff was in a spot of bother. Injury and suspension had devastated his panel. Lethargy had descended upon the boys following the Meath defeat. McEniff had never seen things quite so flat. The walking wounded were everywhere. McHugh was out for the foreseeable future. So too was Paul Carr. Tuohy was still not back. Molloy was struggling with his knee – the Big Man shouldn't be playing football at all. His knee would be operated on before Christmas.

Molloy always had trouble with his knees. He broke his kneecap when aged 14. On leaving school, he worked with John Sisk and Sons in Dublin and twisted his knee in an inter-firms match. That was 1980 and the start of his knee problems:

> I was one of the first people in Ireland to have keyhole surgery carried out on me. I've had six different operations on my left knee and two on my right. It was very hard to come back on eight different occasions. They weren't major operations but I still had to rehabilitate and lift weights.

Training was always a struggle for Molloy. Ice-packs became the norm and had to be applied after both games and training. Matt Gallagher looked on in wonder:

Molloy's knee was the size of two knees and he'd put a bag of ice the size of a bag of spuds on it. You'd ask yourself how he could do it. You'd think of the sheer willpower required to go through the pain barrier all the time. He was just amazing. The strength of the man was unbelievable.

Gavigan's availability was in doubt but for different reasons. Rambo was at the centre of a storm that had already hit the national papers. Ardara and MacCumhaills had met in a league match a week before. The game didn't finish and was abandoned by the referee amid chaotic scenes. In the middle of the confusion, there was intense speculation that Gavigan had been one of those dismissed by the referee. If that proved to be the case, not only would Gavigan miss out on the Dublin game, but his inclusion in the Irish team travelling to Australia for the Compromise Rules series would be in doubt. Martin wisely kept his head down, continued to train with the Irish squad and waited on the disciplinary meeting.

On a positive note, Noel Hegarty's short wait was over and he was in the squad. Already on the fringes, 20 year-old Hegarty rubber-stamped his inclusion with a thundering display as Naomh Columba overcame Killybegs to clinch the Donegal Senior Football Championship

It was against this backdrop of so many injured players that Donegal awaited the arrival of Paddy Cullen's Dublin for the opening game of the 1990-91 Royal Liver National Football League. Dublin never even smelled Donegal. For a side whose preparation was bordering on the non-existent, Donegal really turned it on. It was clear that the players now had a rich reserve of experience and know-how to draw upon as they hit 2-11 to Dublin's 1-9. And it was impressive stuff. The belief was there. Michael Daly was impressed with the long-range point taking and the ball winning abilities on view throughout the Donegal 15. "A win against a side such as Dublin was in the past, something to hope for, at present it is expected," he observed.

Dublin were outwitted on and off the field. Matt Gallagher had Joe McNally, once again, tied up in knots. Brian Murray was the best player on the pitch. Playing at number six was Martin Gavigan. The storm had blown over. In a couple of weeks he would be Australia-bound as vice-captain of the Irish team. He was in the clear and played like a Trojan against Dublin. In Australia, the Aussies would dub him 'the iron man from Donegal'. They got that right. The Aussies, who knew a footballer when they saw one, would have loved Rambo to stay. "I wasn't tempted to stay – there's no place like home," laughs Martin. Astonished by his physical condition, several leading commentators rated him in better shape than many of the fabulously well-paid professional footballers. Gavigan loved it:

It was a professional experience because we went for a month and trained twice a day. It was similar to the lifestyle of professional soccer players. Once we got out there it was all football. To have no other job but to play football for a month was some experience!

I met a lot of the big characters of Gaelic football. Jack O'Shea was the star. All the players you had ever admired were there and to be a part of it was amazing. It was more than I expected. I was bitterly dissappointed for Martin McHugh at the time because both of us put in the same effort in the lead up but James McCartan was better connected and was selected instead to go to Australia.

Manus and Joyce were in deadly form against Dublin, between them notching 2-8 of Donegal's total. And when Donegal needed it, McEniff was in top form on the line. Molloy and Ryan were introduced with less than 15 minutes to go and any chance of a threatened Dublin revival was nipped in the bud. "The show," remarked the Follower, "was back on the road."

Donegal never enjoyed playing against Down, their style of football always caused Donegal problems. A first corrective step was taken a fortnight after the Dublin game when a mediocre Donegal recorded a remarkable draw in Newry. Donegal made their first acquaintance with Peter Whitnell that day. Martin Shovlin – pound for pound probably the toughest man on the Donegal team – had to mark him when he came on as a sub. Shovlin shook his head as he remembered it, "The ball wasn't near us when Whitnell came on and he just walked right over the top of me. I asked myself, 'What kind of brute is this?'"

Down squandered opportunities throughout the game and never managed to pull too far ahead of a dogged Donegal. Then, with 20 minutes' remaining, Declan Bonner got his marching orders and Donegal began playing football. Even so, with seven minutes left, they were still trailing by two points. Then Murray's fist connected with a Manus pass and the ball was in the Down net. Down answered with a point from Peter Whitnell but that was it. Full time. Donegal had just robbed a valuable league point in Newry. The game was also significant in that Noel Hegarty made an appearance with 15 minutes to go and played well. The last piece of the 1992 jigsaw was now in place.

❅ ❅ ❅ ❅

Ulster was dominating the Railway Cup competition at this time and would defend their title in 1991. Martin Shovlin, John Joe Doherty, Gary Walsh and Declan Bonner would all be involved in the winning team in 1991. Always a confidence player, Bonner found his involvement with the Ulster squad to be most rewarding, "I played with quality players like James McCartan, Greg Blaney, Peter Canavan, Mickey Linden and Ross Carr. Playing with men like that helped my confidence no end."

Confidence is everything. Although a member of the All-Ireland under-21

Joyce McMullan

photograph courtesy of the Irish News

winning panel of 1982, Martin Shovlin had been shocked to be asked to a trial for the senior team in 1984. "We went for soup and sandwiches before the game," he recalled, "Michael Carr, Mickey Lafferty and Martin Griffin were all there. I asked myself what was I doing there. I felt so small. I got chatting to the boys afterwards and got over it." Brought into the panel by Tom Conaghan in 1986, his inclusion raised eyebrows. There were those who thought the Dunkineely man wasn't fit for the inter-county scene. How wrong they were. Shovlin would almost burst with pride when he pulled on the green and gold and would, time and again put his body on the line for the cause. Brave to a fault, Shovlin quickly became a favourite with players and fans alike.

In November 1990 he was honoured by the Ulster GAA sports writers and named player of the year. For a man who just went out and played his football, it was an unforeseen accolade:

> It was unexpected. Mickey Linden was in his prime, as was James McCartan, DJ Kane and Martin McQuillan of Armagh, who I thought was probably the best player you could ever watch. It was an honour all right.

❊ ❊ ❊ ❊

November also brought Kerry to Ballyshannon. Jack O'Shea was by then in the twilight of a truly magnificent career during which he had achieved everything there was to achieve in Gaelic football. The man was a footballing god. Those who paid in to Fr Tierney Park that Sunday at the end of November caught a glimpse of his genius as he dominated proceedings for the hour. Even so, Jacko's best efforts weren't enough. Donegal, see, had Declan Bonner. For 50 minutes Kerry led while Donegal stayed in close pursuit but in the final ten the Na Rossa man led the charge that carried Donegal past the winning post by 1-12 to 0-12. The boys were just back from a week in Portugal where they had enjoyed much needed break after an arduous season. Maurice Fitzgerald then, had company in the tanned stakes in Ballyshannon.

Kerry's threat emanated from Jacko and Maurice. Noel Hegarty was in from the start and found himself on the much lauded Eamon Breen. Hegarty wrapped him up. Matt's encounter with his opponent was brilliantly captured by Michael Daly in the *Democrat*: "Matt Gallagher was the master. David Farrell by the end a student who had wished he had not tried to be funny with the teacher." John Joe and Razda handed out lessons too. Reid was on Fitzgerald and again Michael Daly was on form in acknowledging the Killygordon man's important contribution: "Donal Reid struggled against Fitzgerald, the same perhaps can be said of Fitzgerald who against a less res-olute defender would have had free expression for his talents."

With just over ten minutes left and leading by two points, Kerry missed a sitter. Then Declan Bonner, with two points already to his credit, swung it for Donegal. Bonner – always one of the fittest of the squad – left three Kerry defenders for dead and slotted a goalbound-effort past the Peter O'Leary in the Kerry goals. Tony Boyle, hovering with intent, smashed it to the net before it crossed the line. Grand larceny had just been committed on a Rossess man by a Rossess man! Jacko equalised for Kerry but Tommy Ryan was rediscovering old form around the middle and spraying ball into the boys. Kerry were forced to foul Tony Boyle twice, Bonner converted both frees and to put the icing on the cake Gerry Curran swung over a third. Not bad. Three matches played, two wins and a draw.

Meath ended any notions Donegal might be getting about themselves at the beginning of December in Navan. In a niggly and hard-hitting encounter, forwards on both sides came in for special attention. John Cunningham was marking Colm O'Rourke again:

> I had hurt my groin and probably shouldn't have played but the temptation to go out and mark him again was just too great. I took up from where I had left off in Croke Park and started manhandling him and pushing him around. He swung his fist and got me right in the Adam's apple and nearly put it down my throat. I wasn't able to breathe. It was as much as to say, "don't fucking come near me today". I didn't get going at all and was substituted.

As the Donegal defence struggled, a Meath goal after ten minutes set the pace and Donegal were always playing catch-up. When they eventually did equalise through Bonner, who was having yet another good outing, almost 25 minutes remained. That was to be their last score as Meath notched up both the pace and the physical contact. All pretence at discipline broke down. Donegal couldn't outdo Meath at their own game for a second time and – roared on by a fiercely partisan crowd – the home side had four points to spare in the end.

It would prove to be a minor setback. And Christmas 1990 would prove that bit special for Joyce McMullan. When the All-Star team was announced in December, the Four Masters man was in with the best of them, becoming Donegal's fourth All-Star. Joyce had been nominated with three of his colleagues – John Joe, Shov and John Cunningham – but in the end was the only one to make it. It was a richly deserved honour for the Donegal left half-forward ahead of Cork's Paul McGrath and Kerry superstar Maurice Fitzgerald. Shovlin and Gavigan would find themselves in Toronto with Joyce in the New Year – both would be selected as All-Star replacements. Joyce was modest about his achievement, "I had played reasonably well, although not spectacularly well by any means. I was very proud and saw it as an achievement on behalf of the team as well."

Over in Bundoran, McEniff was also a happy man. The latest accolade to come his way was a noteworthy one – All-Star manager. The boys and their newly decorated manager were glad of the festive break but the fanatics among those who followed the green and gold couldn't wait for 1991 and the next instalment in what was becoming an enthralling journey.

❈ ❈ ❈ ❈

There was a school of thought that held Cork should be brought to the back of beyond for the opening national league game of 1991. In the event, the All-Ireland champions were hosted at MacCumhaill Park in February but payback for the inflicted double trip to Lee-side a year earlier was duly delivered when Donegal had three points to spare at the end of 60 absorbing minutes.

Few would disagree that the Gaelic Athletic Association is one of the world's greatest sporting organisations. Unfortunately, in common with all sporting organisations, it has questionably implemented rules. One such rule deemed that players who had served suspension were ineligible for inclusion in the All-Star system. The rule has since been dropped. For a player such as Declan Bonner, this rule fused tragedy with injustice. Bonner's Donegal career was speckled with the occasional sending-off, mostly as a result of being in the wrong place at the wrong time or by picking up two bookings. Dogs on the street, even those who didn't follow the game, knew Bonner as one of the sport's gentlemen.

The man was in a rich vein of form and had been for a year now. It merited an All-Star. Sometimes the rules were an ass. Bonner was still in lethal form, far too good to be tucked away in the corner so McEniff hauled him out to centre half-forward for Cork's visit. It didn't matter to Bonner, he roasted All-Star centre half-back, Conor Counihan, for the hour.

The final score read 1-9 to 1-6. Never mind Skibbereen, this was revenge for Ballincollig. Both goals came from penalties. Dave Barry buried one, Declan Bonner buried the other. It wasn't the greatest Donegal performance – all but one of the scores came from the dead ball – but a win was always a win and Cork were reigning All-Ireland champions. And Tony Boyle was proving to be some full-forward. Niall Cahalane became the latest full-back with no answer.

Noel Hegarty had made himself right at home in the heart of the Donegal defence. His thundering gallops down the middle had a certain Kevin Moran quality to them. The defence, from Gary Walsh out, was watertight but Hegarty brought a new dimension to Donegal's play which was already paying dividends. And Molloy was on the way back, coming in for ten valuable minutes and raising the kind of cheer that once would have greeted Martin Griffin.

Armagh were next up but Donegal now had the whip hand over the Orchard County. Barry McGowan made an appearance in the half-forward line and impressed. Barry Cunningham also made a welcome return and shored up midfield when he came on. James McHugh made a first appearance since the

All-Ireland semi-final and Molloy joined the fray for the second time in a week. And for another of the old hands, Donal Reid, the Armagh match had added significance. Reid had lined out for his county a remarkable 100 times. There was nothing to be said, the statistic spoke for itself.

Sean Bonner was back in the Donegal jersey after a long layoff and came in at full-back in the absence of Matt for both the Cork and Armagh matches. Sean Bonner was something of an enigma. He could take a club game – against all-comers – by the scruff of the neck and turn it on its head. He was equally capable of replicating the feat in a county jersey, and occasionally did, but never displayed the same tenacity and utter ruthlessness that predominated his play in the white and black of Na Rossa. Paddy Hegarty and himself would be the only two players who started the games against Cork and Armagh that spring of 1991 who would not be there on All-Ireland Sunday. Against Armagh, Sean Bonner was magnificent.

Up front the Boyles and Declan Bonner wrecked Armagh. Tony Boyle simply sizzled against John Grimley and was already on the verge of his first Ulster jersey. Declan Bonner was, yet again, the man. According to Tony Boyle, Bonner referred to himself as 'The Legend' although this was in relation to the craic on the back of the bus. Nonetheless, Armagh would have appreciated the label as he hit 2-2 in Donegal's 2-8 to 1-7 victory. Donegal, with a match left to play, were in the quarter-final of the national league for a second year running.

❄ ❄ ❄ ❄

Long bus trips to national league games were the norm for Donegal players throughout the 1980s and 1990s. The dynamics of the seating arrangements were fascinating. Martin Griffin would have held court at the back of the bus on many trips. Charisma just dripped from Griffin. People couldn't help but like him and the younger players would gather around him lapping up the tallest of tall tales. By the early 1990s, it was the old hands that had made the back of the bus their own. "Not just anybody could sit at the back of the bus," remembered Donal Reid:

> You had to earn your place there. You had to be a singer, or attempt to sing, if you wanted to be at the back of the bus. Molloy, Joyce, Matt and me would always be there and we'd initiate the singing on the way home. We could put words and notes to anything. We mightn't have known a song but we would have made an attempt at anything. After winning a game everybody wanted to come down the back but we were always there, win, lose or draw. Our driver Francie Marley had an awful lot to put up with. He must have wondered how we could sing after losing.

"Reid was always good for song or a joke from the back of the bus," recalled Declan Bonner, "And Molloy would often sing 'My lovely old Finn Town.'" A few bottles of beer would help hasten the journey home. "Molloy would sing 'Noreen Bawn' too," remembered Noel Hegarty, "In fact, he always claimed to have been related to her." "Charlie Mulgrew was never far away either," recalled Matt Gallagher:

> Mulgrew might start to sing a rugby song like 'Swing low sweet chariot'. Reid would then pucker his face up and sing a song in German or Italian. It would be absolutely hilarious. Wee Austin Kennedy would come down. He's from Offaly and we'd get on to him about Offaly. We had some mighty craic.

The boys took a bus trip to Roscommon in March with nothing at stake and nothing to play for. The home side romped to a 1-10 to 0-4 win as Donegal tuned out for the hour. Minds had already turned to Offaly and the quarter-final. And championship training had begun in earnest as McEniff switched training to the beach.

The best part of a month elapsed before the meeting with Eugene McGee's Offaly. It was a useful month. McHugh was on the way back, almost ready to rejoin the fray and would make the subs bench for the quarter-final. Molloy's knee was holding out, he too was on the bench. Brian Tuohy had finally bettered his ankle injury and was on the fringe of a first team place. At just the right time, with Cavan ahead in the championship, McEniff's injury list was finally diminishing. A bit of depth was returning to the panel. So much so that in training a few nights before the Offaly game, McEniff played his intended team against the others. The 'others' might well have faced Offaly themselves such was their calibre: John Cunningham, Donal Reid (who McEniff decided to rest for a fortnight), Paul Carr, Anthony Molloy, Barry Cunningham, Michael Gallagher (back from the States again), the two McHughs, Gerry Curran and Charlie Mulgrew. Impressive. John Cunningham was struggling with a groin injury and it would see him miss out on the championship completely.

Tony Boyle was busy too with the under-21s. Captaining them from centre half-forward, the Dungloe man had joined forces with John Duffy and two lads who would win All-Ireland medals as subs in 1992 – Jim McGuinness of Naomh Conaill and Mark Crossan of St Eunans. Burt's Paul Callaghan, who would graduate to become Gary Walsh's understudy, was among the subs. They fell at the hands of a magnificent Tyrone team – on their way to an All-Ireland title – which included Chris Lawn, Fay Devlin, Adrian Cush and a legend in the making, Peter Canavan.

❋ ❋ ❋ ❋

"I want to get into Croke Park as often as I can to play games. We need the experience of playing there before big crowds." The words of Brian McEniff several weeks before the Offaly game. It was not to be and the game was fixed for Breffni Park. Unfortunate, in that Donegal were to defeat Offaly by 1-16 to 0-16 and had the victory occurred in Croke Park an old hoodoo would have been banished.

Donegal made hard work of Offaly, eventually dispatching them deep in the second half of extra-time. It was not pleasant to watch. Old habits best forgotten, illustrated by 27 wides, had returned. There was no doubt about it, the victory had been largely fashioned and executed by the efforts of half a dozen Donegal players. The others merely turned up. New to the squad, Noel Hegarty didn't enjoy the experience of marking Vinny Claffey, "I was very young at the time and maybe if I was a few years older I would have got by. But, from start to finish, Vinny Claffey gave me the biggest roasting I ever got." Claffey finished with three of his county's 16 points.

Yet the game had its moments. It was a day when Manus had a woeful opening period, was substituted and then sent back on. Recovering from a hamstring injury, Manus got three points in the second half of extra time and swung the game for Donegal:

> I couldn't get a kick at the start and McEniff took me off. Mickey Lafferty told me to get showered but McEniff told me to hold on and brought me back on. As soon as I came back on the ball landed in my hands and it was the first time that I had an opportunity to have a go. The last 20 minutes of every game are loose and that's the easiest time to play.

Martin McHugh made a brief appearance but had some way to go. Gavigan the Iron Man, Gallagher from Glenties and Joyce the All-Star were the others who contributed most to the victory. Even though Donegal hadn't done much to dispel a theory ventured some months earlier by Eugene McGee that "you can't make a silk purse out of a sow's ear," it was sweet to put one over on their harshest critic from the All-Ireland semi-final defeat.

It was also the day the Donegal footballing public made an uneasy acquaintance with a former Mayo star, Padraig Brogan, who had declared for Donegal. It was a relationship that never fully blossomed but a few interesting twists lay ahead. Brogan made a decent debut when he came on in the second half.

Padraig Brogan was a Mayo man and scored a spectacular goal for his native county in the 1985 All-Ireland semi-final defeat to Dublin. Things had gone badly for the big man in the meantime. Brogan was friendly with Seanie McEniff, son of Donegal manager Brian and, in 1991, came to Donegal looking for a new start. McEniff took him under his wing finding him employment and bringing him into the county squad. "The Bundoran club took him on," remembered McEniff:

> But while he was a very good player, he wasn't a good squad player.

Although he was quite a clever fella, he was so lazy within himself that he scarcely knew the names of all the lads. At training he'd shout 'Oi, oi, oi,' when he was looking for a pass.

"He could have at least tried to make friends with the lads," felt Martin Shovlin, "But he was the laziest man I ever met. He wouldn't train because he didn't know how to." Declan Bonner found Brogan to be affable, but in this tight-knit Donegal squad that had soldiered together for so long, there wasn't really room for an individualist like him. Bonner thought that he was, "a likeable fella, but just didn't put it in training-wise and that was a bit frustrating for some of the players. He had lots of potential and could turn matches, but he played as an individual."

※ ※ ※ ※

There was no sleep for left half-back Martin Shovlin on the night before the league semi-final against Kildare, but it wasn't pre-match nerves that were keeping him awake:

> I was rooming with Brogan. We had the team meeting and all hands went to bed at about 11.30. I could hear music and thought it must be coming from a disco downstairs. I could then make out that it was traditional music but couldn't work out where it was coming from. I could see movement in the other bed and looked over to see Brogan wearing headphones and listening to Irish music. I roared at him but he never even heard me. This went on all night and I could hardly get a wink of sleep.

For Donegal, it seemed that Croke Park was cursed. Another opportunity to bury the ghost of failure was relinquished – and tamely at that. Another day to omit from the memory bank for players, management and long-suffering supporters.

The Lilywhites in the National Football League semi-final was a prospect that should not have unduly worried Donegal, even though the wily Mick O'Dwyer was now working his magic on the plains of Kildare. Great game but the 1-10 to 0-14 defeat hurt. A lot. Something somewhere was wrong. Leading 1-8 to 0-6 at half time, Donegal were coasting. Donegal's goal had come from the boot of Tony Boyle who has only a hazy memory of it, "I got the goal after collecting a bad kick-out. The full-back slipped and I remember the ball going to my foot, but until I saw it on television that night, I didn't remember where it went."

The second half belonged to Kildare and their rising star, Martin Lynch. They hit the lead for the first time with 12 minutes remaining, and, although Donegal equalised, Kildare had the stamina and know-how to reclaim and hold onto a one-point lead.

Michael Daly was there for the *Democrat*. He was in no mood for taking prisoners. The players were accused of being short on heart. But it was McEniff's performance which mostly fell under Daly's scrutiny. "Too many cooks," he remarked, in reference to the plethora of selectors that surrounded McEniff in the shadow of the Cusack Stand. Too many changes that left both the team and the selectors in utter confusion. It was a view widely held. An opportunity to exploit Gerry Curran's red-hot form was spurned by a slow positional switch. And what was going on with Molloy? Why use Brogan and not the big Ardara man just when he was needed most to lift the team and the supporters? Whatever about Padraig Brogan's reputation in the green and red of Mayo, he was no Anthony Molloy. But 1991 would be the year that Molloy and his manager would not see eye to eye.

The atmosphere in the dressing room after the match was tense, remembered Tony Boyle:

> There were a lot of harsh words in the dressing room afterwards. I remember that I left disgusted because we were so close to a league final and we fucked up. I had played well but I was upset because it was all about getting to Croke Park and finals.

* * * *

There were other issues, but the arrival of Brogan had undoubtedly troubled the boys. He was never truly accepted. Things were a little slack. Rumour was that some of the boys were enjoying themselves too much – McEniff moved on that one and introduced a ban on drink until after the championship.

McEniff understood that the boys would sometimes need to let off steam and, although a lifelong teetotaller, he knew that allowing them to have a drink would permit this. Occasionally he would take them away to a hotel and let them have a drink in a private bar – it wouldn't do to have the word going around the county that the boys were on the piss! Brian Murray remembers one of those occasions:

> McEniff allowed us to have a few beers and me and Shov were the last two to got to bed. Molloy was always one of the last ones to go too. There wasn't a bother on Shov the next morning. Matt, on the other hand, would have been cute. He would have taken a drink but went to bed early to sleep and prepare for the training the next day. McEniff put us through our paces the next morning. It was torture. Molloy and me were lagging behind and were dying.

Shovlin was by far the fittest man on the panel. No matter what Anthony Harkin would set for the players – 20-yard sprints or two-mile runs – Shov would finish first. One night, Harkin turned off the bleep test machine because all the others had dropped out and there was no sign of Shovlin letting the beeps beat him. Shovlin remembers the training session where Padraig Brogan led the way:

> We spent a weekend in Bundoran. It was supposed to be a training session but it ended up as a drinking session. McEniff came into the hotel at about 5am and tried to put everybody to bed. He left at about an hour later and told us that we had training in the morning. The training was at 11 and we hadn't the beds warmed. How bad was it when Brogan won every sprint? He couldn't beat anybody in the squad but he won every sprint that morning and thought he was a great man!

While the defeat to Kildare had been a sickener, in fairness to McEniff his focus and training schedule was directed towards the championship meeting with Cavan at the beginning of June. The boys were still on the sand, the sharpness wasn't there just yet. What Donegal really needed was a leader on the field. That had been missing in recent outings. What Donegal got was Martin McHugh. The General was back in time for the championship.

✳ ✳ ✳ ✳

The Cavan match was McHugh's 100th game for Donegal. McEniff didn't start him but he came on with 15 minutes to go, by then the match was won. A first step, a tentative one at that, had been taken in the defence of an Ulster title. The Donegal performance was nothing to write home about but as Tom Humphries noted in the *Irish Times*, "It is Ulster after all and any win is a good win". The first hurdle had been cleared.

Cavan had the breeze and used it well in the first half. The Donegal forwards found it hard to shake the Cavan-imposed shackles and it took a Michael Gallagher goal a few minutes before half time to level proceedings at 1-4 to 0-7. Cavan had stood shoulder to shoulder – toe to toe – with the defending champions in the first half. It was all to do in the second 35.

That Donegal put eight points between themselves and Cavan by the final whistle indicated a comfortable afternoon at the office. It wasn't quite that simple. Donegal hit a purple patch in the second half and Cavan, in fairness, had at that point endured their fair share of misfortune with the woodwork.

The purple patch was instigated by a classic Martin Gavigan steal from Barry McArdle. With Cavan committed to the attack Gavigan swiped the ball from the boot of McArdle and thundered downfield before unleashing a marvellous kick that resulted in a fine individual point. That score sparked 12 minutes of plunder in the Cavan half of the pitch – a rampage which reaped the bountiful harvest of one goal and seven points; 2-14 to 0-12 read the scoreboard at the town end on the final whistle.

Mulgrew was back in the fray. By the time he was called ashore with six or seven minutes remaining he had run himself into the ground and had been involved in everything. Reid, having availed of the brief rest imposed by McEniff, was back in championship form. "Inspirational," noted the *Irish Independent*. Matt, John Joe and Sean Bonner were in similar form. Before the end the Cavan mentors would substitute their entire full-forward line so dominant were the three boys at the back. Gavigan was the dominant player on the pitch. The Follower was impressed with his style: "His hands were safe, his tackling tenacious and positive and above all else he cleared his lines with authority, speed and intelligence". Molloy was only on a couple of minutes when he had the ball in the Cavan net for Donegal's second goal and the biggest cheer of the day.

A back injury had ruled out Joyce McMullan at the last minute. An out-of-favour Shovlin got back in his place. Tom Humphries noted that there was no sign of Gerry Curran. Further investigation revealed the reason: "Curran, a splendid if erratic half-forward, is doing penance for skipping a recent training session and even McMullan's defection was not enough to win him absolution".

✻ ✻ ✻ ✻

With Cavan accounted for, Donegal's passage to a third Ulster final in four years was virtually assured. PJ McGowan had steered Fermanagh past Armagh but his young side were not expected to create a serious obstacle for the defending champions. And so it turned out at Healy Park, Omagh, and for the second time in three weeks, Donegal had eight points to spare in the Ulster championship.

The team that faced Fermanagh was: Gary Walsh; John Joe Doherty, Matt Gallagher, Noel Hegarty; Donal Reid, Martin Gavigan, Martin Shovlin; Brian Murray, Michael Gallagher; Barry McGowan, Martin McHugh, Joyce McMullan; Declan Bonner, Tony Boyle, Manus Boyle. Hegarty, McMullan and McHugh had replaced Sean Bonner, Charlie Mulgrew and Tommy Ryan from the Cavan game.

As a contest there was little to report. Bonner, who would finish with 0-6, had Donegal on the scoreboard inside the minute. Thirty seconds later the match as a contest was over. McHugh announced his return by putting Tony Boyle clean through for the only goal of the game – the ball duly slammed to the net by the grateful full-forward. As Cliona Foley reported for the *Irish Independent*, it was Declan Bonner who led a potent Donegal attack: "The work-rate of himself and all the Donegal forwards off the ball, combined with some brilliant point taking, had run the Fermanagh backs ragged by half time".

Indeed they had. The *Democrat* would describe McHugh as the "architect" and Bonner as "the executer of the plan". At the interval the score stood at 1-10 to 0-5. Donegal coasted after the break and although Fermanagh matched their tally of eight second-half points, another Ulster final spot was in the bag.

A False Dawn

Fermanagh had been poor – it was difficult to judge Donegal. The Follower noted that "the pace was not championship. It was not even national league." His editor, Michael Daly, agreed a "challenge match-type atmosphere" had prevailed. With Derry or Down destined for the final, Donegal could have done with a sterner test. Even so a necessary task had been accomplished.

*　*　*　*

By the time Donegal contested and won their sixth Dr McKenna Cup title at the beginning of July, it was known that Down would oppose them in the Ulster Final. It had taken Down two games to shake off a Derry side who had already accounted for much-fancied Tyrone. The news was greeted with some dismay by football folk in the county. Derry would have been the favoured opposition. Down had trouble written all over them. Linden, Blaney, McCartan, Whitnell, Kane, O'Rourke and Carr. Dangerous, a county with the arrogance to believe themselves capable of victory against anyone. An arrogance forged in the All-Ireland successes of the 1960s.

McEniff started Molloy in the middle for the McKenna Cup final against Tyrone. In too was Barry Cunningham who had returned from London earlier in the year only to find midfield particularly congested – Cunningham's cause was not helped by Padraig Brogan's continued presence. Leslie McGettigan also got a run-out for the first time since returning from the States. The two-point win revealed little. Molloy collected the cup as captain but didn't appear any closer to regaining his midfield berth for the Ulster Final.

He wasn't. When McEniff named the team he intended to send into battle against Down there was only two changes from the side that faced Fermanagh. Out went Shov and Noel Hegarty. In came Sean Bonner and Mulgrew – Charlie would captain the team in Molloy's absence. Charlie was as surprised as the next:

> I had been captain when we won the McKenna Cup in 1985. I was made captain in the week of the Ulster Final. We weren't prepared for those kind of things at that time. Things were different then and the level of preparation was not as meticulous as it is now. Nowadays every little thing is looked at and discussed. Back then you were made captain and it was expected that whatever qualities you had would be enough to do the business.

More than one eyebrow was arched. What *was* the story with Molloy? His influence and inspiration would be missed. Noel Hegarty could be considered unfortunate but what the hell was Shov, the Ulster footballer of the year, doing sitting in the dugout? McEniff explained his selection to the *Irish Times*:

> I don't believe there is such a thing really as a best 15. I pick the best 15

from game to game. The pitch at Clones is small, so I take that into account for Sunday. The weather forecast isn't good, so I think about that. Down are a tough team, hard and physical, so that comes into consideration. Then I have to think about who is fittest, who is going best in training, who will do the best job on a particular player. I feel for the players who are dropped but I have to do what is best.

In fairness, it was a tough call. Team selection was the part of the job McEniff hated, even fretted about. But someone had to do it. McEniff had now played his cards. The stage was set. Neither Donegal nor Down knew it – no-one did then – but they were both on the verge of history. One would capture that year's Sam Maguire, one would have to wait a little over a year.

※ ※ ※ ※

Preparations weren't all that they could have been. "Down caught us badly on the hop," remembered Charlie Mulgrew:

> We weren't properly focussed on it. We kept a man out of the photograph that day because we were thinking about making money from the team photograph. We were trying to think ahead and all the stuff was filtering through.

"Sam or burst," the Follower had declared. It was burst for Donegal and Down's turn first. Anyway the Anglo-Celt had to be contested beforehand. The national spotlight had turned north once more. Donegal, wrote their old adversary, Liam Hayes, was a team "quietly nursing their wounded ambition". Hayes, like a lot of others, felt that 1991 might just be Donegal's year. Were they to get out of Ulster, well . . .

> With the Ulster title in their possession, and then immediately left to one side, Donegal can seriously consider winning an All-Ireland for the first time. They may look about them and quickly realise that perhaps they are destined to win it. Destiny?

Hayes knew the score in Ulster however. Getting out of it was the problem. "The spirit of Ulster finals has never been very sympathetic towards destiny," acknowledged the Meath midfielder. Derry had been the last team to successfully defend their Ulster title and that was as far back as 1976. Ulster was a minefield. But, like the rest of the boys, Brian Murray was dreaming of another chance. "We really believe we could win an All-Ireland this time, if we just get a second chance out of Ulster," he said in the run-up to the match.

A False Dawn

That second chance didn't materialise in 1991. Down turned the tables on Donegal and it was the Mourne men who left Clones with eight points to spare and an All-Ireland on their minds.

Every game of football has moments that matter and moments that don't. And there are moments when absolutely everything is on a hinge. That moment arrived 18 minutes into the second half of the Ulster final. Down, who had run Donegal ragged and led by 1-9 to 0-5 at the interval, had been clawed back to four points. Then Barry McGowan won the ball and bore down on goalie Neil Collins. His goalbound effort came desperately close but Collins had the measure of it, *just*. DJ Kane cleaned up the spillage and hoofed the ball upfield where Barry Breen was on hand to fire over a point. Matt would have been close to winning the player of the Ulster championship award. When McGowan missed, he could see that chance slipping away. "Barry McGowan could have scored a goal," he recalled:

But the 'keeper made a good save. They came up the pitch, got a point and the game was as good as over. I was disconsolate after the match because I was sure, as were a lot of the other guys, that we were going to win the Ulster final. It was overconfidence rather than confidence and it cost us.

That point was, wrote Philip Quinn in the *Irish Independent*, "like a dagger through the heart of Donegal's championship challenge".

That left the score at 0-8 to 1-10. It was all up. In truth, Down hadn't looked back since the eighth minute of the first half. DJ Kane had levelled matters at 0-2 apiece and then Down proceeded to tear Donegal apart. "Quite simply, Donegal were left breathless by the pace, panache and precision of this Down display," noted the *Independent*. Mickey Linden, a forward who struck fear into the hearts of opposing players and supporters alike, had Gary Walsh picking the ball out of the net for the first time that year in the championship. Linden pounced following a mix-up between John Joe and Sean Bonner and rifled the ball past Walsh to set Down on their way. That man Linden again. For Walsh it was all too similar to a goal conceded in the 1989 replayed final:

As in 1989, two fellas collided and the ball was fed in to Linden. I was at the Rosslea end and he was coming across me. I dived full-length and was only inches away from getting the ball, but he was so quick that he got around me and stuck it in the net.

I always remember the goals in the 1989 and 1991 Ulster finals. Maybe they didn't cost us the games but they were crucial goals at crucial stages. They stemmed from a lack of communication between the defenders. The goals wouldn't have happened if the team had been more settled. At least one of the fellas involved in each of the incidents wouldn't normally have played. When you have the same players playing all the time the communication improves. It shows how important communication is because there was a lack of it for a split second in each of those matches and bang – two goals were conceded.

Liam Hayes had issued a warning in the run-up to the game. "It could be one of those easy days for the Down forwards. If it is and the ball is being played fast and accurately, it is unlikely that the Donegal defence will be able to cope for the entire afternoon," he mused. It was an accurate prophesy. When referee Damien Campbell sounded the final whistle the score stood at 0-10 to 1-15. "We were annihilated," remembered Martin McHugh.

Down playmaker Greg Blaney had hit three sublime points, "The best I've seen from him ever," remarked Down manager Pete McGrath afterwards. And their right corner forward was simply majestic. "Mickey Linden sent a live current through the game with his every touch," noted Tom Humphries. And then there was McCartan, Carr, Mason and Breen. Electrifying. The better team had won. Donegal had been tepid by comparison.

It was Donegal's third Ulster final in a row and Barry McGowan, having made a brief appearance as a substitute the previous year, came in for the dropped Martin Shovlin. Marking him was the experienced Ross Carr who would collect an All-Star award before the year was out. "We weren't prepared for what was going to happen," recalled McGowan:

Down just swept us off our feet that day. Ross Carr thumped into me at one stage and, in my stupidity, I decided to thump him back. I quickly realised that it was the wrong thing to do because he then caught me with an uppercut that knocked me off my feet. He was a lot bigger and stronger than I was and I got what I deserved.

Clones on Ulster final day is no place for half measures.

Some consolation, however slim, would be extracted from Down's eventual annexation of an All-Ireland title. But for now, as some 20,000 dejected Donegal supporters began the slow crawl north out of Clones, the post mortem began. As post mortems go this one would cut deep.

Donegal's middle eight had been annihilated. There was no other way of looking at it. "As a unit the half-forward line of McHugh, Mulgrew and McMullan appears to be finished," declared Michael Daly, adding, "The half-forwards against Meath last August were Martin and James McHugh and Joyce. That line failed then and it was the same three who finished last Sunday. Again they failed."

It was an opinion widely held and the three boys hadn't scored a point between them. Donegal had been found wanting in key positions. That they had lost to a team who would later prove their outstanding calibre by winning not one but two All-Ireland titles was not then known. What was known was that Donegal had failed yet again just when so much had been expected. "The problem was that were were only beating Cavan and Fermanagh to get to the final," felt Martin McHugh. "Down had an exceptional forward unit," remembered Joyce McMullan, "Our performance that day was cat and the only thing we had going for us was that they won the All-Ireland later that year and we took a bit of confidence from that."

Sean Bonner lasted only 15 minutes before being replaced by Noel Hegarty. Bonner had experienced a torrid quarter of an hour and showed his frustration by lamping James McCartan on the way off. The tragedy for Sean was that he was the only one of the starting 15 who would be gone out of the panel entirely by the time Donegal struck solid gold 14 months later. Padraig Brogan and James McHugh had also joined the fray, replacing Murray and Mulgrew respectively.

In the immediate gloom of the Clones aftermath, it was difficult to see a way back. Michael Daly predicted retirements. Others also saw the writing on the wall. The boat that might have carried this team to Croke Park on a third Sunday in September appeared to have run aground.

The Follower penned the words the whole county was thinking.

> Maybe the time has come for a few of our players who have graced the inter-county scene for so long to have a deep self-introspection and conclude 'enough is enough' by sliding gracefully from the scene. Hard, harsh words, but football life is hard and harsh and no room for sympathy or softness of heart when major honours are at stake.
>
> I'll not name names. The players themselves know, know that the bucket will only go to the well so often. They are all honest brokers. They know only too well having lived through the hardships of inter-county footballing life at the top level that it might be in the interests of Donegal football to step aside.

That the man from Dromod, a long-time champion of the players, felt Donegal were carrying "dead wood" was fairly representative of public opinion. Solid Donegal GAA folk figured that was indeed the case that July of 1991. It was over. Donegal had an ageing team. Matt, McHugh, Mulgrew, Joyce, Reid, Sean Bonner were some of the old hands and had been striving in the senior jersey for the best part of a decade. Manus Boyle remembered something Martin Griffin had told him a long time ago:

> Griffin used to say that it was harder to get off the Donegal team that to get on it. That was the way that McEniff managed the team and it's why the older players would have done anything for him. Players like me that spent years under him would have done anything for him but for some reason he wasn't happy that year.

Declan Bonner

While the supporters may have been disappointed with the Ulster Final defeat, the players were devastated. "Walking down the hill at Clones that day I thought we'd never be back to win it," remembered Martin McHugh, "the only plus was that Down went on to win the All-Ireland." Minutes earlier some of the older hands had engaged in a frank discussion in the loser's dressing room. "I was sitting with Martin McHugh and Joyce and we talked about retiring," recalled Donal Reid, "We said we'd give it one more year." Brian Murray was despondent too:

Coming away from Clones, I asked myself if Donegal was ever going to achieve anything. It was the same old story. Bernie Flynn got a poxy goal the previous year for Meath and that day two boys collided to let Mickey Linden in for a goal. I thought that was it and we were never going to get a chance. I was 27 and the team was getting on in years.

❋ ❋ ❋ ❋

Donegal supporters gleaned some consolation from their trip to Clones. The minors, contesting an Ulster Final against Tyrone, were victorious by a point – 1-10 to 1-9. It was the Donegal of Damien Diver, the Boyles – Declan and Mark, Donal Buggy, Ronan McLaughlin and James Ruane. They would fall by three points to Cork in Croke Park in the All-Ireland semi-final.

❋ ❋ ❋ ❋

The following day Joyce McMullan, Tommy Ryan and Charlie Mulgrew headed to Dungloe in search of some peace and quiet. "Charlie told us he was packing in his county career," remembered Joyce, "It was lucky for him that he changed his mind."

The relationship between McEniff and his erstwhile captain Molloy had reached its nadir. In the aftermath of the Ulster Final Molloy retired from inter-county football and headed to New York where he won a championship.

I was still captain in 1991 and Brian and me had a great relationship – we always did and still have. When you're involved at that level you'll have ups and downs. Brogan, was a good enough player, but I don't think he ever fitted into the Donegal style of football. Brian persisted with him but it just didn't work out. Brogan was individualistic and wasn't a team player.

I felt that I should have played in the 1991 Ulster Final. Although I had an operation on my knee earlier in the year I had come back and thought I was playing well. I was given 15 minutes here and there in the matches prior to the final but wasn't selected for the final. Down stuffed us. Things weren't right in the camp. I hung up the boots after that game and went to New York. I had no intentions of coming home to play county football again. I thought 1991 was the end of the road for me.

Manus recalled that things hadn't run as smoothly as they had in 1990:

> Even though we got to the Ulster Final, our preparation wasn't as good as in the previous year. It was not that the preparation changed, things just went better in 1990. Players were picking up silly injuries at training. There were a lot of rows going on. If the County Board wanted us to play at the level set by the likes of Meath and Cork, we wanted to be looked after. Players weren't getting expenses and there were other little things. Looking back now you might say they were petty, but we were training two or three nights a week and working hard on our fitness. Everything was put on hold for football. Nonetheless, as a team, Donegal always went out with the right attitude.

Martin Shovlin agreed that all was not well in the squad:

> Things weren't going that well at the time, especially after 1990 when we did so well. All of a sudden, McEniff was making wholesale changes across the board. I think he made a mistake in dropping men that were available. He was brave enough to stand up and see it through and stuck it out for 1992. He could have walked off the field in 1991 after getting hammered in the Ulster Final.

The jury was out on the manager. Donegal had lost out yet again at midfield and McEniff had chosen to leave Molloy sitting on the bench. The half-back line had been decimated but Shovlin was left in the dugout. Michael Daly remarked that:

> Donegal's lack of morale is something manager Brian McEniff must explain. He has fiddled about with the captaincy, trying to get a player it doesn't bother. He doesn't have a leading figure to lift the side.

McEniff and his squad had made the fatal mistake of underestimating Down in the championship. He had attended the Munster final – a game notable only for the fact that an average Limerick ran an ageing Kerry team to two points – in order to gain some intelligence of Donegal's All-Ireland semi-final opponents. Down hadn't read the script. "It was a very poor display by Donegal," felt McEniff:

> But it was great to see Down going on to win the All-Ireland for the first time in 23 years, we all got a great buzz out of it. Having comprehensively beaten Down in the couple of previous meetings, we underesti-

mated them and were caught cold with an early goal that allowed them to get their tails up. While Down had four or five good forwards, they had a bad defence but we just didn't play that day.

McEniff had a year of his term left to run but wasn't sure if he'd stay or go. The County Board had to be faced a week later. McEniff fielded serious flak: too many mentors; the absence of Molloy, Shovlin and Paul Carr; the uncertainty surrounding the captaincy; unrest in the camp. It was a rough ride. McEniff wasn't sure if he had anything more left to offer. September was in before it was learned that the Bundoran man would see out his third year. "It wasn't the way I would like to go out," he stated in explanation, referring to the Ulster Final debacle.

There were those who didn't know if that was good news or bad. In a bewildering exercise the *Democrat* printed a coupon inviting reaction to some 20 supposed alternatives to McEniff, including Martin Carney, Tom Conaghan, Eugene McGee, PJ McGowan, Martin McHugh and Brian Mullins who had just arrived in Donegal to take up a teaching post in Carndonagh.

In hindsight, had Donegal football lost the services of Brian McEniff in the autumn of 1991, the consequences could have been catastrophic. His going would almost certainly have heralded the end for several of the players who would climb the steps of the Hogan Stand 12 months later. A new man coming in would most likely have tried to build his own team – 1992 might not have happened.

Donegal needed McEniff's continued contribution at that point. Needed a man who would immerse himself in the job the way McEniff did. A man who would approach the task with McEniff's meticulous attention to detail. He wouldn't always garner the favour of the grassroots men, nor indeed the County Board men, but now was not the time for change.

Perhaps a neutral could offer a reason why Donegal needed the Bundoran man at the helm. For a couple of years now, Dublin-based journalists had watched Brian McEniff tick. The now annual sojourn by Donegal to Clones provided them both the opportunity and necessity to explore the enigma that was Brian McEniff. Tom Humphries of the *Irish Times* was the man for the job.

Humphries was a trifle surprised that McEniff wasn't worshiped in Donegal as the football saviour he was perceived to be beyond the county borders. McEniff himself was well aware of how he was perceived. "There are many places in the county where my face doesn't fit," he acknowledged to Humphries.

Humphries struck for gold and, with the professional detachment of an outsider who has listened well, got it in one:

The difficulty is perhaps that McEniff has so many faces. For those in the north of the county, he is a south county man, grounds enough for suspicion. For others he is a rich businessman with three hotels and substantial leisure interests in the Bundoran area. His family are something of a north-west dynasty. McEniff is a boarding school boy. A Fianna Fáiler. A perfectionist. A one-man employment agency for promising footballers. A father of ten. A teetotaller. A disciplinarian. A chancer.

His commitment to Donegal football was total. Extraordinary even. Journalists who had hung around McEniff and asked the pertinent questions of those in the know learned for themselves that McEniff's commitment was not to be found just anywhere. The man lived for Donegal. Humphries, as ever, went the extra mile and dug up a fascinating nugget on how McEniff operated:

'If the phone rings and it is to do with football, it is either a player, the County Board, the press or McEniff,' commented a rival inter-county manager. 'He is on at least once a week. How did your challenge game go? What sort of training are you doing? What are so and so at?' All the time he's fishing for information, looking for clues, yet when you ask him a question you suspect you aren't getting a straight answer. He tells you what he wants you to pass on. If he is upbeat, he is usually unsure of himself.'

Donegal were weary of defeat at the penultimate step but the word that McEniff was to stay was good news when it came. It was worth another shot surely. It could yet come good. He would have to sort the problems over the winter. Clear the air. Settle himself and settle his team and dance the dance come summer.

McEniff had mused before the Ulster final that if Donegal could bring back an All-Ireland the whole outlook would change in Ulster. In the event, it would be Down who would change that outlook. History indicated it was rarely the case that a team could capture an All-Ireland on their first visit to Croke Park. Down had exploded that myth in 1960. More than 30 championships had come and gone and again it was Down that provided Ulster football with the hope it needed. That September, Paddy O'Rourke and the boys from the Mournes planted a beacon firmly in place for Donegal and then Derry to follow. It marked the road out of Ulster and led all the way to Sam Maguire.

RESULTS

National League 1990-91
Donegal 2-11, Dublin 1-9
Donegal 1-7, Down 0-10
Donegal 1-12, Kerry 0-12
Donegal 0-10, Meath 1-11
Donegal 1-9, Cork 1-6
Donegal 2-8, Armagh 1-7
Donegal 0-4, Roscommon 1-10

Donegal 1-16, Offaly 0-16 (q/f)
Donegal 1-10, Kildare 0-14 (s/f)

Ulster Championship 1991
Donegal 2-14, Cavan 0-12
Donegal 1-18, Fermanagh 0-13
Donegal 0-10, Armagh 1-15

13

A Shot at Redemption and the Blues

(October 1991 – April 1992)

"It's never over until the Fat Lady sings."

CHARLIE REDMOND, BREFFNI PARK, APRIL 1992

October, and the promise of winter football. For the diehard supporters it was the return of hurried Sunday dinners, car journeys of varying lengths, an hour and a half spent wrapped up against the elements, kick by kick replays on the way home, and the results from around the country on the car radio on *Sunday Sport* with Des Cahill.

It was a chastened Donegal who prepared for the new-look national league. The summer had stung the boys. "We deserved a lot of the criticism," admitted Martin Gavigan, "It was one of those days – a lot was expected of us and we delivered little. We didn't have the appetite or buzz to win that Ulster Final." Rambo, honest as ever, went a step further, "I felt that had we gone through from Ulster we would not have made the same impact as Down." It was back to basics then.

Officialdom, in the form of the Games Administration Committee, had put on its dunce's hat and, with questionable wisdom, rejigged the league format. Donegal now found themselves in Division 1B with Antrim, Longford, Leitrim, Wicklow and Roscommon. "They're not the Meaths, Corks or Dublins of this world," remarked Declan Bonner. "A disaster for Donegal," agreed Gavigan, "We spent so many years trying to get into Division One, and had just established ourselves there playing good competitive matches against good teams, and then the whole thing is abolished!"

All the speculation about retirements had come to nothing. The boys were all still there or there thereabouts. Molloy had been the closest call and had actually decided to call it a day before changing his mind. Annoyed at not playing in the Ulster Final, Molloy met McEniff at an under-18 club match in Ballybofey:

I don't know if Brian had made a point of being at it but we ran into one another there. I hadn't spoken to Brian since the Ulster Final. Brian said, 'Molloy, it's time we buried the hatchet and had one more go at it'. I went back into the squad but with one or two conditions, such as retaining the captaincy.

Both men needed each other and, in time, Molloy would have cause to be thankful that he insisted on retaining the captaincy.

Bonner had signed for Finn Harps back in August but had committed first and foremost to Donegal. And Sylvester Maguire made a welcome return, back as good as ever after the ghastly leg break that had kept him out of football all year.

McEniff seemed to be on top of things again. The usual plethora of trials and challenge games kept him busy all October. He made sounds about injecting new life and new blood into his squad. This materialised in the form of Liam O'Neill from Malin, Mark McShane from Kilcar and Donal Bonner from Na Rossa. McShane would come closest to making an immediate breakthrough. Mark Crossan, Jim McGuinness and Paul Callaghan also emerged from the trials.

The challenge games saw Mayo defeated in Ballyshannon and significantly Dublin were held to a draw in Parnell Park. It was still there – the ability to mix it with the big boys. The Follower was encouraged, "When you go to Dublin and hold their best to level scores then your team cannot be too bad".

It was the end of October however before the real action got under way. McEniff's first selection for the opening game of the league reflected what he had learned in recent weeks. Nine of those who would play in the All-Ireland final 11 months later were there: Gary Walsh; John Joe Doherty, Paul Carr, Matt Gallagher; Martin Gavigan, John Cunningham, Noel Hegarty; Liam O'Neill, Padraig Brogan; Mark McShane, Tommy Ryan, Declan Bonner; Martin McHugh, Sylvester Maguire, Donal Bonner. Manus Boyle and Barry McGowan joined the fray from the dugout.

Antrim in Casement Park illustrated the futility of the new league. Donegal, at pedestrian pace, cruised to a 1-13 to 0-8 victory. It was a poor performance but top-drawer football simply was not required. "To win with such deficiencies in so many sectors is not going to do Donegal any good in the short or long term," worried Michael Daly, bemoaning the return to a lower grade of football.

The futility continued at MacCumhaill Park a week later. Longford paid a visit and managed a single point to Donegal's 1-7 in truly awful conditions in Ballybofey. Matt had moved to full-back again. The new boys – O'Neill, McShane and Donal Bonner – moved aside. The old faces were re-emerging. Shovlin was back and revelling as usual in the muck. James McHugh, Barry Cunningham and Tony Boyle also returned. The game was incidental.

The Killybegs men were flying too. Having brushed aside Red Hugh's in the county final, Jimmy White's men brought Donegal football some much-needed cheer by progressing all the way to the Ulster club final. Downpatrick were accounted for in the semi-final at Newcastle – a small measure of revenge extracted for Clones. Later, they would fail to lift the title under the most frustrating of circumstances against Castleblaney Faughs, but the point had been underlined yet again. Donegal footballers were as good as anything in Ulster. Maybe even better. John Cunningham remembers it as a chance missed, "We were a far better team than Castleblaney but we didn't bring all our players back from Norway and got beaten by two points. Fishing always affected us badly at that time of the year."

Although captain of the Donegal team in the pre-Christmas league games, John left for Paris early in the New Year. Good well-paid work – something that was in short supply in Donegal – was the attraction, "Brian tried to sort out a few things for me and wanted to set me up with a bit of work but I was not happy and went to Paris".

The final game before Christmas in the national league debacle brought Leitrim to Ballyshannon. In fairness to Leitrim, driven on by the efforts of Mickey Quinn and Declan Darcy, they made a match of it, albeit a poor one. But yet again the result was only ever going to finish one way and the 0-7 to 0-4 win not only put Donegal top of the table but virtually guaranteed a place in the quarter-final with just three matches played. Certainly another league point would suffice. This new league truly was a joke. The Follower spoke for the masses as he took a potshot at the committee up in Croke Park, "A plague upon all their houses I say. Give us back our old league".

Even so, the Leitrim game threw up a couple of interesting asides. Donegal only managed to hit the front, through Manus Boyle, in the last quarter. Notably, this coincided with the introduction from the bench of Anthony Molloy and Barry Cunningham. Brogan, who hadn't put a foot astray, was taken off. Eyebrows were raised. "The time has come to stop messing around with Brogan," instructed Michael Daly.

To all and sundry it was apparent that Brogan was being rejected by the Donegal players. There was no denying it. As far back as the national league semi-final against Kildare in April, it was clear to onlookers that the Mayo man was an outcast. Passes in his direction were not forthcoming that day in Croke Park. Martin Gavigan was aware of the problem at the time:

> He was obviously a little bit rejected due to the fact that when, or if, he got a place in the team then a born and bred Donegal man would be standing on the line. That created a bit of initial hassle. I've no objections to him – if the team is going to go anywhere Padraig Brogan is going to have to be accepted. The whole thing has, and will, affect the team if it's not sorted out. If a player doesn't like the thought of Brogan on the team then it's up to him to prove he's a better player.

The Brogan story had some way to go. Several twists and turns lay ahead and Padraig Brogan would play a role in Donegal's march to an All-Ireland final. Albeit, not in a Donegal shirt nor in a way that could have been predicted then, at the end of November 1991.

It was good to see Molloy back sooner than expected. Molloy in a Donegal jersey was a comforting sight. God was in his Heaven and all was right with the world when Molloy was at midfield. McEniff and himself had buried the hatchet. As 1991 ebbed away football folk were happy to let it go. The year that had promised so much but delivered nothing. Molloy's return to the fold was reason enough for Christmas cheer.

✻ ✻ ✻ ✻

For many people across Europe, 1992 was a synonym for the creation of the Single Market, as, at the stroke of midnight on December 31, 1992, customs controls across the European Community would be effectively abolished. As a border county, this would have more relevance in Donegal than in most places in Europe. The year would be remembered in Donegal all right, but in the northwest corner of the EC, 1992 would be a synonym for sporting nirvana.

As that year dawned there was little reason for optimism among Donegal football supporters that it would be any different from any other with regard to the fortunes of the senior football team. Most thought the chance was gone. And the excitement that the old Division One had thrown up in previous winters was now missing for obvious reasons. Expectations were low. Even the perennially optimistic Follower was wavering, "1992 is our last chance to build on the wonderful supply of proven talent that 1982 and 1987 provided. We may even be gone that one game too far."

The news coming from the camp wasn't all good either. Declan Bonner seemed likely to sit out football for the year. The Na Rossa man was in trouble with a pelvic injury, diagnosed in Dublin by Dr Pat O'Neill as being a hairline fracture. John Joe Doherty had a similar complaint although not quite as serious as Bonner's.

The Cunninghams were out of the country – Barry in the United States and John in France. Indeed it seemed likely that John would remain in the continent long term having secured work on the construction of Euro-Disney. These were four players Donegal could ill afford to do without with two games left in the national league – Wicklow and Roscommon – and the championship ahead with Cavan.

McEniff as ever, was busy with trial matches. A couple of the old hands who'd been out of the side before Christmas were back in action – Joyce, Reid, Murray and Mulgrew. Youngsters Mark Crossan, Jim McGuinness and Paul Callaghan were still catching the eye. Mayo, Galway and an Ulster selection provided challenge games which threw up questions and provided occasional answers. Mark McShane from Kilcar was again knocking on the door and would get the nod against Wicklow in Aughrim. Brian Tuohy was in commanding form at corner back and would also get the nod for Aughrim. Molloy was also coming back to his old form and started at midfield for the first time in what seemed like an eternity. Mulgrew was a surprise choice at centre half-forward. Aughrim would be his first outing since being replaced in the Ulster Final. In hindsight, it was the defining moment of Charlie's year. A good performance against Wicklow and Mulgrew would do his championship ambitions no harm. A bad performance and Charlie was in trouble. The trip to Aughrim would end in defeat, 1-6 to 2-6. Donegal's cause was not helped by the unavailability of McHugh, Murray and Hegarty through injury.

With Donegal now requiring a point from the Roscommon game to ensure quarter-final qualification, McEniff was leaving nothing to chance. The old hands were most definitely back. The team that met Roscommon in Ballybofey had a familiar look to it. Reid, Joyce and McHugh were in. Molloy kept his place in the middle. Murray was in also at centre half-forward.

Charlie Mulgrew was out of the team. He would never kick another ball in the national league. Indeed, his inter-county career was over, bar a McKenna Cup outing and 45 minutes over two matches against Cavan in the championship. Aughrim, as feared, had been Charlie's Waterloo.

And there was still no place for Barry McGowan. The Killybegs man was tearing his hair out on the bench. His gripe stretched back quite a bit at this stage. He'd been surviving for a couple of years as a bit-part player and had already spoken to the manager. McGowan felt he had too much to offer to be sitting on the bench. Versatile to a fault, McEniff would throw McGowan into the fray at any position from corner back to corner forward. What he wouldn't throw him was a jersey numbered two to 15:

> I remember going to Brian McEniff one evening. It wouldn't have been my form to go to him if I was dropped or not selected. I would just take it and say nothing. Having watched other players adopt a different approach I decided that the time had come to ask the question.
>
> I was very frustrated. He'd started to play me in a couple of different positions. After a training session in Donegal I asked him where did he think was my best position. I asked him to give me an idea of where it was and I'd do my best to play the position and make a go of it. He said he saw me as a wing half-back.

McGowan, a forward in his head, had been surprised at the response but decided he would make a go of it. Yet, despite decent performances in defence, he seemed destined to remain on the fringes. His patience was running out.

The Roscommon match in Ballybofey was the proverbial game of two halves. In the first, Donegal were quite awful. Gary Walsh – who had transferred to Burren in County Down – Paul Carr, Donal Reid, Martin McHugh and Tony Boyle had kept Donegal in it. Donegal were very fortunate then to enter the break on level terms, 0-4 apiece, but it could have been worse. John Newton was denied at point-blank range by Walsh just five minutes before the half-time whistle. Up in the press-box the Follower was scratching his head in dismay. Cavan had nothing to worry about in the championship. "I took out my GAA diary at the interval to see where a chap might go on May 24th," wrote the man from Dromod, "I certainly was not going to Breffni to be humiliated."

As it happened, redemption was at hand in the second 30 minutes. Donegal hit points – 11 in all – from all angles and cantered to an 0-15 to 0-6 victory. McHugh was instrumental, kicking five points but excelling as the playmaker. Tony Boyle was in magnificent form and had contributed three points as had Tommy Ryan in the 15 minutes in which he replaced Murray. Ryan wanted his place back and 15 minutes was all he needed. Mark McShane had also impressed but would not be on the panel when it mattered the following September.

After all that they had been through and the speculation they had endured, the old reliables were still to the fore. Molloy, Shov and Matt were three that led from the front in Ballybofey. The couple of league points secured at Roscommon's expense provided Donegal with their first real test in six competitive fixtures. Dublin, in Breffni Park in the national league quarter-final. The last time the sides had met in the league Paddy Cullen hadn't been a wet weekend in charge. Donegal had five points to spare that day in Ballybofey. Since then Donegal had endured pain in Croke Park and Clones and weren't perceived to have the same potency – at least not within their own county. Time would tell if that perception had travelled beyond the county boundaries.

❄ ❄ ❄ ❄

It was a game Donegal folk would never forget. A gallery of hideous images filled the minds of those who had followed this team. Val Daly's goal in 1983. Stephen Conway's point in 1989. Stafford and Flynn in 1990. And now, in the national league quarter-final of 1992, a Dublin duo – Clarke and Murphy, added yet another.

It was worse, much worse, for the players on the pitch. With a minute and a half remaining Donegal were four points up and on their way to the semi-final for the second year running. By the time Paddy Russell of Tipperary blew the whistle for full-time, Dublin had found the Donegal net twice and turned a four-point deficit into a two-point winning margin. Devastation. "Unreal," commented Peter Campbell in the *Democrat*. The gallery was going to need an extension if horror shows like this were to continue.

Barry Cunningham had his ear trained to the radio in New York. McEniff's introduction of Padraig Brogan to the already congested midfield sector had been the last straw for him:

> When Down beat us in the Ulster Final of 1991 I said that I was finished with county football and wouldn't be back. I spent the winter in America and played football for Donegal in New York. I listened to the league quarter-final with an air of detachment. I was a Donegal emigrant listening to the game and felt like no more than a supporter.

In the commentary, Barry heard that Dublin had started like a runaway train. Three points, from Charlie Redmond, Dessie Farrell and David Foran, in the first six minutes indicated that Donegal were in some trouble. It was a false impression, Donegal were merely slow to find their groove but were level within five minutes. Three times Dublin had been undisciplined within striking range of their own posts and three times Manus punished them. Donegal were relishing the opportunity of playing better quality opposition and were stretching their legs for the first time. Martin Gavigan was superb throughout. Twelve minutes gone and Gavigan booted a long clearance in towards Tony Boyle who broke it down ahead of Gerry Hargan to Joyce, arriving on the scene at speed. John O'Leary didn't even see it. Joyce unleashed a mighty effort which almost burst the roof of the net. Now was the time to put Dublin away. Over Christmas, in Donegal football's equivalent of *Urbi et Orbi*, the Follower had articulated an unpalatable home truth. Donegal had a habit of lying on the oars, "Our greatest failing is our inability to bury a team, to actually cremate them and scatter the ashes across the playing field". What Donegal needed now was to pile on the scores on Dublin.

They did. Dublin stepped up the physical intensity of the game but Donegal were equal to it. The Wee Man was buzzing and struck two points either side of a booking shared with Eamonn Heery. Heery should have received his marching orders in the second half for an off-the-ball elbow on Mark McShane but, somehow, escaped unpunished. Sheedy too was dishing it out. Shovlin dished it straight back and was also fortunate to stay on the pitch.

Manus Boyle added another to leave clear daylight between the sides. It could have been more, uncharacteristically Manus then missed two kickable frees. Still, the interval was beckoning with six points to spare. Charlie Redmond had other ideas. He had been causing Tuohy serious problems for the half hour and finally capitalised deep into injury-time with an opportunistic and rather fortunate, goal. Donegal had dominated the half but led by a mere kick of the ball; 1-6 to 1-3. All bets were off as to the outcome.

The preferred outcome seemed back on track within 30 seconds of the restart as McHugh slotted over his third and final point. Tony Boyle added another. The six-point lead was within grasp again. An ominous warning sign came eight minutes in when Paul Carr conceded a close-in free on Mick Galvin which Redmond converted. Carr, like Tuohy, had his hands desperately full.

Even so, Donegal were winning the battle hands down further out the field. The boys had Dublin in trouble around the middle. Reid, Gavigan and Shovlin halted any decent supply of ball getting into the Dublin full-forward line and with Molloy and Brogan lording it over Bealin and Foran, the cracks deep in the Donegal defence were mostly hidden from view. The left boots of Joyce and Mark McShane retrieved Donegal's earlier six-point lead but with 18 minutes left to play, those proved to be Donegal's final scores.

It was back to lying on the oars. A couple of points would have put it out of reach. Scores weren't forthcoming. With nine minutes remaining Dublin had clawed it back to four points. But no further. Donegal were still on top. Then Paddy Cullen withdrew Mick Galvin and Paul Nugent. Paul Carr and Noel Hegarty were glad to see the back of them. Not so good was the sight of their replacements. On came Vinny Murphy and Paul Clarke. It may have been an inspired substitution on the part of Paddy Cullen. It may have been pure luck. Either way, it would prove to be the winning of the match.

Those Donegal supporters who would never sit until the end of a game – always in an inexplicable rush to beat the crowd and the traffic – were already racing for their cars. They were spared what happened next.

With 90 seconds to see out on the clock, Donegal paid a terrible price for their faltering full-back line. The experienced and wise old head of Matt Gallagher – absent through injury and watching in horror from under the scoreboard – was sorely missed now. Goal number one arrived courtesy of Vinny Murphy outfielding Carr and setting up Clarke. There was no sense of panic as Gary Walsh placed the ball on the 21:

> I took the kick out and gave it to Martin Gavigan who was about 50 yards from goal. He won it, turned and took two or three solos and hoofed the ball but it went out over the sideline. We had lost possession and they came down the field and got another goal.

Paul Carr made a fabulous block on Dessie Farrell to prevent a certain equalising point. With the worst of bad luck, the ball broke to Vinny Murphy who drew on it first time and put it past Gary Walsh. Peter Campbell got it right in the *Democrat*, it was "grand larceny".

Watching from the stand was John Joe Doherty. Recently returned from a three-month stint in Paris working on the Euro-Disney project, John Joe had travelled to the game with his club and played in a challenge match with Ballyconnell. "That was my first game of the year," he recalled, "It frightens me how badly out of shape I was. I was so unfit it was unbelievable."

For once the focus wasn't on the forwards – although they had discarded several chances. If Donegal needed evidence that they had a full-back problem, they now had the statistics to prove it. Paul Carr wasn't the culprit – he was merely filling a gap in the absence of a recognised dependable number three. Donegal had been making do with converted corner-backs and half-backs for a long time now. What was needed was an all out full-back in the mould of Martin Griffin. McEniff accepted that he had a full-back problem, "Paul Carr wasn't a happy full-back but he was a very good centre half-back." It was a something that was going to have to be sorted when the shock of the Breffni robbery subsided.

Martin Gavigan, with the aid of hindsight, saw that defeat as a watershed:

We played the best football that day. Defeat was the best kick in the arse we ever got. Letting in two goals, one after the other; six points in the blink of an eye – you're never going to recover from that. But it gave us great confidence for later meetings with Dublin. We knew on the balance of play we could beat Dublin if we didn't concede goals. We felt that if we could stop a repeat of the Cavan goal strike we'd always be in there with a very good chance against Dublin. The quarter-final defeat was a blessing in disguise really.

The Donegal team that met Dublin in Breffni Park – the last encounter between the two sides until their date with destiny a little over five months later – was: Gary Walsh; Noel Hegarty, Paul Carr, Brian Tuohy; Donal Reid, Martin Gavigan, Martin Shovlin; Anthony Molloy, Padraig Brogan; Mark McShane, Tommy Ryan, Joyce McMullan; Martin McHugh, Tony Boyle, Manus Boyle. Sub: Brian Murray for Manus Boyle.

The Dubs were well pleased with themselves. It was a win to brag about. Donegal were as fragile as ever. "It's never over until the Fat Lady sings," sneered Charlie Redmond at Noel Hegarty, going out of his way to cross the Glen man's path following Vinnie Murphy's last gasp winner. Hegarty, who'd had little contact with Redmond during the match, said nothing at the time, but remembered it all the same.

❊

National League 1991-92

RESULTS		
Donegal 1-13, Antrim 0-8	Donegal 1-6, Wicklow 2-6
Donegal 1-7, Longford 0-1	Donegal 0-15, Roscommon 0-6
Donegal 0-7, Leitrim 0-4	Donegal 1-10, Dublin 3-6 (q/f)

14

Ulster Says Yes

(April 1992 – July 1992)

"We played every game as though it was our last."

DONAL REID

Many things needed to fall into place, and quickly. It was April. Six months to Donegal's most famous Sunday – not that anyone envisaged that then – and several of those who would play major roles were nowhere to be seen. Then, just as Dublin administered last rites to Donegal in Breffni Park, destiny took over and the boys who would bring Sam to the Hills began emerging from Lettermacaward, France and the Bronx.

Declan Bonner hadn't kicked a ball since the New Year on the advice of Dr Pat O'Neill. Six months rest was needed for torn fibres of the groin. That was a medical fact. On the Wednesday night after the Murphy-Clarke robbery in Cavan, Bonner turned up at training in Bundoran. It was good to be back. He hadn't really taken the doctor's advice to heart anyway:

> Being told in January to do nothing for six months would have left me in June, right in the middle of the championship, with nothing done. I did nothing for four or five weeks but then I started to run on Dooey beach to keep myself ticking over. I found that when I went back to training in April I was in better shape than some of the other lads. At that time I was training twice a day, before I went to work in the morning and when I came home in the evening.

John Cunningham was back from Paris with less than two months to get into championship mode. There were those that believed Vinny Murphy and Paul Clarke would have had less joy in Breffni had Razda been stationed around the Donegal square. Donegal's problems at the edge of the square were continuing unabated. A week after the Breffni Park debacle Donegal took on Monaghan in Ballybay in the McKenna Cup. "We played on a mucky pitch and hailstones were falling," remembered Tony Boyle:

> We were trounced. That was really a turning point in the season. We went into the dressing room afterwards and the team was on the verge of breaking up. We had a very good chat and it was really that day in Ballybay that we decided to give it one more lash.

Monaghan's Eamon Murphy had been the latest full-forward to wreak havoc around the Donegal goalmouth. Things were at a low ebb, remembered Martin McHugh:

> We stopped for a drink on the way home from the Monaghan match. We chatted about farming and didn't even mention football. Being beaten by Monaghan was the lowest we ever went. A couple of months later we were All-Ireland champions.

Preparation for Cavan continued with a series of challenge games that raised more questions than answers. Tyrone had a goal to spare in Healy Park but that was the least of Donegal's problems. All was not well on the field – a bit of niggle had crept in among the players. And strangely, fitness did not appear anywhere near the level one might expect a month short of a championship visit to Cavan. The only real bonus in Omagh was the first appearance of Bonner since the Leitrim game the previous November.

"Imagine May and no championship football," shuddered the Follower. Donegal were going to have to get used to May and beyond without Padraig Brogan. The big Mayo man had never ceased to surprise the boys over the previous 15 months but his disappearance from Donegal and Donegal football would take some beating. Brogan simply walked away. No explanations, no nothing. Not even to McEniff. He just upped and left at the beginning of May.

"It was a week of sudden departure," wrote the Follower, noting that Brogan had departed Donegal the same week as Bishop Eamon Casey hung up his crozier, albeit in more sensational circumstances. Brogan had always been a free spirit. He would continue to be. Many believed the best goal ever scored in Croke Park came from the boot of Padraig Brogan. He had earned fame in Mayo and now notoriety in Donegal. Padraig Brogan was less than five months away from an All-Ireland medal when he closed the door behind him for the last time in Bundoran.

Three thousand miles away in New York a telephone kept ringing. Barry Cunningham had wintered in the Big Apple but his mind was never far from Donegal. He knew from chatting to his cousin John that there were ongoing problems with Brogan even before the Mayo man's abrupt departure:

Tony Boyle

All of a sudden I was getting 'phone-calls from McEniff. I had received 11 calls the week before Brogan left. I told my girlfriend to tell McEniff that I wasn't home. I really felt I was shafted the year before but McEniff is the kind of man who could bring you around if he got you talking.

After Brogan left I was still ignoring the calls but was chatting about it to my girlfriend and her father, Terry Connaughon, who was high up in the New York GAA and knew his football. He told me that if I thought I was good enough and Donegal were good enough I should do it. I did. McEniff 'phoned again on Monday and I was at training in Ballybofey next night.

The following Sunday, Donegal took on Wicklow in Donegal Town, two weeks ahead of Cavan. Donegal had a 13-point lead at half-time thanks mainly to the sterling midfield efforts of the returned emigrant. Although not fully fit, Barry Cunningham booked a starting place in Breffni on the strength of a masterful hour reminding onlookers of his formidable all-round game. For the first time – bar a half hour's football against Armagh back in 1988 – the Killybegs man would be in for a championship match. Cunningham knew that he didn't have the required championship fitness. On the nights that the team wasn't training, Barry was down at the pitch at Fintra trying to build up his stamina. Training every day of the week was a big commitment, but thoughts of All-Ireland glory drove him on.

It was as low-key as it possibly could have been. All bets were off on Donegal. The darlings of the national media only a year or two before, Donegal were all but written off. Yesterday's news – a team with little left in the tank. That suited McEniff and the boys just fine. Down and Derry were lauded as the teams to watch in Ulster. Tyrone and Armagh wouldn't be far away either. Ulster was bursting with good teams. "One team that definitely won't be coming out of Ulster this year is Down," predicted Martin Gavigan with absolute certainty. He was right. Down would shortly tumble in the defence of their All-Ireland crown at the hands of Derry. Derry had already accounted for Tyrone in the preliminary round at Celtic Park – although not before both sides knocked lumps out of each other – and would then defeat Monaghan at the second asking in Celtic Park in the first round proper.

The hour of battle approached. For a fourth year, it was time to engage with Cavan. Dangerous, unpredictable Cavan. Those who knew Ulster football recognised the dangers posed by Cavan in their own backyard. Any team with Philip Smith, Stephen King, Damien O'Reilly, Ronan Carolan and Fintan Cahill among its number merited a wide berth. And if you couldn't avoid them, they merited respect.

McEniff had given the boys a last chance to stretch their legs in Tuam the Sunday before. He had reason to be happy but kept his counsel. It was coming together. The boys scored 3-15 against Galway. McHugh was back in vintage form bringing everyone around him into the game. Molloy at midfield was the

Molloy of old. Barry Cunningham still hadn't the legs for 70 minutes but was *some* footballer. Matt Gallagher and Noel Hegarty had Jarlath Fallon and Niall Finnegan in their pockets. Mulgrew, Murray, Reid and Bonner all shone. McEniff had options then as he sat down in Bundoran to pick his starting 15. Gary Walsh; John Cunningham, Paul Carr, Matt Gallagher; Noel Hegarty, Martin Gavigan, Martin Shovlin; Anthony Molloy, Barry Cunningham; Declan Bonner, Tommy Ryan, Joyce McMullan; Martin McHugh, Tony Boyle, Manus Boyle.

❄ ❄ ❄ ❄

As exciting matches go, Cavan and Donegal in the first round of the Ulster championship on Sunday, May 24, 1992, in Breffni Park, was up there with the best. Twelve thousand people crammed into one of Ulster's most hallowed grounds and witnessed a thriller. And the last three minutes would live long in the memory for three truly awesome scores – two from a man named O'Reilly either side of one by a genius named McHugh from the Donegal hills.

By the time Jim Curran sounded the long whistle the scoreboard would read Donegal 1-15, Cavan 1-15. The battle had raged for more than 70 minutes. In the end a draw was no less than either side deserved. "The almost hysterical response to the public address announcement that the replay will take place in Ballybofey on Sunday next reflected the mood of the paying customers," noted Pat Roche in the *Irish Times*.

Even so, Donegal had their problems – 17 wides had been recorded over the 70 minutes. The full-back problem was still there – Matt eventually had to move across to curb the lethal Fintan Cahill. And the forwards, some of them anyhow, had footered. The *Independent*'s man wasn't impressed. "This is a pale shadow of the side which trounced Cavan at the same ground three years ago. Donegal's dash has been considerably diluted." Time would tell.

The sides were level pegging on three points apiece with less than ten minutes gone. McHugh was having a hand in everything. Twice now he had left Cavan defenders trailing in his wake, soloing on his left, swinging the ball effortlessly over the bar with his right. "Maybe we're about to see a rejuvenated Martin McHugh this year in the championship," enthused the former Fermanagh great, Peter McGinnity, now providing commentary for the BBC.

Joyce had almost nonchalantly knocked over the third Donegal point. But there was trouble at the other end. Fintan Cahill was on fire, causing palpations in Donegal hearts every time the ball came anywhere near him. One of the great prospects of Cavan football, his promise had been dogged by injury. Not today. It was obvious he was pumped up for this one. The very first contact between himself and Paul Carr saw the Donegal number three shouldered unceremoniously over the sideline. It was Cahill who had brilliantly kicked two of those early Cavan points. In the 12th minute he added a goal.

Cavan won a free around the middle – Molloy adjudged to have committed the foul. Stephen King was thinking faster that anyone. His free was quick and clever. King floated the free into Cahill, who had darted in behind the Donegal full-back. The ball spilled from Paul Carr's desperate stretch and Cahill didn't need an invitation to drill it past Walsh at close quarters despite a heroic effort by Carr to get back for the block. There it was, trouble yet again on the edge of the square. Anthony Molloy was struggling a bit at midfield too. "Breffni Park is a hard place to go and win a championship game. Every dog has its day and Stephen King gave me a fair old roasting that day," he recalled.

McHugh, inevitably, responded to the goal with another point from play. The Wee Man was on song. Peter Campbell and 11,999 others could only marvel at his skill:

If only Donegal could field six forwards with Martin McHugh's brain, as the Kilcar man never wasted a ball. There is no substitute for accuracy, and when not well placed, taking the right option.

Brendan McCormack, the Cavan goalkeeper, then denied Tony Boyle a certain goal with a wonderful point-blank save and the tide seemed to be turning in favour of the locals. Stephen King underlined this moments later with a mighty pointed free, out of his hands, from all of 50 yards. Cavan supporters were upping the ante all around Breffni and their team was responding. With 23 minutes gone Donegal found themselves trailing by 0-4 to 1-6.

McEniff had already acted on the line. He had come under criticism for not acting sooner to shore up the defence in the national league quarter-final. It wouldn't happen a second time. The unfortunate Paul Carr was withdrawn. Carr, a fine defender but not a full-back, was simply a victim of circumstances – none of the boys would ever criticise Carr as they understood clearly that the man was playing out of position. Reid was sent into the action at right half-back. Noel Hegarty moved into the corner and Matt took over at full-back. It was a switch which would pay dividends all year.

Matt had coveted the full-back position for some time. "I was a good organiser," he remarked:

I was always the one who talked anyway so it made no difference to me. To be in the middle made it easier to organise. I think McEniff felt I was a bit small for the position but I didn't agree and told him on many occasions that I could handle it. In the end I think he just got fed up listening to me and put me there.

Gary Walsh had a better view of the full-back problem than most. When he started his county career, Martin Griffin was like a rock in the position. No one had commanded the position since, but Walsh felt Matt was the man for the job:

> If any of the backs were going to do it then maybe Matt was the man because he's so dogged and determined. Look at the big full-forwards he marked later that year. The bigger the challenge the more Matt looked forward to it. We had some great footballers but full-back is a unique position – you nearly have to be born into it. We had some speedy defenders and some strong players but nobody had the complete mix to make a good full-back.

Notwithstanding his perceived lack of stature, the manager was aware of Matt's talents and was happy to see him at full-back, "Matt had the heart of a lion," recalled McEniff. "He was a good two-sided player and knew how to stay on his opponent's dangerous side. For a small man he was outstanding."

Reid's move to half-back immediately settled things. Years of experience and craft were called upon. Launching himself at a Walsh kick out, Reid set off on a solo run down the right wing, transferring the ball to McHugh who kicked for the point on the 24th minute. It hadn't quite the legs to clear the bar but Tony Boyle tracked it all the way as it dipped towards Brendan McCormack in the Cavan goals. Tony's presence was enough to distract McCormack who fluffed the catch and the ball ended up in the back of the net. That Boyle was in the square was of little concern to ecstatic Donegal supporters. "I was all set for claiming that goal," remembered Tony Boyle:

> It must have been the only time the BBC ever put a camera on the stanchion and it showed the footage afterwards. I knew I touched something, but it was the 'keeper's hand and the ball went in directly.

Boyle, buzzing now, scored one of two Donegal points that levelled matters, Barry Cunningham hit the other. Five or six minutes left, level again – 1-6 apiece. Ryan and McMullan traded further points with Carolan and Cahill and Ulster had a real humdinger on its hands.

The Follower had expected a dour, physical battle. Recent history indicated thus. He'd warned the boys, "Nancys will not be acceptable in Breffni. Slaps on the jaw will have to be taken and given with no mouthing at referees." It hadn't panned out. It was hard and tough but never dirty. Both sides were concentrating on the football and playing it well.

It was still level with 22 minutes played of the second half. Worryingly, it was Donegal who had to play catch-up. Tommy Ryan and Tony Boyle, who would both finish with three points, kept pegging away. And then there was McHugh. In time McHugh would become a folk hero to the Cavan faithful, but that Sunday in May he broke their hearts.

Michael Gallagher came on for Manus – who wasn't having a great outing – early in the second half. Declan Bonner was in the same boat – the ball just wasn't coming his way – and was replaced by Charlie Mulgrew with less than 15 minutes remaining.

Carolan secured Cavan's slim lead yet again but despite an eight-minute patch of almost total possession, Donegal failed to get on the scoreboard although Tony Boyle might well have had a penalty during this period. It was frustrating to watch. A Glencolmcille man had watched long enough. Working the ball out of defence with Donal Reid, Noel Hegarty simply kept going. Reid returned the ball and Hegarty hit an inspirational equaliser. There you go lads, there was how it was done. It was the first of a series of remarkable scores.

The next one was classic Donegal. Short passing at its glorious best – the ball swept from player to player at mesmerising speed as the two Cunninghams and McHugh combined to set up Tony Boyle who kicked what looked like the winner. Injury-time – 70 minutes had come and gone. Ronan Carolan had a chance but spurned it. Cavan were about to exit the championship at the hands of Donegal for the fourth year in succession.

Not so. Damien O'Reilly was about to hit the headlines. Inspirational throughout, he would score two points of immeasurable quality in the three minutes that remained. The first was simply breathtaking – the best score in Ulster that year. Aidan Watters pumped a high ball in over the heads of O'Reilly and Matt. The ball bounced out to the left of the Donegal goals and near the end line as the two players sprinted after it. Despite the limpet-like attentions of Matt, O'Reilly succeeded in volleying a truly remarkable point from the most acute angle. Matt still can't believe what happened:

> I thought it was going wide. It was within a foot of the line. I was shepherding him out over the line but he couldn't get around me so he caught me and used me to swing and volleyed it. I saw it fly by and thought 'Fuck, this is in the net,' but it went over the bar. It was a pure fluke. He was just trying to keep it in play.

Goalkeeper Gary Walsh was relieved to see it going over the bar, "O'Reilly didn't know what he was doing. It could have flown across me and into the top corner of the net. It was a great score." It looked like one of the most spectacular equalising points of all time. However, Jim Curran, the Tyrone referee, had more time to play. An injury to Bernard Morris had resulted in a lengthy stoppage ten minutes into the half and he was taken off. Tommy Ryan was seen as the culprit by a large section of the Cavan crowd. "Everybody in Cavan thinks I broke Bernard Morris' jaw, but it isn't the case," stated Tommy:

> Bernard Morris and me went for the ball on the left side of the pitch. I

was goal-side of Morris and just as Shovlin was about pass it to me, Morris hit me in the chest. This kind of thing happened regularly in the Ulster championship and if he'd succeeded, I would have been left ten yards behind him and he'd pick up the ball and clear it away up the field. Just before he got away from me I swung back at him and hit him in the mouth. What I didn't realise was that he'd recently had a dental job done. I picked the ball up and put it over the bar. I was told that I would-n't leave the field alive.

A replay looked appeared imminent. As Gary Walsh pumped the ball outfield following O'Reilly's point, Cavan blundered and committed a foul. A free was awarded, some 60 yards out. Up stepped McHugh. "One of the Cavan players said something to McHugh," remembered McEniff 11 years later, "I can still see him smiling back at him." Two minutes of injury time had elapsed. "All I was thinking about was putting it dead," admitted McHugh:

I went for it and got it. I always find that those long-range free kicks are easier to score than those close goals because the same pressure isn't on you. People don't expect you to get it. When you're taking a close-in free everyone expects you to get it.

The Wee Man's incredible effort had been struck into a swirling breeze. It bisect-ed the posts. "An unbelievable kick," remembered Martin Gavigan. There was-n't a soul in Breffni Park not convinced that they'd just seen the winner.

Except for Damien O'Reilly. Somehow, he had the last say. His earlier vol-ley had been left-footed. Now he swivelled onto his right and struck a splendid point. It was, noted the *Irish Times*, "the ultimate in equalisers". It was all to do in a week's time in Ballybofey. "People said that we were lucky not to lose," said Tommy Ryan, "but if Cavan were there until today I don't think they could have beaten us."

❊ ❊ ❊ ❊

The old saying 'a week is a long time in politics' is equally applicable to football. It certainly fitted in Ballybofey on the last Sunday in May 1992. A week previ-ously a marvellous tit-for-tat thriller had been witnessed in brilliant sunshine in Cavan. In MacCumhaill Park seven days later the heavens opened as Donegal cruised to an easy 11-point victory and a place in the Ulster semi-final.

Donegal were 0-10 to 0-2 ahead by half-time but the game was already long over as a contest. Cavan had been reduced to 14 men which helped their cause little – Philip Smyth sent to the line seven minutes earlier for taking a swipe at Tommy Ryan. Smyth's unprovoked right hook may well have been retribution for the incident involving Ryan and Bernard Morris a week earlier after which Morris was helped from the pitch. However, Morris was fit to start the replay and played for the full 70 minutes.

Tommy, by now the *bête noire* of Cavan players and supporters, remembers the incident well:

> I went down to get a ball in a ruck and Philip Smith came in from a distance and punched me as hard as he could. It was a stupid and blatant thing to do. Another man was put on me and he split my lip open. Austin Kennedy came on and told me that I'd have to come off. There was the like of Manus, Barry McGowan and John Joe Doherty on the line and I was afraid that I'd lose my place if I came off. He stitched me on the sideline.
>
> When I came back on I told the man that hit me that the difference between Donegal men and Cavan men was when Donegal men hit, men stayed down but when Cavan men hit, we wouldn't go down. I said to him, 'You wee weak bastard, your sister would have hit me harder than you did.' The referee was standing beside me and he told me to be quiet. I told him not to worry that he wouldn't get any trouble from me as Donegal had the game won.

In the second half Donegal matched their opening period tally of ten points and, although Cavan managed 1-4, there was little to talk about other than the incessant rain. Sean Kilfeather of the *Irish Times* watched from the shelter of the press box as 16,000 unfortunate supporters got the drenching of a lifetime:

> The conditions were simply dreadful and the man on the public address system who appealed to the public – who had paid to get in to the totally unprotected terraces and who were soaked and miserable enough already – to take down their umbrellas deserved the scornful response he got.

There was no area of the field which Donegal did not dominate. Matt Gallagher utterly quenched the threat of Fintan Cahill. Molloy and Murray had midfield sown-up, the half-back trio of Reid, Rambo and Shovlin were unbreachable, James McHugh was superb while Bonner tore swathes through the Cavan defence. Declan knew he wasn't up to the pace of the game seven days before. It wouldn't happen again:

> I had done a lot of work that week. The team trained twice but I went out for another three nights and kicked hundreds of balls on the Na Rossa pitch just to get some sharpness back. It worked out well.

McEniff had named three changes from the Breffni encounter. Reid, as expected, retained his place at Paul Carr's expense in defence. Michael Gallagher was in at midfield – Barry Cunningham the man to lose out and unlucky at that. And there was no place for Manus Boyle, Brian Murray got the nod instead. In the event, Barry Cunningham, and not the injured Michael Gallagher, would play but at centre half-forward as Murray resumed a partnership last forged with Molloy in 1990. And James McHugh made his first appearance of the championship and a good one at that, in for Joyce who had cried off with a hamstring injury.

Cavan arrived full of confidence. Anthony Molloy erased the memory of his bad display in Cavan:

> Murray and me played well that day, I got two points from play. After the game, Stephen King told me that after drawing with Donegal, the people of Cavan were thinking about winning the All-Ireland!

Donegal set about disabusing Cavan fans of their All-Ireland ambitions as points flew over from all directions. It was a devastating display of point-taking which belied the slippery underfoot conditions. One score as good as the next. The first came from the boot of the Wee Man, converting a free won by his brother. Then Gavigan plucked a ball from the sky, fired it to Tony Boyle as soon as he touched the ground and Boyle transferred to the onrushing Murray for another fine score. John Brady drew Cavan level with five minutes gone but then Donegal proceeded to take Cavan apart. Declan Bonner with three points, Tommy Ryan and James McHugh with two each and Barry Cunningham with one point danced around Cavan and scored almost at will. "It's ominous looking for Cavan," remarked future GAA president Sean McCague in the commentary box for the BBC.

Only 30 seconds had passed in the second half before Cavan knew they were in for more of the same. Bonner sold a dummy and hit his fourth. Then a Molloy point was greeted with the cheer of the day – the Big Man could do no wrong at the best of times in the eyes of his faithful. And so it went. The only blip was a goal from Damien O'Reilly but it failed to lift Cavan out of the rut.

Charlie Mulgrew, on for the injured Tony Boyle, and Manus on for the injured Martin McHugh both contributed scores; 0-20 to 1-6 it finished. Soaked to their skins, supporters were filing out long before Jim Curran's full-time whistle. Donegal, noted Sean Kilfeather, were by then merely "toying with the opposition".

Barry McGowan had also come on replacing Tommy Ryan, but he was not a happy man:

> I was experiencing a third season of championship frustration. I didn't get playing in Breffni and in the replay I was brought on for about 30 seconds which was a joke! Donegal were winning well and I could have been put on earlier and made a claim for a place in the next round. That

day I only had time to hand my substitution slip to the referee when the whistle blew and the match was over.

Barry had reached the end of his tether. He had already talked it over with his family. They understood and saw at first hand his frustration. Others did too:

> Patsy McGowan, the Finn Harps manager, rang me that evening. He wanted me to sign for Finn Harps. 'Surely you're not going to play for Donegal again after being treated so badly?' I laughed at the timing of his telephone call. It was right on cue.

The Killybegs man finally made a decision. It was a decision that would reap rich rewards for himself and his county. He would stick it out with Donegal. If and when the opportunity arose again he would make it damn hard for anyone to displace him. As it happened, his chance was just around the corner. And he would grab it with both hands.

While McEniff was disappointed with the competitive edge of the replay, it seemed likely that Donegal could begin planning for a remarkable fourth Ulster final. The hurdle that was Fermanagh remained to be cleared, but – no disrespect to the Ernesiders – another shot at provincial honours beckoned.

❅ ❅ ❅ ❅

On paper, the 2-17 to 0-7 win over Fermanagh in Omagh meant something. Witnessed in person, it meant nothing. The headline writers in the national dailies judged proceedings solely on the strength of the scoreline. "Donegal shatter Fermanagh," read the *Irish Press*. "Donegal scuttle Fermanagh," agreed the *Independent*. Nearer home the *Democrat* was closer to the mark, "Just not good enough". Because it wasn't.

The basic statistics of the game were simple and straightforward. Donegal trailed by a point at half-time, 0-6 to 0-7. They hit the lead seven minutes into the second half and would eventually catch fire around the 20-minute mark, recording a total of 2-11 while holding Fermanagh scoreless. Roll on Clones and bring on Derry or Down. It was far from being that simple. The boys and their boss knew they had flattered to deceive. It really was not good enough. Peter Campbell in the *Democrat* had called it right. Derry or Down would steamroll them on Ulster final day in Clones.

In retrospect, Donegal were onto a loser playing Fermanagh. Expected to win handsomely, only a complete exhibition would suffice on the day and even then what would they have proved? That the team and management had the maturity to recognise that a 16-point victory in the semi-final of the Ulster championship was just not good enough indicated how high the bar had been raised.

Things were operating on a different level these days.

John Cunningham had started the match at right full-back and he wasn't happy with Donegal's performance in the first half:

> Fermanagh were putting it up to us and we couldn't seem to get going. We seemed to be hungover from the Cavan game. The fact that we were playing Fermanagh really did not lift the focus. It took us a good while after half-time to get going. Tommy Ryan was exceptional and was probably the man who dragged us through the game.

All of ten minutes passed before Tommy Ryan recorded Donegal's first score – an impressive point that started with a Gary Walsh fetch under the bar and reached Ryan via Michael Gallagher, Anthony Molloy, Declan Bonner and James McHugh. Fluent and impressive. But not followed up.

Fermanagh continued to dominate the scoring stakes and had three further points to show by the end of a surprise first quarter. Fermanagh also had a rub of the green, a clutch of defenders somehow denying Tony Boyle a certain goal. There was little excuse for Donegal's poor showing on the scoreboard though. Molloy and Murray were ruling the roost at midfield and sending a plentiful supply of ball into the forwards. And that's were the problems started. Peter Campbell watched as an old ghost came back to haunt his county:

> Time after time they wanted to weave a maze through the Fermanagh defence with very few of them willing to take on and beat his man, and it seemed none of them willing to take responsibility to go for the score.

The Wee Man was missing which didn't help matters – his absence through injury glaring. Joyce was back. Michael Gallagher was in for Rambo – also injured. Barry McGowan was getting his first start, in for Shov who was down with the 'flu.

With a minute remaining of the first half Fermanagh were two up. Then came one of the game's defining moments from a Fermanagh perspective. Declan Bonner had earned the wrath of Fermanagh supporters for a late tackle on Collie Curran but had escaped with a booking. A few moments later Fermanagh full-back, Michael O'Brien, almost took the head off Bonner's shoulders and was sent for an early shower. Bonner just about poked the resulting free over the bar for his team to enter the interval trailing by a point while playing atrociously.

The second half was marginally better. Murray knocked over the equaliser right away but 11 wides were scattered over the 35 minutes. Fermanagh were now a beaten team but Donegal seemed in no rush to expedite matters. With 20 minutes gone they were still only three points ahead. A kick of the ball – although Fermanagh looked unlikely to produce such a kick. Then McEniff sent on McHugh and Donegal finally found their rhythm. In the space of 15 minutes they kicked 2-7. McHugh, while only contributing 0-2 of that total, provided Donegal with leadership just when needed.

The goals buried Fermanagh out of sight. Tony Boyle, Donegal's man-of-the-match, turned playmaker and provided both. The first came from a long clearance from Murray collected neatly by Boyle. The pass from Tony to James McHugh was inch-perfect. James McHugh wrong-footed several defenders and the goalkeeper before side-footing the ball to the net with his left boot.

The second arrived eight minutes later. Two Fermanagh defenders collided allowing Boyle to again set up a goal chance for a colleague. This time it was Tommy Ryan and it really was a peach. "I collected a great ball from Tony Boyle who had drawn a couple of defenders," remembered Tommy. Soloing at full speed he let fly from 21 yards with a glorious left-foot drive that rifled into the roof of the net. "You don't stop those!" quipped the BBC's Jimmy Smith.

The remainder was a rout. Points sailed over from everywhere and everyone. "Donegal are having a training session at the moment in Omagh," commented Smith. Matt Gallagher even arrived up from full-back and stuck one over. His was a wide smile as he acknowledged the rare occurrence to the crowd. "Bonner likes to tell me that we were already 17 points up at that stage, but I always say it was better to be 18 points up," grinned Matt, "I should also have scored a goal that day but Manus wouldn't pass to me!"

Barry Cunningham pulled one of his old tricks on Fermanagh centre half-back Collie Curran:

> At club level I'd often have tried to distract an opponent by calling for a pass. Collie had the ball and was looking to give a pass. I called 'Collie, Collie' and he passed the ball straight to me without looking. I suppose it's underhand but the purpose of it was to put players off. I couldn't believe it when the ball came to me like that in an Ulster semi-final. I've met Collie a few times since then and we've always had a good laugh at it.

Lack of fitness caught up with Barry and he was replaced by Manus Boyle ten minutes into the second half. Manus managed a point. Barry wouldn't appear again for Donegal until 12 minutes into the second half of the All-Ireland semi-final. And Paul Carr got a much deserved 15 minutes for Michael Gallagher at centre half-back. Molloy marked his 100th outing in a Donegal jersey with a magnificent performance. Another for the 100 Club, that at least was worth celebrating.

"A lot of work still remains if Donegal are to assume the role of 1992 champions," remarked Philip Reid in the *Irish Press*. McEniff and the boys didn't need to be told that. That discussion was taking place in the dressing rooms. McEniff wasn't happy with many aspects of the performance and said as much. Over-elaboration, poor shooting and the like. Then McHugh took the floor.

"McEniff was fond of dressing room meetings," remembered Matt Gallagher, "he liked players to have their say." The physiotherapists and other backroom staff were asked to leave. "It was just players and management," remembered Brian McEniff, "there was a fair bit of blood letting." "We told McEniff out straight that the training wasn't right and we weren't fit enough to play the game we were trying to play," said Anthony Molloy. Martin McHugh played a major role in proceedings. "I think his words were 'I'm not turning up for another Ulster final to disgrace myself'" recalled his brother James. The players knew in their hearts and souls that their approach wasn't right. "The resolve was in the team but McHugh stood up and articulated it," felt Barry Cunningham, "the team realised that to go from being a good side to a winning side required enduring pain."

"As a group, we decided to restructure training," revealed McEniff. "We trained like dogs for a month," said Martin Shovlin, wincing at the memory. "Horses wouldn't have done the training we did," agreed Anthony Molloy:

> We'd start off with a 15-minute run and follow that with four 800 metre, four 400 metre and six 200 metre runs. Fair play to Anthony Harkin, he didn't bore us and at training every night he had something different for us.

"As a group we decided that certain players would have to put more in," remembered Tony Boyle:

> Players can train and the training can be hard, but it is only what the players put in themselves that counts. We did more stamina work, ran longer and worked harder. Every so often Martin McHugh would take the training session and it was something that you'd fear because you were in for a tough session.

Everyone had to pitch-in. "We were pushing one another on," recalled Matt Gallagher, "The older guys, including me, started taking more responsibility and horsed men on, especially any slackers." The training on the Tuesday after the Fermanagh game was cruel. Martin McHugh recalled how tough it was:

> We did so much running I was fucked and I cut inside a cone. Barry Cunningham was coming after me. He told me it was my fault that we were doing this training and that I'd have to run around those cones the same as everybody else! We didn't see a football for weeks.

The change in the attitude of the players was the most important thing. The mood was set for the rest of the year, remembered Barry Cunningham:

> All of a sudden the queues at the physio got shorter. Before that, players would be cute and say they had a sore leg to miss out on training. After

that it would only be the one or two who were genuinely injured.

The players were taking more control of the situation after the Fermanagh game. We told the management what we wanted done. McEniff didn't want any club games, not even league games, to be played. We told him that it couldn't be good because ten or 15 of the players aren't getting any football and the players who were starting were only getting one match every four weeks or so. Then they started having league games.

"I think the All-Ireland was won in the dressing room after the Fermanagh game," reflected Martin McHugh, "when the training got harder the spirit in the camp improved no end." Many of the players agreed. The new training regime – 'shock-training' was the term the players gave it – would be one of the main reasons, perhaps *the* main reason, that Donegal made the big breakthrough.

❄ ❄ ❄ ❄

While Donegal players were getting used to their 'shock-training,' Derry beat Down in the Ulster semi-final. The curse on defending Ulster champions had struck again and cost Down their All-Ireland crown. Donegal had expected and hoped that Down would come through. "We had it in our craw to beat Down but it wasn't to be. We never got the crack at Down we wanted after 1991 but PJ McGowan did the business in 1995," said Brian McEniff.

Derry looked formidable. National league champions, undefeated since the 1991 Ulster semi-final and that defeat had been to Down. With the scalp of the All-Ireland champions safely tucked away, Derry were new favourites for the Sam Maguire.

Donegal were boxing clever and giving new definition to keeping a low profile. McEniff's genius for meticulous preparation came to the fore. Lessons learned stretching back to the summer of 1983 and before were implemented. Most of all, lessons learned in the bitter summer of 1991 were written in stone. Derry were favourites, Donegal would merely turn up. Three weeks before the final, McEniff kept a challenge match in Clones against Leinster semi-finalists Louth very quiet. Only a handful of supporters witnessed Donegal obliterate a stunned Louth – 1-22 the boys hit, and that was without McHugh who was hopping around on crutches.

Thankfully the troubling sight of McHugh with his right foot encased in plaster wasn't what it seemed. The Wee Man was simply leaving nothing to chance and was resting an achilles tendon problem. It was an apposite demonstration of McHugh's obsessiveness that summer. The plaster of Paris would be discarded well in advance of Clones.

Those couple of hundred Donegal folk in the know who dotted around the pitch were buoyant. Gavigan and Shovlin were back – big time. Molloy and Murray were awesome. And the forwards were scoring for fun. But it was the display of a gutsy little Glen man that caused the sharpest intake of breath. Injury had kept John Joe out of a Donegal jersey since Christmas and his first run out had pitted him against the undisputed star of Louth football, Stefan White. John Joe and White went back as far as May 1987. Over two games to decide the Ulster under-21 final that year, John Joe had outplayed and outwitted White, then in the white and blue of Monaghan. Five summers had passed and while White's reputation had increased, the result was still the same. John Joe took him apart. So much so that White was eventually substituted

John Joe was desperate to fight his way into the first 15. "For me, every challenge match was a championship match," he remembered:

> I was really pushing it and had White in my back pocket. He was so frustrated that he lashed out at me and I lamped him. Anthony Molloy and all the older players piled in behind me. They were ready to fight. It showed that the spirit was going to be right in the camp anyway. Stefan White just walked off the pitch then. I don't even know if they put on a sub or not. It was just as well there were not too many people about to see it.

The media would again descend on Ballybofey in the days before the final. They got short change. The boys only wanted to play football and were giving nothing away. The lessons of previous years were being put to good use, remembered Anthony Molloy:

> It was all down to experience. We didn't read any papers and stayed away as much as we could from the media. McEniff would always tell us that we had all day Monday for reading about ourselves.

On the Tuesday before Clones, David Walsh, one of the country's best sportswriters, made the long journey from Dublin to the training in Ballybofey: "When the session ended the players galloped past the small clusters of press men. So fast did they move that journalist never got to ask for interviews." If anyone asked – and plenty did – McEniff expressed the opinion that Derry's tag as favourites was quite justified.

Things may have been low-key in the Donegal camp, but McEniff's cunning influence did not stretch beyond the training grounds. The county was buzzing for a fourth summer. Fans would turn up in their hundreds just to watch the team training. Down's demise in Casement had been greeted with some relief. Derry in an Ulster final was one thing, Down another entirely. Derry, went the cry from Malin to Bundoran, were beatable. The boys could take them. It was an air of confidence difficult to sustain when one compared Donegal's 12-month record with that of Derry. Eamon Coleman had guided Derry to victory over Meath, Kerry, Kildare, Down and Offaly in the national league and had just dethroned the All-Ireland champions.

The quiet confidence of the fans was replicated by the Donegal players who had their eyes on the biggest prize of all. "Even though we knew Derry would be tough, we were looking at the bigger picture," remembered Declan Bonner, "Anthony Harkin had been talking about five steps to an All-Ireland. We had got over the first two steps and the third step was the Ulster Final."

Derry folk were certain of victory and had the statistics to back up their claim. Theirs was a team on the up, Donegal were on the way down. Yet there was no shaking the gut feeling that prevailed in Donegal – the boys *would* take Derry. And things were much smoother in the camp than 12 months previously. Then McEniff was at loggerheads with Molloy. Shovlin had been left sitting on the bench. Hatchets had been buried, amicably, in 1992.

There was another motivating factor at play. Fear of defeat. Defeat for several of the Donegal players would mark the end of the road in the green and gold jersey of Donegal. Surely Molloy, McHugh, Reid, Joyce and Matt hadn't long left at this level. Molloy was going from match to match with the aid of anti-inflammatory tablets and ice-packs. He needed to stop playing football if the ability to even move featured in his future plans. "You can't just keep taking tablets. It would be nice to be able to walk in ten years time," he told Tom Humphries.

"We played every game as though it was our last," said Donal Reid. Tony Boyle was the youngest member of the squad and this approach meant nothing to him:

> I was only starting out so it meant nothing to me. It's funny when you look back. In my last few years on the team I was thinking about every game being my last. A lot of players don't think that when they're starting off, or even in the middle of their career. I remember John Connors' father telling me after the All-Ireland to make the most of it because it goes very fast. I used to look at him and think that I had ten or 12 years left. And lo and behold when I look back and I think it went very quick at the end up.

Tony would play on until 2000, but in the summer 1992 Reid was getting weary. Having pulled on the Donegal jersey 112 times, he indicated retirement would follow when the championship adventure terminated. The old hands knew better than anyone that their next game could well be their last.

The team, when it came from McEniff – who was in the same boat as the old hands – contained few surprises. Rambo returned at centre half-back, Shovlin displaced Barry McGowan and the Wee Man was in for Barry Cunningham. The team was: Gary Walsh; John Cunningham, Matt Gallagher, Noel Hegarty; Donal Reid, Martin Gavigan, Martin Shovlin; Anthony Molloy, Brian Murray;

Manus Boyle

James McHugh, Tommy Ryan, Joyce McMullan; Martin McHugh, Tony Boyle, Declan Bonner.

On the bench were Paul Callaghan, Barry McGowan, John Joe Doherty, Paul Carr, Barry Cunningham, Manus Boyle, Sylvester Maguire, Michael Gallagher, Mark Crossan and Jim McGuinness. Brian Tuohy and Eunan Gallagher, both of whom had been there or thereabouts when Donegal took on Cavan in Breffni, were gone. It was desperately unlucky for them. McEniff's old hang-up about leaving lads out of the team was still to the fore. He worried aloud to journalist David Walsh about the fellows in Killybegs who didn't make the team. He'd seen their heads go down that Tuesday night when the team was announced. Back in the Hollyrood he rang Molloy and got the captain to have a quiet word with them.

Barry McGowan couldn't quite believe it. "I thought I had played well enough in the Fermanagh game to keep my place, but I was dropped for the final" he recalled:

> I got to the stage where I thought I'd quit and I felt this was the last straw. I was screaming inside. I felt I played well enough in various positions but was being asked to be the jack-of-all-trades. I was used to plug any holes that appeared in the team. I was probably my own worst enemy. Perhaps I was too versatile for my own good and I suffered for that.

The Derry team was: Damien McCusker; Kieran McKeever, Danny Quinn, Tony Scullion; Johnny McGurk, Henry Downey, Gary Coleman; Brian McGilligan, Dermot Heaney; Anthony Tohill, Dermot McNicholl, Damien Cassidy; Enda Gormley, Seamus Downey, Declan Bateson.

The talking was over. Engagement time had arrived. The whole country expected a Derry win. Raymond Smith, the eminent GAA journalist plying his trade with the *Sunday Independent,* had a gut feeling that Donegal might pull off a surprise win. Yet the statistician in him steered him to make the call for Derry. His old friend in the *Irish Press* agreed. "Football strength and football power should be good enough to bring Derry to victory," predicted Peadar O'Brien. All the hype and expectation that had settled on Donegal 12 months earlier now rested on broad Derry shoulders. Donegal then had nothing yet everything to lose.

�֎ �֎ �֎ ✖

Sunday, July 19, 1992. One of the truly great days in Donegal GAA history. Only that Sunday in September would eclipse it in terms of magnitude. It was the day the boys who brought Sam to the Hills became men. Never had a Donegal team played a game of football like it and never had the green and gold jersey witnessed such an all-round performance of honesty, skill, courage and raw steel in the face of pure adversity. It was the day Donegal finally delivered on the promise of a generation.

St Tiernach's park packed in 35,000 and Clones witnessed one of the games of the summer. For Donegal people it was one of the games of that or any summer as their heroes reclaimed Ulster on a scoreline of 0-14 to 1-9. Clarity in the immediate aftermath was virtually impossible such had been the intensity of the battle. Incident had been stacked upon incident for 70 thrilling minutes. There would be time for analysis later as delirious Donegal eyes saw the talismanic Anthony Molloy joining the small club of men to have lifted the Anglo-Celt Cup twice. God was in his Heaven again.

Less that an hour earlier Donegal supporters were less sure that God even existed. It stood at 0-5 each at the interval but the odds were firmly stacked in favour of Derry. They would benefit from a strong breeze and, more significantly, an extra man in the second half. John Cunningham had been sent off in the 27th minute. A travesty, but a fact. And Tohill had ended Tony Boyle's participation around the same time. The uphill task that faced Donegal was as sheer as the cliffs of Slieve League. That second half would eclipse the first 35 minutes football-wise but not in terms of controversy. The first half had it all.

McHugh unveiled Donegal's intent and Derry malice within seconds as he pounced on the breaking ball from the throw-in and for his trouble was on the end of a crunching McGilligan shoulder into the face. From 60 yards and out of his hands, McHugh drew first blood, launching a huge kick over the bar with the aid of the breeze.

The battle had been joined. Gormley equalised from a free a minute later and then Reid arrived on the overlap for his customary point, albeit a little earlier than usual. It was a fabulous score and one that would give Damien Cassidy something to think about. Reid, marketing manager of Donegal Creameries, had engineered something of a coup for his bosses and for the first time that year the name of a sponsor was emblazoned on the jerseys.

Bonner had the close attention of Tony Scullion for the afternoon. Scullion, an old school defender, was one of the best in the country. Nonetheless, Bonner got the touch that set up the next score – a point from the boot of Tony Boyle. At the other end of the pitch, Matt Gallagher was far from content. "We didn't start the game well," he remembered, "I remember taking a sideline kick and nobody was moving for me, our effort wasn't good."

Like his counterpart Donal Reid, Johnny McGurk, the little Derry wing half-back liked to attack up the right wing. He would score a famous winning point against Dublin to put his team into the All-Ireland final a little over a year later and another spectacular one in the final itself, but in Clones Martin McHugh tracked back to haul him down at the second attempt before the Lavey man could line up a shot. Tohill pointed. It would be his only score of the game. He had only another 25 minutes to contribute.

By the 22nd minute Derry had added two further points from Gormley and

McNicholl – Derry's playmaker – and had the lead for the first time. Then, in the final ten minutes, all hell broke loose. Donegal were about to lose Tony Boyle. Derry would have to do without Anthony Tohill although Shovlin had been magnificent on him anyway.

McHugh had found his full-forward with a short free and as Boyle rounded Danny Quinn, Tohill found Boyle's knee with the full force of his boot. Such was the impact of the kick that Tohill actually broke bones in his foot. "Many people have told me since that they thought he meant it," said Tony Boyle:

> But to me it was a forward's tackle. Still, I'm a forward and it's not a ball I would have swung on. He broke a couple of bones in his foot. I hurt a ligament in the back of me knee but it was one of the lesser ligaments. It could have been a lot worse. I was told if it had been two inches away he would probably have smashed my kneecap and I might not have played again.

Incredibly, Tohill's name did not make it into Jim Curran's notebook. Curran seemed to be saving that for Donegal, but did award Donegal a free. That James McHugh pointed the free was of little consolation to a Donegal side who had just lost the most dangerous full-forward in the land. Worse was to follow, much worse.

John Cunningham was marking Derry sharpshooter Enda Gormley. "I knew that he didn't like it too rough," remembered John, "Looking back I suppose it was stupid, but I hit him over the shoulder and got booked." It was a costly booking. Soon after, John shadowed Enda Gormley as the Derry corner-forward roamed outfield to collect a ball near the sideline. Gormley transferred to the oncoming Dermot McNicholl. Razda lunged at McNicholl with the clear intention of landing a solid shoulder but the Glenullin man saw it coming and easily ducked under it. Cunningham missed his target completely and sailed over the line himself. "McNicholl was a very low-set kind of player," remembered John, "I went to shoulder him but then pulled out of it". Martin Shovlin had a good view of the incident:

> He meant to hit him hard all right – and if John Cunningham hit you, you'd know about it – but he missed him completely. His intention was to shoulder him. McNicholl ducked a little and John grazed his head, but that was it. There was no malice in it at all.

What happened next was incredible. Tyrone referee Jim Curran, for reasons known only to himself, decided it was a booking offence. "I was in shock," said Cunningham, "Matt pleaded with the referee not to send me off but after that all I remember was the long walk to the dressing room on the other side of the pitch." His championship was over. He wouldn't kick a ball again in Donegal's All-

Ireland winning year. The following 12 months would be the lowest of his career.

Donegal folk were incensed. Tohill, Gormley and McGilligan had all escaped the referee's censure. An injustice had been suffered by Cunningham not once but twice. Tom Humphries was there for the *Irish Times* and agreed that Razda had been "the victim of a harsh early booking". Humphries now couldn't believe his eyes as Curran pointed to the line:

> Bizarrely, referee Curran saw fit to dismiss the Donegal corner-back. The linesman most proximate to the incident kept his mouth shut despite the fact that Curran was clearly having difficulty keeping up with the play.

Bonner had just given Donegal the lead moments earlier but as Donegal limped to the break Gormley hit the equaliser from a free. As the teams made their way to the dressing rooms, Derry really had the game for the taking. There was the strong wind, numerical advantage and, as Tom Humphries put it, "the errors of the referee falling in their favour".

Lesser teams would have capitulated. No-one would have faulted Donegal now for faltering. In the aftermath, Brian McEniff would tell journalists that they had taken careful stock of the situation at the interval: "Everyone was very calm at half-time and we decided what had to be done in the second half". Now, long after the heat of battle has passed, Martin Shovlin has a different recollection:

> A lot of niggly things were happening between us and the Derry lads going up the iron steps to the dressing room. There was a bit of pushing and shoving. A bit of a melee got up and McEniff got a clip. Donal Reid and Joyce McMullan were sitting at the far wall of the dressing room when McEniff came in. There were bottles of water on the floor and he lifted his boot and kicked a bottle and it just busted above the two boys. He tore into everybody. 'Do you think that crowd are going to intimidate us going up the steps at Clones?' he roared.

"We had a lot of cross words at half-time," McEniff now admits. "I pinned Joyce against the wall". "It was shit or bust for Donegal at half-time in that match," remembers Declan Bonner, "If we were going to win the All-Ireland we had to go out and beat Derry in the second half." "We knew that the 35 minutes we were facing were either the end of our careers or something big," recalls Martin McHugh. They went for something big.

Barry McGowan had come on for Tony Boyle just before the interval. As the boys left the dressing room someone realised that James McHugh was still in at corner-back. "It was a bit mad at half-time in the dressing room," remembers McGowan:

When I was leaving the dressing rooms I was still at left half-forward but things were hastily changed. Somebody realised that James McHugh was playing corner back and that it wasn't such a good position for him. It's not that it was a much better one for me either. In the heat of the moment somebody made the decision to put me back there. I didn't think anything of it at the time. I knew that it was a bit of a strange move but I ended up in the corner back position. In the second half Donegal started to play particularly well and I was carried along on the crest of a wave.

McGowan had got the break he so desperately sought, but John Joe Doherty was thinking that he'd missed the rising tide:

Barry McGowan went from being a half-forward to being a corner-back. I was thinking, 'This is my chance going. I am a corner-back sitting on the line and half-forwards are coming back to play corner-back'. But it was just a stroke of magic because Barry McGowan went on to become the best corner-back in living memory.

Derry made a couple of blunders of their own in the second half. Gary Coleman was the designated spare man but didn't deliver. Coleman, a man-marker above the ordinary, was like a fish out of water for much of the half. And they left the cumbersome Danny Quinn inside at the mercy of Tommy Ryan. It was a fatal tactical flaw and Donegal exploited it handsomely. "In the second half, we played with just Tommy Ryan and me up front," recalled Declan Bonner:

Derry kept Danny Quinn back and we had to work our balls off to make sure we left nobody loose. Tommy won a lot of great ball and took a couple of great scores. I think Derry erred in leaving Danny Quinn back. At that stage, Derry needed a man out around the half-back line to pick up some ball. Tommy and me ran at them at every opportunity and they had no answer.

Tommy was on top of his game and gave probably his best ever display in a Donegal jersey. "We had the beating of the Derry full-back line," remembered Tommy:

The ball was being played in to the left and right and the spare man, Gary Coleman, wasn't doing his job properly. He was more interested in going up the field and he wasn't defending. Bonner and me were playing in the full-forward line and most of the ball that came into us in the second half was used wisely.

And so began what many believe to be the best 35 minutes of football ever produced by a Donegal team. "It was backs to the wall stuff," said Declan Bonner. It was enthralling to watch. All over the field, Donegal players dug deeper than they'd ever dug before. Heroes stood up everywhere.

Raymond Smith of the *Sunday Independent* had predicted that the duels in midfield would decide the "ultimate destination of provincial honours." He was right. McGilligan had denied Down clear possession over 70 minutes in Casement and it had won Derry the match. Not this time. Molloy and Murray produced a second half display that was unprecedented. Towering. Awesome. Brian McGilligan had just met his match.

There was no love lost between Molloy and McGilligan. The only thing greater than their mutual antipathy was their pride in their respective counties. "It was always a beating match between McGilligan and Molloy," recalled Brian Murray, "They were similar fellas and had great respect for each other. They would shake hands before and after a match and whatever happened on the field would stay there."

"McGilligan and me would always have our own personal battle," said Molloy:

> It didn't matter if it was a McKenna Cup game, league match or a challenge, it was always a nightmare on McGilligan. McGilligan and me would always come out at close to 50/50. That Ulster Final was my day against McGilligan and you'd seldom get those kind of days against him.
>
> He was captain of the Derry team for a couple of years. He was a man of few words but was a fair oul' horse on the field. One of the Derry boys told me that he said in a team talk 'Go out and play your own game and Molloy and me will wrassle around the middle of the field and don't worry about it.'

Speaking to the *Sunday Independent* before the game, Molloy alluded to the intense rivalry between himself and the big Dungiven man. He reckoned he had played poorly on Stephen King in the drawn game with Cavan but there was a sting in the tail of his story:

> A part of the problem that day was that I know Stephen and we are fairly good friends. That made it harder for me. Brian [McGilligan] is a good fetcher, he's having a great year but, the problem I had with Stephen, that's one I won't have with Brian.

Molloy was 35 minutes away from the BBC's Player of the Ulster Championship award. In the process he inspired an entire county. He was, as Sean McCague would later comment, "the hub" of the whole Donegal machine.

Damien Barton was in for Tohill and marked his arrival with a beautiful point soon after the restart. Three minutes in and Tommy Ryan commenced his torture of Danny Quinn. Quinn had to concede the foul and James McHugh levelled matters at 0-6 apiece. Quinn was now dead wood. McGowan and Reid cleverly sprayed ball into the Termon man who rounded Quinn with consummate ease in the ninth and 12th minutes to give Donegal a deserved 0-8 to 0-6 lead. Donegal were cruising. Tommy Ryan was on fire. Fifty minutes had elapsed when Lady Luck looked the other way.

For once Coleman's presence as the free man paid dividends for Derry as he was on the end of a Molloy clearance. The ball eventually found its way to the edge of the Donegal square and after a couple of unsuccessful attempts it was Seamus Downey who toe-poked it over the line. "Most of the attendance reckoned on there being at least one Derry forward in the square before the ball entered," remarked Tom Humphries dryly as Jim Curran consulted his umpires and, inevitably, allowed the goal stand.

"A lot of our players were cross that the referee had been so bad and they seemed to get the bit between their teeth," commented Gary Walsh:

> Seamus Downey scored from a rebound. He had definitely been standing in the square for the 30 seconds before that. At that stage, being a man down and conceding a goal we could have let our heads go down as we might have done in games in the past. Everything looked to be against us. Fair play to the boys, they just raised their game. It was like an avalanche and we just kept going back up the field after that.

The Donegal response was staggering. Everywhere one cared to look Donegal men were playing out of their skins. Martin Gavigan was having the game of his life. It was Rambo who led the revival a minute later with McHugh now orchestrating everything. The Wee Man hit Gavigan with a free and Rambo made it to the Derry 21-yard line before he was upended. Up stepped Declan Bonner to convert the equaliser.

Two minutes later Bonner's assistance wasn't required. Gavigan – heading for the man-of-the-match award – outfielded McNicholl, was fouled on hitting the ground, and McHugh drove the free over the bar against the wind from all of 50 yards. Donegal 0-10, Derry 1-6. Gavigan was invincible. And all around him men were playing out of their skins:

> There was always a lot of determination in those Donegal players as people and personalities. There was a lot of boys there who just didn't like losing. They were competitive people. On that day it shone through in a lot of people. We didn't want to get beaten again. We'd been through defeat, had learned from it and weren't prepared to accept a repeat of it.

It was inner-belief. Everyone dug that bit deeper. The difference between winning and losing is very little. It just requires that wee bit of extra effort. That second half was the best performance we were ever involved in as a team. There was so many players doing so many good things.

Including Murray, another having the game of his life. Nineteen minutes had gone when he fielded a ball above the heads of Heaney and McGilligan to set Molloy off on a solo run down the left wing. By the time Molloy looked for options Murray was on the overlap and struck the sweetest of points with the outside of his right boot. "My adrenaline was up, the team was playing well and everything seemed to be falling into place. It could have gone a mile wide the next day but I felt confident that day," he recalled.

Donegal's vexation with the referee continued when Matt, clearly being fouled, was adjudged to have over-carried presenting Gormley with the easiest of tap-overs from 14 yards. Not for the first time that afternoon Jim Curran heard the displeasure of the Donegal crowd ringing in his ears.

Gormley added a second and with 11 minutes left the teams were level for the seventh time. Donegal however, had victory in their cross hairs. Derry were being made to fight for every scrap of possession in the Donegal half. The Donegal half-back line were described as ravenous. Sean McGoldrick in the *Irish Press* would admire their formation of "a Great Wall of Donegal across the field".

And in behind them Matt was giving sweet nothing away, time and time again he put in the winning tackle. The full-back problem was sorted. Noel Hegarty and Barry McGowan were sizzling. Both operated as the last line of attack and mesmerised Gormley and Bateson with their push-forward mentality. Indeed Bateson was finally replaced by someone Donegal would come to know well in the years ahead – Joe Brolly.

Four scores remained in the game. Three of those raised Donegal banners. Bonner hit the first from a dead ball more than 45 yards from the Derry goals – the free earned by Joyce. A minute later and Donegal were two ahead as Noel Hegarty burst out of defence on one of his trademark thundering solo runs. Bonner, ahead of Scullion yet again, was on the end of the Glen man's pass but had work to do. Shrugging Scullion over the end line he found Ryan. Termon unselfishly found Kilcar and Martin McHugh split the Derry posts.

Derry's last score came yet again from an Enda Gormley free but was wiped out in an instant by a classic Donegal strike. The passage of play perfectly summed up Donegal's mixture of tenacity, sheer bravery and pure genius.

First the tenacity. With possession absolutely crucial from Walsh's kick out, Derry appeared to have the advantage as McGilligan for once fetched above Molloy. He hadn't hit the ground until three Donegal players were onto him. As Molloy, lying full stretch, attempted a hand trip, Joyce parted McGilligan from the ball and Reid lashed it first time out towards the sideline. There was no time for fancy stuff.

Then the sheer bravery. As Heaney sprinted towards the sideline in pursuit of the ball, in nipped James McHugh at the last possible moment to regain possession, skipping over Heaney's boot in the process. It may have been the most important intervention of the game. A Derry sideline would have landed the ball deep in Donegal territory. Job done, Wee James transferred to McGowan – offering support 60 yards or more from his corner-back berth. McGowan off-loaded smoothly to Reid who surged forward. Martin McHugh cut across him offering an option which Reid took. McHugh floated it first time to Shovlin who was tearing in from the wing. Shovlin took the full force of a smashing Kieran McKeever shoulder but as he hit the ground he popped the ball into the hands of Mairtín Beag some 21 yards out from the Derry goal and to the left

Then came the pure genius. Logically, McHugh had to turn back and pass outfield as four Derry defenders, including Henry Downey, were in very close proximity and all goal-side. McHugh had just one thing on his mind however – a point. He threaded a route through the Derry quartet in the space of a dozen magical steps before firing high over the bar with his left foot. "This was as good a score as Martin McHugh will ever be involved in," said Peter McGinnity in the BBC commentary box. It was indeed a magical score, and it perfectly illustrated McHugh's genius for taking on and beating multiple opponents at close quarters.

There was still time for anxiety. McGurk and Gormley combined to provide possession to Cassidy in a crowded Donegal parallelogram but as he thought about the shot Shovlin – who had covered ground at an amazing rate just to get there – lashed the ball out of his hands. Unfortunately it went straight to McNicholl but the Glenullin man was destined to shoot wide not least because Shovlin threw himself on his boot. Sylvester Maguire then made a late, late appearance, as much in a bid to waste time as anything.

But there was more nail-biting action in the Donegal goalmouth. Walsh and Shovlin – utterly exhausted – conceded a 45. It inevitably was dropped into the goalmouth by Gormley and only the joint efforts of McGowan and Molloy diving on the boot of Seamus Downey kept the goal intact. But the ball had spun out for yet another 45. It was another floater but was caught vice-like by Murray. And then, finally, Jim Curran made a decision that met with the full approval of every man, woman and child of Donegal extraction in Clones. He blew the full-time whistle. McEniff made a beeline for Martin McHugh. "The display in the second half was outstanding. I just ran onto the pitch and lifted McHugh like a wee doll. He was super that day," recalled McEniff.

Donegal were in the All-Ireland semi-final. Superlatives were not to be found to describe the display. Michael Daly put it best in the *Donegal Democrat* when he figured that Donegal, "played with the kind of spirit one sees, perhaps, only once in a lifetime". He was correct. Only a truly great football side could have delivered what Donegal delivered that Sunday in July. James McHugh was deadpan, "We had been talking for long enough, it was about time that we produced as a side," he said.

Gavigan, man-of-the-match, was as modest as ever in accepting his award. "It was one of those days when anybody could have got it and nobody would have complained. It's nice to have days like that."

"It was scintillating," stated Matt Gallagher:

The best half of football we ever played. We had decided that the only way to win the match would be by dropping deep and running at them – that was what we were really good at. We were going to commit players to running at them from the half-back line as well as having Barry and Noel running at them. Myself, Rambo and Molloy, the spine of the team, would try to keep it as tight as we could.

"We played the short game as well as we ever played it," felt Anthony Molloy. "Perversely, John Cunningham's sending off actually turned the match," opined Donal Reid:

Our game plan went out the window at half time and the real form shone through in the second half as good players and heart really came through. Everything that was good about Donegal football was there. We knew then that we were good enough to win the All-Ireland.

"We were so fit that when we'd get the ball we'd relentlessly drive forward," recalled Brian Murray, "it was like a machine and Derry couldn't cope with it or find an answer to it." Tony Boyle came in for some ribbing:

Some of the boys told me afterwards that it was only because they got rid of me that they were able to play that style of football. We had been struggling up to that period then I got hurt and John was sent off. The game plan in the second half was not to kick the ball away so we used the short game. We were lambasted for the short game in some quarters, but no team could stay with us when it was played well. Tommy Ryan was the main reason we won that Ulster final. The boys carried the ball a lot, but the odd time they had to kick it long, Tommy won every ball and kicked a couple of good scores.

Tom Humphries in the *Irish Times* had a soft spot for Donegal. He admired the stealth with which they had advanced to the Clones decider. He wasn't leaving the Ulster Final however, without a last parting shot at the man in the middle:

Referee Jim Curran would be well served by a little introspection. His performance was breathtaking in the measure of its incompetence. Donegal lost a goal and a man as a result and while McEniff wisely held his counsel after the game, he also withheld his handshake from Curran.

The Follower was equally sore at Curran. In 50 years of watching football he'd never seen anything like it. And in 50 years he'd never seen anything like Donegal. "Rarely, if ever, have I seen a display of skill, determination, courage and guts to equal the five-star showing in Clones," wrote the man who had seen it all. The man who would become President of the GAA, Seán McCague was in agreement. "It was 35 minutes of as good football as Clones has ever seen by any team in an Ulster Final," declared McCague on the BBC's Ulster Championship programme.

Derry manager Eamon Coleman was perplexed. "I just can't believe it; it will take us a long time to get over this," he remarked to journalists afterwards. Coleman and Derry would only have to wait another year and it would be at Donegal's expense but that was another story. Now belonged to Donegal.

McEniff was a proud, if emotional, man. "It was the most courageous performance any Donegal team has ever given me," he stated. Bigger days lay ahead but McEniff was right. In terms of footballing heroism, when all the chips had fallen and rolled away, it would never be equalled. An old foe, Liam Hayes, agreed. One week before the All-Ireland of 1992, he would refer to that afternoon in Clones: "It was a magnificent 35 minutes of unyielding and unapologetic football, the likes of which no other team has even touched upon in the last four months".

This was a more focussed and determined Donegal side than any previous one. Winning two Ulster titles in three years was a tremendous achievement, but as soon as it was won, the Ulster title of 1992 was set aside. Croke Park beckoned and this time, Donegal wouldn't be happy just to be there. "There was no partying of any kind that night," remembered Anthony Molloy, "we all went home to our own locals and there was no drinking. We trained for an hour and a half on the Monday night after the Ulster Final." Changed times. Only two of the hurdles identified by Anthony Harkin remained.

❊

RESULTS

Ulster Championship 1992

Donegal 1-15, Cavan 1-15	Donegal 2-17, Fermanagh 0-7
Donegal 0-20, Cavan 1-6 (R)	Donegal 0-14, Derry 1-9

15

A Hoodoo Buried

(August 16 1992)

"It wasn't a game we were afraid to lose, we were afraid to win."

BRIAN McENIFF

There had been Sundays like this before. Twenty years before, to the very day, Brian McEniff had been player-manager and right half-back on the first Donegal team to play on such a Sunday. That ended in defeat to Offaly and three times since – in 1974, 1983 and 1990 – there had been similar days that had resulted in deep scars on the very soul of Donegal football. Yet, there had been honour in failure in that quartet of All-Ireland semi-finals.

August 16, 1992. This was different. Never, in the history of Donegal GAA did the county need to win a football match as much as it did now. Mayo had made it out of Connacht and it was they who faced Donegal in the All-Ireland semi-final of 1992. There would be no underdog tag this time – Donegal were deemed red-hot favourites to make it to an All-Ireland final. Donegal had to deliver now or never.

McEniff had continued to box clever. He couldn't avoid the favourites tag thrust his way by the wily Mayo men and lapped up by the media. But he could play it low-key and did. Seldom was a match fraught with more danger than this one and McEniff knew it. The boys were expected to win. That brought its own pressure. The infamous Croke Park hoodoo added to it. Mayo had high hopes of their own. This was the county that had made it to the All-Ireland final three years previously and lost by a mere three points to Cork. Six or seven players remained from that Mayo side and now provided the backbone of this team. Men who knew how to win a semi-final match in Croke Park.

There would be no glory for the boys were they to fail against Mayo. Defeat to the westerners would mark more than just the end of an era. It would damage beyond repair the legacy this team had created for itself over four summers and half a dozen winters. Gavigan, with admirable honesty, hit the nail on the head: "Thirteen members of the Donegal team have experienced the atmosphere of an All-Ireland semi-final in Croke Park. So there can be no excuse for failure. There can be no alibis this time." "We were very nervous and tense," remembered Martin McHugh:

> We were going into the semi-final as favourites and it wasn't good for us. It was hard enough to win a semi-final given that we'd never won one. I remember speaking at the team meeting and saying the semi-final was the hardest game we were going to have. I said that if we could win it that we'd win the next one.

"We couldn't afford to lose another semi-final," said Barry McGowan, "We didn't talk about it in those terms, but everyone knew that we could not afford to lose again. It resulted in a very nervous display."

❊ ❊ ❊ ❊

It was, however, a day of days. That victory was secured was a truth. That Donegal were now a mere 70 minutes away from Sam Maguire was another truth, and a mind-boggling one at that. But that Donegal had laboured throughout and wrapped themselves and their long-suffering supporters in swathes of anxiety was the biggest truth of all. It had been a painful delivery and a whole county was exhausted. But glowing.

Moments before, with the clock showing that 71 minutes had come and gone, the Wee Man got on the scoreboard for the first time. Barry Cunningham had just galloped into the heart of the Mayo defence and had been upended in the square for his trouble. Penalty! Referee Tommy Sugrue indicated that it would be the last kick of the game. Three points ahead, McHugh looked at McEniff. McEniff indicated that he should go for goal, but McHugh decided to disobey orders and tapped it over the bar. "He was right," laughed McEniff afterwards. McHugh's sheer joy from the knowledge that Donegal had at last made it to the Promised Land manifested itself in a dance of delight that ended in the arms of Manus Boyle and Declan Bonner. And with that a whole county exploded. Men and women who had last shed tears over football matters in Carrick-on-Shannon and Roscommon let them flow with abandon. "Magic moments," noted Peadar O'Brien in the *Irish Press*, "Scenes of emotion mixed with utter ecstasy".

The best part of 50,000 people had witnessed history being made. The culchies from the west and the north-west were in town. The Dublin-based media were having a great laugh with it. Orla Bourke of the *Irish Press* looked on as "almost one-third of the Donegal population made the six-hour pilgrimage down to Dublin to watch their boys in green and gold beat the heart out of the wild men from the west. Tweed caps sat atop Mayo red-heads in one half of the Hogan Stand while the other half was filled with Donegal supporters wearing luminous green and gold from head to toe."

At 3:30pm when Tommy Sugrue threw the ball in, Donegal people the world over gathered in nervous expectation and watched the boys go to work with the aid of a slight breeze. Martin McHugh came very close within seconds as Tony Boyle beat Ford in the race to the first ball. "In 90 per cent of the games I played, my plan was to win the first ball no matter what," recalled Tony:

I was struggling with a knee injury and going into that match I wasn't fully fit. I happened to win the first ball and I didn't mind after that. That was how I focussed myself – if I won the first ball, I knew in my head that I had the beating of my man.

A few moments later at the other end, Matt Gallagher beat Liam McHale to the first ball. "I was mentally strong and had worked very hard," remembered Matt:

I was confident. I knew that there would be one or two balls that I wouldn't have a chance of winning but I was intent on giving myself as much a chance as possible by being crafty and doing what I did best – getting under people's skin.

John Joe Doherty played with Matt on many occasions and knew that the full-back had a knack of getting under the skin of his opponents. "Matt would always do his research before a game," laughed John Joe, "He'd find out if any of his opponents had blotted their copybook in the past and if they had, Matt would remind them."

All of seven minutes passed before Donegal raised an umpire's flag – and green and gold flags on Hill 16 – as James McHugh expertly hooked the ball over his shoulder and over the Mayo crossbar despite the convergence of six Mayo defenders. Mayo had already visited the scoreboard twice, points from Finnerty and Jennings had opened their account.

Nine minutes in, Donegal achieved parity but it could have been more. For the first time Donegal unveiled the full potential of their short-passing game. McGowan and Shovlin combined down the right wing to set Reid off on a run. He in turn found Joyce McMullan cutting smartly inside on the overlap. However, Gabriel Irwin in the Mayo goal advanced cleverly to smother Joyce's shot over the end line at the expense of a 45. Bonner duly converted; 0-2 apiece.

The scene was set. That Donegal were the better team was not in question – even though Mayo enjoyed a reasonable first half – but that they were jumpy and apprehensive was equally clear. Peadar O'Brien watched: "There were moments when it threatened to flare to life, moments when it looked as if football style and sense would overcome football nerves and tension, but these were few and far between". Later, O'Brien would note that the tackling wasn't always within the rule book. Six players were booked, among them Matt and Shov, but according to the man from the *Irish Press*, six or seven others could just as easily have had their names entered in the little black book. To biased Donegal eyes it seemed Mayo had set out to play a physical game, perhaps falling into the same trap Donegal had against Meath two years previously. There was little doubt that Mayo were big men, enjoying height advantage over their Donegal counterparts in many sectors.

Maher and Murray traded scores on the 11th and 13th minute and then Donegal hit the front for the first time as Bonner effortlessly fired over a 35-yard free – 0-4 to 0-3. It was a lead held for seven minutes as play skittered and stammered from end to end. Martin Shovlin had come to Walsh's rescue a little earlier, taking up the perfect position on the goal-line as the Donegal number one went to deal with a dropping ball. When it broke across the square, Shov was there to collect. At the other end however, scoring chances were being squandered from play and frees.

Matt had already answered a question or two. "Matt Gallagher has started very prominently indeed at full-back," noted RTÉ's Ger Canning, as Gallagher wrestled the ball from Kevin Staunton to set up another Donegal attack. In the run-up to the game the media had focussed on the 'little and large' confrontation expected to rage on the edge of the Donegal square. Matt had the task of marking Liam McHale for the afternoon and was giving away eight inches in height. It seemed an impossible task but Matt, as ever, proved to be up to the task. McHale did rattle the crossbar with a powerful fisted effort at one stage but that was really about the only trouble he caused Matt. What Matt lacked in height he made up for in pure know-how – all the boys singled him out as being a great reader of the game. "Magnificent," agreed Peadar O'Brien. So much so that Mayo's management gave up and moved McHale out around the middle seven or eight minutes before half-time.

Ray Dempsey twice raised the white flag either side of a James McHugh pointed-free and with 28 minutes gone the sides were again level at 0-5 apiece. A minute later Mayo regained their lead – again the result of a free. A minute before the interval, Bonner was on target again from the dead ball and for the fifth time the sides were level. Molloy had an opportunity just before that to widen the gap but failed to spot Tony Boyle unmarked on the edge of the square and blazed badly wide himself. The score stood at 0-6 apiece at the interval.

Donegal were struggling – things were not going well. Possession was not a problem, conversion certainly was. Peadar O'Brien bore witness to an old Donegal conundrum:

Barry Cunningham

Time and again, the Donegal forward line ran themselves into trouble as they passed too often, ran too far, had their shots blocked, dropped easy shots into the hands of Mayo goalkeeper Gabriel Irwin, or else shot badly wide.

His colleague, Sean McGoldrick, summed it up best, "The Croke Park jinx was whistling through their boots".

The game was passing a few of the boys by. Joyce McMullan was not getting the breaks although it wasn't for the lack of effort. Bonner was quiet from play and had also struggled from the dead ball – although he had converted three in the first 35 minutes. Like Joyce, the breaks were not coming his way. The same applied to Tommy Ryan. With 1-10 to his credit Tommy came into the semi-final as Donegal's top scorer from play in the Ulster championship and second in the overall scoring stakes to Martin McHugh. He had no reason to suspect his football world was about to come crashing down around him. Tony Boyle almost succeeded in putting the Termon man clean through earlier in the half but the flailing hand of Anthony McGarry got a vital interception. Had that ball reached Tommy his future in a Donegal shirt would probably not have taken the most bitter of twists. As it happened, he would get 47 minutes of football before being taken off – replaced by Barry Cunningham – but could not have believed that it would be his last contribution of the championship. "Mayo had beaten us comfortably in a challenge game in Ballybofey before the Ulster final," recalled Tommy:

They fancied themselves in the semi-final. A decision had been made during that campaign that if anybody was getting it tight, you'd help them out. I was playing at half-forward. Martin Shovlin was marking Tony Morley and the entire Mayo half-forward line was cleaning us out. I went back to help out a few times and got caught out.

On ten occasions in the second half the teams troubled the scoreboard operator. Seven of those scores came from Donegal boots, three from the Connacht champions. Yet the result was in some doubt for the best part of those 35 minutes. Liam McHale, now free of Matt's shackles, chipped over a point from the narrowest of angles seven minutes into the second half. He was causing problems around the middle.

Blood pressure was rising in the Donegal dugout. Never a good spectator, John Cunningham was impatiently watching his team mates apparently doing everything in their power to lose the game. He knew how the game could be won:

Barry and me were strategically placed in the dugout. The mentors used to sit on a bench just outside and we made sure we could hear what was going on. It was a dreadful game. We were kicking everything wide. I shouted out 'Jesus Christ, get Manus on'.

Manus remembers that John grabbed McEniff by the collar of his shirt to emphasise the point. McEniff made the change. Joyce McMullan was taken off and Manus Boyle made his first championship appearance since the Ulster semi-final against Fermanagh in June.

Mayo had moved back in front thanks to that McHale chip and increased their margin three minutes later as Jarlath Jennings pointed from the dead ball. Donegal were at sixes and sevens. Manus, primarily sent in by McEniff to end the woeful spectacle of missed frees, didn't help matters with his first effort. Only moments on the park, he found himself preparing to hit what was a scoreable free. He'd had no time to settle at all. "What way is that wind blowing?" he inquired of James McHugh as the Kilcar man jogged past. "Never mind the wind and just hit the fucker," replied a distracted McHugh. "I aimed for the middle of the posts but rattled it off the post," remembered Manus. Nonetheless, he learned enough to allow him adjust his sights next time. The substitution would prove to be inspirational.

Martin McHugh was really buzzing. There would be no repeat of Meath in 1990 when his game had collapsed. This was McHugh producing the goods when Donegal most needed him – providing strong leadership. He was everywhere, roaming the field – sometimes very deep – and carrying the attack into the heart of the Mayo defence himself. Peter McGinnity was up in the commentary box supplying analysis for the BBC. "McHugh, in this period of Donegal ascendancy, is involved in almost everything," noted the Fermanagh man.

It fell to Tony Boyle to begin the Donegal comeback with a point on the ninth minute. Tony was suffering from a poor supply of ball but was causing major headaches in the Mayo defence with anything that came his way. The former Dublin great, Jimmy Keaveney, was watching for the *Independent*. He wanted the ball driven in long to Boyle:

> It must surely have been obvious to everyone in Croke Park that Tony Boyle had the beating of Peter Ford. The most sensible ploy would have been to play the ball into Boyle as quickly as possible but, for some reason, Donegal preferred to weave aimless patterns.

Mayo management played into Donegal hands however by leaving Ford on Boyle when they had, in Dermot Flanagan, a man-marker supreme within their ranks.

Four minutes later Boyle was in action again, drawing a foul from a frustrated yet apologetic Peter Ford, the Mayo captain. Manus stepped up. "Martin McHugh told me that if ever Donegal needed a score, we needed it then," recalled

Manus. Manus obliged and brought Donegal level for the first time since the restart at 0-8 apiece. Donegal pressure was beginning to pay off. They were driving at Mayo in waves. The ball just couldn't keep going wide and so it proved. The last thing Mayo needed now was to hand Donegal an extra incentive to lift their game but that's exactly what their manager, Brian McDonald, did.

Padraig Brogan was brought on. Donegal supporters booed vehemently. "Uncalled-for behaviour," sniffed Tom Humphries in the *Irish Times*. Several thousand voices booing in unison was a picnic compared to what lay in store for Brogan. Meticulous as ever, McEniff had prepared his charges for this eventuality. "We had told the players to up their performance by 15 per cent if he came on," remembered McEniff, "Before he got to his position several Donegal players hopped off him". Brogan had just handed his substitute slip to Tommy Sugrue when Martin McHugh became the first Donegal man to stick the shoulder in him. Gary Walsh was nervous though. He knew what Brogan was capable of:

> Brogan came on and it was a bit like a pinball machine – he was getting hit from all sides and even the smallest men on the field were queuing up to hit him! I was quite nervous when I saw him coming on. He was the kind of fella that could have got a ball 40 yards out and come in and hit his one out of ten unbelievable shots and scored a goal.

Brogan became a reason to beat Mayo and Donegal set about the task with renewed vigour. "We were trouble before he came on and Mayo was doing quite well," recalled Noel Hegarty. That was about to change as the unfortunate Brogan was thumped every time the ball went anywhere near him. "It was a bad call by the Mayo management," thought Matt Gallagher:

> Brogan didn't contribute anything and probably lifted Donegal more than he did Mayo. They should have brought on Willie Joe Padden, he might not have contributed much and Brogan might have played better than him, but it would have lifted Mayo.

Molloy, having a quiet, nervous afternoon by his standards, came to life as did Gavigan. Molloy admitted afterwards that, "there was a fear of going to Dublin and letting Donegal down again. We only played in the last ten minutes." Peadar O'Brien noted the awakening of the Ardara giants, "Martin Gavigan took control with a great spell of football in the last quarter and his power play coincided with a thundering improvement in Molloy's play and Donegal were on their way." Mayo heads were about to drop.

Barry Cunningham had replaced Tommy Ryan in the 47th minute and within minutes made a huge impact, exploding into the game. It was a second astute substitution by McEniff and his mentors. Cunningham was here, there and everywhere – a man in the process of laying down a marker for the All-Ireland final.

The boys in defence limited Mayo to four scores from play. Not bad going in a game of such magnitude. Tony Morley was proving a handful for Reid but he stuck to the task manfully. Barry McGowan had obviously impressed McEniff in Clones. When the team was named for Mayo, McGowan was in from the start – the only change from the 15 that started against Derry. McGowan was staying true to his earlier vow – it would take a good man to dislodge him now. "In my head I always saw myself as a forward," said Barry McGowan:

> I knew that there was nothing worse than to be marking a defender who would attack. A forward's mind is a selfish one. They are always look-ing for possession, to score and enhance their own situation. If a back makes a dart it breaks the forward's concentration. He takes a forward to where he doesn't want to be – the back line. When a manager sees a forward scooting around the back line and running after his own mark-er it brings him down even further and puts him in the bad books. It was the only way I knew how to play in that position.

Two minutes into his first game as a corner back, McGowan's opponent, Anthony Finnerty scored a point from play. He didn't score again and was replaced after 47 minutes by Noel Durkin, an All-Star forward in 1989. He did-n't score at all. As corner-back debuts go, it was impressive.

Noel Hegarty's grip on his corner-back position was vice-like and he too introduced a new dimension to the team by continually surging forward out of defence. The Glen man galloping upfield with the ball seemingly glued to his toe was a sight to behold. A legendary Kerry full-back, John O'Keeffe, sang his praises loudly in the *Irish Times*:

> I've yet to see a corner back like Hegarty come the full length of the field with such confidence and work the ball so cleverly into a scoring posi-tion. We never had corner backs like that in the Kerry team I played in.

It was high praise indeed. O'Keeffe was equally impressed with the Donegal number three, "Matt Gallagher has a big heart and great pace. He's very clever on the ball and he surprised me in that he was so agile and was able to clear everything short." Out in front of Hegarty, Shovlin had yet another excellent afternoon. Everything that came down the right wing was his.

Scores were more rare than wides. In the course of the second half, Donegal would hit one wide more than they would hit points. Exasperated at the inac-curacy up front, Martin Shovlin tried to get on the scoresheet:

> I was clean through at the Canal End. I said to myself, 'If I get this one

over, we'll definitely turn the game. If I can score the rest of the team can.' We needed a score at that time but I blarged it wide. I thought that was it, because there was nobody else scoring anyway.

James McHugh was another to play a significant role – almost as sweeper at times – and was causing huge problems in the Mayo defence. Mayo committed yet another foul on the Bavin man in the 57th minute and Donegal were one ahead thanks to the right boot of Manus. Excitement was mounting around Croke Park. "Is it to be their day at last?" asked Ger Canning, adding, "You can be sure Brian McEniff is living on his nerves." Four minutes later Donegal got a rub of the green. Murray – who had an absolute stormer throughout – put Bonner through but just as the Na Rossa man kicked badly wide he was awarded a fortuitous free. He didn't miss at the second asking and tapped over; 0-10 to 0-8. Donegal eyes were beginning to well-up.

With five minutes remaining Manus opened up a three-point gap for the first time with his third and final point – a real beauty – the free won by the strong running of Barry Cunningham. Manus' unerring place kicking and availability from play was clearly the key which allowed Donegal to put a gap between themselves and the men from the west. The fourth player to be handed the free-taking responsibilities, Manus was the man who delivered. "He really steadied the ship," remembered Brian McEniff.

Jimmy Keaveney – a freetaker of some note himself – was well impressed with the Killybegs man, "The arrival of Manus Boyle unquestionably had a settling effect on Donegal's forwards. Suddenly they had a calm, reliable freetaker but I felt he also contributed handsomely from play." It had proved to be an inspired move on McEniff's part.

Donegal were nearly there but there was scares to be endured. TJ Kilgallon came tearing through the centre of the Donegal defence a minute later. With the fear of a late goal now pulsing through Donegal players, mentors and supporters alike, there was no time for niceties and Noel Hegarty conceded the free. The result was Mayo's last score – a point from Jennings in the 66th minute. "It is still there for the taking – a Mayo goal could send them through to the All-Ireland final," exclaimed Ger Canning, adding to the anxiety of Donegal people watching on television. "It's in the melting pot," warned McGinnity over on the BBC.

The remainder of the game belonged to man-of-the-match Tony Boyle. Tony was so worried about his dodgy knee throughout the 70 minutes that big match nerves simply swept over his head. He fielded spectacularly from a huge Anthony Molloy clearance out on the left wing and cruised past Peter Ford with a terrific burst of speed to reclaim that vital three-point lead. It was the score of the game. As Tony exchanged a high-five with Manus, Ger Canning was giving voice to the thoughts of all Donegal people, "That may well be the point that will take Donegal – finally – through to their first ever All-Ireland final!"

The score stood at 0-12 to 0-9. With injury-time ticking away it was the Dungloe man who again steadied the ship by claiming vital possession. Another huge clearance driven from the boot of Rambo found Tony on the end of it. Barry Cunningham offered support at full gallop with the 'keeper stranded. As the Killybegs man bore down on goal he was unceremoniously hauled to the ground by a clutch of desperate Mayo defenders:

> People have since said to me that I should have taken a shot. I wasn't thinking about it like that. We were three points up and the clock was gone. The corner back was on the goal line and I was at the edge of the large parallelogram. It would have been quite difficult for me to put the ball in the net from where I was. The goalie came running at me. I figured that if I held the ball tight he'd have no choice but to foul me. I went down injured and two minutes were wasted. If I had taken a shot and missed, they'd have had a kick out, or if it was saved it would still have been in play and anything could have happened. I was thinking of the percentage at the time.

All that remained was for Martin McHugh to stick the penalty over the bar. It was the sweetest of moments for a man that had given such a large part of his life to Donegal football. "I knew it from the moment I kicked the penalty over the bar in the semi-final that we were going to win the All-Ireland," he recalled, "I don't know why I felt that way. I just knew it."

That McHugh would have been thinking that way would have come as no surprise to John Joe Doherty, "Martin was probably ahead of his time in that he had a vision of winning an All-Ireland," he said:

> The idea of Donegal winning an All-Ireland had been thrown about in the years leading up to 1992. Everybody had it as a dream but he set to make a reality of it. It wasn't just pub talk with Martin, he'd definitely lead the charge himself.

Donegal's performance was certainly not a thing of beauty. Not by a long way. Sixteen times they had driven the ball wide. Numerous Donegal shots had not even reached the end line. Fifty frees littered the game – albeit the majority conceded by Mayo. But Tommy Sugrue's final blast on the whistle heralded a famous 0-13 to 0-9 victory. The winning margin "could have been 14 or 15 without a trace of flattery," remarked Tom Humphries. Colm O'Rourke, on duty for the *Sunday Game*, agreed, "Seldom can a team have enjoyed so much dominance as Donegal did in the second half of a major game and win by so little". "We could never express ourselves in a semi-final," remembered James McHugh:

> It didn't matter if we played Fermanagh or Cavan in an Ulster semi-final,

it would be the same. Added to that, no Donegal team had ever played well in an All-Ireland semi-final or got past it. Afterwards I remember thinking 'this is it, we had got over the hurdle we couldn't get over'. It was all go from there on. I remember Martin saying to us we'd never lost an All Ireland final.

A hoodoo, albeit one showing some signs of life, had been buried. History had been made. The sigh of relief from Donegal folk in Croke Park was almost audible on the slopes of Errigal. One-third of the population of Donegal, it was said, witnessed proceedings in Croke Park and now most of them swarmed onto the field to greet their heroes. An All-Ireland semi-final is there to be won and nothing else. But this one was celebrated famously nonetheless. No one, not even a dejected Mayo, begrudged Donegal their moment. As Cliona Foley of the *Irish Independent* pointed out, the whole country was aware "that Donegal had been kicked off the second-last step of the ladder an agonising four times". No-one knew that better than the thousands on the pitch.

Barry McGowan was fighting through the thousands on the pitch and badly wanted to find the sanctuary of the dressing room. "I had picked up an injury to my shoulder midway through the second half," he explained:

> I was shouldered – it was nothing out of the ordinary – and I seemed to get tangled with one of my own players. It felt sore at the time but the adrenaline was pumping and I played on. It turned out that I had badly damaged the ligaments in my shoulder.
>
> We didn't get off the pitch for half an hour after the match. In that time I had started to cool down and I could feel the pain kicking-in. After the match, supporters were slapping me on my back. They meant nothing but the best but the pain nearly brought me to my knees. I'm sure people were wondering what was wrong with me that I was staying away from them. All I was doing was minding my injured shoulder and trying to get to the dressing room.

If Donegal players needed reminding of the enormity of the task ahead, that reminder came from the Mayo captain almost a half hour after the final whistle. Congratulating Donegal on their win, Peter Ford added words of wisdom that were forged in bitter experience, "Remember lads, you are in an All-Ireland final. We were the same in 1989. You may only get one chance. We blew ours. Do not let the same happen to you."

The Mayo players and management had a torrid few weeks ahead of them. The players would issue a statement making themselves unavailable while Brian McDonald remained as manager. Stories of pushing cars around training grounds and general unhappiness with a brusque style of management would litter the papers – the implications of the thin line between success and failure illustrated as Mayo washed their dirty linen in public. "If that Mayo team had been well prepared, it would have beaten us," felt Martin McHugh.

Matt Gallagher, high on adrenaline, made a prediction as he struggled back to the dressing room, "The whole county will go crazy, they are football mad and they've been waiting for this for so long". He wasn't wrong. Already, on the streets around Croke Park, all talk centred on one topic. And for five weeks that topic would dominate life in Donegal like no other. Tickets. The third Sunday in September, as always, would be All-Ireland Sunday. The opposition was still to be determined – a week would pass before Dublin took on surprise Munster champions, Clare. Donegal folk didn't give a damn who their team met in the final as long as they could secure that little piece of card which guaranteed admission to see it.

In the dressing room under the Hogan Stand, Brian Murray was taking it all in and chatting to Vincent Hogan of the *Irish Independent*. The two of them were keeping an eye on an emotional Brian McEniff. "People have no idea what he goes through," Murray told Hogan, "What he probably needs most now is a good night's sleep. Because that man just doesn't sleep in the week of a big game."

Sleep was far from McEniff's mind which had turned to the final, he had a few quiet words with Barry Cunningham. Having come on as a substitute, Barry was pleased with his performance:

> I was as frustrated as anyone else. The boys were playing without any conviction or belief in themselves. It looked like we were going to lose the game. The game was loose and the ball kept coming to me but the game still had to be won.
>
> After the game McEniff came to me in the dressing room and told me that I wouldn't be starting in the final. He knew that there might be speculation that I would start in the final but he was getting my head ready even at that time.

"Barry was our super-sub," remembered McEniff:

> He could have played in the middle of the park with any team but Molloy and Murray had something special. The two lads complemented each other very well. I felt sorry for Barry in that respect. He would always have wanted to play.

Nine years before McEniff had been inconsolable after his team had been defeated by Galway. McEniff's evening would not be spent in a lonely Dublin Park this time around. It would be a different journey home. "God knows, we've had our share of bad homecomings," remarked the man himself. Half of

Bundoran would be waiting on the steps of the Hollyrood at a quarter to three in the morning to welcome him.

Analysis raged in the days that followed. "A quicker release of the ball will be necessary if they want to win an All-Ireland final," reckoned Kerry legend John O'Keeffe. His old sparring partner, Jimmy Keaveney of Dublin, agreed, "Donegal must be more direct". But the wily Dub saw beyond the nerve-ridden semi-final – he knew that Donegal had fought through an immense personal psychological barrier. Keaveney recognised the "immense heart" of Donegal and, dismissing Clare's chances, sent a chilling warning to a former team-mate, "I see Paddy Cullen's men having their hands full trying to outwit this Donegal team."

※

RESULTS

All-Ireland Semi-Final 1992
Donegal 0-13, Mayo 0-9

16

A County Goes Daft

(August 17 – September 20 1992)

"The word 'defeat' never came into it.
We were going to win the game, it was as simple as that."

DECLAN BONNER

And so the All-Ireland adventure began. This was uncharted territory for Donegal folk. A week after the Mayo game, Dublin booked their place in the final at Clare's expense – five points the margin. Suddenly all talk centred on the sky blues. The names Curran, Barr and Heery rolled off every tongue – the much feared Dublin half-back line was discussed with trepidation in every corner of the county. Charlie Redmond was another. And no one had forgotten Vinny – the Trinity Gaels man had posted a stark reminder in the semi-final against Clare when 2-1 stood to him alone.

Donegal's training was continuing at a frenetic pace. Men were pushing hard to win a starting jersey for September's third Sunday. Training games were played at championship pace – there were no half measures and slaps were given and taken. Barry McGowan was wary of his injured shoulder, but it had taken him so long to secure a place in the starting 15 that he wasn't about to give it up. "I got a hard knock on my shoulder in a practice match and fell over," he remembered:

People thought I was finished. The knock had been to my left shoulder and even though I felt the pain in my right shoulder, I just gritted my teeth and played on. The way I dealt with that particular knock proved to the selectors that I would make it.

On the Saturday before the final a training match was held in Donegal Town. Declan Bonner was knocked out and carried off, Donal Reid and Joyce

McMullan beat the heads of each other and Rambo chased Murray up and down the field. Tension hung thickly in the air but there were some moments of mirth. "Charlie Mulgrew was pushing really hard to make the team," remembered Matt Gallagher:

> He was very difficult to mark. He was strong and two-sided but he was-n't the best finisher. Rambo and him went for a ball and Mulgrew went to toss Rambo but Rambo just threw him head over heels. I lay down laughing. He got as mad as hell. 'What are you laughing at?' he demanded. 'I'm laughing at you,' I replied. It was so serious between the two of them for a moment but I couldn't help myself and was dou-bled over laughing at them. Then Mulgrew started to laugh.
>
> What was very good about that was boys like Mulgrew, Sylvester Maguire and Manus were all pushing so hard to get a place. This made everyone else push hard.

"Even at training you'd want to beat somebody," agreed Martin McHugh:

> Martin Gavigan definitely improved my game. I'd say Bonner would tell you that Noel Hegarty improved his game or Tony Boyle would tell you that Matt improved his game. They have all proven since that they were fabulous players. At that time people wouldn't have realised that. Boys like Barry McGowan, Noel Hegarty and Declan Bonner carried their clubs for years.

❋ ❋ ❋ ❋

Donegal got a chance to test themselves against Dublin's most recent opposition when Clare made the long trip to Trummon for the opening of Naomh Brid's new ground. It was an interesting exercise from a number of perspectives: Donegal defeated Clare by eight points; McHugh scored a truly magnificent goal while masterminding the entire game; and a major punch-up ensued as matters between John Joe and Padraic Conway got out of hand. But by far the most interesting development was that McEniff started the six forwards that he would line out in the All-Ireland final three weeks later: James McHugh, Martin McHugh, Joyce McMullan, Declan Bonner, Tony Boyle and Manus Boyle. The warning signs were there for Tommy Ryan who started on the bench.

Barry McGowan was struggling with his shoulder while Reid had picked up a bad slap in a club game. In their absence John Joe and Paul Carr had the opportunity to attract McEniff's attention. John Joe certainly did, not least because himself and Conway battered the heads off each other, but in between fisticuffs the Glen man was as sharp as ever at corner back.

In half a dozen positions players were worried and others hopeful. Bonner had been quiet by his own high standards in Croke Park. In Ballintra he hit 1-4 to remind himself and onlookers just what he was capable off. Tommy Ryan knew he was now in a battle for a starting jersey. In Ballintra he came on for Tony Boyle and rammed home a goal in double quick time to underline the fact that, prior to his Mayo nightmare, he had been the in-form forward. Barry Cunningham was in a similar position. Every time he pulled on the jersey he was impressive but with Molloy and Murray on song around the middle his chances of a start in midfield were slim.

McEniff had used the Clare match to take a close look at Manus Boyle. "He told me that he wanted to see me do things other than scoring," remembered Manus, "He wanted me to pass the ball, tackle and work. Clare got stuck into us and we responded in kind. We played that game the way we played the first ten minutes against Dublin in the final."

Brian Murray was based in Leixlip, County Kildare. He'd undertake the 160-mile trip by road to Ballybofey in the company of selector Seamus Bonner and panellist Michael Gallagher. Murray had also been detailed for some extra training by McEniff. "Although he could go up and catch a ball, Murray would often reverse when he'd land," recalled McEniff, "I wanted him to bound forward so I suggested he train with Kieran McCready."

Dublin-based McCready was a great Donegal supporter who had been involved with McEniff's back-room team in the mid-1980s. McCready had a strong background in boxing and he set up a gym where he would put Murray through a training regime taken directly from boxing. Shadow boxing, footwork exercises and pummelling became part of the routine. "McCready was 63 at the time but would participate fully," remembered Brian Murray:

He'd pummel my stomach and then I'd do it to him but it was like hitting a wall. He'd know where to hit me too. He'd hit me hard and would tell me, 'No fucking Dublin player will hit you as hard as that. You can take anything they try.' It was so different from the training I did in Donegal but it was great to train with him.

McEniff, meantime, was chatting to an array of football men at the Hollyrood – Larry Tompkins, Jack O'Shea, John O'Mahoney and Pete McGrath among them. Art McRory, an old friend in Ulster, was another consulted by McEniff as he searched for nuggets of information, however small, that could make a difference on All-Ireland day. "We picked the best of of what we could find out from the successful teams of previous years," recalled McEniff. Letters, faxes and calls flowed into the Hollyrood wishing the owner well in his quest for Sam. Every third or fourth call was someone chancing their arm in the equally crucial quest for a ticket.

A County Goes Daft

Sean O'Neill of Down wasn't concerned about tickets when he called McEniff. Three times an All-Ireland winner with Down in the 1960s, O'Neill was regarded as having one of the keenest football brains in Ulster. The hairs stood on the back of Brian McEniff's neck as he scribbled down the notes O'Neill directed down the telephone line:

> It was the Sunday night before the match when he finally caught up with me. I took the call and he was talking at me rather than to me. I made notes of what he said and these were what I referred to before we left the hotel the following Sunday. He said that McHugh would have to go down the barrel of the gun, namely Keith Barr.

Martin McHugh was in the best shape of his life and would ram himself down the barrel of the gun in the final. "The All-Ireland was the game I prepared best for," remembered McHugh:

> We used to do runs around the field at Ballybofey and Martin Shovlin was always the fittest player. On the Thursday week before the final I passed Martin Shovlin in the run around the pitch. I knew then that I was right. I had never passed Shovlin before or since.

While the boys worried about the game and McEniff schemed, the rest of the county pulled in favours owed in the hunt for tickets. Bandwagon-hoppers appeared out of the woodwork here, there and everywhere with genuine GAA folk fearful they might be overlooked in the clamour. Fifty thousand people would scramble for less than 10,000 tickets – 9,130 to be precise. An extra allocation of 1,000 or so came into the county at the last minute but thousands of people would suffer disappointment. Phone-calls down the country were made and often proved fruitful as GAA folk kindly passed tickets northward. "The biggest problem at the time was tickets," remembered Noel Hegarty, "everywhere I went people were looking for tickets. It was bedlam." "In the lead-up to the game there was no talk about the game or how we were going to play," recalled Martin McHugh, "all people were talking about was tickets."

As the weeks passed, excitement reached fever pitch. Training in MacCumhaill Park now took place in front of crowds that would have rivalled many an attendance at national league games in days of old. People were not going to miss a single moment. There was little room left on cloud nine. The days leading up to the All-Ireland were truly a wonderful time to be in Donegal. Written off by the entire country, a contented confidence seeped through the county in those September days. The weather was unseasonably fine, the hay had been saved and Donegal were in the All-Ireland final. It was already a time to celebrate but it was about to get so much better.

While the people of Donegal basked in the reflected glory their team had earned for them, the players left nothing to chance in preparing for the biggest day of their footballing lives. Anthony Harkin's training programme had got them into the best shape of their lives. "Anthony Harkin kept up to date with training methods not only, in Gaelic football but in rugby, basketball and soccer too," remembered Martin Gavigan:

> He was familiar with the training regimes of the All-Blacks. He would introduce their methods into training and apply it to Gaelic football in a sensible way. He made it as professional as he put ball-work at the centre of it. His programmes didn't just materialise overnight, he put lot of work and research went into it.

"When he first came, most of the squad wouldn't have known who Anthony Harkin was," remembered John Joe:

> It probably took him some time to earn the respect of the squad. When we started to win we began to see the bigger picture. Anthony was always a very fair trainer and did not have any favourites. He had a very powerful voice and when he shouted at you you'd hear him.

There was still time for the bizarre in the Donegal camp. The boys landed for training in Donegal Town one Tuesday night only to find the dressing rooms locked. No problem, figured McEniff, turning to the smallest man around – Wee James – and hoisted him up onto the window ledge of the dressing room. McHugh – not used to breaking and entering – grabbed the window but the whole frame came away in his hands and walloped the manager below.

The press were back in Ballybofey. And getting soaked for their trouble as the rain poured heavily and steadily. "Welcome to Donegal. I apologise for the weather," grinned McEniff, as he and the boys spent an evening trying not to say too much to the hacks from the capital. Nothing much was given away. Donegal wouldn't be altering their game plan though, that much McEniff was willing to confirm, "We play a running game and we will stand by that".

By the time the hacks went to print, all the old yarns about Donegal football had been dusted down and revived. Like the one about the Kerry man instructing the Donegal man on how to accept the Sam Maguire Cup in Croke Park. "Keep one hand free to shake hands with the Queen," warned the Kerry man. Puzzled, the Donegal man pointed out that the Queen is never in Croke Park. "She will be when Donegal wins the All-Ireland," retorted the wit from the Kingdom.

McEniff's association with Donegal's success in 1972, 1974, 1983, 1990 and now in 1992, was chronicled in detail. McEniff didn't mind telling the odd self-deprecating story, seemingly saving a different one for every journalist he met.

One was from a Connacht final replay in Castlebar when Mayo were all over Sligo in the opening minutes. It was 1975 and McEniff was the Sligo trainer. Debate was raging among the many Sligo selectors about what changes should be made. McEniff, said to himself, "I don't need this," and walked up along the sideline. Just then a Mayo supporter shouted in, "McEniff, you know more about frying chips than you do about football". Somebody in the Sligo squad evidently knew something about football as the county won its first Connacht title in 47 years.

Gavigan was attracting extra attention from the press men. He was to be married on the Saturday after the game. "Please don't mention a draw," he laughed, with the practised air of a man who had that conversation a thousand times.

And there was poignant moments too. Peadar O'Brien spoke to John Cunningham about that sending off against Derry. "It was terrible. I was so down, and I was so embarrassed. And worse still, I have been unable to regain my place since." Although his suspension had amounted to just two weeks, his place in defence had gone to Barry McGowan. O'Brien concluded that he hadn't seen anything like the raw football enthusiasm throughout Donegal since Tyrone had made it to the final back in 1986.

Players were trying to cope with the hype. It wasn't easy. One man who understood what they were going through was former Dublin star, Brian Mullins, then living in Carndonagh:

> Living in a rural community where the players are trying to live their lives normally while waiting for the game is difficult. Every time they go for a sliced-pan, a fill of petrol, into the post office or wherever – everybody they meet wants to talk about the game! That creates a terrible burden for the players – it's almost as bad for some as asking them to make a speech in the Dáil.

There was hardly a telegraph pole in the county that wasn't wrapped in green and gold. Flags, banners, bunting and signs were everywhere. Pillars, kerbs and road markings were painted green and gold. Shop window mannequins were clad in Donegal jerseys. "How do you think it'll go?" inquired stranger off stranger. Masses and Novenas were being offered. Rosaries were being prayed. Margo was never off the radio "Walking Tall in Donegal". Donegal really had never known anything like it. Diehard GAA fans didn't know whether to laugh or cry at the utterances of the newly converted. Those who wouldn't know whether the ball was blown up or stuffed could now be heard pouring forth on the merits of Donegal's short-passing game, McEniff's options on the bench and how Dublin liked to launch attacks from their own 40. It really was new territory. It was abundantly clear that McEniff and his boys had captured the imagination of the entire county. And beyond. In North America, Britain, Australia and various corners of the world, Donegal people's thoughts were with the boys in green and gold.

Martin Shovlin

Up in the capital, Paddy Cullen had announced solemnly that his squad had been struck down by a mystery virus. The Follower was less than sympathetic, "Like all Dubs he thinks that anybody outside the Pale came down with the last shower". The man from Dromod was expecting war, "I say the final will be open naked warfare under the guise of sport". If Donegal's recent encounter with Clare over in Ballintra was anything to go by, the boys wouldn't be found wanting if war was declared. Yet, they had learned a lesson in 1990 when they forgot about football altogether and got stuck into Meath with abandon. A happy medium would have to be found for the Dubs.

McEniff would have no problems if the boys had to hit hard. Speaking to some journalist or other in the lead up to the final, McEniff smiled as he told a story that revealed a steely interior:

> Because I am the Donegal team manager and because of my business interests in the county, some opposition players like to take a swipe at me on the football ground. I have only one answer to that. Retaliate first!

Practice matches at Donegal training sessions were tough affairs. Players on the fringe of the team were pushing desperately hard for a place on the final 15. "I used to referee some of those matches," recalled McEniff, "I'd throw in the ball and not sound the whistle again. I'd let them at it hammer and tongs. That's what made them such a tough side to beat."

McEniff wasn't always content to simply referee the game. Relatively fit for his 49 years, the manager would occasionally take part in A versus B games. On the Tuesday before the All-Ireland he fielded at left corner-forward on the B side. He won a ball and shimmied past Noel Hegarty to score a point. "I told him 'That won't do against Dublin,'" remembers McEniff:

> He hit me hard when the next ball came in. He was a 6'1" sheep farmer and as hard as steel – I felt like delft that was about to break. I wouldn't satisfy him and got up and played on, but was sore for about three days afterwards.

❀ ❀ ❀ ❀

Tuesday, September 15. Things were tense as everyone in MacCumhaill Park waited on the announcement of the team. As the players stretched they bantered with each other. Manus Boyle – who had scored 2-10 for Killybegs in a recent league match attended by McEniff – asked Tommy Ryan if he had received a 'phone call from McEniff. Tommy hadn't and neither had Manus. Was that good or bad? James McHugh was listening in and put their minds to rest when he told them that Martin hadn't got a call from McEniff either!

The time had arrived when McEniff would name the 15 who would go into battle against the Dubs. McEniff had hoped to talk to the boys individually but in the event the team was announced for the first time in a crowded dressing room in Ballybofey. A pin dropping would have sounded thunderous as McEniff began to speak. Gary Walsh. Barry McGowan. Matt Gallagher. Noel Hegarty. Donal Reid. Martin Gavigan. Martin Shovlin. Anthony Molloy. Brian Murray. James McHugh. Martin McHugh. Joyce McMullan. Declan Bonner. Tony Boyle. Manus Boyle. All the wondering – all the speculation – was over. Disappointment, albeit expected, for John Joe, Razda and Barry Cunningham. Desolation for Tommy Ryan.

"The story had been leaked to Donal Keenan of the *Irish Press* before the team was announced to soften the blow," remembered Tommy Ryan:

He told me that Manus Boyle was going to play in the final. I told him to tell me something I didn't know. It was a good decision to select Manus and he was definitely there on merit. But I hadn't played at left corner-forward all year so the choice wasn't between me and him. I think the final decision was between Joyce McMullan and me. Unfortunately, none of the selectors were close to me. Mickey Lafferty knew Joyce very well and Seamus Bonner was there too. I don't blame anyone for it, if I was a selector choosing an All-Ireland final team and a clubmate of mine was involved, I'd do my utmost to make sure he was on.

I can accept that Manus had to play but I don't like the way it was orchestrated. Brian was never man enough to tell me what happened when they sat down to pick the team. It was nothing to do with Joyce. He got his chance and held his corner against Paul Curran who was a very good player.

"Joyce was used in the final because he was physically strong and had always played reasonably well on Paul Curran," Brian McEniff outlined:

Curran was one of the best players in the country at the time but Joyce horsed him out of it several times. We took Curran out of the game by putting Joyce on him, it was one of the strategies we had worked out.

We needed a free taker on the big day and that's where Tommy lost out. I felt so sorry for Tommy. It was a very difficult decision but one way or another, I had to have Manus on the team.

Although Gaelic football is a team game the team is made up of individuals. Tommy Ryan was dismayed at his exclusion and while he couldn't hide his disappointment, the team ethos kicked-in almost immediately. "I'll never forget Tommy Ryan's reaction when the team was announced," said Sylvester

Maguire, "It said an awful lot for the squad." "Tommy was disappointed," remembered Martin Gavigan:

> But he was still man enough to stand up and say that the team winning was the important thing. He was fully behind the players. He said we were 26 players that had made the same sacrifices and it didn't matter what 15 went out to play. That took heart.

❋ ❋ ❋ ❋

Disaster was about to strike Shov. On the Thursday night before the final the boys had a final training session in Ballybofey. Nothing serious – just a bit of ball-work. What happened next is seared into Martin Shovlin's brain forever:

> I can still see it – everyone was watching themselves and conscious of not picking up an injury. A ball was dropping in my general direction. Fuck it, I thought, I'm not going in for that or I might get hurt. But whatever way I turned I jarred my neck badly.

Shovlin knew immediately that he was in big trouble. He got a lift home that night with the Kilcar and Glen men. "He mentioned to me that he'd hurt his neck and doubted that he'd be able to play," remembered John Joe Doherty. John Joe started preparing himself mentally for the eventuality of playing in the final.

McEniff sent Shovlin to Sligo for physiotherapy. Murray was already attending a physiotherapist who was treating his leg injury and the two of them headed off. Shovlin is convinced to this day that if he hadn't gone for physiotherapy, he might have made it:

> There was no examination properly done. I told the physio that I hurt a neck muscle – it might have been something else – but she gave me a wild going over instead of maybe getting it looked at and x-rayed to see what was the exact extent of the damage.

Shovlin returned home very sore and now extremely worried. Cortisone injections kept the pain at bay but he was now in a desperate race against time. By the time the team left Donegal for Dublin, the Saturday newspapers were already reporting that the Dunkineely man was doubtful.

Yet Shovlin got encouraging news in Dublin from a surgeon by the name of Tim O'Brien who told him that he'd play the following day. It seemed, with the aid of pain killers, that Shovlin might yet take his place in the starting 15.

❋ ❋ ❋ ❋

That the Dubs, some of them anyway, believed the widely-held assertion that they merely needed to turn up to receive their All-Ireland medal was apparent in the words of their captain Tommy Carr. Speaking to Michael Daly in the days before the game, it was clear that Carr – despite some protestations to the contrary – was supremely confident. Even if things were to go wrong. "Even if they do [go wrong], I still feel that we are strong enough to go on and win, strong enough not to allow setbacks or problems to affect us." His manager, Paddy Cullen – mesmerised that Dublin were installed such heavy favourites – was rightly worried that his charges were beginning to believe the media – that it would be a cakewalk, or even a catwalk! He would surely have balked at Carr's final comments to the *Democrat*:

> People expect Dublin to win All-Irelands, rightly so. They have won them in the past and are used to winning them. Now Dublin are in an All-Ireland final against a team who are there for the first time.
>
> What more can a player say than Dublin should win the game; sure they should win it, but we're not taking anyone for granted. It's an All-Ireland final that we have been aiming for for the last number of years and we intend to win it.

Undoubtedly, the Dubs were beginning to believe their own media's hype. What lay ahead of them would come as a terrible shock. Sam Maguire 1992 had their name on it. Losing to Donegal didn't come into the equation. "A lot of the Dublin team, were doing silly things and giving silly interviews," remembers Manus Boyle:

> They were falling into the trap. We were kept away from the media and had one press night. Fellas would give interviews but they'd only give yes or no answers. We kept it very simple, kept a low profile and it worked. The Dublin lads got caught up in the hype. I feel sorry for the Dublin players. They sell papers but they're only ordinary fellas and they still have to go to work.

Barry McGowan, Manus' Killybegs team-mate agreed, "In hindsight, you'd have to feel sorry for them. Paddy Cullen had an unenviable task of trying to keep the Dublin players' feet on the ground".

One man with his feet on the ground was Anthony Molloy. The Donegal captain knew how to handle the media. Interviews were always given and Molloy would always be courteous, but there would be no hubris or grand-standing. No one was going to make the mistake of handing Dublin any moti-vation, not that Dublin – self-appointed champions-elect – would have noticed anyway, busy as the players were with fashion shows, personal appearances and advertising campaigns.

Acres of newsprint covered all the angles. Donegal football had never come under the spotlight like this. Yet, the consensus among the experts was that this was a bridge too far. In the previous 40 years, only Down in 1960 had managed to win an All-Ireland in their first final appearance. It just wasn't done.

Former greats and eminent GAA figures were wheeled out to predict and analyse the man-to-man clashes throughout the field. It made for fascinating reading. Mick Lyons did the honours for the *Irish Independent*. Full-back when Meath accounted for Donegal in 1990 and a regular battler with the Dubs, Lyons knew both teams well. In his opinion, the winning and losing of the All-Ireland depended on the outcome of a handful of key confrontations.

The clash of Matt and Vinny Murphy on the edge of the Donegal square was crucial. Lyons had vast experience when it came to marking Murphy and he had advice for the Donegal number three – "Matt Gallagher will want to establish his mark early". However, Lyons scored advantage to Dublin in this sector.

At the opposite end of the pitch, he expected Tony Boyle to just shade it over Gerry Hargan. "Boyle is the complete full-forward with excellent ball control and scoring ability. He can scoop the ball up quickly and is very good at laying it off. He will be a handful for Hargan." At midfield, Lyons felt Donegal also had the edge, acknowledging that Molloy and Murray "have a great understanding".

And so it came to the Donegal half forward line versus the Dublin half-back line. Lyons was emphatic – man for man, Curran, Barr and Heery would account for McMullan, McHugh and McHugh and that advantage would win Dublin the game. "Martin McHugh needs to take on Barr and run at him if he is to be effective and impose himself on the game," argued Lyons. Yet, he was sure that Barr would overcome the best McHugh could throw at him and become the influential figure in a Dublin victory.

There was little doubt but that the clash between Keith Barr and Martin McHugh was pivotal. It could well decide the outcome of the game. Barr was the key man on the Dublin team – their playmaker operating from centre half-back. And he was more. Tom Humphries wrote that Barr was, "Essence of Dub. Hero of the Hill. The centre back from hell. The man the culchies love to hate." Humphries was writing half in jest but he wasn't wrong. Keith Barr was no ordinary Dublin footballer. But neither was Martin McHugh an ordinary Donegal footballer. Paddy Cullen was well aware of the importance of the Wee Man to Donegal, "Everything goes through him and Keith Barr will have to be careful."

And so the predictions went. "Dublin have the form, the experience, the strength and the knowledge," wrote Peadar O'Brien, adding that he would be mildly surprised if Donegal were to emerge with the honours. Bonner and the two Boyles "will trouble the Dubs full-back line, but not often enough to be effective," he added with certainty. Donal Keenan was another big name journalist who opted for the Dubs, suspecting that the pre-match hype would have a greater "debilitating effect on Donegal than Dublin". "The more you'd read it the more it would madden you," said Martin Shovlin, "according to the media, there was no point in us turning up. McEniff and Harkin told us to ignore it."

Martin Breheny in the *Sunday Press* agreed with his Fourth Estate colleagues. "Dublin to lift Sam," he predicted, for three reasons:

> One, teams rarely win All-Ireland finals in their first appearance; two, Dublin have been in the top three sides for the past five years, and three; Croke Park is worth a few points to them against less experienced teams. Put the three together and a six-point win for Dublin looks a possibility.

The bookies also illustrated the widespread belief that this All-Ireland was Dublin's for the taking – Dublin were 4/9 favourites while Donegal trailed at 7/4. Yet, 31 counties were hoping for a Donegal win. "They have generated the most extraordinary surge of emotion at home, equalled only by the Papal visit, Euro '88 and Italia '90," reckoned Keenan. There was no doubt that Donegal's appearance in the final had also captured the hearts of the nation – outside the capital. Goodwill was emanating from all corners of Ireland.

And now, on the third weekend of September 1992, a large chunk of Donegal's population was in Dublin. A weekend like no other was had. It is said that 25,000 Donegal folk packed the streets of the capital – 10,000 of them bereft of that all important ticket but desperate to sample the once-in-a-lifetime atmosphere. Every hotel, B&B and floor of relations and friends in Dublin was taken up. Donegal had invaded en-masse. The only question remaining was if the county would return with the silverware. "Nothing has been left undone," McEniff had assured all and sundry. Time would tell.

❀ ❀ ❀ ❀

The squad stayed at Finnstown House Hotel in Lucan. They had also stayed there for the semi-final. McEniff was trying to keep everything low-key and familiar – the last thing the boys needed now was disruption. The lads were relaxed and supremely confident. "We were a better team than Dublin and couldn't believe that we were seen as the underdogs," remembered Donal Reid, "I was more confident of winning that game than any other championship game I ever played. I don't know why, but it was just how I felt."

Some of the lads headed to Shelbourne Park for a night at the dogs. Joyce, Molloy, Matt, Manus and Murray, the usual suspects, played cards. There was a bit of an edge in the air and the game finished early, but not before Murray had won a few pounds. He took it as a good omen.

The boys went to bed at a reasonable hour. The sleeping arrangements had been changed. McEniff put each line of the team into one room. It didn't meet with universal approval. "I used to room with Joyce McMullan," remembered Matt Gallagher, "but the night before the final I roomed with Barry McGowan and Noel Hegarty. We were a bit squashed." The full-forward line of Declan Bonner, Tony Boyle and Manus Boyle – dubbed the Killer Bs by the national media – came to grips with the new arrangement. "Tony and me always roomed together anyway," remembered Bonner:

> We went into the room and I got one of the outside beds and Tony got the other leaving Manus with the middle. I told Tony that he'd got it all wrong and that he'd better take the middle bed and Manus should take the one on the left!

Everyone had their own worries as they headed off to bed that Saturday night, but for Martin Shovlin in particular, it would be a restless night.

❆ ❆ ❆ ❆

The others knew Martin Shovlin was in trouble but didn't think, for a moment, that he wouldn't be able to play. "Shovlin would go in where no one else would," said Brian Murray, "He's one of the bravest players I've ever seen. He had great heart and would never, ever give up." It was different this time. Player and manager put it to the test before the dew had lifted from the grass on Sunday morning. Team doctor, Austin Kennedy, gave Shovlin the medical OK. They found a nearby rugby pitch and McEniff put Shovlin through his paces. It was looking good. Kicking wasn't a problem. Shovlin caught a few balls into his chest and above his head. Fine, no problem. Then it happened. "Brian threw a ball along the ground," remembered Shovlin, "I stooped and the pain shot straight down through me. That was it."

"Shovlin was a man of steel but there were tears in his eyes when he told me that he wouldn't be able to play," remembered Brian McEniff. Martin Gavigan had roomed with Shovlin on the Saturday night and although aware that Shovlin had a bit of a sore neck, he had no inkling that it might cost him his place on the biggest stage. "I told him he'd be grand in the morning," remembers Gavigan:

> It was a real blow when I heard it. I couldn't believe it that he wouldn't be playing. That was the most courageous decision any player could ever make. I played in a couple of games that I shouldn't have played in. To make a decision like that on such day showed some courage, but that's Martin Shovlin for you.

Manus Boyle, too, was struck by the decision Martin Shovlin took. "I wouldn't have done what he did," Manus admitted, "I would have tried to play with one leg hanging off. His honesty was second to none. It says a lot about the man that he did what he did."

The lads were devastated for the man from Dunkineely. This was the man who had put his wiry frame through hell for them and for the county. Yet there was a limited amount of time for sympathy as the bus swept towards the city centre and their date with destiny. In less than two hours they would be on the hallowed turf of Croke Park. They had to get their own heads right. "We'll do it for Shov," agreed the boys.

McEniff had an inkling that Shovlin wouldn't make it and had prepared a contingency plan. He had been in Glenties a few weeks before to watch a couple of games in the Donegal championship. Naomh Columba were playing Gaoth Dobhair and John Joe Doherty was out to impress. "I knew McEniff was coming to watch," admitted John Joe, "and players will try harder when they know the manager is watching." John Joe must have tried very hard because McEniff said he had never seen a better display in club football. John Joe had put himself to the forefront of his manager's thoughts.

Now that Shovlin was out, McEniff's dilemma was whether to switch the defence around as both Barry McGowan and Noel Hegarty would have been seen as natural wing half-backs. He knew the Dublin full-forward line possessed great aerial power and decided height in the full-back line was vital and left the corner-backs where they were. Declan Bonner believes it was a good decision to interfere as little as possible with the line-up:

A less experienced manager might have panicked at that time and started to make changes. Although John Joe had never played at wing half-back for Donegal, and the word was that maybe Noel Hegarty or Barry McGowan would move out there, McEniff left it as it was and players weren't unsettled by being moved about. It worked well.

John Joe would take Shovlin's position but the decision wasn't taken lightly, John Cunningham, sent off in the Ulster final, had come into the manager's thoughts. "I felt sorry for Razda," recalled McEniff, "I had great grá for him as a person and as a footballer. He always played with a lot of heart but John Joe had more pace and was the man for the job."

Needless to say, John Cunningham was disappointed. He knew that Shovlin had been struggling. When the word came out that Shovlin wouldn't make it, a couple of people approached Cunningham and told him what he was already thinking – that, against the odds, he had a chance of starting in the All-Ireland final. After all, Cunningham had played in four Ulster championship games while John Joe had struggled with injury all year. "In the corridor I saw

Mickey Lafferty had gripped John Joe by the arm and was saying something into his ear," remembered John:

> That's when I clicked that John Joe was on. The next man I came across was Brian McEniff. I grabbed him in under the arm and said, 'What's going on here?' Brian is a real diplomat but I wasn't very pleasant to him. I said, 'You bastard, you're shafting me.' Brian being Brian, told me that I'd get my chance.
>
> There was no better man than John Joe Doherty, it couldn't have happened to a nicer man to be honest. We went to the meeting and of course everybody was devastated for Shovlin and that kept me in my place. He was in a worse state than me and Tommy Ryan was in bits too.

It had been a strained and emotional morning. The players gathered their belonging, knotted their ties, put on their jackets and boarded the bus. The thoughts and hopes of Donegal people everywhere rested with the occupants of that bus as it sped through the streets of Dublin under Garda escort. Many of the team were still reeling from the news that Shovlin had failed the fitness test. Others had withdrawn into themselves and were preparing for the match ahead. The bus was quiet and tense. What was needed was a moment of levity. As the bus neared Croke Park, the Lord, in that mysterious way of His, saw to it that such a moment would arise.

The Bishop of Raphoe, Seamus Hegarty was a Kilcar man and former principal of Falcarragh school. John Cunningham knew him of old and takes up the story:

> The Bishop, wearing all his regalia, was sitting in the front seat of the bus. A massive Donegal crowd had converged on the road at Quinn's corner and the traffic stopped. One of the fans held up an inflatable, life-sized adult doll with a Donegal scarf around her neck. He held it right up to the window and the Bishop couldn't miss it.

The tension evaporated as the players dissolved into laughter.

❊

John Cunningham

17

One Sunday in September
(September 20, 1992)

"We were floating going out on to the field
and floating coming off it."

DONAL REID

Shortly after 3pm on Sunday, September 20, 1992, the Donegal team, led by captain Anthony Molloy, emerged from the tunnel between the Canal End and the Hogan Stand to a massive roar that erased years of footballing heartbreak for Donegal. Donegal folk in the 64,547 crowd rose as one to acclaim their heroes. "It doesn't matter what you do, there's nothing in your life that will surpass that feeling," said Molloy, "It was the greatest day of my life and I'll never forget running on to the field. We had the support of 31 counties and that was a big help. For me, I felt lucky to be there at the right time and in the right place."

"The crescendo of noise was unbelievable," remembered Barry McGowan:

Jack O'Shea had told us what to expect and we had read various things about the experience, but nobody ever told us about the noise we'd experience on the day. The Canal End was thronged with Donegal supporters. The noise was deafening. The decibel level must have been extremely high because I remember having a pain in my head. It was like the noise from a pneumatic drill. The level of noise was such that I wanted to cover my ears with my hands but I couldn't do that because you'd look stupid to do that on All-Ireland final day.

Noel Hegarty was affected by the noise too. "We weren't ready for it," he recalled, "The noise was unreal when we came out of the tunnel. My legs went weak and just about carried me as far the bench where the team photo was to be taken."

Those watching the final on RTÉ television missed this historic moment as the station was on an ad-break but Charlie Collins and Michael McGee were there for Highland Radio. "What a scene we see here, in the Canal End, the Cusack Stand and around us in the Hogan Stand," relayed Charlie Collins to the thousands tuned in at home. The sight of the Canal End, with hundreds of green and gold flags, interspersed with the orange and white flags of Armagh, fluttering in the light breeze has remained with John Joe Doherty, "It was just a sea of green and gold there and it seemed to stretch around three sides of the ground".

Around the globe Donegal folk were on the move too as they packed bars and social centres in London, Manchester, Birmingham, Leeds and Glasgow to watch proceedings live from Croke Park. In Paris, Munich, Amsterdam and Brussels they would also be glued to the big screens. Across the Atlantic the story was the same in New York, San Francisco, Boston, Chicago, New Haven, Cleveland, Philadelphia, Washington, Detroit, Santa Monica, Los Angeles and New Jersey. And in Canada, Donegal folk flocked to centres in Toronto and Edmonton. Those who couldn't get near a big screen were tuning into the BBC's World Service which was to provide regular reports. Never in the county's history had so many of its sons and daughters been united in common cause.

Anthony Molloy made his way to the middle of the park and posed for photographs with referee Tommy Sugrue and Dublin captain Tommy Carr. Molloy won the toss and took a few moments to indicate his decision to the referee. Donegal would play into Hill 16. Molloy's delay was theatrical; it was always Donegal's intention to play into the Hill. "Molloy hadn't lost a toss all year and we played into the Hill," recalled Martin McHugh. "We weren't going to allow Dublin to get into the match. It was a big decision. Had Charlie Redmond been hitting the penalty at the Hill 16 end, it would have made a big difference."

All-Ireland final day is high on ceremony. The teams complete their warm-up, line-up to meet the President and parade behind the Artane Boys' Band before standing for the national anthem. There isn't half the pomp before an All-Ireland semi-final and the ever-meticulous McEniff set about preparing his squad for this eventuality. Two Sundays earlier, the Donegal squad gathered to watch the All-Ireland hurling final and take note of the rigmarole that Kilkenny and Cork participated in. They knew what they were in for but it didn't help the time pass any more quickly for goalkeeper Gary Walsh:

I found the time before the game to be an awful drag. What goes on before the game nearly seems longer than the game itself. When we were waiting for Mary Robinson I looked into the crowd in the Hogan Stand. I thought to myself that I'd been playing for ten years waiting to get to this stage and wanted to go out and play my best.

As the teams stood to attention for the national anthem, John Joe Doherty's mind flicked back and recalled his first sight of an All-Ireland final. "I saw the 1974 final in a neighbour's house on a colour television," he recalled, "before the game we all stood to attention in the living-room for the national anthem." John Joe remembered the Dublin goalkeeper saving a penalty from Galway's Liam Sammon. That goalkeeper was Paddy Cullen, manager of the 1992 Dublin team.

The anthem ended, the Artane Boys' Band left the pitch and all thoughts switched to the 70 minutes of football ahead. Dublin were seeking their 22nd All-Ireland title, Donegal were seeking their first.

❄ ❄ ❄ ❄

From his position in the press box, Highland Radio commentator Charlie Collins commentated on the opening moves:

> Keith Barr gives Martin McHugh a little nudge, I'm sure there will be one or two of those before this game is out. The game is on. Brian Murray knocks it down to Anthony Molloy, Donegal gets the first possession. Molloy knocks it forward looking for Tony Boyle. Boyle is out in front of Hargan but he was fouled by Hargan and Donegal are going to have a free from 40 metres and this free is going to be taken by Martin McHugh.

Tony Boyle did what he set out to do in every game, he won the first ball and then knew he had the beating of Dublin full-back Gerry Hargan. The Dubs had expected that Hargan, full-back on the 1983 All-Ireland winning Dublin team and holder of two All-Star awards, to have the experience to handle the man from Dungloe. After all, he had curbed Boyle's influence in the league quarter-final back in April. Anyone making assumptions about Boyle based on league form was working with faulty intelligence. Tommy Ryan could have told them what to expect:

> Tony Boyle wouldn't try a leg in national league football and this fooled the Dublin men, as it had the Mayo men. McEniff roared at Tony for weeks to rise him for the game. Tony is one of those players that when you put a championship jersey on him he'd raise his game and that's testament to how good a player he was.

Martin McHugh took the free and it drifted to the right of the posts. McHugh and Manus Boyle had struck thousands of balls at the pitch in Towney in the weeks leading up to the final. Free-taking had almost cost Donegal the semi-final and this was a nervous start. "I made the decision that I'd take the frees in the final," said McHugh:

> I didn't lift that first free. It was funny because I felt good, it was the best

I had ever prepared for a match. I had practised frees and did everything right. It works for you sometimes and doesn't work for you other times. We got another free and Declan took it and of course Manus didn't miss a free.

As John O'Leary placed the ball on the edge of the square, Keith Barr had words with the Wee Man. "Barr suggested to me that I hadn't the balls to do it," McHugh told TG4 years afterwards. "I said straight back to him that we'd see who had the balls at the end of the game."

Coming into the game the Dublin half-back line of Curran, Barr and Heery had been lauded as the best half-back line ever to have played Gaelic football. If Donegal were to win, Sean O'Neill had warned McEniff, Martin McHugh would have to go down the barrel of the gun.

❄ ❄ ❄ ❄

In the closing moments of the first half, Dublin right half-back Paul Curran found himself on Donegal's 45-metre line. He was brought to the ground by John Joe Doherty and Joyce McMullan. Free. McEniff had selected Joyce for his physical strength. "We put Joyce on him to negate his attacking game," McEniff recalled. "Joyce had an advantage over him in upper body strength and horsed him out of it a few times." Joyce stumbled over Curran and Curran lashed out. A little bit of what Charlie Collins would term "argy-bargy" broke out. Referee Sugrue didn't appreciate some of the Donegal players disputing his decision and moved the free to the 21-metre line. It was an easy tap-over for Charlie Redmond to make it 0-9 to 0-7 but the response of the Hill was muted.

Gary Walsh's long kick out broke to James McHugh who delayed his fisted pass to brother Martin. Keith Barr was breathing down Martin's neck. Eamon Heery arrived too but McHugh jinked and turned, found space and swung the ball over the bar with his right foot. "Now who has the balls?" snarled McHugh to Barr. No reply. "I knew I had the psychological battle won then," recalled McHugh. Manager McEniff knew it too: "When McHugh ran through the centre of the Dublin defence and carried the game to them I felt that we'd cracked it. Croke Park didn't exist any more and it was just 15 against 15." Charlie Collins, watching gleefully from the press box, noted the change in Barr's demeanour: "Keith Barr had a word with Martin McHugh when he missed a free at the start of the match. He doesn't appear to be saying much to him now."

Three points up and half-time almost upon them, McHugh had reason to feel pleased:

Barr must have decided to watch my left foot and I happened to turn on to my right. I felt that was the most important score of the game and I'm not just saying that because I scored it. We were two points up and it was the last score before half-time. It was important to get it and I always think the last score before half-time is very important.

The first half had passed at a frenetic pace. "McEniff had told us to go at them like the waves of Tory," remembered Donal Reid, "and that was how it turned out. It was almost as if we had written the script ourselves."

✳ ✳ ✳ ✳

"The Dublin half-backs were singled out before the game in all our preparations," James McHugh now freely admits:

Our plan was to stop them attacking at all costs. We were to keep fouling them until we got two straight scores. We kept running straight at them. Many players, particularly big-name players, don't like it when you come at them and that Dublin team wasn't happy defending.

John O'Leary's first kick out had been won by Keith Barr. Manus Boyle clattered into him from behind and then held up his hands in mock amazement. "We didn't mind giving away a couple of frees. Unless you are very unlucky, a referee won't book you early and you can get away with a push," grinned Manus. Barr was on the ball twice in the opening minutes and twice he was fouled. On his third time on the ball he bounced it twice and conceded a free when he could find no way through a wall of green and gold jerseys. The plan was paying dividends.

Dublin announced their intention early on and hoofed a high ball into full-forward Vinny Murphy. Molloy, Hegarty, Gallagher and McMullan all gathered under the dropping ball but Murphy made a magnificent catch and won a free. The high ball into Vinny came as no surprise to Matt who'd spent the previous five weeks working on this in training with Tony Boyle and Brian Murray – and getting the odd elbow in the jaw for his troubles. "The game plan was to concede possession to Vinny if we had to but to defend the goals," he revealed:

His forte was to field the ball either behind of, or in contention with, the full-back and then use his physical strength to burn the defender off. He wasn't the quickest full-forward I ever marked but he was definitely one of the strongest. He'd use his physical strength to burn you off and usually put you to the ground.

Matt wasn't left to deal with Murphy on his own. Molloy, Murray and later in the second half, Barry Cunningham, would drop back to deal with this serious aerial threat. This was part of a long-standing Donegal game plan. "I would always have lain back and left any attacking to Murray," said Anthony Molloy:

> Vinny had one fault and we knew it. He was a great man to get the ball in the air but he was a bit selfish – he wouldn't lay it off when maybe he should. Matt played him well and crowded him out. Matt would have been one of the best markers around at that time – after all, he did a tremendous job on big Liam McHale in the semi-final.

As the game wore on, it became apparent that Dublin had no alternatives to the long ball into Vinny. It was meat and drink to the Donegal defence.

The first score of the game came in the second minute as Charlie Redmond converted the 13-metre free won by Murphy. Redmond had once described his free-taking method as: "Seven steps back, three to the side, four Hail Marys, two Our Fathers, lick the fingers, and if it goes over God did it and if it goes wide I missed it." God was with the Dubs as Redmond tapped over the easy free.

Dublin were on top in the opening ten minutes. "For some reason we took five or ten minutes to settle down in every game that year," remembered Molloy. Dublin had the ball in the net in the third minute when Vinny Murphy shouldered Gary Walsh over the line after the goalkeeper had comfortably collected a short kick from Niall Guiden. Free out. "He was just letting me know he was there," said Walsh, "but I was expecting him anyway.

Barry McGowan was marking Mick Galvin, a player with many years experience of playing in the corner. McGowan hadn't taken his place in the stand with the other players to watch the minor match between Armagh and Meath. Instead, he stayed in the dressing room while Dr Austin Kennedy gave him a pain-killing injection for his shoulder injury. It was McGowan's sixth championship start and only his second full game in the corner-back position. "If I had been five years older I wouldn't have had the nerve to do that," he admitted, "but it was a once in a lifetime chance and I grabbed it." Galvin scored Dublin's second point before the fifth minute elapsed. McGowan was fuming:

> I was very orthodox in marking him and just followed him around. I hadn't the nerve to go on any attacking sprints. I decided to stick with him as best I could and shadowed him the whole day.
>
> He got a point in the first half. On that occasion Donegal stupidly lost the ball on the wing. I tried to get back but was tripped up and ended up flat on my face on the ground. By the time I got up Mick Galvin had the ball and by the time I got to him he had popped it over the bar with a very deft touch. I was livid. Even though I was only a rookie in the corner-back position I was really angry with the rest of the defence at the time. They had played poorly for a couple of minutes.

"The good start Dublin were feared for seemed to be arriving," wrote Michael Daly in the *Democrat*. Donegal nerves were still in evidence as Tony Boyle kicked wide, Martin McHugh misplaced a short free and Anthony Molloy kicked a ball over the sideline.

Eight minutes had elapsed when Declan Bonner was fouled 50 metres out and near the Hogan Stand. He hoisted a high, dangerous ball into the Dublin goalmouth where it broke to James McHugh who had stolen a yard on Eamon Heery. McHugh had only one thing on his mind:

> No matter what kind of ball came in I would never jump and the ball landed in my hands. I knew where I was going and I knew what I wanted to do. McEniff always talked about aiming high for the crossbar. O'Leary was definitely beaten. If we had got a goal at that stage, we might have been able to express ourselves more – we didn't win by as much as we should have.

The ball ricocheted off the crossbar and broke out to Martin McHugh. "Manus was going for it too and I nearly pushed pushed him out of the way to get to it," laughed McHugh. It was fitting that Donegal's first ever score in an All-Ireland should come from the boot of the Wee Man. "All doubts were dissolved," wrote Micheál Ó Muircheartaigh in the *Irish Press*.

What happened next rocked Donegal. Following a scramble in front of the Donegal goals, Dessie Farrell got a light push from Noel Hegarty in the parallelogram and blasted the ball wide. The referee sounded his whistle, threw out his arms and signalled for a penalty. "Things weren't looking good at that stage and I though to myself, 'Ah Jeez, not again,'" said Martin Gavigan. "I didn't think it was a penalty, it was a big decision for the referee to make so early on," thought Noel Hegarty.

Charlie Redmond was Dublin's penalty taker. Four years previously he had famously missed a penalty at the same end when Dublin needed a goal to draw level with Meath in the Leinster final. He was in good company as the Canal End goals were rarely breached by penalty takers throughout the 1980s – Kevin McCabe, Jack O'Shea and Mikey Sheehy had all missed at that end in big games.

Thoughts of the Canal End jinx weren't on the mind of Gary Walsh though. He'd taken a prophetic 'phone call from his brother Declan some days earlier: .

> He told me that he'd dreamed that I saved a penalty in the final by diving to my right. I stood there all nervous and didn't know whether to go to my right or left. If I had dived to my right and Charlie had driven it to the left then my brother might have had a thing or two to answer for.

Charlie Redmond drove the ball to Walsh's left and well wide of the post. "Will this lift Donegal?" wondered Charlie Collins on Highland Radio. Charlie Redmond had a stark assessment of the miss after the game, "The penalty lost it for us, it changed the whole game". It had certainly knocked his confidence and his contribution from play for the remainder of the game was muted.

The penalty miss upset them more than it did us," felt Noel Hegarty. "If it had been scored I wouldn't have liked to bet on us." The Donegal supporters raised the din by a few decibels. "The support got up after the penalty miss and they could sense something," remembered Joyce McMullan. "It was like we had got a sniff of something and said to ourselves, 'there's something on here'." John Joe Doherty felt the referee tried to even things up afterwards:

> The penalty decision was harsh, but after that the Dublin players would probably have been aggrieved with the referee because we seemed to get every call that was going. Referees tend to favour the team the majority of spectators are supporting. I would say the referee probably sensed there was a massive support among neutral supporters for Donegal. I am not saying he wasn't a good referee – he was – but Dublin would probably feel hard calls were made against them.

Manager Brian McEniff was impressed with Sugrue's refereeing, "Tommy Sugrue was an outstanding referee, and I'm not just saying that because he refereed our final. He set a standard for other referees to follow."

Donegal upped the pace of their game and started to make things happen, but not before Vinny Murphy got on the end of a long ball from Jack Sheedy and scored his first point from play. Charlie Collins wasn't convinced, "The umpire had a better view of it than we did, but from where we look, that ball certainly seemed to drift wide." Neither Gary Walsh nor Barry McGowan were convinced they'd conceded a point and made their feelings known to the umpire but it counted for nothing. The point stood and Dublin led by three points to one.

Good work down the right sideline led to Donegal's second score. Mixing their famed short-passing game with pinpoint kick passing, James McHugh found himself on the end of a four-person move and scored a super point from an acute angle far to the right of the posts. "I always played on the right and was very confident of scoring from there," he recalled. Owen McCrohan writing in the *Donegal Democrat* was effusive in his praise:

> During the early tentative minutes when his side were often struggling to keep their collective heads above water, the man who raised the standard of revolt was James McHugh. It was his utter defiance and brilliant football brain that got the side moving.

"Brian Murray carried the most pressure into the match because he was working in Dublin," remembered Martin McHugh. Murray was a Dublin-based guard and was quite friendly with Dublin half-forward Jack Sheedy. When Sheedy held on to a ball after a free had been awarded, Murray shouldered him hard. "The Donegal man came out the better in that one," adjudged Charlie Collins. "Murray threw his shoulder into Sheedy and Sheedy hit the ground like a stone." To those watching it looked like Murray had perhaps settled an old score. It was nothing of the sort. Murray was raised and hadn't even noticed what player he had hit, "He was trying to waste a bit of time. I went over and gave him a dunt. I didn't notice, but I was told afterwards that he fell on his arse. I just gave back the ball and that was it." Still, it signalled the intent of the entire team. Donegal weren't going to be knocked around.

The resultant free was driven long from the ground by Keith Barr. Vinny Murphy rose above a posse of Donegal players to make a spectacular catch. He released the ball to Jack Sheedy who was none the worse for his altercation with Murray and he pointed from 20 yards. "Donegal's self belief on the day was epitomised in their response to Dublin's good start and in Matt Gallagher's refusal to panic as Vinny Murphy made catch after catch," wrote David Walsh in the *Sunday Independent*. Donegal were two points down but the tide was about to turn.

Murray won an O'Leary kick out and released to James McHugh who drew a foul 25 metres from the Dublin goals. It was well within Martin McHugh's range but with two poor kicks from the ground behind him, McHugh – demonstrating a maturity gained over 11 championship campaigns – handed the responsibility to Declan Bonner. It was something of a surprise for the Na Rossa man but he composed himself and silenced a jeering Hill 16 by chipping the ball between the posts. "McEniff had told me to concentrate on general play in the training before the final and I didn't kick too many frees in that time," Bonner recalled. "When Martin called me to take it I didn't have time to think about it. It can be daunting kicking into the Hill and I was glad to see it going over, it helped settle everyone."

Donegal had got their tails' up. Martin Gavigan, back helping Matt Gallagher, hoofed a ball long up the field. Bonner, buzzing after scoring his first point, came out well in front of Tommy Carr and laid it off to Molloy. Full-forward Tony Boyle takes up the story:

> Declan won the ball and gave it to Molloy who gave a massive fist pass to me. Over the years, that hand pass went into folklore and stretched from 25 yards to 70 yards! I collected the pass and had a good few yards on Hargan. I knew that if I ran at him I could cut back inside on my left. For a split second I was going to take a shot myself but Deegan moved across and I saw Manus was in a better position. I would have put my house on Manus, of all people, sticking it in the back of the net.

Tony released the ball to Manus and with John O'Leary stranded, the Killybegs man had the goal at his mercy. His left-footed shot hit the top of the crossbar and went over for a point. "If Dublin win this one they should take that crossbar and put in Parnell Park as a souvenir – that's two that have bounced off it," exclaimed Michael McGee on Highland Radio. "I was trying to keep it high and had aimed for the roof of the net because O'Leary was so quick at closing forwards down," remembered Manus. "It was a good thing it didn't rebound out the field but I never thought any more of it." The sides were level for the first time but Dublin were still on top. Jack Sheedy ran strongly through to point on the run despite Martin McHugh's close attention.

Matt Gallagher then followed Vinny Murphy far out the field and intercepted an intended pass. "We were happy to push him further out the pitch – it suited us to have him out there," said Matt:

> As he got the ball he started to fall and I knew he was going to flick it off to my right. I read it, took a chance on it and got it. I gave it to Bonner and that was it. My job was to mind the square, it wasn't to be scoring points. While I would have loved to have gone up the field, I think McEniff would have lost his life if I had!

Donegal sliced through the Dublin defence with intricate short passing. Bonner found Molloy who played it short to Martin McHugh. McHugh shrugged off the tackle of Keith Barr and ran 30 yards into the heart of the Dublin defence and scored his second point of the day with his left foot. Level. McHugh was relentlessly going down the barrel of the gun. "You could see the chests puffing out and the shoulders lifting," recalled Manus Boyle as Donegal moved effortlessly up through the gears. Moments later Donegal moved into the lead for the first time as Declan Bonner perfectly completed an exquisite move by pointing with his left from 25 metres. Twenty-two breathless minutes had passed and the score stood at 0-6 to 0-5. "That's Donegal at their best, short passing and men coming on to the ball at speed," enthused Charlie Collins.

The Dublin defence was looking vulnerable as the Donegal forwards ran relentlessly at them. Chants of "Donegal, Donegal" rang around the ground as Martin McHugh knocked a free into the right corner. Once again Tony Boyle was out in front of Gerry Hargan and the full-back conceded the free. Manus Boyle nonchalantly stroked the free between the posts and high into Hill 16. His free-taking style was described by Eoghan Corry in the *Irish Press* as "cool as a Killybegs breeze". Neither Corry nor the Dubs had seen anything yet.

Brian Murray was lording it at midfield. He nearly hadn't taken his place at all and just five days before the final his participation was seen as extremely doubtful. Suffering from an Achilles tendon injury, he had spent most of the week prior to the final receiving physiotherapy and, on the advice of Sean Boylan, immersing himself up to the waist in the cool Atlantic waters off

Rossnowlagh. Sea water must be a great healer as Murray was the pick of the midfielders on view. "One of the things that stood in my favour when it came to selecting the team was that I played club football in Dublin and would always have played well against Dublin," recalled Murray. "I would have known Paul Clarke and knew, as did Seamus Bonner, that I had always done well on him."

John O'Leary sliced another kick out towards the Hogan Stand. While Jack Sheedy won it, it worked out to Donegal's advantage as John Joe Doherty nudged him over the line. John Joe had a shaky start on Sheedy but was now coming to terms with him. Ever alert, Joyce McMullan took a quick sideline kick as Donegal pressed harder and harder on the Dubs. Tony Boyle won the ball and laid it off to Manus. Tony remembers it thus:

> Manus, as Manus always did, turned to see if he could get a shot on goals but he was well closed down. He knocked it back to me. I bounced it – Paul Curran dived in and nearly tipped the ball away – and broke through two players and it opened up for me. In my early years I would not have been noted for my scoring. I was a target man and I was happy to throw the ball to Declan and Manus because I knew if they got it in a bit of space it would go over the bar. It was the only score I got in the final and I enjoyed it. It was typical of a lot of the scores that I got where I would get the ball and use my strength to break by a couple of players.

Tony Boyle had become the fifth Donegal forward to score and only 25 minutes had passed. With the score at 0-8 to 0-5 and the Canal End going berserk, Dublin were at sixes and sevens and unable to deal with the rampant Donegal forwards. Eamon Heery stemmed the tide and broke through three Donegal tackles as he surged powerfully forward and released a long ball in the direction of Vinny Murphy. Twenty-one year-old Dessie Farrell nipped in front Noel Hegarty and cleanly won that ball. "It must be a goal," screamed Charlie Collins, but thankfully Dessie wasn't listening and he blasted the ball well over Gary Walsh's crossbar to leave just two points between the teams.

Twenty-seven minutes into the first half and Keith Barr became the first, and only player, to enter the referee's notebook following another high tackle, this time on Anthony Molloy. "Dublin had the name of being a dirty team but that wasn't the case that day," recalled Molloy, "Keith Barr had tried to rough the Wee Man but we soon sorted that out." Barr's afternoon was an unhappy one. He was felled by several of the Donegal players and had no answer to the direct running of Martin McHugh who was ripping holes through the heart of the Dublin defence. "Barr came into the game with a big reputation," remembered Martin McHugh. "He was a tremendous footballer and would have been player of the year had Dublin won the All-Ireland." Such was the havoc McHugh had wrought that Barr was already out of the running for an All-Star award.

Paul Curran was underneath the Cusack Stand when he hoisted a speculative ball into the Donegal goalmouth with about half an hour gone. The Donegal fans in the Canal End gasped as goalkeeper Walsh, Jack Sheedy and John Joe Doherty all seemed to go for the ball. "We'd worked a lot on dealing with high balls for both the semi-final and the final," remembered Walsh. "I came out and tried to get a fist to it but was lucky that it deflected off me and Sheedy and John Joe picked it up." "I stumbled and remember a massive roar from the Canal End behind me which seemed to push me forward before I passed the ball to Joyce," recalled John Joe. "It was nearly the crowd that cleared that ball because we had been doing our best not to get rid of it. Somehow we managed to clear it up the field."

Moments later Brian Murray fielded but spilled a Mick Deegan free, but the referee said Murray had been fouled. Charlie Redmond kicked the ball into the Ard Comhairle in a fit of pique and Sugrue promptly moved the ball forward. Murray hit the free into Manus Boyle who fielded above Mick Deegan and scored his third point. "Murray was a fine striker of the ball," said Manus Boyle:

> We knew the three Dublin full-backs were smaller than us. Murray could kick it 50 or 60 yards from the ground and wouldn't send in the ball out of his hands and have it falling from the sky. At this stage, I was happy to be on Mick Deegan. He was playing me from behind and this suited me – any forward would be happy with that.

It had taken Donegal some time to settle but they were cruising now and led by 0-9 to 0-6. Redmond would score a close-in free and McHugh would go down the barrel of the gun once more before half-time.

The last action of the first half was a Charlie Redmond foul on Anthony Molloy who had covered back and won a long ball intended for Vinny Murphy. Referee Tommy Sugrue sounded the half-time whistle and the teams made their way towards the tunnel and a Canal End resplendent in green and gold. "The memory of the Donegal support from three sides of the ground as we came off at half-time still makes the hairs stand on the back of my neck," said Declan Bonner.

The acclaim of Croke Park was no more than the men in green and gold deserved. It had been a consummate team performance. "When the likes of Martin McHugh or Declan Bonner have been knocked off the ball by Dublin men, Gavigan, Molloy and Murray have been quick to intervene," noted Charlie Collins. They had weathered an early Dublin flurry, conceded a penalty, missed two goal chances and ran down the barrel of the gun. The All-Ireland final debutants were good value for their three-point lead as they headed for the dressing room and enjoyed a well-earned but brief break. "Leading by 0-10 to 0-7 at half-time is something that not even the keenest Donegal supporters would have imagined in their wildest dreams," said Michael McGee. Wild dreams were about to be fulfilled.

❆ ❆ ❆ ❆

Half-time passed in the blink of an eye. Confidence was flowing throughout the Donegal support as they anticipated the second half. Donegal made no changes but Dublin introduced Paul Bealin for Dave Foran at midfield. "The atmosphere is unbelievable here, Donegal people are on a high," Charlie Collins told Highland Radio listeners.

Even at the start of the second half, Dublin persisted with the long ball into Vinny Murphy. Keith Barr continued to slow the game down by taking frees from the ground, giving Donegal time to crowd out Murphy. It was one thing winning the ball – and Murphy won plenty – but quite another thing finding the space to use it. Donegal lapped it up. "Dublin didn't prepare well for the match," felt Martin McHugh:

> The only tactic they had was using Keith Barr to kick frees from the ground into Vinny Murphy. Keith Barr was so slow in taking the free that by the time he kicked it, Anthony was back in defence. Vinny Murphy won a lot of ball but there were two or three players around him when he hit the ground. Dublin persisted with that tactic. Rather than Keith Barr kicking the ball short, taking it back and putting me under pressure he persisted with this. We also fouled a fair bit out the field and slowed the game down to suit us.

A quick ball into Murphy led to Dublin's first score in the second half. Matt Gallagher shepherded Murphy into the corner but Vinny crossed the ball into the centre where it broke to Mick Galvin. Barry McGowan had been caught out. "The point came from some loose marking on my part," he recalled, "and Mick Galvin didn't need a second opportunity to pop it over the bar." There were only two points between the teams again. Joyce McMullan, relatively quiet from play in the first half, won a free when he ran at Paul Curran. Referee Sugrue moved the ball forward and into Manus Boyle's range following a comment from a Dublin player. Slightly to the left of goals and about 35 metres out, Manus chipped the ball and the reaction of the supporters packed into the Canal End confirmed that the three-point margin had been restored.

Confidence was running through Manus' veins, but then it always did. A big-game player if ever there was one Manus didn't have nerves of steel, he just didn't have nerves at all. "You need players who are prepared to stand up on the big day," said John Cunningham. "Some people freeze on the big day while it brings the best out of others and Manus seems to be one of those."

Joyce McMullan and Declan Bonner came more into the game early in the second half and combined to find James McHugh who waltzed around half the Dublin defence before shooting narrowly wide. Declan Bonner was clearly getting the better of Tommy Carr, the Dublin captain. "I was delighted that he was playing at left corner-back," said Bonner:

> I had watched him playing and I had read something where he said that he didn't like playing corner-back and wanted to be further out the field. Knowing that he didn't like playing corner-back meant that I had one up on him before the game even started.

Mild controversy arrived when Gary Walsh collected a Dessie Farrell shot under his bar. As he made his way out to the right his attempted hand pass was blocked by Mick Galvin. Initially the umpire signalled for a 45 but following a few words with the big goalkeeper he changed his mind. Walsh is still adamant that it was wide. The Dublin faithful on Hill 16 were incensed and donated some of their hard-earned pennies to the clearly misguided umpire. "Maybe the umpire is getting caught up in the excitement of the whole thing," was the opinion of the most composed man in Croke Park, Charlie Collins.

Dublin hit three or four wides early in the second half. On the sideline Brian McEniff was feeling a little anxious. "I was a wee bit worried that we weren't settling in the second half," he said. He'd soon be called on to make a change, albeit one that he had anticipated. Joyce McMullan again won a ball in the Donegal half-back line and released it to midfielder Brian Murray. Murray carried it forward and gave it to Manus Boyle who was fouled. Free in. Murray was hobbling, his calf muscle had ripped and his game was over. On the sideline McEniff gave Barry Cunningham the shout. "I was so keen to get on that I tripped getting out of the dugout," remembers Cunningham:

> I ran down the sideline to warm up. People were throwing rosary beads and scapulas over the fence. I picked them all up and gave them back to the people that had thrown them. I told them to keep them and remember the day. I told them that it would be all right and that we were going to win the All-Ireland.

In the summer of 1977, nine year-old Barry Cunningham caught his first glimpse of the Sam Maguire Cup at an Irish fair in London. Every county in Ireland had taken a stall at the fair and the Sam Maguire was the centrepiece of the Dublin display. Mesmerised, the young Cunningham went over to get a better look at this glittering trophy. "I was wearing a wee green and gold rosette and the woman on the stall asked me where I was from," he recounted. "I told her I was from Donegal. She told me to take a good look at Sam Maguire because it was the closest I'd ever get to it." As he warmed up on the sideline, Barry Cunningham was just 25 minutes away from getting his hands on the cup as a winner.

There was no way Murray could continue and he hopped off the field of play. "I was totally drained coming off the field," he recalled:

> I had worked so hard with the injuries. I felt that I had done well in the
> game and would have loved to finish it. Getting injured and having to
> leave was hard. I was applauded as I came off. When I went to the
> dugout Charlie Mulgrew clapped me on the back and said 'well done'.
> Then the whole lot just seemed to come on top of me and I started to cry.
> I don't cry that often but the whole lot just came out. Someone said,
> 'leave him' and then I stopped as quickly as I began and watched the rest
> of the game. It was tense but I knew we weren't going to lose.

While the change was taking place, Manus had been standing patiently over the
ball waiting to hit the free. Paul Curran got involved in a little bit of gamesmanship and tried to move the ball back but 20,000 indignant Donegal voices alerted
the referee and he placed the ball on the correct spot. Did the delay disturb Manus'
concentration? Not a bit. At the much quieter Hill 16 end, Matt Gallagher marvelled at the thousands of Donegal and Armagh standards waving in the breeze
and even though more than 25 minutes remained, he knew the day was won:

> The sun was setting over the Canal End where there was a huge array of
> Donegal flags. Manus struck the ball over the bar and we moved four
> points up. I said to myself then that we weren't going to lose.

Manus was making only his second championship start of the summer and his
selection was controversial. But he repaid his manager's faith in him. Every
team needs an accurate free taker and in Boyle, not to mention the McHughs
and Declan Bonner, Donegal had them in abundance. Barry Cunningham had
got up to the pace of the game immediately. He remembers it clearly:

> Martin McHugh gave me a pass and the whole pitch opened up; you
> don't expect that in an All-Ireland final. Getting that good early touch
> and winning the free settled me. I was in good shape mentally and phys-
> ically and there are some days when it will go for you and some days that
> it won't. The ball seems to follow you around if it's going well. There's
> nothing you can do about it and the ball just lands for you.

Paul Curran was forced to pull the rampaging Cunningham down just outside the
14-metre line. Tommy Sugrue once again signalled for a free and Manus said
thank you very much as he tapped over his easiest free of the day. The gap had
opened to five points. Donegal were overrunning a bewildered Dublin team in
all sectors of the field. The only leaders on the field wore green and gold, there
were none to be found in sky blue. Plan A of hoofing the ball into Vinny Murphy

wasn't working but there was no back-up plan. The Dublin management failed to make any changes as their All-Ireland aspirations petered out in the second half. This wasn't supposed to happen to Dublin. This team of all talents, so memorably beaten by Meath in an epic four-game encounter the previous year, deserved an All-Ireland. They only had to turn up and send Donegal home with another hard-luck story. John O'Leary still hadn't got over the shock of it when he collaborated with Martin Breheny in his 1997 biography *Back to the Hill*:

> I don't want to take away from Donegal's historic triumph, but I genuinely feel we left that All-Ireland behind us. Of all the championship defeats I experienced down the years, this was one of the hardest to take.

Shock was a common feeling among the beleaguered Dublin defence. Donegal crashed at them like the waves of Tory. "Donal Reid, wearing the number five jersey, went past me a number of times," a stunned Tommy Carr told Raymond Smith of the *Irish Independent* after the game.

Dublin had been five points down with only two minutes left in the league quarter-final in April. Dublin had stolen a victory they didn't merit and it confirmed all their notions about Donegal's brittleness. But there was no doubts in Donegal players' minds this time. They'd experienced that sickening defeat and learned from it. "We knew we had matched Dublin every time we played them in the years leading up to 1992," said Barry Cunningham. "We always knew that we could beat them and it was just a matter of performing on the day." "Dublin really underestimated us," recalled Brian Murray:

> I knew that a few of the Dubs were ordinary players, but I suppose they could say that I was an ordinary player too. We had some exceptional players but they didn't really have any. Keith Barr was a very good player but after that you'd have to look very, very hard to find an exceptional player. We had very, very good players who could, on their day, destroy a team. The three boys in the full-forward line could win a game on their own.

The game had started at a frantic pace and had continued at that pace throughout. A ball broke behind Martin Gavigan and he acted instinctively:

> I was racing back towards our own goals and the ball was in front of me. I just pulled on it before Vinny Murphy could pick it up even though he was going in the opposite direction. The ball went flying over the sideline. Everyone was just giving it their all at that stage.

Dublin sent the ball into the Donegal parallelogram from the resultant sideline kick where it was eventually claimed by Barry Cunningham who won a free. Twice on the ball since coming on to the field and twice he had won important frees.

✻ ✻ ✻ ✻

Of all the people in Croke Park on All-Ireland final day, those with the worst view of the action are the substitutes. "All you can see is a forest of legs," commented Tommy Ryan. Martin Shovlin couldn't get accustomed to watching the match from the dugout and longed to take his place at left half-back. "It makes a while difference when you're not on the field," he said:

> I was in a daze during the game, looking out and wanting to be there but I wasn't fit. There wasn't a hope that I could play. It stayed with me for such a long time afterwards. It was a real setback. There's not a day goes by that I don't think about it and it was 11 years ago now.

It was similarly disappointing for Charlie Mulgrew who had made his championship debut back in 1981 when he was still under-21:

> It was extremely difficult and it can still hit me. I was involved with Donegal for 12 years and what I ultimately wanted was to be involved with Donegal in Croke Park and win an All-Ireland title. There was quite a bit of satisfaction from being involved but the regret will always be there that I didn't get to play.

Most distraught of all was John Cunningham who had believed he had a chance of replacing Martin Shovlin only to discover that the management chose John Joe Doherty to fill the position. Cunningham had spent the first half ruminating on an altercation he'd had with McEniff in the dressing room before the team had taken the field:

> I was keeping to myself in the dressing room before the game but then Brian said: 'There are men in here that don't want to be here. They're not up for this game.' Nobody knew that I had been talking to him in the hotel and this was directed at me.
>
> Then I had another go at him. I was still in the dressing room and I got him over in the corner on my own. I said: 'If I play for Donegal I'll play.' Brian told me that I'd get my chance and I suppose maybe he was thinking along those lines but it just never happened. I was warming up all right but it just didn't work out. That was my All-Ireland.
>
> I had devoted my whole life towards that day. In footballing terms it was the worst day of my life, that's being honest. It was a funny emotion. Everybody around me was so high and I was down but tried not to show

it. It's difficult to explain. Football is a team effort but you're still an individual. People can say whatever they want but if you're among the subs it's not the same – not to somebody like me who had always played and was a winner. I was annoyed at the time but I'm all right now.

❋ ❋ ❋ ❋

While the subs were experiencing mixed emotions the game thundered on. Eamon Heery launched an attack and found Keith Barr. Maybe the half-back line could produce something for Dublin. Barr surged forward but found his attempted pass blocked by Martin McHugh. The Wee Man was everywhere. "Barr had thrown caution to the wind and went forward so I had to follow him back," McHugh said matter-of-factly. The ball broke to Paul Curran but his attempted pass into the danger area was brilliantly intercepted by Noel Hegarty and cleared out the field. Charlie Collins was calling it as he saw it. "It's all harem-scarem and helter-skelter in the All-Ireland final. Dublin have it all to do. They were everyone's favourites but find themselves five points down."

Dublin earned a free and pumped the ball into their full-forward line. For once the Donegal defence didn't sweep up the ball and Niall Guiden nipped in for his first point to leave the score at 0-13 to 0-9 with 14 minutes gone in the second half. A minute later and Manus confounded everyone in Croke Park as he kicked a ball wide from far out on the right wing. "I was disgusted," he remembered "I was having one of those days when everything went over the bar and wondered why the umpire didn't flag a point. I was sure it was over, as was Tony Boyle and we said as much to the umpires."

"Gerry Hargan has never played against a better full-forward," opined Charlie Collins as Tony Boyle beat him to yet another ball and was fouled. Brian Mullins writing in the *Irish Independent* agreed. "I was especially sad for Gerry Hargan because I can never remember him being given such a hard time by a full-forward before." The free was 35 metres from the posts and only ten in from the Hogan Stand sideline. "It was my most difficult kick of the match," recalled Declan Bonner, "but I was confident of putting it over. Once I struck it I knew it was over." The ball curled majestically over the bar. Three sides of the stadium rose to acclaim the score which put Donegal five points in front again.

A sustained period of Dublin pressure followed in which Jack Sheedy shot wide and Rambo, who commanded the centre of the Donegal defence throughout, collected a blocked shot from, of all people, Mick Deegan. Gavigan had an impressive afternoon. "I started by marking Charlie Redmond," he recalled:

I had the pace on him and I knew I was stronger than him too. I won the first couple of balls that came in. I didn't fear any of the Dublin forwards so I didn't mind who came out to mark me. I knew I was in as good a shape as I possibly could be and I was going to be able to compete. I was-n't going to win every ball but I was going to be there.

Dublin were trying everything but the Donegal defence stood firm. Paul Bealin was starting to win a lot of ball in the middle of the field and after fetching one of Gary Walsh's kick outs, returned it in to Vinny Murphy. Matt Gallagher blocked him. "Matt had been like a leech all day," recalled Brian Murray. Murphy collected the ball after the block and released it to Charlie Redmond. Redmond bore down on goal and Rambo threw himself at him. Redmond spun away and had a shot but three Donegal players, Walsh, John Joe and Matt combined to block it. The ball fell to Barry McGowan who took a knock from Redmond:

> I took a hard knock and went down. I was glad to hear Tommy Sugrue blowing the whistle for a free kick. I didn't want to jump back up again too quickly, I wanted to wait a moment to, first of all, see if I was injured badly and, if so, to get a wee bit of a rest. After a few seconds I knew I wasn't that badly injured. I just took a few seconds to gather my thoughts again before I played on.

"Those are the sort of moments that win All-Ireland finals," exhaled Charlie Collins. Charlie Redmond was screaming at the referee but Sugrue paid no attention to him. Noel Hegarty saw his chance. Redmond had taunted him when Dublin won the league quarter-final in Cavan by telling him the game wasn't over until the Fat Lady sings. "I told him I could hear the Fat Lady singing then," Hegarty recalled. Redmond made no response. Touché.

Redmond, who had a very quiet game after the penalty miss, was involved again moments later. Barry Cunningham had conceded a free outside the 45-metre line and Redmond elected to place it on the ground and drive it in to Vinny Murphy. Cunningham was determined to make up for conceding the free and sprinted back to the goalmouth. "Vinny Murphy had won nearly every ball that went in there," recalled Cunningham:

> He was like an Australian Rules player in a lot of ways and needed the run to get the jump so I stood in front of him to try and stop his run. The trajectory of the ball from the free kick was very low and he couldn't reach past me. I caught the ball in front of me rather than above my head. It was one of those things, the ball was just running my way.

Another free won by the Killybegs man who certainly made a big contribution when he came on. "Barry Cunningham was magnificently constructive in everything he did from his arrival on the field until the end," wrote Micheál Ó Muircheartaigh in the *Irish Press* the following day. In the pages of the *Irish*

Times Paddy Downey wrote: "Barry Cunningham was the one that this reporter would make man-of-the-match".

Keith Barr won another free and played the ball in long. It broke to Charlie Redmond, who was by then operating at corner-forward. Coming in from the left of the parallelogram a goal chance presented itself. From out of nowhere, Barry McGowan came rushing across and blocked Redmond's shot. "It hit my foot," recalled McGowan, "Vinny Murphy then knocked the ball wide on the other side and then appealed for a penalty. There were two or three Donegal players there at the time and it would have been a brave man to give a penalty at that stage."

More coins were donated by the denizens of Hill 16 to the collection being taken by the umpires. "I got hit with a couple of coins that were thrown from the Hill," remembered Walsh. "We collected the coins and gave them to the umpire. I met him at the Burlington Hotel the following day and he told me he got enough for a couple of pints out of it!" McEniff had come down to investigate and got involved in a stand-off with Dublin selector Pat O'Neill. "Strong words are being exchanged but I don't have to tell you who's not pleased with who," reported Charlie Collins. Donegal men were standing toe-to-toe with the Dubs all over the pitch and McEniff was no different. The years rolled back as the two former All-Star half-backs marked one another on the endline at Croke Park. With several thousand Dubs on the Hill screaming obscenities it wasn't a comfortable place to be but McEniff never flinched.

With Donegal leading by 0-14 to 0-9 Charlie Collins demonstrated remarkable restraint when he declared, "Donegal are playing brilliantly, this is one of the best performances we've ever seen from them". Molloy who won more frees than any other Donegal player in the final, won another in the middle of the park. Martin McHugh played it in to Tony Boyle who again had the beating of Hargan. He slipped the ball to Manus Boyle on the left wing who remembers the score thus:

> Deegan was pulling at my jersey and I was wondering what had to happen for me to get a free. I just looked up and hit it. I had no option other than hitting it – I thought I would lose the ball if I soloed it. The defence was closing in on me and there didn't seem to be any other forwards around, so I decided to have a go and it went over.

As simple as that really. "What a brilliant score from the Killybegs man," exclaimed Charlie Collins, his voice an octave higher as the end of the game drew near. "He has answered all the questions today." Donegal were now six points up and looking good. "We want Sam, we want Sam," started off as a fervent, almost prayerful whisper at the back of the Canal End. Belief was spreading through Donegal fans as they gave throat to the mantra. The whisper became a roar and the chant echoed around the stadium: "WE WANT SAM, WE WANT SAM".

Paul Clarke scored from a 45 to reduce the margin to five points but it barely raised a ripple of applause on a shell-shocked Hill 16. Only seven minutes remained. Vinny Murphy picked up a poor pass from Tommy Carr moments later and blasted the ball over Walsh's bar from a very tight angle. Four points between the sides. "Memories of the quarter-final in Cavan come into the minds of some Donegal supporters," wrote Michael Daly in the *Democrat*, but he might have added that they never once entered the minds of the players.

Tommy Carr had switched with Eamon Heery and Heery now found himself at corner-back marking Declan Bonner. "We started to lose our shape for a period and Heery wanted to go forward at every opportunity," remembered Bonner. On one of his sallies Heery scored a point – Dublin's third in less than three minutes – to leave only three points between the sides. The score stood at 0-15 to 0-12 as the game entered its final phase.

McEniff had left the dugout a few minutes earlier. As he left, he told Naul McCole, selector and County Board chairman, that he was going to spend £600. "Roscommon had Meath almost beaten in 1991," McEniff said:

> Marty McDermott, the Roscommon manager told me that he saw the game slipping through his hands. I wouldn't let the game slip through my hands.
> The Dubs had pushed our half-forwards back down the pitch. While McHugh was doing Trojan work back there, I needed him in the other half. I went on and had hard words with Molloy. I remember Rambo looking at me strangely because he couldn't believe what I'd said to Molloy. I was using what my mother would call 'soldiers' talk'. I got over to the Hogan Stand side and had some words with the half-forwards. I wasn't satisfied that I had done enough damage so I ran back across the pitch. We were fined but nowadays you'd get a sideline ban too.

A quick free taken by Noel Hegarty from between the 65s found Tony Boyle once again trailing Gerry Hargan in his wake. Hargan had been persuaded out of retirement earlier in the year but there must have been times that Sunday as he watched the green number 14 speed away from him once again when he rued the decision to return. Hargan committed the foul and presented Manus Boyle with another easy scoring opportunity. From inside the 20-metre line, Manus restored Donegal's four-point lead.

James McHugh was doing great work in defence. Mick Deegan played a high ball down the line for Paul Bealin who stood at 6'2". James McHugh is 5'7". McHugh leapt up and punched the ball away from the Dublin substitute. It brought to mind a mighty tackle he committed on another giant, Brian McGilligan in the closing moments of the Ulster final two months before. His brother Martin was now playing in the Donegal full-back line. "These Donegal lads are playing as if their lives depended on it," intoned Michael McGee. With five minutes remaining in the game Mick Galvin earned a 13-metre free. Five Donegal men spread across the goal line and Redmond chipped the ball over the bar.

Three points between the teams. There was tension on the pitch, tension in the stands and tension in the dugout. With only five minutes remaining Brian McEniff called on Sylvester Maguire to start warming up. For Tommy Ryan, this was the final straw. Having started in all five championship matches prior to the final, Tommy had every right to feel aggrieved when he lost his place for the biggest game of all. As he saw it, he could have been compensated in a small way by coming on as a sub. "I didn't mind being fucked once, but I couldn't stand for being fucked twice," he said. "I told McEniff that if he wanted to see the end of the game he'd better not bring Sylvester on before me. The two of us warmed up but neither of us got on." Ryan, adopts a philosophical view now:

> I went to St Eunan's College and played on good soccer and Gaelic foot-ball teams there. At the age of 24, I was the only fella left playing. The rest of them were either hurt or had just stopped. I was lucky enough to play on and I'm still playing – or trying to.
>
> The All-Ireland was the only time in my life that I ever got the chop, but talk about bad timing! It just so happened that it came that day. Unfortunately things didn't go to my liking on that day. There's no point cribbing or crying about it, it just didn't happen for me. Whatever happens in a football match, whether it's a club game or an All-Ireland final, you can't change anything when the final whistle goes. The next game will come and you'll pull on the jersey and play no matter who it's for.

Back on the field, Barry Cunningham won a kick out from Gary Walsh and set up Manus Boyle for a point made in Killybegs. "Manus had been playing full-forward for Killybegs since we were under-12," said Barry Cunningham:

> Mick Deegan was probably fed up with Manus and didn't know what to do with him, so he decided to play in front of him. I won the ball at mid-field. I bounced the ball, looked up and saw Manus behind Deegan. I thought to myself that if could get the ball over Deegan's head Manus would be clean through. When you kick a ball into a forward that's com-ing out you'd normally try to hit it with a low trajectory. I adjusted my technique and kicked a looping pass. It landed in his hands. It was something we had done at club level countless times.

Manus was clean through and with a magnificent eight-point haul already to his credit he was thinking of a goal:

> The goal was on my mind. I could see Eamon Heery filtering back and I thought I'd just put it over. The worst thing about an opportunity like that is

that you get the chance to think that a goal is on. In my head I knew a point would put four between us. I wasn't thinking about four points as I hit it, but I'd noticed the scoreboard and clock a minute or so before that and realised that if I got another point the game would be won. The Dubs weren't going to get a goal; the defence was closing everything down. Bonner was coming in but he stopped. If he had kept going we would have had a goal. O'Leary would have had to come to me and I could have slipped it to him.

The ball glided over the bar and all over Donegal thoughts turned to finding fuel for the bonfires that would light up the night skies for the following week.

Nine points in the All-Ireland Senior Football Championship final. The man-of-the-match award was only going to have one home after a performance like that. Those who had followed his career knew that the bigger the stage, the better Manus would perform. Martin Breheny compiled the player ratings in the *Irish Press* the following day: "Superbly confident every time he went for the ball, he destroyed Dublin. Never beaten for possession, never fumbled the ball and never lost concentration. Ten out of ten." "To this day, nobody can understand why Mick Deegan was left on Manus for the entire match," said Anthony Molloy. "It goes to show you what preparation Dublin had done. Mick Deegan was a small man and suited Manus down to the ground."

Dublin knew the game was up and poured forward in vain. Donegal forwards poured back alongside them and almost everyone on the pitch found themselves between the Donegal endline and the 45-metre line. A sideline ball was fed to Paul Clarke who was promptly dispossessed by Joyce McMullan. The ball broke loose. "I hoofed the ball over the sideline," remembered Joyce. "I should have picked it up but my emotions were running high at the time and it wasn't easy to make the right decision." Matt Gallagher was trying to remain calm:

> I knew the match would be over at five to five. By this time the clock was creeping on for ten to five. It was the Alamo for us. That was probably the only time in the game that we cracked in terms of possession. We possibly got too many men behind the ball but it worked for us. If we were a wee bit more disciplined we might have won by more. Dublin were losing the All-Ireland final by two or three points at their home ground, of course they were going to throw everything at it. They might as well lose by six points as lose by two.

Dublin worked the ball into the parallelogram where it was scooped up by Donal Reid. Vinny Murphy dispossessed him and made a desperate final goal attempt. "He hadn't got a great angle," recalled Gary Walsh:

> I would have seen one of my great strengths to be my ability to close

down a fella the closer he got to goals. I would always have had a better chance of saving a ball the closer a fella would get to goals. It was an ordinary enough save. I got down quick to his feet and was brave.

The ball went out for a 45. Paul Clarke took the 45 and with it, scored Dublin's 14th and final point. The stands were in a state of blissful mayhem. Donegal men, women and children surged towards the perimeter wire of the pitch. History was about to be made. Donegal was about win its first All-Ireland title and become the 16th county to do so. Photographers were gravitating towards Donegal's dugout.

Martin McHugh was still running at Barr. He picked up a ball from Barry Cunningham and played a one-two with the Killybegs substitute. Cunningham hit it into Declan Bonner who skyed the ball. Tony Boyle had been in a better position to score than Bonner but he followed the ball in and knocked John O'Leary over the endline. Spectators were already scaling the wire. O'Leary struck another poor kick out and Joyce McMullan collected the ball. "O'Leary didn't catch it too well and he hooked it a bit," remembered Joyce. "It was just sitting there to be won. I took it down and wee James was going past. The obvious thing to do was give it to him as he's a good carrier of the ball and good at taking on defenders."

Joyce is a master of understatement. Nothing is obvious in the frantic, dying moments of an All-Ireland final. James McHugh hopped the ball once and released it to the onrushing Declan Bonner who takes up the narrative:

> Heery was on me at this stage. He knew I was going to go on to my left foot, I knew I was going to go on to my left foot – I was just waiting on the opportunity and then I put it over. Tommy Sugrue had said there was about two minutes left and I knew that once we had the four point cushion we were safe. I raised my fist in triumph. That salute was shown over and over on TV. I always told Manus and McHugh that there wasn't much point in kicking all those points, that you have to wait and kick that last point as that's the one that's going to be remembered!

Four points the margin. Eighteen magnificent points. Sixteen tremendous players. One All-Ireland title.

Dublin had one final attack but Jack Sheedy was off balance as he struck the ball wide. Barry Cunningham claimed Gary Walsh's final kick out and hand passed it to Declan Bonner who headed straight for the sideline. Paul Clarke robustly tackled him and Bonner went to ground. Seconds later Tommy Sugrue blew the full-time whistle and started wrestling with Martin McHugh.

"We talk about the Battle of Clontarf, we talk about battles here and there, but when the history of Donegal is written, the battle of Croke Park will be emblazoned across the pages," said Michael McGee.

18

Sam's for the Hills
(September 20-25, 1992)

"Sam's for the Hills."

Anthony Molloy – September 20, 1992

A few yards from where Declan Bonner lay sprawled, Tommy Sugrue and Martin McHugh were grappling with each other. Just seconds before, Sugrue had brought the final curtain down on the All-Ireland football final of 1992. Now McHugh wanted the match ball. For five or six seconds the Kerry official clung gamely to the leather but it was a lost cause. McHugh had stood toe to toe with Keith Barr for 70 minutes and had not been found wanting – Tommy Sugrue stood little chance. McHugh got the ball. "I was so confident of winning that I decided before the game that I was going to get the ball at full-time," remembered Martin McHugh:

> I was watching where the ball was in the dying minutes. I was running after it everywhere to make sure I'd get it. I got all the lads to sign it and I still have it. Tommy Sugrue wanted the ball as well but I wasn't going to let go. At the end up he had to let go.

Declan Bonner smiles at the memory. The Na Rossa man had been in possession at the finale. Lying along the sideline having shipped a heavy wallop, he had let the ball roll from his grasp. "I should have held on to it," he laughed, "but I wasn't thinking as quickly as McHugh!"

Bonner had little time to nurse his wounds. Croke Park simply erupted. Donegal folk, poised in their hundreds to scale the wire that surrounded Croke Park, now sprang onto the pitch. Bonner made a speedy recovery:

I had to get up – even if my back had been broken I would have had to get up! I was right under the Hogan Stand and the crowd was in immediately. It was some feeling. I was carried along to the steps of the stand.

There was no holding back Donegal supporters. The wire fence that surrounded Croke Park was a difficult enough proposition if viewed in reasonable circumstances. These were far from reasonable circumstances. Men, women and children cleared eight feet of wire with the confidence of Olympic hurdlers. The urge to get onto the pitch to greet the boys was primal.

"I looked up to heaven and savoured the moment," was Joyce McMullan's reaction to the full-time whistle:

The thought of it still makes the hair stand on the back of my neck. It was a great sight to see the place come alight. People were clearing the fences around the pitch and there was an almost manic ferociousness about them. A friend of mine came running at me and he was so emotionally charged that the eyes were standing in his head. The whole place went bonkers.

Manus Boyle was, like many of the other players, immediately engulfed by the crowd:

What annoyed me was that I couldn't see Mick Deegan. I had just won an All-Ireland but losing one must be the hardest thing. I didn't get a chance to commiserate with him then. I did about ten interviews and I didn't get back to the dressing room for an hour and a half after the game and I met Mick then.

At the other end of the pitch, Barry McGowan was overwhelmed:

It was just sheer relief and I just looked up and threw my arms up to the heavens. It was a basic reaction to one of the greatest moments of your life. Very often when one experiences a heightened sense of nervousness and fear you think of the man above. It's a natural reaction.

I remember the crowd coming on to the pitch and being buffeted about all over the pitch with all these euphoric people. It was a marvellous thing and the scene were unbelievable. I was pushed towards the Hogan Stand and the cordoned off area. I had to get over the railing then. People realised that I was one of the players and I remember being physically and unceremoniously thrown into the area. I met the other players and waited on the steps of the Hogan Stand to lift the cup. There was nothing artificial about the occasion. Natural emotions shone through.

I would liken it in many ways to a traumatic experience. People often block out traumatic experiences. I know people will wonder how I can liken winning an All-Ireland final to such an experience, but it is due to the heightened emotions. Perhaps such instances are closely related.

"Getting across the railing and up the steps was harder than the game," remembers Tony Boyle:

> I met so many people, they were coming at me in waves. Sometimes people don't realise how tired you are when they're hitting you on the back. You're physically exhausted. I was among the last to get to the steps of the Hogan Stand. I remember making my way up past the subs.
>
> To win an All-Ireland was fabulous and to beat the Dubs in their own back yard was an added bonus. To play like we played was very satisfying. We got so much stick after the Mayo match and I think it worked to our advantage. I like to think that we put in one of the best performances in All-Ireland finals of the 1990s.

The scene on the pitch was that of a tribe celebrating its greatest victory. Donegal players were hunted down and engulfed in a sea of unbridled joy. Hundreds, then thousands, of people in assorted hues of green and gold swarmed onto the hallowed sod. Sixty seconds after Tommy Sugrue sounded the final whistle, the pitch was already a heaving mass.

Noel Hegarty was uncomfortable with the crowds. The closing minutes of the game had been a blur for him. "I looked up at the clock at the Canal End but I might as well have been looking at the wall. I couldn't focus on it all," he recalled:

> I would not like all the back-slapping. There was a lot of people running around and slapping you – it can be rough enough. I wanted to get as close to the Hogan Stand as I could to get out of it.

Donal Reid was trying to take it all in. "Knowing in your heart and soul that Donegal were good enough to win an All-Ireland title and then having won it was great," he recalled:

> My wife was the first person I wanted to see and I eventually found her. Somebody put a straw hat on me. People were excited and running onto the field, many were delirious. I saw people from different clubs with arms around one another's shoulders. I saw old men and women crying. I was an older player and I stood back, looked at it and enjoyed it for what it was.
>
> I was delighted for Brian McEniff. I looked at him and saw that he was very calm and collected. He had put a lot into football over the years.

Tommy Ryan

I was delighted for my team-mates, some of whom I had played with since the under-21. It was great for the county. I wasn't taken away with my own success. I was thinking of my family and what they had to put up with and hoped they were enjoying the occasion.

Brian McEniff had been collared by Mick Dunne of RTÉ for an immediate after-match comment. McEniff managed to utter a few words to the veteran broadcaster before a wall of green and gold engulfed the little huddle and swept them down the field. Interview over. McEniff was enveloped by well-wishers. Moments earlier, just before the final whistle, an excited supporter had scaled the wire and entered the Donegal dugout. "What's the story with him?" someone asked McEniff. "Ah, leave him be," answered McEniff, "he's one of ours." Now, as McEniff made his way across the pitch that same supporter strode by his side, one arm looped around the Donegal manager's shoulder. He was Seamus Braid from Downings and had travelled to Dublin from London for the match. He would die in tragic and violent circumstances on O'Connell Street some ten hours later.

Up in the press box, hacks gazed down on the happy mayhem below. The Follower was emotional.

A personal life's ambition has been achieved for me by the dedicated efforts of players and management. Words, even tears, cannot express my personal gratitude and the gratitude of so many like me who kept the faith in the leanest and darkest days.

Down on the pitch, an ecstatic Molloy made it through the mayhem, shepherded by Croke Park ard-maor John Leonard. "I hadn't time to see any of the team or shake anybody's hand because I was swept across the pitch," he recalled:

It was great looking down on all the players gathering on the steps. It's a day I'll never forget and I have very special memories. Many people, young and old, were crying with delight. People were going crazy.

It's hard to describe lifting Sam because it's totally electric. You'll never do anything in your life as good. It's a day filled with emotion. The place is teeming with colour and people go mad and are crying. It's hysterical stuff.

Out around the middle of the field players were enduring hearty slaps on the back and were being hoisted onto the shoulders of supporters. It was utter chaos. James McHugh finally made it to the relative safety of the cordon at the foot of the Hogan Stand. He'd managed to elicit a tin of coke from someone but before he could take some much needed fluid on board an excited Donegal supporter leapt on him knocking the tin from his grasp – it was that kind of day.

One by one the boys made it through the throng and poured up the steps of the Hogan Stand to watch the presentation. Peter Quinn, the Fermanagh man who would have the distinction of greeting three All-Ireland winning Ulster captains during his presidency, began to speak.

A minute later it happened. Quinn turned to Anthony Molloy, captain of Donegal, and handed him the Sam Maguire Cup. Molloy had waited a lifetime for this moment. Thousands had dreamt of such a moment. Now, here it was. Donegal were All-Ireland Senior Football Champions. Molloy was about to get his hands on the Cup. A mighty roar shook the famous old stadium as 25,000 Donegal voices greeted the spine-tingling sight of the Ardara man hoisting the Sam Maguire high above his head.

The full vent of that cry of joy might only have lasted five or ten seconds but they truly were magical hair-raising moments. Grown men – hard men who plied their trade on GAA fields from Gaoth Dobhair to Malin – cried like babies. Everywhere one looked tears were falling with utter abandonment. Croke Park temporarily became a little corner of Donegal. A shared sense of elation swept through the crowd as they saw Donegal become the 16th county to win the All-Ireland title.

Molloy composed himself. He'd shared a word or two with President Mary Robinson, Taoiseach Albert Reynolds and other dignitaries. Now he would address the multitudes. Dermot Gilleece was watching for the *Irish Times*:

> The sea of green and gold made famous by countless Kerry teams, pro-
> vided a familiar camera shot when the climatic moment came. As sight
> merged with sound, however, the richly distinctive Gaelic of Anthony
> Molloy, lent unmistakable emphasis to this, a uniquely different, occasion.

Indeed this was different. This was history in the making. Molloy had some Gaeilge but it had been 20-odd years since he'd had cause to use it. The Ardara man had enlisted the help of his friend Pól MacCumhaill from Gaoth Dobhair during the week to help out with his speech. And then he forgot to bring it with him! It mattered little as Molloy made one of the great Croke Park acceptance speeches:

> A Uachtarán na hÉireann, a Uachtarán Chumann Lúthchleas Gael, a
> chléir, agus pobal na hÉireann; cuireann sé lúcháir an-mhór orm an corn
> Sam Maguire a ghlacadh ar son muintir Dhún na nGall. Is lá aoibhinn é
> seo; bhíomar ag fanacht de i Dhún na nGall le ró-fhada, ach is fiú é anois.
>
> President of Ireland, president of Cumann Lúthchleas Gael, clergy
> and the people of Donegal: we've done it! We in Donegal have waited
> far too long for this day to come but it was worthwhile in the end.
>
> There's a lot of people I'd like to thank. I start by thanking our team
> mentors, Mickey Lafferty, Naul McCole, Seamus Bonner and Anthony

Harkin. I would like to give a special word of thanks to our trainer, Anthony Harkin. As you can see, we were in magnificent shape out there today. I would also like to thank our physios, Karen Crawford and Catriona Fitzpatrick, our masseur, Angela McMenamin and the doctor himself, Austin Kennedy. I would like to thank my own wife and family for the patience and support they have given me all year; I say this on behalf of all the team and the whole Donegal squad. I would like to thank also our former players who wore the county jersey and have contributed to this success here today. I also wish to thank yourselves, the supporters, who have been brilliant to us down the years.

Another man who didn't make the squad today, he had to pull out just before the game started, I'd like you all to put your hands together for Martin Shovlin.

You probably thought I'd forgotten somebody, but I want you to put your hands together for the greatest man in Ulster at the moment, Brian McEniff! For the past 30 years Brian has given his life to Donegal football, and indeed Ulster football, and he got his just reward there today. Thanks very much Brian.

I would like you to put your hands together and give three rousing cheers to the beaten Dublin team. Hip, hip …

And then, seizing Sam Maguire once again, he uttered the immortal words, "Sam's for the Hills!" And the crowd cheered deliriously one more time. One by one the boys made it up the steps and lifted the most famous piece of silverware in Ireland high above their heads. And each was cheered by the masses below. McHugh was still hanging onto the match ball. Shovlin got a special roar of approval as the crowd acknowledged his massive role in getting the team here. Razda and Tommy Ryan were in the same boat. Charlie Mulgrew, Paul Carr, Sylvester Maguire and Michael Gallagher all got their moment of glory having put in many tough hours in a Donegal jersey. The younger lads – Mark Crossan, Paul Callaghan and Jim McGuinness – were acclaimed too.

Michael Lyster was live on air for RTÉ. "I don't remember enjoying an occasion of football in Croke Park like that for a long, long time," said Lyster. "Absolutely phenomenal, I am absolutely delighted for them," said panelist and Meath manager Sean Boylan. "Magnificent, every single one of them," agreed John Maughan.

Down in the bowels of Croke Park Jim Carney was talking to some of the Donegal lads. "It was just fabulous to see Molloy going up and picking her up," quipped an emotional Matt. "I'm just over the moon," said Martin McHugh, "we've done it for the whole of Donegal." "Unbelievable here at the moment," said Bonner at a loss for words. "It's great to win but even better to win with such panache and style," was the opinion of Pauric McShea.

Sam's for the Hills

❈ ❈ ❈ ❈

Up in Donegal the streets and roads had been practically deserted for almost two hours. It was almost eerie – traffic levels were similar to Christmas Day. "Abandoned," noted the *Irish Times*, "while 15 men in green and gold kicked their way with deadly accuracy over the bar and into Gaelic football history." Now the whole place came alive. In towns and villages in every corner of the county people spilled onto the streets in celebration. The Diamond in Donegal Town seemed to fill within seconds. Almost 1,000 people had watched proceedings on large screens in the Abbey Hotel, now they took their singing and dancing to the street. The party had begun.

❈ ❈ ❈ ❈

It was a long time before the boys made it back to the dressing rooms. In the corridor outside half a dozen Donegal players leaned against the walls and chatted to journalists. The quotes were flying. Vincent Hogan of the *Irish Independent* was chatting to James McHugh. "Well James, did you ever think you'd see this day?" "Naw, no way. Not in a hundred years. I never believed this could happen to ordinary bucks like us." Hogan was mightily impressed by McHugh's refreshing modesty. "Ordinary bucks indeed!" he wrote later, "Ordinary bucks don't play football so sharp, so crisp, so full of confident rhythm it defies containment".

Matt Gallagher, for once, was finding it hard to string a sentence together. "Words? There's none can describe this. Jesus, God. Lord help us, what have we done? Look at us. Would you ever have believed it?"

Reid was on cloud nine. "I'm just in a state of shock right now. I can't actually feel my feet. It's like being mad drunk without drinking!" And then Vincent Hogan reminded Reid that he had promised to hang up his boots after this one. "Retirement?," smiled Reid, "Ach sure I'll maybe stick around for the league games between now and Christmas. It's going to be fierce hard to walk away from this team. And you know, when the evenings start getting long again…"

McEniff too was rolling off the sound bites, "I told the team to keep running at Dublin, to come at them like the waves of Tory". The press liked that one. "This victory is not for me. It's for the people of Donegal," he told Tom O'Riordan of the *Irish Independent*, "I love my county and bringing home the Sam Maguire Cup will be something that I know I will cherish for the rest of my life."

John Joe Doherty was beside himself with delight. "I didn't have time to get nervous," he told Vincent Hogan, "One minute, I was ready to take my place in the dugout. The next, I'm thinking about marking Charlie Redmond."

The journalists were caught up in the sheer romance of what they had just witnessed. "One of the greatest finals for many years," reckoned Tony McGee in the *Irish News*. The great Gaelic games commentator Micheál Ó Muircheartaigh was fulsome and sincere in his delight for Donegal:

> An All-Ireland victory is sweet at any time but when it is achieved on the county's first ever appearance it becomes an exhilarating experience for all connected with it, players, mentors and followers combined.

The feature writers, some of them anyway, would lose the run of themselves entirely with every fishing cliche known to journalism. "Reeling in the Big One" wrote Miriam Lord in the *Irish Independent*, managing to drop the words 'catch', 'hooked', 'landed', 'wave', 'cod', quota', 'net', 'sea' and 'herring' into the first couple of paragraphs.

Outside the Dublin dressing room it was a different story. Paddy Cullen was dejected. It was difficult not to feel sympathy for the usually bubbly Dub. His match analysis, as relayed to Tom Humphries, was in staccato bursts. "The best team won. We played badly. We did everything wrong. We played well for ten minutes and then just stopped. It's hard to figure out. Hard."

Keith Barr was equally devastated and equally generous. "That's the way sport goes. Somebody has to be the loser. It was us. Somebody has to be the favourites. We didn't live up to it. They crowded us and harried us. The best team won."

John O'Leary reckoned that Dublin simply froze but, like all the Dubs, was generous in his praise of the victors, "They played a running game and they played it well. A team that does that can destroy you. We let them win all the breaking ball and they kept on running at us."

Humphries watched as James McHugh waited patiently outside the Dublin dressing room and then offered words of consolation to his marker Paul Curran as he left. McHugh made plans to meet Curran for a drink the following day. "No team has ever been beaten by a nicer group of men," noted Humphries. Sean Kilfeather was also down around the Donegal dressing rooms:

> An hour after the final whistle had blown several players had still not reached the showers. They seemed reluctant to don their street clothes, apparently afraid that the great feeling of elation might be washed away in soap and shampoo.

Kilfeather watched as Barry Cunningham swept into the dressing room with his arms aloft shouting "Where's the Queen?"

The whoops and hollers ringing around the walls indicated the sheer euphoria of the players coming to terms with the fact that they had just won an All-Ireland. It had all been so different a little earlier. Joyce McMullan battled his way back through the throngs and made it as far as the Donegal dressing room. As he made his way through the door he couldn't believe the sight that greeted him:

> I walked into the dressing room with Matt Gallagher, having just given an interview to Charlie Collins, and the place was like a morgue. The players were sitting round looking at me. I shouted obscenities at them asking what was wrong with them – we'd just won the All-Ireland! Seamus Bonner, who was big buddies with my brother Gerard, was in the corner and I could see a tear in his eye. I knew something was badly wrong.

Something was badly wrong. McEniff had been approached before the game and told that Joyce's brother Gerard – who had been ill with leukemia – had died. The news threw McEniff. He made the difficult decision not to tell Joyce and in doing so allowed the Four Masters man to enjoy the once-in-a-lifetime opportunity to play in an All-Ireland final. Now, a couple of hours later, the time had arrived to tell Joyce the terrible news. The boys who had made it back to the dressing room ahead of Joyce and Matt had been told and were struck dumb. "The dressing room went from euphoria to total silence," remembered Martin McHugh.

What happened next is forever imprinted in Joyce's mind:

> Bishop Hegarty arrived with Austin Kennedy, who was Gerard's doctor. With McEniff and Lafferty, they took me to a quiet corner and told me that Gerard had died that morning. I told them that couldn't be the case because I had been talking to my sisters, Rosaleen and Maureen, outside the dressing room and they had told me Gerard was delighted.

Joyce was understandably stunned. Gerard was indeed ill and hadn't attended the match because of the risk of infection. He'd had a transplant to treat the leukemia he was suffering from and was bitterly disappointed that he couldn't go to the match. Joyce had been chatting to him the day before and Gerard had wished him good luck. Now he was being told that Gerard was dead:

> I kept repeating that they'd got it wrong and that I'd been talking to my sisters outside but they said no, it was true. This was the Bishop, the doctor and my manager telling me this – I had to believe them. Meantime, the team was sitting outside in silence looking at one another with the cup in the middle of the floor. Donal Reid put a scapular in my hand which I still have to this day. After ten minutes of this the emotion caught up with me and I cried.

Joyce made his way back into the dressing room and was comforted by his teammates. Matt, who knew the loss of a brother himself, came over and said that he would go home with Joyce to Donegal Town. Plans were made to arrange a taxi for the boys. It was the days before mobile 'phones, yet, no one had rang the McMullan home in Donegal Town to find out for sure. McEniff would eventually do this, but for now was caught up in the moment. The Donegal dressing room, having just won an All-Ireland, was a sombre place indeed.

Joyce's sister Maureen, who was near the area, became aware that things were subdued in the Donegal dressing-room. She asked one of the stewards outside the door what was going on. He told her that a relative of one of the players had died and they were just after telling him. The steward didn't know which player it was but Maureen quickly realised it must have been Joyce. Ten minutes later she eventually persuaded the stewards to let her into the dressing room. Joyce can still see the scene:

> Maureen came in – the players were still all sitting around the dressing room with bags and dirty gear lying on the floor and the cup sitting on the table – and she said 'It's not true, it's not true!' I gave her a hug and the relief was unbelievable.

In the meantime McEniff ran up to the Highland Radio crew in the press box and managed to secure a 'phone. Knowing McMullan's telephone number off the top of his head, he dialled, got through and learned for himself that Gerard was quite well. The drama was over at last. Joyce eventually got to a 'phone and spoke to Gerard.

> He was over the moon. By this stage there was a whole party going on at home. My father, who has died since – God rest him – was 90 at the time and had stayed at home. All the neighbours had come around and the place was abuzz. They were having a real party when I rang and I half told them the story but they didn't really comprehend what had happened.

The relief in the Donegal dressing room was tangible and loud. As Joyce says, "It really made the occasion even more amazing that it already was." It was like a miracle. Smiles spread again, and the boys raised a din.

Where the rumour began no-one knows, including Joyce:

> How do rumours get out? A wee story in the morning can become a huge story by nightfall. I don't know where it came from but I don't think it was malicious. Some guy from a newspaper rang me the next morning before I got up and asked me if I thought it was the Dubs that had spread the rumour. I told him I didn't think that for one moment – you can imagine what he was going to do!

Charlie Mulgrew

❄ ❄ ❄ ❄

The craic on the streets of Dublin was mighty. Myles McEntee of the *Irish Press* was in the middle of it:

> A sea of Donegal flags and flavours swamped the city. As cars blared their horns down O'Connell Street, and buses from McGlynns, McGinleys, McGuinness' and anything beginning with McG, waited in vain for their passengers, a lone bagpiper led a group of cheering Donegal supporters down the central promenade of Dublin's main thoroughfare.

Bars and clubs across the city were jammed to bursting point. Many Donegal folk were also making their way slowly home. Bus after bus and mile after mile of cars made their way triumphantly through towns like Carrickmacross, Castleblaney and Monaghan. Navan, Cavan and Enniskillen saw and heard similar convoys. Many of the supporters had stayed in Dublin on the Saturday night and, time permitting, would have loved to meet their Dublin hosts after the game to indulge in a little good-natured banter. Never had a set of supporters been so sure of victory before a game than the Dubs that weekend.

The after-match celebrations for the players got underway in the ballroom of the Grand Hotel in Malahide. The 500 guests rose to their feet to welcome Donegal's newest son, Sam Óg Maguire, as he was paraded to the top table by the manager and his captain – McEniff and Molloy. Those who hadn't obtained tickets for the celebration dinner crammed into the hotel's public bar. The number 42 bus had never done such a roaring trade.

RTÉ's Ger Canning and Marty Morrisey conducted interviews for the live link-up with that evening's *Sunday Game*. Michael Lyster was back in the studio with Colm O'Rourke. Few were the occasions when O'Rourke raised cheers from Donegal supporters but they were certainly forthcoming when he announced Manus Boyle as man-of-the-match. Peter Quinn spoke for the masses, "It's not often I agree with Colm O'Rourke – in fact, I rarely agree with him – but on this occasion I am in total agreement with making Manus Boyle man of the match".

Manus had just written himself into the record books. He, more than anyone, was the man who had destroyed the Dubs. "The nine points that he scored is a huge haul that sees him enter GAA folklore alongside such legendary All-Ireland final sharp-shooters as Mikey Sheehy, Jimmy Keaveney and Frankie Stockwell," wrote Owen McCrohan.

Martin McHugh sought out team trainer Anthony Harkin at the function to thank him for the part he played in winning the All-Ireland:

> I give him a lot of credit. He was man enough to take the criticism and turn the training around. He could have taken it the other way and asked us

who we thought we were. That's the reason we won the All-Ireland – the meeting in that Omagh dressing room and Harkin changing the training.

Music at the Malahide hotel was provided by Hugo Duncan. It was the first of many gigs that Hugo would play during the celebrations prompting Gary Walsh to remark, "Hugo Duncan must have had a contract with the County Board. Wherever we turned up, he turned up."

Martin McHugh was in rip-roaring form. RTÉ asked him about Donegal's poor record at GAA headquarters. "Well," replied McHugh, "We haven't lost an All-Ireland final there yet." The Donegal players were kitted out in their Magee blazers and were looking the part. Vivienne Clarke was covering the celebrations for the *Irish Press*:

> Irishmen are not noted for their hugability. Meet one after ten years and the best you'll get is a tepid handshake. But in the Grand Hotel in Malahide restraint and caution were thrown to the wind as hundreds of Donegal men indulged in a massive love-in.
>
> It was an orgy of goodwill for the men and women celebrating their county's first All-Ireland football title. Every player was kissed, embraced, fondled and hugged.

The boys, some of them anyway, celebrated through the night. Joyce had recovered from the trauma of the dressing rooms to enjoy his evening. Yet the events had taken their toll and at around one o'clock he found himself retiring to bed. His thoughts were still with Gerard:

> He died the following year. My sister gave him a bone marrow transplant but it was a severe form of leukemia. He was a great fan of the team and had gone everywhere to see it. I was delighted that he lived to see the All-Ireland.

McEniff finally got to bed around 3 a.m. It had been a long day day but yet sleep was slow in coming. Flicking through the television channels he came upon Channel 4's coverage of the game. "I saw Anthony Molloy receive the trophy, and then I could sleep happily," McEniff told Sean McGoldrick next day.

✳ ✳ ✳ ✳

"It was the following morning before the enormity of it struck me," remembers James McHugh:

> Martin and me went down for breakfast and the *Evening Herald* wanted

pictures. We went out for a walk and people were congratulating us. There had been a huge build-up all summer. Every aspect of your life is geared toward the All-Ireland and you're on a merry-go-round. But we were mature enough to handle it. Still, I found it very difficult to come back after the All-Ireland.

On Monday the hour arrived to depart for the Hills. The chosen method was by special train to Sligo, a wise decision as cavalcade by bus and car would have caused a tailback stretching 150 miles! For Brian Murray it was one of the highlights of the week, "It was the first time that we had gathered together after the game," he remembered:

> It was brilliant. Our families were with us on the train and we had a bit of grub and stopped at a few places on the way down. The team, wives and girlfriends all retired down to the bar. It was the best bit of craic we had. We all got up and sang. We didn't want the train to stop at all.

As the Iarnród Eireann executive train – renamed *Express Sam* – made its way through the midlands people came out all along the way to pay homage to the heroes from Donegal. Dromod, home of the Follower and former abode of Gary Walsh, was Leitrim's only station and a more that a thousand people turned up to greet the passing warriors. Three and a half hours after embarking they finally pulled into Sligo. "We had great sport in all those little towns in the midlands," recalled John Joe Doherty:

> Coming home from Dublin via Sligo was unusual. The reason was that the train would be faster, but we seemed to stop in every wee village. We did not care at the time and if we were told we were going home by Cork nobody would have argued.

There were 10,000 people to greet them at Sligo railway station. The roar that greeted the players as they stepped from the train was deafening and it got louder as Molloy hoisted the Sam Maguire above his head. The *Irish Times* man was watching:

> The scenes at the Sligo station came close to pandemonium as the crowd surged forward for a closer look at Sam and their heroes, who brought him back. It was something of a happy mob scene as Molloy, the cup held high, struggled his way through the crowd with everyone stretching out to touch the prize.

Slowly the team made their way to a platform in front of McEniff's Great

Southern Hotel. The scale of the welcome became apparent to the players for the first time. Jim Carney of RTÉ individually introduced the boys to a delighted crowd. Eventually, much later than anticipated, they set off on the last leg of an epic journey:

> Gardaí had difficulty clearing a passage for the coach that was to take the victorious team in a triumphal procession to the Donegal border 20 miles away. Hundreds of Donegal cars with their horns blaring full blast, formed a cavalcade behind the coach. It took them half-an-hour to get out of the crowded streets of Sligo.
>
> All along the route to the Donegal border, hundreds of well-wishers lined the side of the road waving Donegal flags and cheering as the coach passed through Sligo county and a narrow strip of Leitrim. Every few miles bonfires lit the darkness along the roadside and in the surrounding fields.

It was a sight that has remained with Brian Murray:

> At one stage I looked back and could see nothing but miles and miles of cars following us. There were bonfires in big barrels at the Donegal border. Molloy and McEniff got out and walked into Donegal. It was something else to witness it. It was the first time Donegal men had brought Sam Maguire to Donegal.

That emotional and highly symbolic moment for the team and mentors occurred just before 11pm. As the bus reached the Donegal border, something special happened. Molloy and McEniff, disembarked from the bus. Charlie Collins was on board broadcasting for Highland Radio. He recounted what happened next to David Walsh of the *Sunday Independent*:

> Everybody went fairly quiet, the two boys were going to walk across Bundrowes Bridge into Donegal. It was dark outside, we could see the bonfires burning on the Donegal side of the border.
>
> We watched as they walked into Donegal with the Cup and everybody – I mean players, their wives, girlfriends, selectors, county board people, the physio, the doctor, Seamus Marley the busdriver – had tears in their eyes.

Sam Maguire had just entered Donegal, not as Margo had prophesied, "across the bridge at Lifford", but over the River Drowse. Coloured lights had been strung across the bridge and the names of all the players had been painted on the road. It was a magical and breathtaking moment.

Bundoran was reached and entered on foot, its most famous son carried the cup into the town. Stephen O'Brien of the *Irish Independent* had followed the Donegal bus all the way from Sligo:

> Bonfires, banners and frantically waving supporters lined the 25-mile journey from Sligo to Bundoran where McEniff's 83-year-old mother Elizabeth was waiting to welcome him home to the Holyrood.

Also there to greet McEniff was the great Sean O'Neill from Down. He'd driven all the way from Belfast just to congratulate the Donegal men in person.

"There was no toilet on the bus and by the time we got to Bundoran we were bursting," recalled Brian Murray:

> Three of the women were pregnant and we used them to get through the crowd. 'Pregnant women coming through,' we shouted. People must have thought we were ignorant but we were just busting to get to the toilet! It was chaos.

The cavalcade made its way to Ballyshannon. "The crowd roared approval as Sylvester Maguire, Gary Walsh and me got off the bus," recalled Brian Murray. A convertible Mercedes was going to take the three players to where the reception for the team was, but the streets were so thronged it had to be abandoned. It was an emotional moment for the big midfielder:

> It was great coming back to my own town and meeting all my buddies who I had played with and socialised with. I met people who had introduced me to football.
>
> Working in Dublin and beating Dublin in the All-Ireland final takes some beating. We won it for all the supporters who followed us for all those years. They followed us in good times and bad times – and there were probably more bad times. To see the joy in people's faces, young and old, after winning the All-Ireland made it worthwhile.

In Ballintra, Matt had his moment, and an emotional one at that, in the local community centre. McHugh too remembered his old team-mate from 1982, Pauric Gallagher. The Wee Man said a prayer at Pauric's grave.

The final destination was Donegal Town – the sight there was amazing. Upwards on 30,000 people jammed into the Diamond to greet their heroes. McHugh was amazed at the sight. The boys were just beginning to realise what they had achieved. "The whole crowd were singing along to the Tina Turner song *Simply the Best*. It kind of sunk in then – we really had achieved something big!" recalls McHugh. One of the most memorable moments in Donegal Town was when Tom Conaghan was brought on to the stage and Brian McEniff took his arm and raised it to the crowd. The most public of acknowledgment for the role Conaghan had played in Donegal's greatest day.

Celtic goalkeeper Packie Bonner, who had been in Croke Park, was bitterly disappointed that he was missing out on the homecoming – he went back to Glasgow on Monday. When he got there he would collect on his £20 bet with Celtic manager Liam Brady who had favoured his native Dublin. Bet aside, the big goalkeeper was in euphoric mood in the *Irish Press* and spoke for Donegal exiles everywhere: "You have no idea how much this victory means to people from the county. So many of us have had to leave and earn a living abroad. But for one glorious afternoon we were united in pride."

Donegal had never seen anything like it. There was nothing in the history of the county prior to then with which to compare. A county celebrated in a fashion never dreamt of before. "The hills of Donegal were alive with a wild joy," wrote the *Irish Times*. There was no rule book, people did their own thing. Michael McHugh was on hand all week to record things for the *Democrat*:

> Never before has there been such an atmosphere of joy and happiness throughout Donegal and indeed the whole of the North West.
>
> By their heroic exploits in Croke Park, the Donegal senior football team have done more for the morale of the people of Tir Conaill in 70 minutes than the total efforts of governments and politicians alike since the founding of the State in 1922. And that is not an insult to either, as the sheer joy, emotion and joy that followed Sunday's victory could not be replaced even by the investment of millions of pounds or the opening of a new factory.

The county was alive like never before. The sense of pride was tangible. New signs had been commissioned and constructed, now welcoming the All-Ireland champions. For a week the boys criss-crossed Donegal. They brought the Cup to every part of the county, "I saw little places that I hadn't seen before or since," commented Brian Murray.

On Tuesday night Shovlin took to the stage in Dunkineely. Afterwards he described the moment to David Walsh:

> I told them how proud I was to see the Cup come over Storm Hill (a little hill on the approach to the town) and that, no matter what, my neck would be okay and I'd be playing for Dunkineely in the intermediate county final against Milford on Sunday week.

Same old Shov. That same night the Donegal victory party snaked its way into Kilcar. Again Walsh watched as they pulled into Bavin:

Five bonfires blazed on the hills around Bavin on Tuesday evening, a hundred or so people gathered at the gate of the McHugh household. They waited until the team coach passed and loved the moment when Martin and James McHugh greeted their parents and showed the cup to their neighbours.

Ardara was equally memorable. Molloy and Gavigan carried the Cup into the town. Another speech but this really was home and the emotion was getting to Molloy. "The words are beginning to get scarce," he told his friends and neighbours. As David Walsh wrote, "Those who came to pay their respects understood". Walsh had a way of unearthing gems. He spoke to Molloy's sister, Catherine, over from New York for the game. There were 12 Molloy siblings, only three remained in Donegal and Catherine was one of six in New York. "Anthony," she said, "was always a special brother. He had a way, he'd never say 'pass the salt' but 'Kate, a little salt would swing it.'"

And so it went. "We stopped outside Glenties to go to the toilet and saw sheep that had been dyed green and gold," recalled Brian Murray, "where else would you find it? It was surreal." Rambo would remember a fella in Kilcar with about 30 lights on his bike. Up in Glenish someone had put lights on a ram's horns! On the Wednesday night Donegal took on the rest of Ireland in Ballybofey to raise funds for GOAL and Somalia. On Thursday night they found themselves in Termon. McEniff took the microphone outside the Lagoon Bar, uncertain of the reception he would receive. "I know I am in Tommy Ryan country here," began McEniff. He acknowledged the disappointment of Tommy and the people of Termon but went on to explain that he had hoped to bring Tommy on "but such was the magnificence of the men on the pitch that it wasn't possible". The explanation sufficed. McEniff was applauded generously. Now was not the time for recrimination, GAA folk, who knew the score, kept their notions to themselves.

Nothing had prepared the county for this. "Nobody had planned what we would do if we won it because everyone was afraid to think that way," remembered Tony Boyle, "maybe that's why the celebrations went on like they did." Even the normally meticulous McEniff was at something of a loss. "I hadn't thought about what would happen afterwards," he recalled, "It was an older team and we were determined to celebrate the victory."

And for the week Donegal folk welcomed the heroes in their own townlands, villages and towns. There had never been a week like it in the county before and there hasn't been one since. Never had the achievements of a single day been celebrated thus. Owen McCrohan, a wise old head guesting for the *Donegal Democrat* captured it to perfection, "It was a day that will be savoured in Donegal for as long as grass grows and rivers run".

18

Another Go

(October 1992 – July 1993)

"It was a terrible way to lose the All-Ireland title."

JOHN JOE DOHERTY

The boys turned their attention to football again in October when Mick O'Dwyer's Kildare visited the backyard of the new All-Ireland champions. Donegal ran onto the field in Ballybofey to a Kildare guard of honour and the enthusiastic acclaim of 10,000 voices as man, woman and child rose to their feet in salutation. A quick glance confirmed all the old hands were still, more or less, on board. McEniff, as expected, was still clutching the reins having agreed a further 12-month term at the October County Board meeting. And, despite the enforced absence of a handful through injury, the old faces were still there. Including Big Molloy – bad knee and all.

And it was the captain himself – with the not inconsiderable assistance of a versatility-player par excellence from Killybegs and a disenchanted Termon man – who pointed the way to an eventual 1-9 to 0-6 victory. The first half was something of a wake-up call for the boys – then in the midst of epic celebrations – who struggled throughout. As the rain lashed from the high heavens the two teams managed five scores between them in the first half. Tony Boyle, Manus Boyle and Joyce McMullan hit Donegal's points, Kildare answered with two of their own.

The opening 30 minutes had proved an education for All-Star Martin Lynch, playing at full-forward and marking Matt Gallagher. Time and again he learned he was no match for the best full-back in Ireland. Mick O'Dwyer, not known as a slow learner, moved Lynch to the middle for the second half and it paid immediate dividends. Eight minutes into the second half the Lilywhites hit the front, 0-5 to 0-4.

Enter the three boys. Barry McGowan moved outfield and immediately clipped Lynch's wings. The first kick out was caught by the Killybegs man and slipped to Molloy who thundered through a bevy of white shirts before firing between the posts. Parity. Points were traded before McGowan proved his outstanding versatility by cutting through the Kildare defence with all the swagger of a long-time attacker to kick a point of his own.

And then Tommy Ryan made the most welcome of returns. On from halftime for an ill Martin McHugh, Tommy slid home Donegal's first competitive goal since the Ulster semi-final. That had been against Fermanagh, had been one of the scores of the championship, and had come from the same left boot. Termon's favourite son was back – a little wiser, a little sadder and forever damaged but still playing football. Five or six minutes from the end it was the same Tommy who fisted over the last point of the game.

It was the beginning of a new winning streak – and the continuation of an old one – that was destined to run and run. That it stretched back the entire length of the championship to the McKenna Cup defeat by Monaghan the previous April only added to the aura of invincibility that now surrounded the boys. "Donegal, once the team of a thousand insecurities, no longer believed they could be beaten," Vincent Hogan would later remark in the *Irish Independent.*

Gary Walsh earned the plaudits in hospitable Carlow a fortnight later as the boys marched on with an 0-12 to 0-5 win that was much trickier than the scoreline suggested. "Our biggest mistake was not resting during that league campaign," felt Anthony Molloy, "I had been at a function in Glenties until all hours the night before the Carlow match and got very little sleep." "It's easy to say now, but we should have rested players for the league," agreed Martin McHugh:

It was our first time to win an All-Ireland and every man wanted to play. We went down to play Carlow and stayed up until six in the morning drinking and celebrating. We beat Carlow easily but we didn't realise the effect partying and playing was having on our bodies. Injuries had to happen and they did catch up with us.

Carlow saw the first tear in the fabric of the 1992 squad. Charlie Mulgrew, warming the bench since the Cavan replay the previous May, decided he'd had enough and hauled off his county jersey for the final time. Almost 32 years old, Charlie saw little future in the subs and walked away. The bus would be quieter in his absence and, despite his demotion in more recent years, football folk noted his going with some regret. Looking back, Charlie now feels that he should have stuck it out. "I got very fit in 1992 and was playing better club football in 1993-95 than I had been previously," he remembered, "I don't regret it anymore but, with hindsight, I should have stayed on."

There were others missing off the bus for a variety of reasons. Shovlin was still in trouble with his neck and it would be some time before he would land one of his trademark tackles again in a county jersey. Razda too was out with injury and had been advised to rest for the winter. His cousin Barry had returned to New York. James McHugh was having a short-lived break and it was also Martin's intention to rest weary legs. Circumstances dictated otherwise – the Wee Man was needed. He made a brief appearance against Carlow and was pencilled in again for the visit of Leitrim to Ballyshannon.

McEniff didn't know it then but the injuries that were besetting his side would, like the winning streak, run and run. In time those injuries would play their part in the relinquishment of the All-Ireland crown. Time-out for some of the lads was a necessity. But, as McEniff says all these years later, "Everyone wanted to keep on playing on that team". Every opposing team Donegal now met wanted to be the first to claim the scalp of the All-Ireland champions but the boys were determined to defend their position as the best team in the land. Even Big Molloy was still in there doing battle in the number eight jersey despite the ongoing trouble with his knee.

Leitrim, it had been feared, would provide the most difficult challenge to date. The worries were unfounded as Donegal went through Leitrim for a short cut in front of the biggest crowd ever seen at Fr Tierney Park. John O'Mahoney was the new director of operations on the sideline for Leitrim and at centre half-back the Connacht men had the much-lauded Declan Darcy. In 1994 O'Mahoney would deliver to Leitrim a famous Connacht title – the county's first since 1927. Later still he would steer Galway to two All-Ireland titles while Leitrim would lose the services of Declan Darcy who would declare for the Dubs. That was all in the future. In front of 8,000 spectators, Donegal, sans McHugh, ran riot hitting 1-14 to Leitrim's 0-6. Exhibition stuff by the boys from goalkeeper to left corner-forward. "I have run out of superlatives for Matt Gallagher," remarked the Follower. The same could be said of Tony Boyle and the rest of the gang as waves of appreciative applause rippled around the ground at the teamwork now in evidence.

Twelve of the men who started the All-Ireland final were in action – Gary Walsh, John Joe Doherty, Matt Gallagher, Donal Reid, Martin Gavigan, Anthony Molloy, James McHugh, Noel Hegarty, Joyce McMullan, Declan Bonner, Tony Boyle and Manus Boyle. They were joined by Paul Carr, Mark Crossan and Sylvester Maguire and the 'new' boys were not found wanting – all three would repeat their performances a fortnight later in Cavan. Murray made an appearance for Molloy and Jim McGuinness from Glenties got a first run out, coming in for Joyce.

Cavan suffered a similar fate to Leitrim, albeit by a point less, in Breffni as the boys cruised to Christmas unruffled. Some of them were still celebrating like there was no tomorrow but they had reserves of stamina and football know-how that were now second to none. The man mostly responsible for those reserves was to be found – splendidly attired in his winter woolly green hat – looking on from the Donegal dugout. The evidence of Anthony Harkin's now legendary training regime, which had carried the boys through the summer, was still there for all to see. They were now cruising on a different level to ordinary souls and it was enough to see them past teams who had nothing to celebrate and a couple of evenings a week free to run around mucky pitches. Hard and all as it was to believe, there were those who decried the extent of the celebrations. As amateur players who had undertaken a professional training regime and won the greatest prize the game had to offer, most people felt that the team was entitled to whatever type or extent of celebrations it liked. Yet there were those who sniffed and sniped. Fortunately, all right thinking people ignored them, as did the players.

The Follower, who'd skulked out of Breffni on days gone by with his head hung low, enthusiastically embraced the new order:

What style, what confidence, what grandeur and what panache. To win a competitive game by ten points in Breffni is special not alone for Donegal but for any team in Ireland. A new era has finally dawned and let us rejoice.

Against Cavan it was difficult to know who to single out for special praise – Tony Boyle had taken the breath from all in Breffni with a truly magnificent goal strike that almost burst the netting. Then again there was Paul Carr. Comfortable now that he was no longer expected to play in a position completely alien to his footballing constitution, Carr was proving his worth. Then there was Matt. Still being Matt. John Joe being John Joe. Joyce had run at Cavan like the Tory waves. And new boy Mark Crossan was winning admirers every time he pulled on the jersey.

On paper it appeared that McEniff would have selection problems come the New Year – McHugh would be back for sure, Shovlin was doing all possible to get back, Tommy Ryan was determined to prove a point, Razda had a similar point to prove, Barry McGowan had proved a point and wanted a regular jersey in lieu, Big Murray was another who could not be ignored and Barry Cunningham would surely be catching a plane come the stretch in the evenings. It was a good complaint for McEniff to have.

As Christmases went, Christmas 1992 was an eventful one. Several of the boys would scale richly deserved heights. The Wee Man seemed to be picking up national awards by the dozen. The prestigious *Sunday Press* Players' Player of the Year came his way. "That one meant a lot to me," said Martin McHugh. McEniff, with unrivalled authority, then paid a compliment that didn't require a presentation. McEniff simply spoke it. "Martin McHugh is the greatest player Donegal has ever produced."

Thirteen Donegal men were nominated for All-Stars awards – Gary Walsh, Matt Gallagher, Noel Hegarty, Donal Reid, Martin Gavigan, Martin Shovlin, Anthony Molloy, Brian Murray, Martin McHugh, James McHugh, Manus

Boyle, Tony Boyle and Declan Bonner. Tradition dictated that the All-Ireland champions might expect half a dozen statues at very best, in the event they managed seven – an impressive tally but one reflective of their heroic battle out of Ulster and spell-binding magnificence against the mighty Dubs.

The names McEniff, Monaghan, McHugh and McMullan – Donegal's four existing All-Stars – were joined by Gary Walsh, Matt Gallagher, Martin Gavigan, Anthony Molloy, Martin McHugh, James McHugh and Tony Boyle. The boys had a black-tie night out in the Burlington just before Christmas and took the place over. Such was the year Donegal had enjoyed that there was understandable disappointment for more than a few of those who'd missed out.

It was the first year that players could be selected in positions other than those they had played in. "I got the left full-forward position and had a great bit of slagging with Declan Bonner and Manus Boyle," remembered Tony Boyle, "Everywhere we went we were introduced as the three best corner-forwards in the country. It really topped off the year for me." Declan Bonner was interviewed by Highland Radio and signed off, tongue in cheek, by thanking Tony Boyle and Enda Gormley for collecting his and Manus Boyle's All-Stars.

Bonner might have expected to make it. Hegarty and Reid hadn't put a foot wrong all year. And Shovlin's great disappointment in missing the All-Ireland would have been marginally reduced had he picked up a deserved All-Star. Manus, with his magnificent nine points on All-Ireland Sunday, had reason to be hopeful. It was not to be. Donegal would have to make do with a mere seven All-Stars!

It could have been less – at county Convention the following January, Thomas McBrearty, secretary of the referees' board, would claim that up to four of the players who received All-Star nominations could well have been sent off in domestic games since September but, fearful of being responsible for depriving players of awards, referees had turned a "blind eye and a deaf ear". Such impunity had been a long time coming.

"Maybe my performances in the league games before Christmas were what swung it for me," thought Gary Walsh:

> I didn't have much to do in the All-Ireland semi-final or final but keeping two clean sheets helped. I had probably played better in other Ulster championship campaigns. I think the team can win the All-Star for you. There was probably a feeling that Donegal had to have a certain number of representatives.

The McHughs made history by becoming only the third set of brothers to win All-Stars on the same team. Pat Spillane had shared All-Stars with his brothers Mick and Tom in 1985 and 1986 respectively. "I had won an All-Star in 1983 but it was great to win one with James and the other Donegal boys," remembered Martin.

Another Go

"Winning the All-Star was the highlight of my career," said James McHugh:

It was a big honour for both Martin and me. We had reached the pinnacle. Winning an All Ireland was great, it was something you worked for but winning an All-Star is a great achievement. We met players from different counties and had a good old night. When Martin won one nine years earlier he didn't know nobody. The Donegal lads took over the place in 1992.

The Wee Man wasn't finished yet. The 1992 Texaco Footballer of the Year Award was his – the first Ulster man to win it in 24 years. Joining footballing greats from the previous 35 years, Martin McHugh was now in the company of Jim McCartan and Sean O'Neill of Down, Kerry's Mick O'Connell, Mick O'Dwyer, Jack O'Shea and Pat Spillane, Dublin's Jimmy Keaveney and Meath's Colm O'Rourke. "The Texaco award was a nice award to get," said Martin McHugh, "All of a sudden, a wee Kilcar man from a sheep farming background ended up mixing with some of the leading athletes in Irish sport."

Yet all the awards in the world couldn't capture the essence of McHugh. He was never going to be remembered in Donegal for his medals and silverware. Rather, individual moments of unrivalled genius which terrorised defences with a lethal combination of wizardry, bravery and utter conviction. Footballers like McHugh came along once in a lifetime.

❅ ❅ ❅ ❅

The New Year brought with it some much needed escapism as a Donegal party of 85 went to Tenerife. All the boys were able to avail of the holiday except Tommy Ryan who had just changed his job. As it happened, Tommy was on hand to accept the prestigious RTÉ/Ballygowan Team of the Year Award on behalf of the squad at a star-studded banquet in the Burlington Hotel.

Although the County Board was awash with funds – figures released at Convention showed a surplus of more than £155,000 – a disagreement broke out between the treasurer and the squad over holiday spending money for the players. The amount of money, in the context of swollen County Board finances, was negligible but the issue was allowed to fester for too long before eventually being sorted.

A trial game in the middle of January allowed McEniff take a look at adding new players to the panel. John Duffy was one, although he picked up an injury in the course of the hour. Shovlin also finished the trial in discomfort. Despite intensive physiotherapy stretching back to September, his neck injury recurred. Declan Boyle was another McEniff hoped to add to the panel but the mercurial Killybegs youngster was engaged with Finn Harps and on a path that would eventually bring him to Celtic Park in Glasgow.

Sam's for the Hills

The wily old head of The Follower had words of wisdom for McEniff before January was out, "If he feels that winning a NFL title would interfere with Sam returning to the hills then in my book he has only one course of action. Forget the league." Were Donegal to go all the way to a national league final they would be in action just four weeks before the 1993 championship quest began. Something would have to give. Injuries and even suspensions could become a factor. Yet the whole county, players and mentors wanted to keep winning – Donegal had what Vincent Hogan called "champions' dignity" to defend. The boys were caught between a rock and a hard place and the Follower's wise words would be forgotten.

The winning streak was kept going when Dublin were held to a draw in the Charlie Gallagher Memorial Tournament Final in Cootehill. New Dublin boss Pat O'Neill – a dejected Paddy Cullen had walked away from the sky-blue hotseat following the All-Ireland defeat – threw everything at Donegal in an effort to prove a point but the boys were equal to the task and give as good as they got.

Donegal went to Glasgow to play Mayo in the Willie Dowds Challenge Cup. Mayo had come under the stewardship of Kerry great, Jack O'Shea. Brian McDonald had resigned the Mayo post on the very night the boys brought Sam back to Donegal. Even with Jacko as manager, Mayo were no match for the All-Ireland champions as Donegal claimed the cup. Barry Cunningham was back from the Big Apple for both the Dublin and Mayo games and was motoring well. Yet, the Follower saw cracks appearing in Glasgow:

We dug into our reserves of pride and confidence that Sam has given. We can send that particular bucket to Sam's well of confidence and experience once too often. The celebration circuit has finally caught up.

Peter Campbell was also warning that the "bid to retain the All-Ireland must begin now and that should mean an end to the social circuit". It wasn't easy for the boys. The invites to functions and presentations flowed in unabated. Yet they met a couple of times in early February and the focus shifted to the task ahead – retaining Sam.

By the time the boys resumed the business of the national league they were now bereft of the services of James McHugh who had picked up a shoulder injury in Glasgow. Joyce, injured in a car crash, was also missing in Semple Stadium but despite a mediocre performance Donegal had three points to spare over Tipperary, 1-12 to 1-9 the final score. It was the poorest performance to date and didn't augur well for the survival of the unbeaten run as Cork were next up.

Revenge for Ballincollig had already been taken in Ballybofey. Defeat would send Cork packing to Division Two. McEniff started with 13 All-Ireland men. Peter Campbell and 7,000 spectators watched as Tony Boyle inspired Donegal to a sixth successive league victory, "The difference between the sides was the stubbornness of the Donegal defence and the total dominance of Boyle and Bonner in the front line." Donegal were now putting teams away.

Longford were next in their own Pearse Park. Donegal put 3-16 past them as John Duffy marked his debut with an impressive 1-2. Murray, operating from midfield, matched Duffy in the scoring stakes while Manus hit 1-4. Shovlin made a welcome return as did the Wee Man. For a second year Donegal had come through the league undefeated with 57 points to spare over all-comers in seven games.

For the fifth time in six league campaigns, Donegal had qualified for the quarter-finals – Derry would provide the opposition this time. Yet the achievement was overshadowed by events within the county. Manus had raised a few hackles by calling a spade a spade in an interview with the *Irish Times* and pointed out that the merry-go-round of functions and appearances hadn't come his way. The comments annoyed some but Manus, as ever, was quite prepared to stand by his remarks.

Derry inflicted a first defeat in 11 months. But not in the league quarter-final – the McKenna Cup fixture came along first in mid-March. Eamonn Coleman had predicted that his Derry side would triumph and was proved correct as both teams fielded without the services of several regulars. There were those who felt Derry begrudged Donegal the All-Ireland. Having defeated All-Ireland champions Down, it was said some of the Derry squad had an All-Ireland won in their heads by the time they met the boys in Clones – 14 Donegal men ended that notion.

The McKenna Cup game in Ballybofey was barely 18 minutes old before it exploded. While prone on the ground, Molloy received a boot and his teammates piled in. It was indicative of the poor refereeing and increasing bad blood between the sides that high tackles flew unchecked between then and the finish. By then Derry had amassed 1-9 to Donegal's 0-6, with talkative substitute Joe Brolly rattling in 1-2. The boys and McEniff didn't seem that annoyed and the Derry men were by far the more anxious to progress anyway.

A couple of weeks later there was much more at stake – a place in the semi-final of the national league. The local derby continued, this time in Breffni Park. Derry, the defending league champions, were anxious to repeat their McKenna Cup success over Donegal. "We are," previewed the Follower astutely, "playing the second best team in Ireland." Ten thousand turned up in Cavan – many of them later than anticipated due to the belligerence of Crown forces at Border checkpoints – and saw Donegal and Derry clash at championship pace. McEniff sent out 13 of his All-Ireland men – Rambo, Hegarty and Joyce were unavailable through injury and 'flu but Paul Carr and Shov more than cancelled out their absence. Breffni was no place for those with weak tickers as the two teams tore into each other. It eventually proved costly for Donegal when Kieran McKeever felled substitute Tommy Ryan off the ball. Tommy, the man who terrorised

Derry in Clones the previous summer, was stretchered off with a broken jaw and McKeever was sent to the line. He would serve a two-month suspension.

McEniff got a dig from a Derry player while on the pitch making a positional switch and at the final whistle a Derry official had to be restrained from attacking the Donegal boss. McEniff was also refused entry to the Derry dressing room. The players unanimously agree that their most dour battles over the years were with Derry – the national league quarter-final of 1993 certainly supports that theory. The boys once again were not found wanting, neither in the football stakes nor in standing up for themselves, and by the time Brian White sounded the final whistle they had a point to spare – 0-10 to 2-3. It was impressive stuff after the apparent flatness of a few earlier league games. The last 15 minutes had been played at a phenomenal pace as the boys upped the ante and the opposition had no answer.

Derry had thrown everything and Donegal threw it back. Gary Coleman was hitting the Wee Man exceptionally hard. The Wee Man sorted him instantly, got booked and proceeded to play like a demon. Few were the teams that could match Derry's physical intensity at that time but this Donegal team certainly could. Matt Gallagher, Barry McGowan, Donal Reid, Brian Murray, Declan Bonner, John Cunningham, the McHughs and Tony Boyle providing the backbone. Molloy renewed hostilities with Brian McGilligan. Martin Shovlin, witness to many wrestling matches between the two midfielders, remembers this as one of the worst:

> While the two of them had many tussles, that one was unreal. It got so bad that McGilligan stood in the middle of the field, took his gloves off and challenged Molloy 'All right Anthony, just me and you'. Of course Anthony didn't back down. How frustrated was McGilligan when he was shouting like that? Anthony got awful stick about it afterwards.

The bad blood grew darker in the week that followed. Derry griped at County Board level and McEniff, uncharacteristically, snapped back. Harry Chivers, the Derry chairman, claimed that McEniff had ensured that Mayo, and not Derry, travelled to Glasgow a few months earlier. McEniff didn't deny it – Donegal met Derry often enough in Ulster as far as he was concerned. It was tactical. Mayo would do him fine. In response to Eamonn Coleman's criticism of the referee, McEniff snapped, "I can't go out and kick the frees over the bar for them. We got frees, we gave them away too but I'm not going to allow any team go out and tramp over us". The next meeting between the teams would make for interesting fare.

Clare, busy proving that their status as Munster champions was no fluke, had come through at the expense of eternal bridesmaids Mayo. It was another day out in Croke Park, halfway through April, against another team the boys might expect to defeat. That they managed and found themselves in a first-ever national league final. All talk of the league trailing the championship in terms of importance went by the wayside. A second national title was now within striking distance, not something that came Donegal's direction every year. It would have to be availed of.

Clare had put up a spirited challenge but never remotely troubled the All-Ireland champions who were well worthy of their 1-12 to 1-7 victory. Fifty thousand attended the league semi-final double header at Croker and saw Tony Boyle tear Clare apart. Not only did he strike three points himself – bringing his league tally up to 2-21 – but the Dungloe man fed the boys around him as Murray, Molloy and Cunningham freely sprayed the ball in his direction. Barry Cunningham was the man who got the Donegal goal, rifling the ball off a Clare defender and into the back of the net. As Michael Daly remarked, he "looked quite pleased with himself". Good performances were to be found all over the field. However, the victory came at a price for Barry McGowan when he damaged his hamstring. "I tore my hamstring for the first time in that semi-final," he revealed, "and it started a bad decade for me with that injury. I seemed to be permanently receiving treatment, I just couldn't shake it."

Bonner didn't finish the Clare game however, adding to the ominously increasing list of injuries that now included Martin McHugh and Tommy Ryan. All winter Michael Gallagher had also lost out through injury. With Molloy, Murray and Cunningham on song around the middle, the Glenties man was receiving little gain for the sacrifices required in wearing a Donegal shirt while making a living 150 miles away in Dublin. But his time was coming again.

Dublin supporters, in Croke Park themselves for their later semi-final with Kerry, gave Bonner some grief as he left the pitch. Tony Boyle, not realising the seriousness of Bonner's injury was in stitches on the pitch as Bonner was stretchered off in the closing minutes:

> You could clearly hear the Hill chanting, 'Declan Bonner is a wanker'. I laughed at that. It was a bad injury and Declan was in hospital for weeks after it – we didn't realise how serious it was. We had some laugh about it in the dressing room. Of course Bonner later said that at least the Dubs knew his name, they weren't singing at anyone else!

Those same Dubs would be back in Croke Park on the first Sunday in May as Donegal and the metropolitans renewed old acquaintances – a national league title at stake this time around. But neither side could claim it for themselves on May Day. It finished 0-9 apiece in front of 51,179 spectators as Donegal rescued a game, two-thirds of which belonged to the Dubs. Significantly, the third which belonged to Donegal was the final one.

Some onlookers argued Dublin let the title slip that day, others pointed out that the game finished prematurely with Donegal on the ascendant and Dublin two men down. Either way, few neutral punters left headquarters disappointed.

Tom Conaghan

photograph courtesy of Irish News

As a game, highlights – and lowlights – were plentiful. Trailing 0-2 to 0-6 and with Dublin playing all the football, Noel Hegarty came on for 'flu victim Rambo at half-time and was instrumental in swinging things back in favour of the green and gold. Barry McGowan, Manus Boyle, Brian Murray and Big Molloy suddenly slipped into fifth gear. Reid was superb and McHugh started running down the middle. Match on. John Joe Doherty drove Charlie Redmond to distraction. "It was my best performance for the county," thought John Joe, "I would say that I got my All-Star because of that display. Redmond didn't seem to want to play. He fouled men all over the field before he was sent off."

With 22 minutes gone in the second half Donegal drew level at 0-7 apiece. The Dubs were in trouble and they knew it. Twice more they took the lead but on both occasions the boys levelled within a minute. Noel Hegarty set up the first and fired over the second having thundered down the right wing on one of his trademark get-out-of-my-way solos. If the Dubs wanted their football tough and uncompromising – and it seemed they did – Hegarty surely was their man.

Dublin had spent much of the half cynically hauling Donegal players down just outside the range of free-takers. Eventually Charlie Redmond tested the patience of referee Brian White once too often. With 59 minutes showing on the clock Charlie found himself in the dugout watching proceedings. A minute later Keith Barr joined him, losing the run of himself entirely and lunging wildly at Molloy. However, despite the various stoppages, Brian White lost his courage and played less than a minute and a half of added time, drawing proceedings to a close with tempers broken, Donegal threatening the winner and scores level at 0-9 apiece.

"We should have won that day and to have won the national league would have been the icing on the cake," said Brian Murray. "A terrible refereeing decision cost us the game," felt Matt Gallagher, "Manus had scored a legitimate goal but it was disallowed."

The battle was rejoined a week later. Different story. Dublin were well worthy of their four-point winning margin, 0-6 to 0-10 the final score. Donegal had produced what Michael Daly termed "an inexplicably flat performance". There had been good reason for the optimism radiating from Donegal folk before the throw-in. A few of the boys – Mister Consistency, Tony Boyle, among them – played poorly the week before, that was unlikely to occur two weeks running. And the Dubs, minus Redmond and Barr, weren't exactly causing knees to knock. Five minutes into the replay, Tommy Carr became the third Dub to make the long walk. Carr, never a favourite of opposing supporters, signalled his vicious intent by drawing his boot petulantly off Murray in full view of White. It would earn him a six-month suspension. (What followed was an unprecedented media-driven campaign to have the suspension reduced. The campaign was successful and the suspension was eventually reduced to four months.) But, as is often the case, the 14 played like men possessed and outwitted and out-scored the opposition. Donegal understood. They'd done it to Derry in more fraught circumstances. "We got lazy," remembered Noel Hegarty, "we had a spare man but everyone was leaving their man loose."

There wasn't much to be said. The boys were disgusted at Dublin's cynicism which negated against decent football, yet few could argue that the better team hadn't won. "It was, at all times, a rough, reckless battle of football's biggest guns," wrote Vincent Hogan, adding that referee White had found himself "amidst a thicket of high elbows, clenched fists and low morals" for a second week running.

Pat O'Neill, love him or loathe him – and most Donegal supporters enthusiastically chose the latter – had injected a harder edge into the Dubs. It was a more cynical sky-blue outfit who faced Donegal under the guidance of the doctor than the outfit guided by Paddy Cullen a summer before. It would finally win them an All-Ireland in 1995.

Donegal had squandered chances and were strangely disjointed all over the pitch. The presence of McHugh and Gavigan was sorely missed – victims of 'flu – although both did come on. For a second week Brian White got a tongue lashing from players, the Donegal boys more vocal this time. The media agreed. "The time has come when the GAA must introduce more professional referees to take charge of major games," wrote Tom O'Riordan after the drawn match. Good referees were "as scarce as hens' teeth," commented Owen McCrohan dryly in the *Democrat*. Referee or no referee, the sky-blues deserved their NFL medals. The Dubs were seven points up at half-time. In the dressing room O'Neill asked his 14 if they wished to be remembered as the team that surrendered a seven-point lead and a league final. They didn't and wouldn't. "Dublin had more reason to win it than us," felt James McHugh, "I don't remember anyone being too bothered about it afterwards."

The boys looked tired. It had, after all, been a long road. Only a second defeat in 18 competitive games was hardly something to moan about. A national league title would have been the icing on the cake but no more. The boys had given the county yet another delightful taste of the big time, despite their duties with Sam, and had further enhanced their status. Before the replay, Donal Keenan had paid tribute, "Donegal have become a very good side, finally realising their great potential". One defeat, league final or not, changed nothing.

❅ ❅ ❅ ❅

Early in the 1992 Martin Gavigan had predicted that the then defending All-Ireland champions Down would be toppled in Ulster. He was right. Now, as the summer of 1993 arrived, all over Ulster inter-county footballers from the Mournes to the Sperrins were making similar predictions about Donegal. The task of getting out of Ulster had been a bridge too far for so many defending

Ulster champions – 17 years had passed since last an Ulster title had been successfully defended. Donegal could not even consider back-to-back All-Irelands – like Meath in 1987 and 1988, and Cork in 1989 and 1990 – until the provincial route was negotiated. Would the boys suffer the fate of Down? How much had the national league run taken out of them? "McEniff cannot know how much ambition was shed on the celebration trail last autumn/winter," added Martin Breheny in the *Sunday Press*.

As May drew to a close and Antrim lurking in the long grass, more and more of the boys were picking up niggly injuries. Against Dublin in the drawn game McEniff had managed to start with 14 of those who played on All-Ireland Sunday plus Shovlin – Noel Hegarty the sub who came on. In the replayed league final Donegal were close to All-Ireland Sunday strength – 14 started plus Shovlin while Rambo and the Wee Man made substitute appearances. McEniff would have few opportunities of fielding his All-Ireland squad again – Donegal were about to be decimated by injury.

A fortnight before Sam was put on the line for the first time, the injury list was worringly long. John Joe, Molloy and Rambo all featured – their injuries picked up or exacerbated in club games. Declan Bonner was still not himself since that back injury against Clare and it was known that Tony Boyle's knee, as ever, was causing problems. By the time Antrim visited Ballybofey it was Tony's shoulder and not his knee which betrayed him. James McHugh was another watching injury-stricken from the bench with a trapped-nerve in his back. In all, the boys had to defend Sam short a third of the All-Ireland starting 15 – four of them All-Stars. Gone were Big Molloy, Rambo, James McHugh, Tony Boyle and John Joe Doherty. Their places went to Barry Cunningham, Razda, Jim McGuinness, Tommy Ryan and Noel Hegarty – it was still a formidable outfit. Tommy Ryan was in for his first big game since his All-Ireland disappointment. Only eight weeks had passed since he'd received the broken jaw against Derry in the NFL quarter-final.

The expectation throughout the county that the boys – injuries or not – could take Antrim with one hand tied behind their back didn't help. In fairness though, Antrim was a most favourable draw. As the Follower pointed out, "In the past 12 months we have scaled football's Everest. They have trawled, none too successfully, football's deepest troughs." Donegal did just enough to scrape through.

Enough but no more, as the final score of 0-12 to 0-9 indicated. A three-point lead was apparently deemed enough by the boys, they achieved that after three minutes, went in three up at the interval and still had three to spare when Pat McEneaney blew for full-time. The display had been nothing to write home about but carried the boys into a fifth consecutive Ulster semi-final. McHugh, captain in Molloy's absence, illustrated how much he had been missed against Dublin as he led from the front with yet another man-of-the-match display. "Moments of majesty to remember," noted Donal Keenan in the *Independent*. Yet, overall, it had been a tired, strangely lethargic, performance. Ordinary even. "Is it good? No. It's tedious," groaned a bored Tom Humphries in the *Irish Times*. All through the second half the *Irish Times* man was praying for someone to say, "It's raining. Next score wins."

Gary Walsh; Barry McGowan, Matt Gallagher, Noel Hegarty; Donal Reid, John Cunningham, Martin Shovlin; Brian Murray, Barry Cunningham; Joyce McMullan, Martin McHugh, Jim McGuinness; Declan Bonner, Tommy Ryan and Manus Boyle had started. Sylvester Maguire, Mark McShane and John Joe Doherty all came on. "Donegal are a bit understrength today. 33% to be precise," quipped Humphries. Nonetheless, the performances of Walsh, Shov, Joyce and Murray were up there with McHugh as 15,000 spectators – among them Derry boss Eamonn Coleman – watched the champions brush over the first hurdle.

McEniff had moved to plug up the gaps by drafting Kilcar's Mark McShane onto the panel. There was yet more plugging to be done as Jim McGuinness departed the Antrim game with a dislocated collar-bone. "The players are tired because they are playing too much football," McEniff told the press afterwards.

All football talk around the country centred on Donegal's battle to defend their title short four illustrious All-Stars. Already, the odds on them getting out of Ulster had lengthened dramatically. Martin Breheny of the *Irish Press* graphically illustrated Donegal's dilemma:

> Could Dublin defend Leinster short Mick Deegan, Paul Curran, Jack Sheedy, Paul Clarke and Vinny Murphy? Or Derry short Johnny McGurk, Henry Downey, Anthony Tohill, Damien Cassidy and Dermot Heaney?

That was the enormity of the task facing Donegal. The Wee Man, now contributing a column in the *Sunday Independent*, agreed:

> The core of our team are out through injury. Most people would agree that our strength in winning last year's All-Ireland was up the middle with no fewer than six of our seven All-Star awards going to centre men.

The race to get Tony Boyle back in the number 14 jersey was desperate. The loss of his ball-winning and distribution ability in attack was enormous. Meath manager, Sean Boylan, was enlisted to treat the Dungloe man with his much sought after herbal remedies. Tony would make progress but wouldn't kick a ball in the defence of Sam. Molloy's troublesome knee was subjected to a fifth operation – micro-surgery this time – in an effort to prepare him to once again scale the dizzy heights.

McEniff's head was wrecked but finally he made a decision. He would field only boys who were fully fit. It was all that he could do. He needed cover for his All-Stars. He turned to John Duffy and Big Michael Gallagher again. And he looked no further than Killybegs for one of the game's most exciting prospects –

although it was thought likely even then that Donegal would lose him to professional soccer – 19 year-old Declan Boyle. Sylvester Maguire was pencilled in for a start, but he too joined the war wounded, ripping his groin in training the Tuesday before. Barry Cunningham was another in nursing a groin strain but was available on the bench. In the end, McEniff replaced Cunningham and McGuinness with Mark McShane and John Joe Doherty and hit the road for Breffni.

When the boys brought Sam to the Hills, John Duffy was among the 30,000-something Donegal supporters who encircled Croke Park. Nine months later the Ballyshannon man was the toast of those same supporters as he swapped the terraces for the sod of sun-drenched Breffni Park – somehow the sun always seemed to shine on championship Sunday in Cavan – to score the precious point that kept Donegal in line to retain Sam. Duffy had been sent into the fray with 57 minutes gone and his team trailing by three points. On too came Big Michael Gallagher. "It called for a miracle," reported Tom O'Riordan in the *Independent*, "Donegal's epitaph was engrained on the minds of the milling 22,000 crowd." It was McEniff's last cast of the dice – Sam was slipping away. The next 13 minutes – on the hottest day of the summer – belonged to John Duffy and Michael Gallagher.

The teams would hit another seven points in all before the final whistle. Five of them would come from Donegal boots, with Duffy, in particular, involved in everything. Manus Boyle and Declan Bonner were now equally industrious. On the field two minutes the subs combined with an old hand – Bonner – to put the show back on the road. Two points down. Matt – in his 100th game – was uncharacteristically conceding frees to Armagh men like there was no tomorrow, and handed one back a minute later. Another couple of minutes and Duffy drew a foul which Manus pointed. Back to two. Generous to a fault, Matt then fouled one of the Grimleys – three the margin again. Duffy, creating havoc every time the ball came his direction, was fouled yet again, allowing Bonner slot over from 35 yards. Two, the margin again. A couple of minutes later, Noel Hegarty's dismissal for introducing Jarlath Burns to the sharp end of his elbow went practically unnoticed as the boys kicked into top gear in an attempt to halt the Orange march. They were cutting it fine; 69 minutes had come and gone before Bonner, showing all his old dash, drew yet another free. Manus, having missed a sitter just before, hit a beauty from a more difficult angle. One down, 0-14 to 1-12. Hundreds of bandwagon-hoppers and half-hearted Donegal supporters were already nearing their cars and buses, having decided earlier that the dream was over. They missed the conclusion of the Duffy and Gallagher show. Shovlin, the undisputed master of going in where it hurts, would have been proud of the ball won by Michael Gallagher half a minute into injury time. The hard-won free was cleverly used. No time wasted, Gallagher took responsibility and delivered long and true into his Civil Service teammate. Duffy collected, made the space and hit the sweetest of equalisers with the outside of his left foot. Donegal 0-15, Armagh 1-12. "The age of miracles is with us still," exclaimed Paddy Downey in the *Irish*

Times. Close call. But still in the championship. "I don't think we'd have come back like that two years ago," Bonner told the press. Bonner had played his part in that comeback and hit a magnificent seven points.

It was only later, when Donegal heart's recovered from double-time, that anything resembling analysis could be considered. Still there maybe, but at a huge cost. Barry McGowan lasted 13 minutes before tearing a hamstring – Mark Crossan replacing him and having a stormer. The unfortunate Razda had joined the casualty list with a hamstring injury even before the throw in and had to be replaced by Paul Carr. Joyce broke a finger but played on. Even more heroic was Donal Reid. Somehow Reid managed almost 40 minutes of championship football with a badly injured shoulder. Grimly sticking to the task despite the all too visible pain, Reid allowed McEniff the luxury of retaining his subs for a tactical emergency. McEniff did and won the draw. In a team of men who put everything on the line for their county, what Reid did that day in Cavan was above and beyond the call of duty and spoke volumes of his commitment to his county. And then there was the loss of Hegarty – he was facing a month's suspension for striking. Donegal finished the game with just eight of their All-Ireland starting 15.

Armagh had hit hard and fouled often. They had man-marked tightly and the boys hadn't broken free. McHugh had spent a fruitless afternoon in the restricting company of Kieran McGeeney who had followed him everywhere and Matt had better days guarding the edge of the square. Advantage Armagh then, as the replay beckoned a week later and the team now down to half their All-Ireland heroes.

The next instalment from this bunch of extraordinary footballers was remarkable. In the space of seven days they turned things upside down. The team that took the field for the replay against Armagh could not have been envisaged even a couple of weeks before. Walsh, Matt, John Joe, Murray, McHugh, Joyce, Bonner and Manus were joined by Shovlin, Paul Carr, Mark Crossan, Declan Boyle, Michael Gallagher, Mark McShane and John Duffy. That they proceeded to annihilate Armagh by 12 points was noted with trepidation throughout Ulster and beyond.

Eighteen thousand headed for Breffni. Donegal folk got their money's worth in the first 15 minutes – the remaining 55 minutes were free. By the time that devastating quarter of an hour was over, Donegal led by 2-5 to 0-0 and football watchers the country over knew that the boys were back in business.

And how! A lot had been learned in the week. McHugh, marshalled out of it in the drawn game by up-and-coming young lion Kieran McGeeney, put it all on the line. McGeeney, who would go on to lift the Sam Maguire Cup himself nine years later, was about to be taught a footballing lesson by an old master. As the teams ran into position for the throw-in the Wee Man kept running and positioned himself on the edge of the Armagh square. Manus switched out to the 45. McGeeney followed McHugh and found himself isolated on the edge of his own square with the 1992 footballer of the year. It took McHugh 15 seconds to hit his first point. For the 15 minutes that followed, he ran the show and ran McGeeney into the ground. By the time Armagh switched Damien Horisk onto the Wee Man, Donegal had recorded 1-4. Armagh needed to watch more that the old master, the new boys – Paul Carr (0-1), John Duffy (1-1) and Declan Boyle (0-1) – were equally up for it.

Horisk would spend the remainder of the afternoon hanging out of McHugh but it was a lost cause. McHugh had stood up to better men than the Armagh number five. "Horisk's attempts to cut down McHugh's influence owed more to the art of wrestling than to football," commented Seán Kilfeather in the *Irish Times*. It mattered little, with midfield claiming everything, McHugh and Murray linked up to put Mark McShane through for a second, killer, Donegal goal. For good measure McHugh himself added another point and with 15 minutes gone the game was over.

Donegal had qualified for an unprecedented fifth consecutive Ulster final. It was as good a 15 minutes as a Donegal team had ever strung together. Devastating. Around Breffni people were comparing it with the second half showing against Derry in 1992. It was hard to figure just how good Armagh were, but it certainly was a better showing from the All-Ireland champions than they had given the week previously! The forwards went on to score almost at will and by Michael Cranny's final whistle they had amassed 2-16 to Armagh's 1-7. But the day belonged to others as well as the forwards. Nowhere had the side been found wanting. Matt handled Ger Houlihan and then John Grimley with absolute authority. John Joe Doherty had former minor-star Des Mackin in his pocket while new boy Declan Boyle had a flawless debut. Mark Crossan, Michael Gallagher, John Duffy, Paul Carr were equally flawless. And Murray, the leader around the middle in the absence of his old partner Molloy, rose to the challenge and earned a piece of Belleek China. It had been an impressive demonstration of strength in depth.

The injury list was still running to a couple of pages. As players were scored off the list and another would immediately replace him. James McHugh made a late appearance in the replay but it was for Bonner who had hurt his back again. Barry Cunningham had also made a late appearance, replacing Mark McShane who had picked up a severely bruised shoulder. That appearance would be Barry Cunningham's last in a Donegal jersey. He aggravated his groin injury two weeks before the Ulster final and it has never properly healed. Permanently on the injury list it seemed were Rambo, Tony Boyle, Barry Cunningham, Razda and Donal Reid. Molloy was close to ready – he had 20 minutes in him at least. The press men were agog at his unquenchable desire to play for Donegal. "Molloy's left knee really ought, at this stage, to be donated to medical science," wrote John Brennan in the *Irish Press*. "I had thought about retiring after the All-Ireland," revealed Molloy:

Another Go

But some of the boys said to me to hang in for another year to see what happened. I had another operation on my knee and it was hard to go through another spell of rehabilitation and use weights to build up my knee afterwards. I was the kind of player that needed every bit of training I got.

With so many out of action, McEniff chanced his arm and got the County Board to request a one week postponement of the final from the Ulster Council. Predictably, it was not forthcoming.

And the opposition? Derry. The general consensus was better Derry than Down but this one was going to be tough missing so many of the boys. And Eamonn Coleman's side hadn't always got the credit they deserved. National league champions in 1992, they had lost to eventual All-Ireland champions in both 1991 and 1992. As Derry prepared to join battle with their western neighbours they did so as favourites.

It was all down to the wire. Predictions were impossible. Rarely had defending champions put their provincial and All-Ireland titles on the line missing so many of the previous campaign's stalwarts. By the time the boys set off for Clones, McEniff had exactly two-thirds of the team that finished the All-Ireland available to defend it in Clones. The team he choose for battle was: Gary Walsh; John Joe Doherty, Matt Gallagher, Barry McGowan; Mark Crossan, Paul Carr, Martin Shovlin; Michael Gallagher, Brian Murray; James McHugh, Martin McHugh, Joyce McMullan; Declan Bonner, Manus Boyle, John Duffy.

Donegal and Derry folk and neutrals alike eagerly awaited the clash. Statisticians figured it was the first time in almost a quarter of a century that the same sides met in consecutive Ulster finals. The Follower had a sneak look at revamped Clones and was impressed, "I will go so far as to say that despite the work not being finished you will see the Ulster final in more comfort that ever". Roll on Ulster final Sunday then and another trip up the hill in Clones in the sun.

❅ ❅ ❅ ❅

Sunday came and with it the rain. Donegal cars and buses crawled through the downpour and snaked their way towards Monaghan. Others with yellow number plates made similar journeys from the heart of County Derry. All talk speculated on whether the game would come off at all. Could the pitch, with its new sod, take such a fall of rain? No announcements were relayed on the radio and a fateful trip was made in monsoon conditions, bumper to bumper, to logjammed Clones.

Inside, it was even more difficult to envisage an Ulster final taking place. Those on the slippery grass-banks of the famous Clones Hill were sure that an announcement confirming that the pitch was unplayable would be forthcoming. Up on the hill it was an ordeal just to remain standing – it would become dangerous as the crowd filed into the grounds in large numbers. Down below, the pitch resembled a paddy-field. To play football on it would surely be asking for trouble – it had danger written all over it. It was time for a brave decision by the Ulster Council. Instead they sent the minors of Tyrone and Derry out into the rain. Tyrone became the minor champions but the folly of playing football in Clones that Sunday was soon graphically illustrated for all to see and hear – the Ulster Council included – by the cries of pain that rang around the ground following a broken leg sustained by Derry's Cathal Scullion.

In the senior dressing rooms, both Donegal and Derry were certain that common sense would prevail. They were overlooking a simple fact however – common sense was not necessarily a condition of office for certain posts in the country's greatest sporting organisation. The game would go on. Regardless. Donegal, defending Ulster champions, were being told to put their coveted All-Ireland crown on the line in a dangerous quagmire by men who cared little for the welfare of the organisation's greatest asset – its players. For once Donegal and Derry players found themselves in agreement. The pitch was unplayable. Come back another day. Allegedly Eamonn Coleman was of the same opinion. And prepared to stand up to the man who governed everything that moved in Ulster GAA circles. According to McHugh, the referee – Tommy McDermott of Cavan – indicated that the matter was out of his hands and in the hands of the man in the suit. It was time to stand up to officialdom.

The most serious criticism of Brian McEniff the boys have was that he didn't stand up on that Sunday in July and tell a certain official where he could put his orders. What could the official have done had we refused to play, ask the boys? Too many sacrifices had been made to play a game as prestigious as an Ulster final on such a pitch. A youngster had just broken his leg as a direct result of the conditions. What more justification would you have needed to call off a fully committed senior game with so much at stake? Indeed, such was the traffic chaos surrounding the ground that there were serious problems getting the ambulance carrying young Scullion out of the ground.

"We were diverted on our way to Clones such was the flooding and congestion," remembered Tommy Ryan:

> We saw the condition of the field and there was no way the game should have been played. We were All-Ireland champions and I don't think we would have been turfed out of the championship for not playing. With the Derry minor breaking his leg McEniff had all the grounds he needed. All he had to do was go to the press room and get the journalists to start writing and we could have all come back the following Sunday.

The pitch had been torn up by the minors. The issue should have been forced. And a week gained would have benefited Donegal greatly – some of the lads might well have made it off the injured list. It didn't happen. The fight wasn't fought. The game would go on.

It did. And the boys surrendered their heroically won provincial title of 12 months standing. And they surrendered the opportunity to travel forth to Croke Park and defend their right to keep Sam in the Hills. The adventure was over. It all slipped under the murky waters of a Clones paddy-field on the third Sunday of July 1993.

"We had trained on the pitch the week before," remembered Brian Murray, "While we were there they were watering the pitch. I stepped on to the pitch on the match day and went up to my ankles. The match should have been called off, it was no day to play football." "It was a washout and should never have been played," agreed Declan Bonner. "It was an insult to both teams to ask them to play," felt Manus Boyle, "there was a complete disregard for the safety of both the players and spectators."

Much of the 70 minutes of football was lottery-like in execution by both sets of players. Derry, who defeated Down in similar conditions in Newry, made the better of the heavy going. "They powered through the mud and muck and fashioned a win, a win, I believe, due as much to the elements as to their ability," wrote the Follower after the Newry game. He could well have filed the same report in Clones. Same difference only worse. The statistics in Clones were simple. At the interval Donegal led by one point, 0-5 to 0-4. In the second 35 minutes, Derry doubled their first half tally while Donegal added a single point. Full-time score: Donegal 0-6, Derry 0-8.

"The match, as was to be expected, was littered with errors, some of them quite hilarious as the ball squirted hither and thither in the muddy pools which formed on the pitch," wrote Seán Kilfeather in the *Irish Times*. "I went low for a ball and lost my balance. I must have slid on my backside for at least 20 yards. I just couldn't stop," recalled Mark Crossan.

In the aftermath a fierce debate would rage regarding the state of the pitch. It was impossible to kick the ball along the ground. At times the ball literally floated. Some of the decisions of referee Tommy McDermott were also rightly questioned. But the simple fact was, while the bigger stronger Derry men had undoubtedly adjusted better to the conditions, they were also the better team on the day. In addition to their two-point winning margin, Derry had hit nine wides compared to Donegal's five. Inspired by the wonderful athleticism of Anthony Tohill over 70 minutes – McEniff would declare him the best footballer in Ireland – Derry would go on to overcome Dublin by a single point in a thrilling All-Ireland semi-final and would have a goal to spare over Cork on All-Ireland Sunday. Sam was coming back to the hills after all – the Sperrins. If Donegal were to surrender Sam, they could do worse than surrender it to the men from Derry. "Fair play to Derry, the team adapted to the conditions and went on to win an All-Ireland," said Manus Boyle, "I went to the All-Ireland and outside of the Derry players, no one was happier than me to see them do it."

Gary Walsh had picked up an injury with the last kick out of the first half. "I had been having problems with my thigh muscle that year," he remembered:

> When I took the last kick out in the first half it felt as if the muscle had fall-
> en off my leg. I struggled into the dressing room and told McEniff that I
> couldn't feel my leg as it was numb. McEniff had often taken similar risks
> in the past, but he hadn't listed Paul Callaghan in the first six substitutes.
> He asked me if I could play on and I told him that I could stand there. I
> tried to take the first kick out in the second half but the ball only went
> about ten yards along the ground. I thought I had hit it with full force but
> it was like kicking with a rubber hammer – I couldn't feel the ball.

Matt Gallagher took over the kicking duties. Gary Walsh played on but the injury has never fully healed. "My kick out faded after 1993 and I lost at least ten yards off it due to that muscle injury," he recalled:

> I had terrible problems with that injury but how it was dealt with left a
> sour taste. While you were playing county football you were great but
> we lost the Ulster final in 1993 and I never heard another word about my
> injury from any member of the County Board. I left Clones that day
> hardly fit to walk. If we had won that game I'd have been with a doctor
> in Dublin the next morning. My club, Burren, sent me to a physiothera-
> pist in Belfast to have it treated.
> The weakness in that leg that has never left me. Even now when I
> play football it will cause me trouble. On the day after a game I can hard-
> ly move my leg.

Derry choked the fight out of Donegal within seven minutes of the second half throw-in. Trailing by a point at the interval, Tohill had Derry level pegging within a minute of the restart – the Swatragh man was pulling all the strings. Damien Cassidy, Damien Barton and Enda Gormley added three more and although they wouldn't score for the remainder of the game, they had enough power and strength to keep Donegal at bay. Duffy converted a close-in free in the 21st minute to leave the score 0-6 to 0-8 but that was it. Donegal had a cou-ple of half chances for goals but none was converted. McEniff threw on Mark McShane for Bonner and in a last desperate effort to match Derry for strength sent in All-Stars Molloy and Gavigan. It wasn't to be.

Donal Reid, nursing a fractured scapula, watched forlornly from the bench:

> It was probably one of the saddest days in my football career. I felt help-
> less. My whole footballing career was fading away in front of me, the

sacrifices, the endless endeavours, the unfailing commitment and most of all, the Sam Maguire.

The boys had hit Derry very hard early on and two or three of them – including McGilligan – needed treatment. Titanic struggles were going on all over the field and in many quarters the boys were holding their own or winning outright. Matt Gallagher, John Joe Doherty, Barry McGowan and Paul Carr had matters well in hand. Murray and Gallagher were doing okay in midfield while the McHughs and Shov were scrapping successfully for everything. Joyce was the pick of the boys throughout – he was everywhere carrying the game to Derry. Duffy was also causing problems. At half-time, leading by that point, things looked a hell of a lot brighter than they had 12 months previously when Donegal climbed the steps into the dressing rooms with neither Razda nor Tony Boyle. Donegal folk were optimistic. Donegal had not been found wanting and had matched Derry score for score and more. The game was the boys' for the taking. But, in 1993 it was Derry's turn to turn up the heat, and four points within seven minutes of the restart put their name on the Anglo-Celt Cup. "It was a terrible way to lose the All-Ireland title," felt John Joe Doherty, "everything seemed so glum. There wasn't even a cover over the dugouts and the subs got drenched. Nothing about that day made sense."

"We had a lot of mileage on the clock," said Matt Gallagher:

Conditions didn't help. Derry put out a team to play in the conditions and Anthony Tohill did what he did best: play against Donegal. He played against us in four finals [two Ulster and two NFL] and was, I think, man of the match in three of them. He loved playing Donegal.

Brian McEniff was proud of how his depleted team had performed but naturally disappointed with the outcome:

I can't put my hand on my heart and say that we would have gone on and won the All-Ireland in 1993. We had a lot of injuries at the time. Qualifying for the closing stages of the national league took too much out of the team. We wanted to beat Derry and got the opportunity to do so in the quarter final. We would have been better to lose that game.

What Donegal didn't know was that Derry had found their road to Damascus after the national league quarter-final the previous April. Just as Donegal's pivotal moment of 1992 had occurred in the dressing-rooms after the Fermanagh match, Derry's moment was equally recognised when it came. Mickey Moran, speaking to Eoghan Corry in *Oakboys*, had no doubt that was where the decision to win the All-Ireland was made:

After the Donegal fiasco in the quarter-final of the league, when we flopped in the second half, we got together the next Monday night and said we are just going to try everything possible, to look at every avenue to put things right.

Anthony Tohill, one of the most gifted footballers of his generation, had no intention of losing to Donegal in a second Ulster final. For him, attitudes had changed a year earlier as Anthony Tohill revealed to Eoghan Corry:

Hurtful as it was, losing the 1992 Ulster final to Donegal changed attitudes on the Derry team. It was that defeat that was decisive in the make up of this team. In view of what Donegal went on to achieve, it just stiffened our resolve.

The recriminations about the conditions lasted for a week or so. "Were this a club game it most certainly would not have been played," mused the Follower. "The worst summer conditions I have ever seen," commented former Galway player Jack Mahon in the *Democrat*. Criticism was not merely restricted to Donegal-friendly sources. "I don't wish to detract one bit from Derry's victory but this match should never have gone ahead," argued former Kerry great Páidí O'Shea in the *Irish Independent*, "I wouldn't have played a junior league game on such a surface, not alone an Ulster final." Seán Kilfeather was equally shocked at the Ulster Council's decision to proceed in "the worst conditions experienced in championship football in recent times".

Even Tohill, on his way to another All-Star award and with an Ulster title under his belt, would join the criticism. "It was a disgrace that the Ulster final should be settled in those conditions, no matter who won it." Martin McHugh agreed but was generous in losing, "We were beaten fairly but that game should never have been played". James McHugh felt that Derry were a better team:

I don't think we would have beaten them on a dry day. They had seen Down win the All-Ireland in 1991 and us winning it in 1992. There was pride in them and they wanted it more than us. They wanted to rub it into the champions.

On the full-time whistle supporters on the hill, far from the comfortable seats occupied by members of the Ulster Council, were simply glad it was all over. It had been an unpleasant ordeal. The drama unfolding on the field below had become secondary. The famous Clones hill now bore all the appearance of an entry in the National Ploughing Championships. Derry and Donegal supporters clung to each other as they slowly exited the slope. A plague of frogs of almost Biblical proportions had descended on the hill adding a further surreal element to a dreadful day. Muck and dirt rode up as far as knees and all around unfortunate supporters were falling in the mud, most of them facing a four-hour journey home in the most unpleasant of circumstances. Everyone agreed on one thing: it was a good job neither side had scored a goal. Had a goal went in and an inevitable surge of celebration occurred on the hill, the Ulster Council could have had a major tragedy on its hands. It would only have taken a few people to slip to trigger an avalanche of falling bodies. Everyone concerned was fortunate to escape a disaster equivalent to those of Hillsborough or Heysel Stadium.

Devastated Donegal supporters speculated what it would have been like had the likes of Molloy, Hegarty, Rambo and Tony Boyle been available fully fit to stand shoulder to shoulder with Derry men for 70 minutes in the mud of Clones. Then Donegal folk could have accepted that they had defended the honour of Sam in circumstances that were acceptable. Pete McGrath, manager of Down, was sure that the conditions had given Derry the edge. "When it comes down to the final analysis," he told the *Irish Press*, "the ground conditions were what decided this Ulster football final. They favoured Derry." Brian McGilligan was equally disappointed that the final had been played in such conditions. His reason? "On a dry day you would have really seen what this Derry team was capable of. As it was we still showed Donegal that we can play the short-passing game as well as anyone."

There had been controversy on the pitch too. Manus had got his marching orders near the end, frustration finally getting the better of him – Johnny McGurk bearing the brunt of the Killybegs man's fury. "A harsh decision in the eyes of all who braved the rain and mud to watch," commented Eoghan Corry. The bad blood between the players and management had continued, on and off the field. Kieran McKeever certainly won no new Donegal fans with his application of man-marking. On one occasion he stood almost on top of his marker as McEniff issued instructions near the sideline. "Cop yourself on Kieran. Stick closely, yes, but don't make a fool of yourself," chastised Jack Mahon. McEniff was the centre of some after-match aggravation. An umbrella-wielding Derry supporter connected and another threw a punch before the Donegal boss was surrounded by a protective cordon of supporters and escorted to the safety of the dressing room.

McEniff seemed to have the knack of raising Derry-men's hackles. Eamonn Coleman wasn't a huge fan. "Myself and Brian McEniff are totally different types of people. He's a big-time hotelier and I'm an ordinary bricklayer, but we're good friends," he told Eoghan Corry. Friends or not, McEniff turned up in Bellaghy a couple of months later, and managed the Rest of Ireland team against the new All-Ireland champions, Derry, and got the biggest cheer of the night when he came on and scored a point. "The tales of great bitterness between Derry and Donegal were overstated," felt Brian McEniff, "Eamonn Coleman came to Bundoran before the All-Ireland semi-final and I gave him all the information we had gathered on Dublin."

Sam's for the Hills

Tom Humphries, with his soft spot for Donegal, was generous in his praise of the fallen champions. He observed their "awesome grief" and had a tribute to hand.

Yesterday was among their finest hours. An afternoon when, with the heart and spine ostensibly ripped out of the team, they walked and breathed and ran Derry to the wire. Once upon a time we thought that Donegal teams lacked the nerve for the big occasion. Yesterday they died with dignity.

They had. But their story didn't end there. On the bus on the way home from Clones the boys' sense of unity was as strong as ever. Molloy made his way up to the front of the bus and sat down on the edge of the seat nearest McEniff. They'd come a long way together, the two of them. "You'll stay on for another year, old man," suggested the captain. The old man knew the logical answer to that one. It wasn't the one he gave.

RESULTS

National League 1992-93
Donegal 1-9, Kildare 0-6
Donegal 0-12, Carlow 0-5
Donegal 1-14, Leitrim 0-6
Donegal 1-16, Cavan 0-9
Donegal 1-12, Tipperary 1-9
Donegal 1-8, Cork 0-9
Donegal 3-16, Longford 0-7
Donegal 0-10, Derry 2-3 (q/f)
Donegal 1-12, Clare 1-7 (s/f)
Donegal 0-9, Dublin 0-9 (f)
Donegal 0-6, Dublin 0-10 (r)

Ulster Championship 1993
Donegal 0-12, Antrim 0-9
Donegal 0-15, Armagh 1-12
Donegal 2-16, Armagh 1-7 (r)
Donegal 0-6, Derry 0-8

20

The Long Goodbye
(October 1993 – October 2003)

"Most of us have remained friends even now, 11 years on.
We will remain friends into our more mature years."

DONAL REID – JULY 25, 2003

I t was over bar the shouting. There was football, plenty of it, to be played but the remarkable odyssey of the boys who brought Sam to the Hills was nearing its end. As Sam slipped under the water in Clones, so too did the heart and soul of the greatest football team Donegal had ever known. It would take a while for it to show. But it would show.

They took up the cause again in October of 1993 when the national league called for football to be played. It was still there – the old magic. Down – who had an All-Ireland in them still – came to Ballyshannon but the boys had nine points to spare. Nine games they played in total over the winter, winning five, losing four. Derry hit 3-16 in Casement against them that October. The boys managed 0-7 in reply but, coming a day after the Shankill Bombing which killed ten people in the city, no-one was too concerned about football.

McEniff would give football to some of the newer lads that winter but, here and there, the boys still featured. When the Dubs came to MacCumhaill Park old pride was at stake. Four points the margin again – Dublin weren't going to beat the boys at home. Yet morale was low that Christmas, the expenses row was still lingering. A release of steam was much overdue – it came unexpectedly in the defence of the Willie Dowds Cup over a weekend in Glasgow. Derry and Harry Chivers got the match they had lost so much sleep about a year earlier. Donegal travelled with a strong squad and would account for Derry by 1-9 to 0-10. "A defeat would have put us back years," McEniff claimed afterwards, wisely making no mention of the war of attrition that took place on Scottish soil. In Glasgow that weekend, Donegal and Derry had some serious unfinished business to attend to.

The two teams were staying in the same hotel yet relations were so bad that – as late as the Saturday night – the organising committee were considering calling the game off. In the event, it went ahead. In a setting far from home and in a game which held no disciplinary fears, scores were settled right, left and centre. No more, or less, than the rest of them, Shovlin took his opportunity:

> We played on a wee tight rugby pitch and a fair few heavy hits went in. There was a report in a Scottish newspaper and the journalist said he couldn't understand how two men remained on the field, namely, Matt Gallagher and Martin Shovlin. We were even going out over to the line to get involved. It could have really got out of hand!

And, the craic was good too. Manus came back in the New Year following a family tragedy and hit four points against Mayo in MacCumhaill Park. The show kept ticking over and the boys found themselves in a play-off to decide progression to the quarter-finals. It was back to Breffni. In a great game of football the boys were well able for Down. Ten of the September 1992 boys were on, plus Razda. It fell asunder for Donegal and Razda in Croke Park in April. In a poor performance the boys lost by a point to Laois and Razda was the victim of yet another unfortunate sending off. For John Cunningham, nothing was going right:

> I put in a massive effort which was obviously a kick back from not playing in the All-Ireland; I was an honest trainer but I was never that athletic. It was a fantastic game against Laois. I remember the sending off vividly. I got the ball and passed it to Noel Hegarty. This fellow came across to block me so I put out my hand and shoved him. It happened in front of the Hogan Stand and the whole stand erupted. I was running on to take the ball back off Hegarty. Referee Tommy Sugrue let play go on but yer man lay on the ground and Sugrue came back. I continued to play and the linesman put the flag up. That was me sent off.
> Naul McCole and me went up to the GAC. There was a danger that they would double any suspension because I had been sent off for striking in a club game. It was off the ball and there was an extra month then for such incidents. There was a danger that I might get two or three months. I made the appeal and got a month.

Razda was feeling the pressure and didn't feel that he was playing well at the time, "The whole thing was backing up on me then." John felt he was trying too hard and was in a bad state:

> I was safe enough for the Antrim game [in the upcoming championship]

PJ McGowan

so I went to Brian about a week or ten days into the suspension and said to him that I needed to get away, to go on a holiday and clear my head. Brian said, 'Fair enough, away you go'. I went to Crete for a week. I came back refreshed and decided to have another go at it. It was very close to the championship. In fairness, Brian always fancied me for the championship – the only day he didn't fancy me was the day of the All-Ireland final!

That April brought with it a piece of good news. Dungloe and Aodh Ruadh met in a reserve game. Back, playing football for the first time in almost a year, was Tony Boyle. Just in time for the championship of 1994.

The last hurrah then. But the team was already minus the services of a few good men.

❈ ❈ ❈ ❈

Charlie Mulgrew was long gone from the Donegal scene by the summer of 1994 but still had more football to play. St Eunan's were about to re-emerge as a force and Charlie, as ever, would be prominent. They won, and then lost on paper, the county final of 1997 as controversy raged about the legality of Leslie McGettigan. Yet, the highlight of Charlie's career was still ahead of him – the 1999 Donegal senior final. Like 1997 it was against Ballyshannon. This time the result stood and for the first time in 16 years St Eunan's were the Donegal senior football champions.

When the time came Mulgrew would help his old friend Bonner with the county seniors. He now manages St Eunan's and dreams of doing well in an Ulster club championship. Still bustling after all these years.

❈ ❈ ❈ ❈

As he wanders into the Bayview in Killybegs in July 2003, Barry Cunningham looks hardly a day older than the long-haired warrior who tore the hearts out of the Dubs. On his way from training the Killybegs minor side, Cunningham is putting it all back in. When he talks of football it is with assurance. Measured. And discerning.

He wouldn't be there either for the championship of 1994. That summer he was 27 years of age but his glory days in a county jersey were already well behind him. An old injury finally caught up:

I originally got injured when I was 14 and the same injury was there for ten years. I didn't have it at all in 1992 but it came back as soon as I started playing the league in early 1993. It was a severe groin injury that was probably brought on by the training the year before. I aggravated it two weeks before the 1993 Ulster final and never kicked another ball for

Donegal after it. I haven't been the same player for the club either – I can even feel the injury even now.

That was probably a throwback to the amount of football I played when I was a kid. I remember playing five games a week during the winter when I was at school in Falcarragh between soccer and Gaelic. It had to take its toll.

Now he has taken a first tentative step towards management at county level. In 2003 he was a mentor with the under-21 side managed by Seanie McEniff. With the passion Cunningham has for Donegal football, it isn't difficult to envisage the Killybegs man taking the managerial reins at club or county level. He has strong opinions on the state of Donegal football and even though those opinions were expressed prior to Donegal's long summer of football in 2003, they remain valid:

My big regret with Donegal football is that we never built on 1992 and, as far as I'm concerned, it has been downhill all the way. The only way to change that is bringing the youth up. Guys that are 15 now will be 18 in three years' time and that's not a long time. What they're doing with the school of excellence is the only way to go. More has to be done in the schools.

It seems likely that Donegal hasn't seen the last of Barry Cunningham. Football in the county will surely be the better for it:

If there's something that you can do you have to at least consider doing it – no more than me deciding to come back from the States. I would like to give other people the same chance that I got because it is fantastic. It is the memory of your lifetime.

❋ ❋ ❋ ❋

One of the most honest combatants ever to pull on the Donegal jersey was also gone by that summer of 1994. Michael Gallagher, or 'Big G' as the boys called him, hadn't arrived on the scene until 1989 but had won many admirers with his hard grafting. He gave up after the defeat by Derry in 1993, "My career came to an end because of the long travel – I was living in Dublin and I just couldn't keep it going. I had a young family. I worked as a carpenter on the sites so it just all took its toll." As much as any of them he had good times and bad. 1992 was special:

It was such an achievement for a crowd of lads who were in the twilight of their careers. Personally, it was the one year that I carried injury for most of the championship and it curtailed my own ambition but being part of it was still a great thing.

Sam's for the Hills

Football has now taken a back seat. Sort of:

I gave up the club scene two years ago. I was in an accident and suffered a broken pelvis, so that put an end to it. But I'd never say never. It's very hard to hang up the boots. I keep in reasonable shape so, who knows, I might play reserve football next year!

❈ ❈ ❈ ❈

If 1992 was seen, even at the time, as the last hurrah for the boys, 1994 was surely the last possible quest for Sam by the vast majority of the class of 1992. First up was Antrim in Casement Park. McEniff was in a position to name all but two of his All-Ireland 15: Gary Walsh; John Joe Doherty, Matt Gallagher, Mark Crossan; Barry McGowan, John Cunningham, Noel Hegarty; Anthony Molloy, Brian Murray; James McHugh, Martin McHugh, Joyce McMullan; Declan Bonner, Tony Boyle, Manus Boyle.

Rambo, Reid, Ryan and Shov were watching on as the boys won, 1-12 to 1-9. Tony Boyle was back to his brilliant best with Bonner revelling in his presence. Barry McGowan and Molloy – for all the mileage in his weary legs – were also very sound. Rambo eventually came in for a tired Molloy while Tommy Ryan also made an appearance.

The end came on Sunday, July 26, 1994 in Breffni Park against Tyrone in the Ulster semi-final – 0-10 to 1-15 the final score. The Tyrone of Canavan, Cush, Lawn and Donaghy were fully worthy of their eight-point winning margin. Donegal were, on paper, as close to full-strength as could be. McEniff started the same team as started against Antrim. John Duffy came on for an injured Martin McHugh after 27 minutes. Tommy Ryan replaced Joyce, and Rambo, his own career in tatters because of injury, came on for Big Molloy.

"A special team have finally come to the end of the line," sighed Michael Daly in the *Donegal Democrat*. They had, and they knew it. Big Molloy was dejected as he made his way to the sideline that afternoon in Cavan. As Donegal supporters filed out of the grounds they knew there would be changes ahead. In the dressing room under the Breffni Park stand, the break up of the greatest football team Donegal had ever seen was taking place. The dressing room door was locked. Applause could be heard. And then, one by one, the boys filed out ashen-faced. Molloy, the greatest warrior of all, had tears streaming down his face. It was all over. McEniff confirmed that he had called it a day. The Old Man was gone. And with his going the break-up began. The boys who brought Sam to the Hills would never field in such numbers again in the green and gold.

❈ ❈ ❈ ❈

The Long Goodbye

The disintegration of the team was difficult even for those remaining. One of the youngest members of the panel was Paul Callaghan, the young goalkeeper from Burt. He has a particularly poignant and telling memory. "When I joined the panel in 1991 it was impossible to get the back seat on the bus. That was were all the craic was. After 1993 it got easier and easier to get a seat there. Eventually no-one sat there at all."

❋ ❋ ❋ ❋

It was the end of a glorious odyssey for Anthony Molloy. In his going, Donegal supporters lost a favourite son. Never again would they see Molloy scatter bodies as he inspired all around him by pulling a ball out of the sky. Now, all these years later, the man who lifted Sam sits in the Nesbitt Arms Hotel in his native Ardara and remembers the day it all ended in Breffni:

> McHugh shipped a heavy knock and was carted off. I was taken off five minutes later and I knew that was my last day in a Donegal jersey. It was a sad moment. I remember walking over to the dugout and thinking to myself that was it. I knew we were going to get beat and that I wouldn't be there the following year. It was also a wee bit of relief. It was becoming harder to do everything. It was harder to go to training, to ice my knee and take the anti-inflammatory tablets. It was time to call a halt. There was no more enjoyment in it.

Molloy is still Molloy. As likable as they come. No airs or graces – the same Big Molloy. What's his favourite football memory outside lifting Sam? The answer is pure down-to-earth Molloy:

> We played Ballyshannon in 1983 and they had seven under-21 county players while we had one – me. We drew with them the first day and beat them by a point the second day. Those were my two best ever games at club level. They were the kingpins of under-age football. I got great satisfaction from that.

Martin Gavigan also remembers that game well. He headed off to Limerick to sit exams the following day with a finger that was in bad shape. Now, as Molloy walked away, Rambo was sorry to see his old friend go. It wouldn't be the same without the big man. "We played a lot of games together and got involved in a few scuffles along the way but Molloy would fight for you always," recalled Gavigan, "You always had somebody on your side when Anthony was about."

Before 1994 was out Molloy was appointed manager of the county minor team – the first of two three-year spells. "It's the best thing I have ever done. I

got great enjoyment out of doing that," says Molloy. In 1996 he steered the
minors to an Ulster title. Along the way he made decisions managers have to
make. One stood out:

> I made a decision that I'll regret for a while in the Laois match [the All-
> Ireland semi-final]. We were eight or nine points down that day and I
> knew that we'd have to have a good spell at some time in that match –
> and we did. We got a free with a minute to go to equalise. I decided to
> bring on the man who had already done the same thing for me in the
> Ulster final. It worked out that day but it didn't work out against Laois.
> I think we could have won the All-Ireland minor title that year.

Molloy enjoyed the management side of things, "The respect was there and I got
great satisfaction out of it". He missed playing every Sunday and this was the
next best thing. Management of the Donegal seniors seems inevitable:

> It's a hell of a big job. Brian would have put a lot of pressure on me to
> take it over early in 2003. It's a job for a retired person. I met Páidí Ó Sé
> in Dingle recently. He sat back and closed his eyes and told me that to
> be a manager you have to go to bed thinking about it and wake up think-
> ing about it. That's the way it would have to be if you were to do it right.
> I'd never rule it out. I think we have enough natural footballers in
> Donegal. People say that we don't have the talent but I don't agree. There
> are certain eras where a good crop of players might come together. I don't
> know about the senior job but I'd definitely think about coming back
> again to the minor or under-21 posts. I feel we have an awful lot of raw
> talent at under-age in this county, it's just a matter of focusing it.

Everywhere he goes strangers greet him by name. The man who lifted Sam is a
living legend. There will be other footballers who will wear the green and gold,
but without a shadow of a doubt, there will never be another Molloy. "Anthony
Molloy, like the memories of 1992, will never be forgotten," wrote Ciaran
O'Donnell in the *Derry Journal* shortly after his going. After all, the image of
Molloy raising Sam Maguire is indelibly imprinted in the minds of Donegal
people everywhere.

❋ ❋ ❋ ❋

With McEniff gone, the Donegal job was up for grabs. PJ McGowan, the man who
had the Midas touch with the vocational schools and the under-21s of 1987, was
interested. So too were Donal Reid and the Wee Man. When it became known that
McHugh's hat was in the ring, it looked very much a one-horse race. He wanted

the position in the context of player-manager he said. Not a problem, thought an entire county of football supporters. What transpired was very different.

McHugh didn't know it then but he had kicked his last ball for Donegal. Nine years later, sitting in the foyer of the Cavan Crystal Hotel, Martin McHugh is talking football. Heads turn. Elbows and fingers are pointed to draw attention to the man in the grey suit. Hands are raised in salute. Cavan folk, it appears, revere McHugh as something of a messiah. McHugh is talking about the events of August 1994 when he went for the Donegal job. Cavan hadn't got him then:

> I wouldn't have gone for the Donegal job unless I thought I was capable of doing the job. People look at records – I trained the Kilcar team in 1985 and we won the championship. I managed the club team in 1987, 1988 and 1989 and we contested three consecutive county finals. We were beaten by Killybegs by a last-minute goal in 1988. I felt Ballyshannon had one of the best club teams in Ireland and they beat us in 1987 but we beat them in 1989. We also won two leagues. We contested three All-Ireland Gaeltacht finals and won two of them. The club had achieved a lot.
>
> Questions will be asked if I would have been able to drop or manage fellas that I would have played with. My next door neighbour and best friend was captain of Kilcar in 1989 and I dropped him for the county semi-final. He was off form, I dropped him and he accepted it.

McHugh recalls the fateful evening he learned he wouldn't be the next manager of his county:

> I was interviewed for the job by a committee. The following three years of Donegal football was at stake and I had my plan drawn up. The meeting was called for, say seven o'clock and I arrived at 6.30 p.m. Some of the committee started arriving at seven – I thought it was terrible organisation for dealing with the future of Donegal football. I went into the meeting but they hadn't a question made out. I told them that I'd put my plan to them and they could ask me questions about it.
>
> I always had good time for Mickey McLoone. I had met him beforehand and asked him to be a selector with me. He immediately told me he would do it. Having a person like that behind me was good. I had put a lot of thought and time into it. That's why it was so disappointing. It would have been great to have Mickey McLoone involved in Donegal football. He'll probably never be involved in it now.
>
> I outlined my plan and they then started to ask questions. Looking back, I'd have to say some of the questions were ridiculous. One man even asked me if I was serious about Mickey McLoone – as if I would joke about that. Looking back, I wasn't going to get that job even as I went into the meeting.

We were called over to be told the outcome. Donal Reid was to be called at 6.30, I was to be called at 7.00 and PJ was to be called at 7.30. I arrived at 7.00 and Donal still hadn't been called in. The three of us were sitting there in Heaney's Bar. Reid was called in first. One of us told the other that neither had got the job. It was a bad way to handle it. There was to be a County Executive meeting followed by a full County Board meeting afterwards. I was told the vote was unanimous and that the five on the committee went for PJ. I went in anyway and they told me I didn't get the job and they started to tell me the reasons for it. I told them to stop, said thanks and walked out.

Donegal folk would never get the opportunity to see McHugh as player-manager. According to McHugh, that was one reason given for him not getting the job:

This is a rare thing, but I always found it was easier to be a player-manager than managing from the sideline. I could manage a team more easily from the field because I could see what was going on better. If you're on the line your nerves are at you and you're all hyped up, whereas if you're on the field you're playing and concentrating on your own game and I could always see things better when I was on the field. I had good men with me and they were going to call the shots on the line. The selection committee told me that I couldn't be a player-manager. I think that is totally and utterly wrong.

If the selection committee were unsure of the merits of player-managers, McHugh would argue they needed look no further than the likes of Dublin's Tony Hanahoe. And there was an example closer to home – Brian McEniff himself. There is more than a trace of regret in McHugh's voice as he talks about it now:

I was very hurt about the whole thing. The reason I haven't taken the Donegal job since has nothing to do with sour grapes. I felt that I deserved a chance at that time. I didn't know the politics of it. Up until the last minute I thought I was going to get it. When I was a player I would have often represented the players and looked for gear and argued about expenses etc. – the board didn't want me. I didn't canvass anyone. McEniff has recently publicly said that he should have backed me at that time.

All McHugh needed from McEniff was a nod in the right direction. It wasn't forthcoming. "Martin would have been disappointed that maybe I didn't support him," McEniff told TG4 years later. McHugh was well aware of it:

I would have backed him in 1987 and 1989. It's too late now. I would love to have worked with Murray, Gavigan, Declan Bonner and Barry McGowan. Donegal had a lot of good players and I would have loved to work with them. There were new players too – Declan Boyle and John Duffy were fabulous footballers. I thought there was a lot to work with. I thought Donegal was the most talented team in Ireland at that time. Other teams were improving but the talent was there. I felt I was right for the job at that time. I really wanted it.

When it came down to it, McEniff had no vote. Nine years later McEniff recalls the events:

> PJ McGowan, Martin McHugh and Donal Reid went for the job. Donal was only putting his hat into the ring – he later managed the under-21s. Martin never asked me to be a selector with him. Maybe later I would have returned refreshed and returned as a mentor. At that time I thought I had done enough and had to get out.
>
> PJ McGowan had a great CV and a good record of winning All-Irelands. He was also a member of the County Executive and may have been on the Ulster Council at a time.
>
> Naul McCole, Danny McNamee, Tom Daly, Connie Maguire and Hughie McClafferty, were, I think, the board chosen to select the manager. The vote for PJ was 4-0. Martin was upset about it. It's a shame that Martin didn't stay on because I'm quite sure he and PJ could have worked together. I was sad because I felt that together, PJ and Martin could have at least won an Ulster title. PJ took them to a national league final so the residue was still there.

Now, almost a decade on, it is easier for McHugh to be more philosophical about the whole thing:

> Not getting the job might have been the best thing that ever happened me. If I had taken the job I might have fallen out with a lot of the players because I would have been ruthless enough to drop them. I felt we could have won an All-Ireland. The County Board didn't want me. It could have sent me to my grave and might have cost me money. At the end, perhaps they did me a big favour by not giving me the job.

There are others who regretted that McHugh didn't get the reins – those who felt the Wee Man could have squeezed something special out of Donegal. Molloy's boots were already hung up but he felt McHugh was the man for the job:

> It was handled badly by the County Board. PJ McGowan was – and still

is – a very good friend of mine and went for the job. But McHugh had the support of that bunch of players. Most of them knew him and knew what he would have wanted. The County Board should have worked something out but they cut McHugh off completely.

Molloy reckons that McHugh, had he been given the job, would have recaptured Sam:

> I think so, without doubt. He proved himself by going to Cavan and bringing a Division Three team to Division One. Some of the players didn't perform for him in the All-Ireland semi-final against Kerry but he still wasn't far away. McHugh was a born manager. There was nothing he didn't know about the game – he proved that with Cavan. He was around a long time and the boys had a lot of respect for him.

Molloy's old midfield colleague, Brian Murray, was equally appreciative of the Wee Man's managerial capabilities:

> When you think about what he achieved afterwards with Cavan – everybody thought he was the right man for the Donegal job but other people felt he was too close to some of the players. Maybe he was the right man for the job when you see what he did later. Maybe Martin would have got more out of other players. He would have taken no shit and pulled no punches. He was very well respected.

Some supporters felt that PJ McGowan's undoubted managerial strength lay at under-age level. Yet PJ deserved his chance with the seniors as much as any man. Declan Bonner, who would succeed McGowan as manager, appreciated that it was a difficult situation:

> I don't know if McHugh could have squeezed an All-Ireland from the team at that time but maybe he could have. It was a difficult job for PJ McGowan to come into as maybe 18 or 20 of the players had All-Ireland medals. The County Board may have been reluctant to make a change like that but the players wanted Martin. Martin had played with us and was a good leader. It was a difficult time.

Manus Boyle has no doubts about what McHugh might have achieved:

> There is no doubt whatsoever that McHugh would have squeezed an All-Ireland out of the team. The 1995 team was the best team to emerge since 1992. Players were starting to play very well. McHugh knew the play-

ers and could have done very well with them.

Noel Hegarty is of the same opinion as Manus:

The thing about Martin McHugh was he was very strong-minded for a start. He was a good man. He wouldn't be afraid of telling you where to get off when other people might have been. He stood us up in the dressing room in Omagh in 1992 and said 'we start today'. If we hadn't started the hard training, we'd have never have made it. That will have to go down to him.

Martin Gavigan is utterly sure that McHugh was the man for the job:

Another chapter that should have gone a different way. McHugh should have been there. Everybody might have got a second chance. McHugh would have took us well on the way to another All-Ireland. We saw what he did with Kilcar for years, then Cavan and then with Sligo IT. Donegal had a lot of players and some good young fellows and I think McHugh deserved a chance at the time. I would have been all for it.

Others are not so sure if there was another All-Ireland in the team. Martin Shovlin thinks maybe the glory days were gone by then. Yet he appreciated McHugh's breadth of knowledge of the game:

I think the backbone of the team was probably past it at that stage. His players were gone by then. It was a matter of rebuilding.
    But Martin was a great reader of a game in all fairness. He could see weaknesses and strengths no bother. He'd often speak out. I don't mind boys speaking up as long as they know what they're talking about and McHugh knew what he was talking about.

Barry McGowan was also unsure:

At that stage the team was at a juncture. There were really two teams. We had a lot of young players coming in. I do not know whether Martin McHugh could have succeeded in winning an Ulster title. I can only speculate. But he was a very good manager.

Brian McEniff, the man who proclaimed McHugh as the greatest Donegal footballer ever, thinks Sam was beyond the team of 1995, "I don't know that there was another All-Ireland in them, I think our last chance of an All-Ireland was 1994".

Speculation was irrelevant. Martin McHugh's association with Donegal senior football stretching back 138 games to the winter of 1980 was over. The most decorated Donegal footballer of all time was lost to the county. McHugh says:

> The chairman of Cavan had approached me before I went for the Donegal job but I told him I wasn't interested in talking to him as the job I wanted was Donegal manager. When I didn't get the Donegal job, Cavan came back again. In fairness to PJ McGowan, when I went for the Donegal job it meant that my career with Donegal was over. I couldn't be there and undermining PJ. If I had got the job I could have played on for another year or whatever. It was an easy enough decision to make when Cavan came back to me. Yet it was hateful because I might have been able to play with Donegal for another year or two. I regret that but I had no option. As soon as I went for the job I left myself with no option.

And so, in 1994, McHugh took on a Cavan team that had lost its way. They had last won Ulster in 1969 and weren't expected to do anything. But McHugh brought his huge reputation as an achiever with him to Cavan. While the Wee Man was inexperienced in terms of inter-county management, his playing achievements were such that people sat up and listened. He had a huge effect on the Cavan players. He went the Donegal route but in a fraction of the time. He marched them from Division Three to Division One and then tackled the championship. He took them to an Ulster final in 1997 where they beat a Brian Mullins-managed Derry. Cavan's long famine was over and a wee man from Bavin had proven a big point. Seldom was an Ulster final victory celebrated with such emotion and delight. McHugh became an instant folk-hero in Cavan.

Along the way his Cavan had met Donegal in Clones:

> It was a sad day for me when Cavan beat Donegal as it was the end of Donegal that day. Players retired after that. It was PJ McGowan's last day so I ended up beating him in his last game as manager after both of us had gone for the job three years previous. I have a great grá for Donegal. I had grá for Cavan too, but it's different.

McHugh was back in Croke Park where Kerry provided the opposition. Cavan lost 1-17 to 1-10 but put up a good showing. McHugh had decided that 1997 was to be his last year with Cavan as there was a lot of travelling involved. Many seasoned observers saw it a little differently. Cavan were not the most talented football team in the country and many believed that the mercurial McHugh had taken this team as far – maybe further – as it could go. He moved on. Shrewdly.

Since then he has most notably turned his managerial gaze to third-level football and steered Sligo IT to Sigerson Cup success in 2002. Many onlookers felt it even surpassed his exploits with Cavan. It started off as a "one-night a week" job but soon he was hooked and training was upped to three times a week. He used to train the team at 7 a.m. on Friday mornings to allow the lads go home that evening. Without any irony whatsoever, McHugh modestly complimented the students, "That kind of commitment you don't get from everybody."

McHugh's face continues to be well known in Ulster and beyond. A regular analyst on the BBC's coverage of Gaelic games, the Wee Man from Kilcar is as famous as ever almost a decade after his last campaign for Donegal. Now, at the end of July 2003, McHugh sits in a Cavan hotel and ponders the question a whole county occasionally occupies itself with – do you think you'd ever take the Donegal job?

> I'd never say never. I've always said that I'd love to manage Donegal but the time is not right at the moment. When I do something I put my whole life into it. When I was managing Cavan my whole life was Cavan football. There was a huge level of professionalism brought to the job. It would have been great to do that with Donegal. I'm not taking it away from Cavan – I enjoyed my time there – but it would have been nice to do it with Donegal footballers.
>
> When I went back home after the Cavan job my little daughter hardly knew me. That was lost time. It's not worth it for that reason alone. It's all right for the likes of Mick O'Dwyer, his family is reared now. I'd love to manage Donegal at some stage. It's nothing to do with me not getting the job in 1994 even though people will say that. I'm a very single-minded person and I make up my mind about what I'm going to do. That issue is over now.

❊ ❊ ❊ ❊

There was another victim of the 1994 managerial race. A victim whose story almost got lost in the hullabaloo about McHugh. Donal Reid had played 135 times for the Donegal seniors. And expected to add to that tally. He'd had his fair share of injuries down the years but the most cruel blow of all didn't manifest itself until the Ulster semi-final of 1993:

> We drew with Armagh in the first game and I cracked my shoulder blade. That was my last ever game for Donegal. I couldn't play in the replay. We couldn't find what was wrong with my scapula until a week or two before the Ulster final when a scan revealed a crack in it. I couldn't play, even with an injection.

Even so, as the summer of 1994 approached, Reid was still thinking football. He wouldn't kick a ball that summer but was still burning with intent. So much so that he applied for the Donegal job when McEniff called it a day. He was beaten but had no regrets:

> I felt PJ McGowan was the man for it because he had won All-Ireland titles at under-21 and vocational schools levels. In my opinion he was the natural successor. I went for the interview as I was marking my card for the future. Martin McHugh also went for the job. The emphasis was on McHugh and PJ and not me. I feel that I did a very good interview for the job. I thought my interview went too well because I was afraid I'd actually get the job. I know Martin was annoyed that he didn't get it.

Reid was happy enough with his experience. He'd taken from the interview what he wanted:

> I didn't really want the job because I still wanted to play for another year. Martin probably should have got the job. I don't know how his interview went but maybe it was the way the board perceived Martin, after all, he was still a player. I don't think it was a personal thing, I think it was because he was young. Martin McHugh proved himself afterwards and showed himself to be an exceptional manager.

Reid had to have an operation on his knee in September 1994 but was hoping to be back in action for the seniors in the New Year of 1995. What the Red Hughs' man didn't know was that his career was over. He would never kick another ball for his beloved green and gold. He no longer fitted into future plans for Donegal football. It wasn't quite how he had envisaged the end:

> Because of the way 1993 ended for me, I wanted to play on. I had given so many years to Donegal and still thought there was half an hour or 20 minutes left in me. I felt I could have been a steadying influence coming in and played a panel role. I thought that would have been good for the morale of the team. I had been with Donegal in good times and bad times. I think it's important to have players like that on any panel.

Reid says he was the only player dropped from the previous panel. Others that didn't play retired or moved on of their own accord but not Reid – the man wasn't ready to retire, "I felt I could put back into football what I got out of it. I enjoyed the game. I went for the position of under-21 manager with Red Hughs but lost it in a vote."

He was appointed Donegal under-21 manager in October 1994, replacing PJ McGowan, the man who defeated McHugh and himself for the senior post. Reid,

Sylvester Maguire

Michael Gallagher

Paul Carr

photograph courtesy of Irish News

378

assisted by Seamus O'Reilly, would go on to claim an Ulster title with the under-21s in 1995. Donegal beat Cavan in a replay in Enniskillen by 3-11 to 1-11.

Martin McHugh and me ended up on opposite sides of the fence when I managed the Donegal under-21s and Martin managed the Cavan under-21s. I beat Martin's Cavan in the Ulster final. I suppose we were pitting our wits against one another. I was glad for him when Cavan won the Ulster Senior Football Championship because he was a friend of mine, and still is a friend. He proved his point. Some people didn't like what he did, but for me that is neither here nor there. I don't have an opinion on that, nor did I have an opinion on it at the time when he was managing Cavan opposite me. He had a job to do and I had one to do. He chose Cavan and I chose Donegal. We shook hands after the match and there were no ill feelings. I respected Martin McHugh as a player and a manager and I still do.

Donal has since successfully coached and managed at club level in Tyrone although he insists that 2003 is his last year. "I'm taking a year out of football next year. I've had enough, the battery has gone flat." Sitting in Jackson's Hotel, Ballybofey, in the summer of 2003, Reid's immense passion for Gaelic football is clear to see. He says he is going to try to be selfish over the next couple of years and look after himself and his family. That said, it is difficult to see him ever being without football:

I enjoyed football immensely. We give out about football a lot but I have a passion for it – I'll always be involved in it. I cannot see myself not being involved in it. My family has talked on several occasions about moving to South Africa. It is another passion of mine – my wife and I love the country, we have friends out there and have been there on holidays a few times. When we've come close to emigrating I've changed my mind because of football. I'm not even playing – I'm managing, albeit a senior club in Tyrone. I've held back from emigrating because of football! I know in my heart and soul that I'd miss it too much. I suppose I'd be on the Internet checking results. Football is in my blood and I can't change that although there are times when I'd love it not to be there.

Reid knows there is more to life than football. He had a good friend in – and went back a long way with – Seamus O'Reilly, the man who assisted him with the under-21s in 1995. Indeed O'Reilly took over from his friend as manager when Reid stepped down. O'Reilly died suddenly and young in April 1999. Football men and women who knew him were stunned. Reid was heartbroken and penned an eloquent and moving tribute.

Just listening to Donal Reid for an hour is an education about the sacrifices made by the boys who brought Sam to the Hills. Much of Reid's story can be mapped onto the lives of others. It is a story told without bitterness. Although some of the comments below have been used earlier in this book, it is worth reading again. Reid speaks in facts and tells it the way it was:

There were many, many funny incidents that kept us going. Some of them would be below the belt and some of them would seem cynical but they were good fun to us. You could write a book and let people see what a footballer's life is like. We made nothing from football – I didn't make a red cent out of football. However, I did make a lot of friends and my social circle revolved around that. I had hard times as well. I spent time in hospital. I lost money from work and travel. I missed my children growing up. I missed them from they were babies until they were at national school. People never see that. People go to matches on a Sunday and see players in a jersey. Spectators criticise us as amateur players.

If someone has inadvertently made a few pounds from football then I will make no apologies for it. I have sacrificed so much. On the day that my first child was born, I went to the hospital, collected my wife Maura and brought her and the child back to the house. I didn't even have time for a cup of tea and took my boots and went off to training at Murvagh beach. At the start of the year, Tom Conaghan had told us that barring death, we were to be at training. That is how serious it was. I wouldn't do that nowadays. I put football before everything; I put it before family and work.

Football has to be put into its proper place. In hindsight, we didn't do that. We deserved an All-Ireland title, we deserved three All-Ireland titles but did not get them. We were professional footballers in an amateur era.

If people only knew the real story. Many's the night we trained on snow at Murvagh or Inver beach. The manager would put on the lights of his car and we had to run to it. We used to run for five or six miles on the beach. We would go around a corner and find Conaghan waiting on us with his hands in his pockets and roaring us on. We were up to our knees in sand and the froth was hanging from our mouths. We had to round him and run back up the beach. That was tough. I had a friend, a black fella from South Africa that I had met at college, staying with me at that time. He was shocked. He was watching from the dunes and couldn't believe the training we were doing as amateur footballers. He told me the SAS wouldn't have done the training he saw us doing.

People put you on a pedestal and expect you to behave accordingly. Even as a club player you are an ambassador for your club. There is a fine line. As I tell my players in Aghyarn, if they are misbehaving when they're out they are letting both themselves and their club down. By playing football they are making a statement and must treat football as it should be treated.

It has gone over the top at county level. Players do not get thousands of euro, they never have and never will. It actually cost us money to play inter-county football. People sometimes look at us and think we're worth fortunes but we're not. Those of us that are grounded would have used football to further our careers. I have done three courses since I finished playing football – courses that I should have done while I was playing. I have studied physiotherapy and physical therapy over six years. I'm now a qualified physical therapist and I did not have time to do that when I was playing football. It cost me about €10,000 to do these courses. These are qualifications that I should have had a long time ago. It's a safety net for me and my family. At least I will have something to fall back on because football wouldn't have provided that. Football won't put bread and butter on your table or shoes on your wain's feet.

I could go on. I would love to be able to write a book without fear of recrimination and tell the real stories of what is behind it all. I would write about the craic we had, the tears we've had and the fall outs we've had. We cried together and laughed together – we were very close as a team. If any footballer has had the same time in his career as I have had, they will have had a good time. I had a good time. Football was good to me and I was good to football. That time was the best years of my life. Most of us have remained friends even now, 11 years on. We will remain friends into our more mature years.

✻ ✻ ✻ ✻

Joyce knew it was time. Knew that the team hadn't really risen to the challenge in 1994. There was a lot of wear and tear and burnout in the side. He felt the edge had been dulled with the sense of achievement that came from winning an All-Ireland for the first time. It was difficult to train and get worked up for games in 1994. The decision to walk away, when it came, was no longer hard to make:

It was an easy enough decision. We had found it difficult to prepare for the Tyrone match. The whole championship was a struggle that year. I had been involved for 13 campaigns and the time was right to leave.

He's still playing football though. He looks every bit as fit as he did when a player all those years ago as he sits talking football during lunchtime in Donegal Town:

I'm still playing a bit of reserve football with the club. It's still great to get out and do a bit of training. It's good to go out and train with the young lads for state of mind or whatever you want to call it.

And good times were had with the boys in the green and gold, "We made a lot of friends and had a lot of craic and had many good days and nights out".

❄ ❄ ❄ ❄

Paul Carr had soldiered a long time. His was a lengthy tenure in the Donegal jersey. One of Conaghan's boys of 1982, Carr had been a valuable commodity through several eras since. Now, 12 years later, it was time to go and like the old soldier he was no-one had to tell him:

I joined the panel first as a 16-year-old under the management of Sean O'Donnell around 1980. I was there or there abouts right through until 1994 mostly under the management of Brian McEniff and I can tell you I saw a lot of changes during that time.

It came to an end in 1994 after we went out of the championship. Brian had stepped down and I had moved home to Sligo – although I did play for one more year for Sligo after that which was a mistake.

Like the others, he had his special memories:

It was up in the Hogan Stand when we lifted the Cup. I remember getting my hands on Sam and turning around to the Hogan Stand and catching my father's eye – now that was special to me.

Paul and Brian Tuohy are currently looking after a club in Sligo and Paul has made a few appearances as a player. He was involved in the Donegal team which defeated Dublin in the All-Ireland masters final in October.

❄ ❄ ❄ ❄

PJ McGowan, the man who had tasted glory with the vocational schools and the 1987 under-21s, was now in the hot seat. And why not – after all his football CV was an impressive one:

I did expect to get the job because I had managed at inter-county level, I'd also played for Donegal under Brian McEniff and I would have been involved with Brian for a number of years, going away back to when I was the trainer of the side. I'd managed Fermanagh and I'd managed school teams and the under-21 teams, whereas the other boys were still playing. Martin McHugh should still have been playing that year, but I suppose he didn't feel like playing when he didn't get the job, and he headed away to Cavan.

The Long Goodbye

The whole managerial race had left its share of bad taste but that was neither of the making of PJ McGowan nor of concern to him. He had a job to do and he set about doing it. Sometimes though, it wasn't easy:

> It was an ageing team in many ways, a lot of them had All-Ireland medals, Anthony Molloy had retired by that stage and the side was in need of rebuilding. Some of the fellows didn't want to quit. They enjoyed inter-county football so much and it had been good to them. I suppose it was my unenviable job of easing these boys out, and bringing new boys in to shape a new team and that was fraught with difficulties.

He steered Donegal to the national league final in 1995, scoring wins along the way against Down, Derry, Dublin, Meath, Kildare, Clare and Laois. McGowan remembers the Down game well:

> The very first game I was involved in the senior team was a national league game against Down in Newry. It was Down's first game after winning the All-Ireland final and we set up a guard of honour for them. We waited and waited and they didn't come out. The boys broke up and then we heard they were coming so we formed up again. They came out of the dressing room and ran past us and entered the field at the other end. Some of the boys said 'To hell with this'. It was a real snub. We went out and beat the lining out of them.

Who else but Derry awaited in the league final. And it was Derry who added to their national league title of 1992 – the boys falling by 0-8 to 0-12.

By the time the championship of 1995 came around, another of the boys had fallen by the wayside.

❋ ❋ ❋ ❋

It's the mid-morning of a blazing hot summer's day in Kilmacrennan. In at the back, in a quiet spot of his bar, Tommy Ryan sips water and drags on a cigarette. The story he has just told has been one of incredible highs and harrowing lows. Now, several years on, he recalls the end of the road:

> Things that happen in GAA always come back to haunt you. Myself and PJ McGowan never got on after what happened in the All-Ireland under-21 final. He never started me in a game. I asked myself what was the point of holding up the bench when I'd been playing for the previous five or six years. It wasn't that I was even a fringe player; I wasn't getting on. We were playing against bad teams by this time and the quality in Ulster

was starting to dip. I wasn't able to get on the team so I decided to leave. There was no big hullabaloo about it. I just said to myself that I wasn't going to travel around the country to be a sub. I might have been working in Mayo and then driving back to training. It was just the way things happened. The bottom line is that the manager didn't play me and, as manager, that was his prerogative. It wasn't the way I wanted to leave. I would preferred to leave when I was finished. If I was capable of playing at 19 and 20, surely I was capable of playing at 27 and 28.

There was football left in Tommy. He turned his attention to his native Termon and plugged away. And picked up the odd medal along the way and more to the point, enjoyed his football. And he's playing still. Termon surprised everyone by making to their first ever county senior final in October 2003. Tommy took his place up front but having struggled with injury all year, he was forced to withdraw early. Unfortunately there was no fairlytale ending for Termon, or Tommy, as Four Masters claimed their first senior title since 1984.

❆ ❆ ❆ ❆

Sylvester Maguire has been good to Donegal football. It's over now for Sylvester and Donegal. It was a long road and in the end he sort of faded away:

> At the end of 1994 club championships I was team captain in Ballyshannon and we won the championship that year in Donegal. We were through to the Ulster club and beat Errigal Ciaran in the first round. Then we were drawn against Bellaghy so I stayed away from county football at that stage to concentrate on the club. Then I came down with a viral infection and had to hold back and take a break on medical advice.
>
> I went back for a county trial around the turn of the year and did quite well but I didn't get called back. I think myself, Reid and Joyce were let go then. That was under PJ McGowan but there was no personal animosity between PJ and me. He made a call and it was hard to take at the time, but I've had to make similar calls as a club manager and under-21 selector. Every manager has to make a call and it's just one of those things. If your time's up, it's up.

That wasn't to say that football had seen the last of him. Like a lot of the boys he has too much football knowledge not to share. Aodh Ruadh have benefited.

> I've been managing club for a number of years and we won the championship for three years in a row. I was player-manager for 1997, 1998 and 1999 I and finished up at the end of 2000. I came back as manager in 2002

and in between I managed other teams in the club and was involved in school teams. But I've two children now and just want to spend time with my family.

Sylvester is a great man for the stories. Every time he meets Martin Gavigan he tells him the same story. Rambo laughs as he passes it on:

Ardara were playing Ballyshannon in a game and Anthony and Sylvester used to be at one another regularly! One day Sylvester got past Anthony after getting a good shot and was delighted with himself. Then he looked up and saw me coming! All he could do was close his eyes!

❄ ❄ ❄ ❄

Before the All-Ireland series in 1992, Martin Gavigan was bemoaning the fact that Donegal wouldn't get to have a crack at Down. "We owe them a beating, after what they did to us," said Rambo, in reference to the Ulster final disappointment of 1991 when Down had eight points to spare in Clones.

Donegal finally got their chance at Down in Clones in the summer of 1995. By then Down were the defending All-Ireland champions. McGowan had a lot of the boys still available to him – namely Gary Walsh, John Joe Doherty, Matt Gallagher, Barry McGowan, Rambo, Shov, Big Murray, Noel Hegarty, James McHugh, Tony Boyle and Manus Boyle. Bonner would come on as a sub with Paddy Hegarty, Mark Crossan, John Duffy and Mark McShane completed a formidable line-up. It was one of McGowan's greatest days as senior manager as the boys ran through the All-Ireland champions, hitting 1-12 to Down's 0-9.

PJ was enjoying himself – even in the lead up to the match:

In the lead-up to that match, between the national league and the McKenna Cup, we played something like ten matches in 12 weeks. The training required was minimal. All that was required was some ball work but the team were going fairly well although Derry beat us in the national league final. We had Down the following Sunday. Tony Boyle got injured in the league final and, with being beaten in that, nobody expected us to win.

But, by some miracle – and with the help of the back room boys and loads of holy water and one thing and another, Tony recovered – he spent more time in the sea than in his bed! We got him fit and he had a clinker of a game as we beat Down.

It was also a memorable day for Barry McGowan. It was the one and only time he had to mark Mickey Linden. "Thankfully, it was only once. He was an unbelievable player – a real nightmare. Thankfully, Donegal played out of their skin that day and it lessened Linden's effect."

The euphoria of that win was torn asunder in Ballybofey a couple of weeks later as Donegal fell badly, 0-8 to 1-14, to Monaghan. It was one of those days when nothing went right. A huge opportunity was thrown away. McGowan says he saw the signs:

> We had to wait four weeks to play Monaghan and complacency set in. Monaghan swept the board with us. It was a big blow. I could see the signs but I couldn't get it through to the boys to be wary of Monaghan.
>
> We sussed Monaghan completely and we wanted to watch videos one night but the boys had other places to go. After we beat Down, the All-Ireland champions, they thought 'Here we go again to All-Ireland glory', but, believe me, you can fall far short.

❅ ❅ ❅ ❅

Martin Gavigan is as easy-going as they come. The Iron Man from Donegal is a real gentleman. Football is discussed for a couple of hours at his home outside Stranorlar on a Friday night in July 2003. He sinks into a soft chair after a hard day's work and casts his mind back.

The end of the road, when it came, was inevitably linked to his knee and its missing cruciate. Even Rambo, for all his fitness and great strength, could only push it so far. Even so, he was still there in 1995 when Donegal dethroned Down in Clones. Then Monaghan in Ballybofey and disaster. It was his last championship game for the county. By then in the twilight of his career, Martin was not impressed:

> The preparation for that game was brutal. We were doing piggy-backs at training – us with bad knees! We went to Heaney's on the Thursday before the game and boys went all over the town to watch the rugby for an hour – the All-Blacks were playing. There wasn't the right focus. Players thought that Monaghan was going to be a doddle compared to Down. I was disappointed with the whole set-up – it was very unprofessional.

He had a bit of football left to play but it was all over really. Gavigan, the man who believed in always giving one hundred per cent, knew his time was up, "If you're not able to train and be at the top of your game what the point? There was younger players coming on the scene. Leave it with them was my feeling."

And he did. Rambo, the man people paid in to see was now a spectator himself. "It's harder going to games than playing. At least when you're playing you have some say in things!" he laughs now. He sees the boys rarely.

The Long Goodbye

"Everybody is doing different things and has families now," he says, although he did bump into Molloy at a game in Ardara recently.

Sometimes, looking back, he wonders how they did it at all. How they gave the level of commitment they did. At least he was based in Ballybofey. He shakes his head in disbelief as he talks about the boys from Glen:

> That gives you an idea of the commitment that people made. That is dedication to drive from there to training – it was like a day's work for those boys. Year in year out. And the oul' chat that used to go on in the County Board about the few pence expenses and the boys taking cars to training! Noel Hegarty, John Joe and the boys from Kilcar. Rarely did they miss training. There used to be the odd story about them stopping off in the pub on the way back to discuss things. They used to have it all figured out!

But then so too had Martin Gavigan.

❅ ❅ ❅ ❅

An indication of the team's potential was apparent during the national league campaign of 1995-96. For a second year running the boys made it to the final, beating Clare, Tyrone, Laois, and drawing with Meath, Derry and Kildare along the way. Cork were accounted for in the semi-final but yet again Derry proved their worth and had seven points to spare in the final in Croke Park.

And so it went. Old faces and new faces. In 1996 Down had their revenge in the championship, albeit just about, one point the margin in Clones. It was the infamous day that Gary Walsh was alleged to have stepped over the goal-line with the ball. Still on board was the aforementioned Walsh as well as Razda, Matt, Hegarty, Shov, James McHugh, Tony and Manus. New faces, who would write their own chapter, were now established on the first 15 – Damien Diver, James Ruane, Dessie McNamara and Brian Roper. The times were a-changing but PJ McGowan was laying down solid foundations for the future.

An old friend hit the big time in 1996. The minors, under the guidance of Molloy, won the Ulster league and added the championship, beating Derry in the Ulster final by 0-9 to 1-5. The Big Man was back in Croke Park – working with the likes of Barry Monaghan and Michael Hegarty – although his charges would lose by a point to Laois in the All-Ireland semi-final.

The football was becoming mediocre. The national league of 1996-97 was disappointing. Seven games played – only Cavan were beat, draws with Cork and Tyrone and defeat by Kerry, Meath, Derry and Kildare. It was sliding alright. The end was in sight.

The 1997 championship brought Antrim to Ballybofey. "Donegal always struggled against Antrim in the first round of the championship," sighs PJ

McGowan. On this occasion, they again scraped by, 2-12 to 1-13 the score. Paul Callaghan, understudy to Gary Walsh for so long, got a championship debut. Matt, John Joe, Razda, Barry McGowan, Big Murray, Hegarty, Bonner, Tony and Manus were still there. Jim McGuinness made a championship appearance for the first time since 1993. And a new face, Adrian Sweeney from Dungloe, made his first championship appearance.

The McHugh/Donegal saga was about to come full circle. Next up was Cavan in Clones. McHugh and the men from Breffni were on the march to a famous Ulster title and Donegal – with Callaghan, John Joe, Hegarty, Shov, Murray, Bonner, Tony and Manus on board – were next to fall victim. Cavan had six points to spare and McHugh was a match away from becoming a legend down Breffni way. For PJ McGowan, the man who defeated him three years previously in the pursuit of the Donegal job, it was the end of the road. For now.

❄ ❄ ❄ ❄

The Legend was finished. A recurrence of an old injury meant the championship of 1997 would prove to be Declan Bonner's swansong:

I picked up an injury against Wicklow in the national league in 1996. I passed blood when going to the toilet in Virginia on the way back. Dr Kennedy took me straight to Cavan hospital and I had a major operation on my kidney. I didn't play for the rest of that year. I played in the championship the following year but the defeat to Cavan in the 1997 Ulster semi-final was my last game. I got a slap in the same spot and broke two ribs and went off after five minutes of the second-half.

Not everyone expected what happened next. Bonner went for, and got, the Donegal job. The Na Rossa man, at 32 years of age, was the new boss. Almost immediately it seemed Donegal were back on track. Bonner had seen and done it all. He knew about winning as a player at the highest level.

"In my first year we played one of our best ever games against Offaly in Croke Park in the national league semi-final," he recalls. Indeed Donegal had sailed to that semi-final, beating Derry and Armagh along the way. Cork were dispatched in the quarter-final. But Offaly, on their way to their first league title, would prove a bridge too far in April 1998 and Donegal were on the wrong side of a 1-14 to 3-10 scoreline.

❄ ❄ ❄ ❄

Gary Walsh, the greatest goalkeeper to stand between the posts for Donegal, sits forward on the couch of his home in Derry and recalls his final championship.

The Long Goodbye

And how he was quite happy to embrace it when it came:

My last game was in 1996 and I was a sub in 1997. The infamous goal incident against Down took a lot out of me emotionally. Whether it was a goal or not, I can never say but the way the referee gave it and the whole attitude was hard to take. I took it very badly and I still get hung up whenever I think about it or someone talks about it. I met a fella in Clones [at the replayed Ulster final 2003] and he passed a smart comment on it. I just turned and walked away from it. Even worse for me was the fact that I was working in Down at the time. I got an anonymous phone call the following morning from some smart alec.

I didn't play well that year and Paul [Callaghan] had been on the panel for a number of years and definitely deserved his chance in 1997. Nobody likes being left off, but I knew I wasn't playing well enough to be selected in the 1997 championship. I fully agreed with PJ McGowan's decision to play Paul Callaghan in 1997.

Gary was beginning to feel the pain of a dozen championship campaigns. He is honest in his appraisal of his role in Donegal football. He had no doubt his weary body was telling him that time was most definitely up:

I've had bother with my back in recent years. Kicking the ball off the ground requires a lot of force. In training you do a lot of diving and are hitting the ground a lot. You feel great at the time but I was 31 in 1996 and was feeling my age for the first time.

Walsh, the 'Quiet Man' as the boys christened him, called it a day. Six years later a 'phone call from Bundoran would initiate another dalliance with the green and gold – this time as goalkeeping coach. Walsh loved it. The summer of 2003 stretched long for Donegal football folk as a new squad of boys made it to an All-Ireland semi-final. It was an opportunity for Walsh to watch McEniff in action one more time:

He's a great man. People criticise him and it's easy for people to criticise someone who puts himself up there. I can see the amount of things he does for Donegal football. If anybody has more pride in Donegal football, I have yet to meet him. He's a great man and I owe him a personal debt of gratitude for taking me into the panel in the first place and giving me a chance. His dedication to Donegal football has never waned. He rang me after the Fermanagh game [in June 2003] and we spoke for half an hour. I'd say he may not have slept all week and he looked like a fella that hadn't slept all week. He looked like death warmed up after the Fermanagh game.

I see a different side of him now. The role of manager has changed, even since I left in 1997. Young people are even more headstrong now. I know we had a lot of headstrong fellas on our panel but players are probably a bit more difficult to handle now. I think the manager now must be a personnel manager, psychiatrist, accountant and organiser. It's not based around football so much now, it's based around getting the best out of fellas. Managers have to know how to handle their players on and off the field.

Gary enjoyed his time working with Tony Blake. And Sean Sweeney from Gaoth Dobhair he reckons is a great prospect between the Donegal sticks. It brought a new focus and a new dimension to his summer. Gary Walsh still occasionally stands between he posts, voice booming, for Aodh Ruadh's junior team. It's hard to leave it behind. He could chat football for Ireland – certainly he would chat football all evening. "Don't post me a book," he says, "Come in with it and sure we'll have a chat about football."

❋ ❋ ❋ ❋

July 2003. It's a Thursday night in Dunkineely, around nine o'clock. Naomh Ultan are training. A variation of backs and forwards is played at great speed. The trainer is spraying the ball in all directions. Varying it. Sometimes the forwards become defenders and the defenders forwards. One man catches the eye. Darting here and there. Socks up to his knees.

Martin Shovlin is still as fit as a fiddle. Running around a field with a bunch of young fellows, some of them half his age, and able for any of them. Afterwards he sits in a car a stones throw from the half constructed new clubhouse and for a couple of hours reminisces about old days. Like his football, Shovlin is straightforward in the telling of his tale, "I kept going until 1997. The last game was against Cavan. McHugh was manager of Cavan. They beat us in the semi-final in Clones. It was the end."

They probably exist – they always do – but few people have a bad word to say about Martin Shovlin. Everyone had good time for Shov. He was at the epicentre of a memorable row one Sunday in Burt. Later he swore, tongue in cheek, to the County Executive that the Burt boys produced hurleys and used them. There wasn't a witter of truth in the statement but the next time the two teams met there was still 15 Burt men willing to shake the likeable rogue's hand. A whole county of admirers were gutted for Shov that Sunday in September. "There are days yet that I still say to myself, 'Imagine, I missed the All-Ireland'" he says softly, "It wasn't to be." He still sees some of the boys from time to time:

We meet an odd time. We had a reunion at Christmas and it was mighty. At the GAA banquet, the 1982 squad got together and they would not meet as often, except for the lads that went on to senior level. We have just lost track of some of the lads. Donny McCole is in the States and Maurice Carr is in England, but the other lads would still meet fairly regularly. Of the local boys, I would meet Tommy Ryan a lot, Declan Bonner regularly, and Molloy. As regards Joyce and these lads, I would meet them maybe and chat to them once every couple of years.

The times we had together were great. I played with Molloy and them at 18 years of age and I'm now 40, that's nearly a lifetime. When you play with men for years a great bond is built. The car loads that travelled to training were closer again. The friendship was mighty. We had some great weekends away. I know they are distant now, but we have memories that will stick with us forever.

There has never been another footballer like Shovlin. It is unlikely there will ever be. The boys would say Shov probably broke the mould himself.

❋ ❋ ❋ ❋

By the time Martin McHugh's Cavan sunk Donegal in the summer of 1997, John Cunningham had already kicked his last ball for Donegal. Razda, one of only a handful of Donegal men captain an All-Ireland winning team, didn't need telling. Honesty to himself and to his team was always his strong point:

I was captain of the team for a year or two. I was playing reasonably well. I always seemed to play all right for the county. I never had any real nightmares. I suppose in the last game I played against Antrim I began to come unstuck. I was never the fastest to begin with but that day I definitely knew my pace was gone for county football anyway. I was at corner-back and Matt was beside me and it was his last game too.

John is now busy with the Killybegs club. Putting it back in. In the middle of July 2003, on a beautiful summer's evening, he is to be found in Fintra in charge of the Killybegs under-10s. It's a long way from the battles Razda used to find himself in. He wants to win of course, but this is fun. Parents and youngsters roar encouragement from the sideline. The manager offers advice and encouragement. His charges are much too young to yet appreciate the rare achievements of the man teaching them the fundamentals of Gaelic football.

The day they do they will realise that their's was a privilege indeed.

❋ ❋ ❋ ❋

Matt Gallagher, the best full-back in Ireland in the year of 1992, sits talking about football in his home in Ballintra. It's late, midweek, and there's work to go to in the morning, yet Matt is as accommodating as ever. Late or not, he'll chat. By the time he played his last game that summer of 1997 he knew he was operating on borrowed time:

> I played against Antrim and played poorly and was taken off at half time. I didn't play against Cavan. Then PJ lost the job and Declan approached me and asked me to be a selector. It wasn't hard to make up my mind that I wasn't going to play any more, I probably should have done it the year before. It's hard to walk away from something you've been involved in for a long, long time.

With his old friend Bonner providing him with the chance to stay involved, Matt was accorded the opportunity to wean himself slowly from the inter-county scene. For a football mad youngster from a football-mad household, the whole experience – stretching almost two decades – was all his dreams come true:

> The fact that you were there and were involved in all those exciting times was really something! When people talk about Donegal now they still talk about that team. There is a great reverence about that team. You're still recognised and treated with a bit of respect. Even yet, people have a fantastic memory of that time. I suppose the highlights are the places you've been and the people you've met and made friends with. It opens a lot of doors for you.
>
> I'm from a very small club. To be able to compete, be involved and make it to the very top is my outstanding highlight. To be able to say to my two sons that I was probably the best full-back in the country is good. For them to realise that when they get to 15 or 16 will be great. I know that I was up there. I won four Railway Cup medals with Ulster. Tony Scullion was the absolute best defender of the period – he was fantastic. Kieran McKeever was the best man-marker. I played with these two guys and was more than able to hold my own when we played against the best players in the country. That is the most satisfying aspect to me. If I played badly against a fella I learned my lesson and it didn't happen a second time.

It wasn't all plain sailing. When the county learned of the tragic death of Pauric Gallagher in Boston in 1989 there was widespread shock and sadness among football folk who knew him. Matt has many warm memories of his older brother:

> We spent so much time together. We were brothers – he was a year older than me – and we were very close. We went to school together and played a lot of football together. We won an under-21 All-Ireland togeth-

er and that was a fantastic thing for brothers to do. Naomh Bríd is a very small club and to have two club members win an All-Ireland was just off the wall. We were part of history. Because the club was so small we were playing as a third or fourth division team at the time.

Pauric was fantastic. He was a real leader on the pitch in the years that we won the county junior and intermediate championships back to back, 1986 and 1987. He was a fantastic influence on the pitch, much better than I was. He could get through to guys a lot better than I could.

He suffered a bit from being a good soccer player and a good Gaelic player. When he was a student, soccer paid the bills. He played soccer for money. There was a lot of soccer at university. He was a fantastic Gaelic player and full-back was probably his best position. It was ironic that I should win an All-Ireland at full-back because he was a better full-back than I was. His best game for the county was probably in Monaghan in the 1981 Ulster final when he was drafted in to play full-back. He was absolutely superb.

He featured a lot in my life at that time. The thing that hurts most was neither Pauric nor my father were there to see the All-Ireland win. My father died two or three days after the Ulster final in 1991. My father was a huge influence on me growing up and he was a huge GAA man. He taught us how to play football. It was painful that they weren't around. It would have made the experience complete.

※ ※ ※ ※

Bonner's first championship as manager was memorable. He almost delivered the sweetest of Ulster titles in 1998. Operating now with no more than a small cohort of the 1992 team, Bonner came tantalisingly close to the Anglo-Celt Cup.

Paul Callaghan, Mark Crossan, Barry McGowan, Noel Hegarty, Jim McGuinness and Tony Boyle were on board when they beat Antrim in the opener in Belfast. Manus Boyle and Brian Murray came on that day. And Bonner introduced a new face to championship football in the person of Brendan Devenney from Newtowncunningham.

Defending Ulster champions Cavan were accounted for in Clones by 0-15 to 0-13. Paul Callaghan was replaced by Tony Blake, and apart from a brief appearance as a sub in 1999, Callaghan's championship career was over. John Joe Doherty was in from the start while James McHugh came on as a sub.

The Ulster final that July, in the end, belonged not to Declan Bonner's Donegal but to a gifted footballer from Dungiven by the name Joe Brolly. Geoffrey McGonigle, another Dungiven man, set Brolly up for a last gasp winning goal. Brolly, memorably, acknowledged his teammate's role, "He has an arse like a bag of cement. You can't get near him when the ball comes in, yet he

Jim McGuinness

Mark Crossan

Paul Callaghan

has the most delicate skills."

Brolly still had work to do when he got that ball but for the first time in the 70 minutes he had broken free of Barry McGowan, waltzed around a stranded Tony Blake and blasted the ball to the net. Donegal 0-8, Derry 1-7. As Brolly theatrically blew kisses to the crowd, Donegal kissed goodbye to an Ulster title. Of the boys that brought Sam to the Hills, Barry McGowan, John Joe Doherty, Noel Hegarty, Manus Boyle, Tony Boyle and James McHugh suffered that cruel defeat together.

It really was the end of the road for the old men. There were other leagues and other championships to be played under the guidance of Bonner. But with new faces. The manager knew himself that it was the end of an era, "We lost to a late Joe Brolly goal in the 1998 Ulster final and Brian Murray, James McHugh, Barry McGowan and Manus all stepped down after that," he recalled.

❋ ❋ ❋ ❋

Nobody played football with the style of Barry McGowan. Princely, someone once said. He can be found these days on the Dunkineely side of Killybegs. Soccer highlights flicker silently on a television in the corner as Barry recalls the injury that finally brought his career to an end:

In the national league semi-final of 1993 I tore my hamstring for the first time and it started a bad decade for me with the same injury. I seemed to be permanently receiving treatment. Various physiotherapists will testify to this because I had them plagued. I had to contend with tearing hamstrings every year after that.

My last game was in 1998 and we played Derry in the Ulster final. I was 32 years of age. I could have played on but my battle with injuries was too much. I was afraid of making a quick sprint and tearing a hamstring – I got to know how far I could push myself. The injury was holding me up. I didn't want to kid myself that I could still play at inter-county level while having to contend with such injuries. If a player can't play at one hundred per cent he will be found out. After that I decided to give up.

Barry spent many Sundays down those years in the company of Joe Brolly. The Killybegs man smiles as he recalls those epic clashes with one of the great characters of Gaelic football:

He was very unorthodox and even he didn't know what he was going to do next. It was very hard to mark him. He was a left-footed player which was a blessing in one way – if he had two good feet nobody could have dealt with him.

He was a very pleasant character. He always tried to get a player involved in conversation. I don't know whether it was to calm his own nerves or being tactical in trying to gain a player's confidence and give him a false sense of security. I never bothered with the chat because I knew what he was at.

I remember the national league final in 1995. I was swapped onto him at a late stage in the game – I remember running over the pitch to mark him. When I was still 20 yards away he held out his hand to shake my hand. I avoided his hand and gave him a good shoulder. I got a lot of criticism for doing so and people thought I wasn't very sporting. I knew exactly what he was at! I'm sure he'd tell you himself that the time to shake hands is at the start or end of a game. He was a good character and a good player. He gave me a lot of trouble – he had great pace. Most of the time I tried to annoy him by trying to get him to follow me – I knew he hated that.

He was a devil. It was all mind games with Joe. In that department I would like to think that I was his equal and would have taken him on. I was able to hold my own. I am sure he thought I was half mad because I'd shout at him and play the hard man even though I was never the hard man.

On that same day in Croke Park Brolly broke his wrist as McGowan and him went for a ball. McGowan had nothing to do with the injury but was sorry all the same to see his old sparring partner stretchered off in obvious pain. "I felt bad for him," remembered McGowan, "I rang him up and inquired after him. We talked for a good while and he said he was none the worse." It was fitting therefore that it was Brolly who was there to bookend McGowan's career with that famous last-gasp goal in Clones in the Ulster final of 1998:

The 1998 final seemed to be a wrestling match. I thought I'd be sent off at one stage. The referee went to book me. I thought he'd booked me earlier in the game and I pleaded with him not to send me off. Brolly couldn't stop laughing at me when he saw me panicking because I thought I was going to be sent off.

McGowan enjoys bumping into the boys now and then. He enjoyed the craic they had in Bundoran at Christmas 2002:

There were all there except perhaps one or two. It was a very enjoyable night. As the years go by there will be more of these functions and people reminiscing. It is only now dawning on people how hard it is to win an All-Ireland and the magnitude of such an achievement.

It is a pity that we don't meet more often. It's not easy to meet. Everyone went their own way and it's hard to get a group of lads together. You bump into some of them occasionally through work or whatever. It happens less and less, but that's life.

He talks about his friend Manus and the football Manus is playing in 2003. In doing so Barry reveals that he finds matches hard to attend now that he has stopped playing himself:

I don't go to matches. Perhaps I dislike them because I miss the game. I feel uncomfortable watching them. I have such happy memories and nothing replaces playing. I don't like just sitting and watching a game and criticising so I don't go to matches like other players do.

This year in Killybegs people are talking about Manus just like they did ten years ago or more. He seems to be in great shape and enjoying it. If a player still enjoys it they should keep playing. Injuries took the fun out of my game. I always said that when the enjoyment ceased I'd stop. It is understandable that people were disappointed that I didn't keep playing for another couple of years. The last few years I spent so much time on the treatment table and I felt it was time to move on. I didn't want to start hating the game but I had stopped enjoying it. I just wanted a break from it. I will probably go back to it at another stage. At this stage I want a break and I want to recharge my batteries.

Some people say that I have to give something back at this stage. You never stop giving. You give the game the best years of your life and you enjoy and love the game. I shall resume giving at a later stage. This is just the end of a chapter.

❅ ❅ ❅ ❅

Manus, the man two Donegal teams needed to win an All-Ireland, is at it still – playing the kind of football in 2003 that electrifies those watching. John Joe Doherty, who marked him many, many times, heard all about it in Anagary. "He's still doing it. He scored four goals and six or seven points in a recent match." Manus shrugs off the accolades. Sitting in his home halfway up the mountain, overlooking Fintragh Bay, he worries about the future of the fishing industry in Killybegs. Football sometimes needs to be put into perspective. He remembers the day he pulled the plug:

I got very sick at the end of 1997 and lost a stone and a half. I wouldn't have been the same player in 1998. I played against Cavan that year and did all right. Barry McGowan and me have been friends since we were very young. Coming back in the car from the Ulster final in 1998 I said to Barry that I'd never play for Donegal again and he said neither would he. Declan Bonner was after me to come back and he was a very hard man to say no to. He must have called me 20 times. I told him it was nothing to do with him, it was just a decision I had made. Barry and me met him in Donegal Town. He offered to make Barry captain and to play me at centre half-forward. Bonner would have known that I always wanted to play at centre half-forward. It was too late for me then though, I would have needed to get it in 1994 or 1995.

Manus was always sure of himself. He was sure now. It was time to bring the county journey to an end. He stuck with his decision and Bonner understood.

These days the Killybegs maestro still doesn't look a day older than that Sunday in September when he swept the ball over the Dublin bar a magnificent nine times and ensured that when 1992 is spoken of, the name Manus Boyle trips simultaneously off the tongue.

❄ ❄ ❄ ❄

Kilmainham is where Big Murray is still to be found. The Ballyshannon accent hasn't deserted him one bit. Probably drives the Dubs mad. Another culchie on the dirty streets of their capital. In Kilmainham Garda station, Murray pours forth on football and his leaving of the green and gold:

Two weeks before the 1998 Ulster final I got injured in a Mickey Mouse challenge match at the opening of a pitch somewhere. Michael Lawlor tackled me in the closing minutes and tore ligaments in my shoulder. I got a lot of treatment and felt I was nearly right. I was disappointed not to get a run versus Derry. Heaney was playing that day and I had always done well against Derry.

It wasn't hard to pull the plug then, I was 34. I had intended to retire the year before but the boys asked me to come back. I trained and got back into good shape. I knew when we were knocked out in 1998 that I would retire. It was getting too much. I had a young family and there was a lot of travelling involved. It was the right time to bow out.

I was disappointed though because Derry went on and played Galway in the semi-final and lay down. We had a good enough side to put it up to Galway had we got past Derry. Donegal had played well throughout the game. Derry brought on two big fellas that day – Heaney and Geoffrey McGonigle. Geoffrey stuck out his arse and laid a ball on to Joe Brolly and he put it into the back of the net.

It was a little strange playing under an old teammate like Bonner:

It was short but a bit strange. We would have been good buddies. We started off with Donegal around the same time and had played under-age together. We knew each other very, very well. In a way I was delighted that I was asked back. There was a couple of games that I didn't get a run in and wondered why. It was just a pity that we didn't pull it off that day. It would have been nice for Declan and the whole lot of us.

Brian transferred from the Civil Service club to Kilcock in 1996. He built a house out there and has been living in the north Kildare town for seven or eight years now. He's still playing football. "I'm still enjoying it but it's coming near the end," he says with a grin. Eleven years to the day after the boys brought Sam to the Hills, Big Murray was back in another final on the third Sunday of September. Kilcock made it to the Kildare senior final and although they fell to Round Towers it was a man from Donegal who led a second-half revival. Big Murray, still hustling after all this time.

❄ ❄ ❄ ❄

James McHugh's honesty is almost disarming. He's just in from a day's work and is chatting about politics and tribunals in Dublin. No problem there. Then the conversation turns to football. As his dinner boils dry, James says things none of the others have said:

Looking back on it, we did not win as much as we should have. We did-n't get enough out of it – if we had won an All-Ireland earlier we might have. It was a good football team. I watched a lot of that team play club football – that was a very good Donegal team. But in saying that, when we got to the All Ireland in 1992 most of the players were boiling – going over the top. I have regrets that we didn't win more. But the other side of the coin is we are lucky to have won an All Ireland.

James feels that the same desire for success was never there among the boys after the heroics of 1992. And more success would have been forthcoming had things been different before 1992:

We would have won it earlier if we had the desire in ourselves. We had quality for years before that. Had Donegal won the Ulster title in 1989, we would have had a good chance. That was a very strong side. If we had broken through a wee bit earlier ...
    If you look at that Donegal team, they had to come through at some stage. Maybe it was our own fault we didn't come earlier. It wasn't a fluke in 1992. There were a hell of a lot of good players. It is a pity we didn't go on afterwards. It's very hard. I don't care who says what, but it is very hard

when you reach your goal. So many of us had reached the goal but a two-in-a-row wasn't enough of an incentive. We should have won 1993 and 1994. But, at that time we were too happy. We just packed it in. We were too content with what we got. I found it very hard to come back after the All Ireland. If we had won two, we could have won three or four. It's a disappointment now but at the time I was like everyone else, I had enough.

James was caught in a very awkward situation when Martin went for but didn't get the Donegal job. To his credit he continued playing football:

I still feel that the 1995 team was the closest team we had to 1992. Maybe even to the point where it bordered on being a better team. They were a balanced side. By 1994, a lot of the 1992 team were more or less gone as players. When that team went, that's when new players came in. In 1995 we still had a lot of the All Ireland team plus a new group of players. That was a good side.

We could have unleashed another championship. At that stage of the Ulster championship, we had ten players with medals and that would have been a big advantage. There was no back door. You had only one game to play and you were in an All-Ireland final. And anything can happen in an All-Ireland final.

That team of 1995 could have gone a stage further. I believe that if Martin had got the job, we would have progressed. We would have come close. The fact that Martin didn't get the job probably upset a lot of players, myself included. It was hard for me to go back. PJ McGowan who was manager is a nice fella and I wouldn't say anything against him but I was left in a hard situation.

Injury put paid to football in 1997. By the time he made a return to the green and gold Declan Bonner was in his first year in charge:

I came back in 1998 but it was not for long. I had fierce trouble with my back for years – I wasn't fit to do the training. I came back and Donegal had beaten Antrim in the first game. Then we met Cavan. I came on as a sub in the Cavan game with only two weeks' training behind me. Then there was four weeks to the Ulster final. And I missed the next two weeks and my career was over.

❄ ❄ ❄ ❄

The national league of 1998-99 was mediocre. Bonner was team-building again, it was time to build Donegal from scratch. That winter they won three and lost four. Bonner had them right when the summer came around and they gave Armagh all the bother they wanted over two matches. They drew the first day in Ballybofey – only Noel Hegarty and Tony Boyle remained of the 1992 starting 15 – and lost the replay by five points in Clones. Armagh took Derry in the Ulster final and were emerging as the dominant force in Ulster. They would lose to Sean Boylan's Meath in the semi-final that year but their name was on a future Sam.

The Bonner era came to an end in June 2000 in Ballybofey. Fermanagh turned up in MacCumhaill Park and inflicted a two-point defeat. Bonner was happy to walk away. He'd done his time and played his part:

> I enjoyed my time as manager. It was very time consuming; you're looking after the needs of 25 or 28 players. You're always on the 'phone. That chapter is closed now. I've played for and managed my county and enjoyed it while I was doing it.

Three years later and Bonner is still playing football with his beloved Na Rossa. They've just lost a championship match to Burt on a Saturday night in July in sun-drenched Lettermacaward. Bonner is as amicable as ever in the aftermath – even to two Burt lads – and gives generously of his time to chat of days gone by. He still sees some of the boys:

> A lot of the lads work on the road. I would meet the likes of Donal Reid, Charlie Mulgrew, Tony, Noel and John Joe. Donal Reid does some physiotherapy work now and he's very good at it. I wouldn't see much of Shovlin, but I see Matt fairly often. We had a great night as a group in Bundoran last Christmas – a ten-year reunion. Many things were meant to have been done but they never materialised. Maybe they will some day.

❄ ❄ ❄ ❄

There is an old Donegal bag lying by the back door of the house in Ranafast. From the kitchen window you can see planes landing a couple of times a day at Carrickfinn Airport. It's July 12, 2003. John Joe Doherty has a couple of hours to chat about football. Then he has to make his way down the coast to Carrick – Glen are playing a league match this evening. Sure what else would he be doing? Hardly marching anyway.

While Donegal lost two finals in 1993, John Joe Doherty performed well during the season, so well that he impressed the All-Star selectors who placed him at right full-back on that year's All-Star team. Playing for Donegal meant everything to John Joe. He was bursting with pride to captain his county:

> I was captain when Declan Bonner took over the team. It was a big hon-

our for me to captain the county. There were a lot of new players on the team at that stage and I was one of the older players so I enjoyed that year. Getting beaten in the Ulster final of 1998 would probably go down as my biggest disappointment. Things were looking up. We were very unlucky to get beaten in that Ulster final. If we had won that match I feel that the story of Donegal football in the years since could have been totally different.

One of the last of the boys to depart the county scene, he recalls the end:

The Ulster final of 1998 was my last championship match. Then in 1999 I got sent off in Corrigan Park in the McKenna Cup and was suspended for three months. The referee got it wrong. I was still playing with the team because I knew I could still be back, but then pulled my thigh muscle – I've struggled a lot in club football ever since.

In 1999, Donegal drew with Armagh in Ballybofey and the replay was in Clones. Declan Bonner approached me after the drawn match because my suspension was up the next day and I would safely say that had I been fit I would probably have been playing in the replay. I had to tell him that I wasn't fit.

❄ ❄ ❄ ❄

Paul Callaghan, the blond-haired goalkeeper from Burt, might have expected a longer career between the sticks following the departure of Gary Walsh. In 1997 Callaghan was the man and again in 1998 was in for the opening game of the championship against Antrim which Donegal won 1-11 to 0-11. Then it all went wrong. "Two weeks before the semi-final I tore my calf muscle at training and missed the Cavan game," he remembers. Tony Blake took over and Donegal advanced to the Ulster final. It marked the end for Callaghan. He would replace an injured Blake a year later in Clones when Armagh won the day but 1998 marked the beginning of the end.

Like his friend Jim McGuinness, the world seemed to be Callaghan's oyster back in 1991:

A neighbour called and told me that Brian McEniff had rang and wanted to talk to me. We had no 'phone at the time so I had to walk down the road to a telephone box which was about half a mile away. I phoned Brian at the hotel and he said he'd seen me playing under-21 and had also seen me playing on an Inishowen team against Donegal at the opening of the Urris pitch at Clonmany, and he asked me to come join the panel, and that was me in the squad then.

McGuinness, Crossan and himself were the babes of the team. But old enough to appreciate what had been achieved in the summer of 1992.

> Panel members were treated the same as players, it had been a panel effort and everyone was a hero. The crowds were great, we felt like The Beatles!
>
> McHugh had fans everywhere. I remember the scenes in Burt hall. One man at the front of the hall kept asking, 'Where's Martin McHugh? Where's Martin McHugh?' When McHugh finally came onto the stage the man just gave a contented sigh, 'Awww, Martin McHugh.'

Paul is now the county hurling coach and has been very involved in the work of the hugely successful GAA summer camps which have been held in Donegal for several summers now. He is playing still with Burt and boasts an incredible penalty-stopping record complemented by an equally incredible penalty-scoring record.

※ ※ ※ ※

With Bonner out of the picture Donegal found themselves under the guidance of a Derry man – Mickey Moran, who was there with Eamonn Coleman when Derry won their All-Ireland in 1993. Mickey's first league campaign was innocuous and the championship foray was nothing to write home about either. Fermanagh caught Donegal napping in their first game of the summer 2001 but as it was the first year of the back-door system there was to be a second bite at the cherry. Fermanagh lost a week or two later and found themselves facing Donegal yet again. Donegal progressed but only as far as Newbridge and there Kildare called a halt to progress.

※ ※ ※ ※

Tony Boyle has just driven from Omagh and is glad of the cup of tea in a quiet corner of the Mill Park Hotel in Donegal Town. Later he'll point his car for Carrick and drive to meet up with some of the boys for a 'celebrity' soccer match being organised by Noel Hegarty. He can't wait – the craic will be good with the boys, it always is.

His last game was in the qualifiers of 2001 against Kildare in Newbridge. By then he'd been pulling on the senior jersey for over a decade, yet it all passed by in a flash. These days he doesn't see the boys as much as he'd like to:

> There are probably five or six of us that are working on the road and you would meet that way, but I wouldn't see much of them socially. McEniff had a do in Bundoran over Christmas and that was the first time we got

together. I would see Reid occasionally, when I was playing I would have got a bit of treatment off him. I wouldn't see Shov from one end of the year till the next unfortunately. Similarly with James McHugh and Barry McGowan.

❄ ❄ ❄ ❄

It's a tough question. If you were to have one teammate standing beside you, who would it be? Tony Boyle only had to think for a second. There would be several, but if he had to pick one, he'd pick Hegarty, "Noel and me would have been close and soldiered together for a long time. He would always give 100%. He would tell you what he thought of you and whether he liked you or not!"

That day in Newbridge when Tony called it a day, so too did the man from Glen who'd been in many battles alongside him. Noel Hegarty's great service to Donegal football came to an end. Two summers have passed since and Higgs has an hour or more to chat about that and other football matters in his Slieve League bar in Teelin. After that he'll be off training with the Naomh Columba:

> I was in fairly good shape in 2001. But Mickey Moran was only using me as a sub. The Kildare game was probably the best game we had that year. I had no qualms about being left off. I said fair enough, play away with what you've got and I'll come on. But that day in Fermanagh, when Fermanagh beat us, there was no point in me sitting on the bench as they were beating us. I was only 29 or 30. I was disappointed in that. I played my last game against Kildare in Newbridge then.

Regrets. Hegarty, no more than the rest of them, has a few:

> We were better than one All-Ireland. We should have won a league or two. We met Derry in two league finals and they were probably better and more organised than us but we should have won one of them.

He has great memories of the fun they had together. No more so than the banter in the car all those nights back and forward to training in Ballybofey:

> We used to have great craic going up to training – the two McHughs who always travelled together, myself and John Joe. Before we travelled together, the men in the car wouldn't have got on. There was great rivalry between the players and the supporters of our clubs.
>
> We used to stop afterwards for a few pints together. James was a great character. Martin would be more serious. Every night Martin would be talking about what team would work. One night on the way to

training in 1994, everyone in the car had to pick their preferred team. As it turned out, I was the only one of the four that ended up actually getting on for real – James, Martin and John Joe weren't on. I can tell you I was laughing hard the whole way home that night.

✤ ✤ ✤ ✤

Another dull winter followed but in 2002 the championship sparked to life again. Cavan were beaten in Cavan. Down were hammered 3-12 to 1-6 in Ballybofey. There were two points to spare over Derry in Clones in the semi-final. Another Ulster final beckoned. Armagh, propelled by Joe Kernan – the man who led Crossmaglen Rangers to three All-Ireland club titles – escaped Clones with an Ulster title leaving behind a Donegal team who never fully recovered from conceding a goal in the second minute. Armagh would go on to win the All-Ireland.

Mickey Moran's side advanced, via the back door, to the All-Ireland quarter-final against Dublin in Croke Park and drew, 0-14 to 2-8 – a result that for a week or so revitalised Donegal football. Yet it was the events of those weeks that in the end sunk Donegal football to a new low. Some of the team remained in Dublin to celebrate the draw. Twelve days later Dublin played them off the pitch and, back home, all hell broke loose. Allegations and counter-allegations were hurled back and forth. The end result was that Mickey Moran packed his bags and departed for the Sperrins. Just in time for the Derry job. And Donegal were rudderless.

✤ ✤ ✤ ✤

Mark Crossan is playing still. The St Eunan's man was 22 years old when Donegal struck gold in 1992. Eleven years later he is the old man of Donegal football. It wasn't always thus. It only seems like yesterday that he was a whole lot greener and attending a county-trial game in the New Year of 1991. He remembers that Paul Callaghan and Jim McGuinness were there too that day in Ballyshannon. All three played well, McEniff gave him the nod and that was the 1990s sown up, "One thing that stands out in my mind was the step up in training from the under-21 team. It was nothing like what we were used to and was totally new to us."

Crossan's chance came in the championship of 1993 against Armagh and he seized it with both hands:

> I remember sitting on the bench, watching the game, which I had got used to, when Barry McGowan got injured and then Brian gave me the shout. It was a bit of a shock. I went in corner–back and marked Diarmaid Marsden and did fairly well on him, and I've played ever since. Strangely enough it was Diarmaid I marked in my first championship game against and in my last in 2002, when I got injured in the Ulster final.

The Long Goodbye

Now in the twilight of a career that has spanned the reign of four managers, Mark is as optimistic about his football in 2003 as he was that day in Ballyshannon in the winter of 1991 when he played his way onto a squad that would win an All-Ireland:

> I'm still playing for the club, and at this stage I'm going to relax until after Christmas, and then see what happens. You know, we're not that far away. Mickey Moran took us to an All–Ireland quarter-final, and Brian took us to the semi–final this year, so there is a good team there.

❄ ❄ ❄ ❄

Jim McGuinness is no longer the long-haired student of 1992. A decade and a bit on he is, like Crossan, one of the elder statesmen of the county scene. His role in recent times has been more limited but there was a time when McGuinness, just 18 years-old, had the whole world at his feet. He remembers it well:

> In 1991, I went to Boston to play for the summer. I came home for Christmas with the intention of going back out again. I'd lived there for eight or nine months. There was a trial in Ballyshannon over Christmas, and the club asked me to go up to it. On the day I played fairly well, I scored 1-3 or 1-4 in an A versus B game. I was only 18 at the time. After the match, Brian McEniff came over to me when I was coming out of the dressing room and asked me would I be interested in joining the panel. I couldn't believe it. I couldn't wait to get home to tell my parents. It all happened so fast; just one game and then I was in the panel.

Like Crossan, his chance came in the summer of 1993 – Antrim in Ballybofey:

> It was great. There was a great buzz around the county, with Donegal being the All-Ireland champions and it was a great honour to be on the team. I played fairly well that day but in the final minutes one of our own men, Mark McShane, caught me from the side when I went up for the ball. I broke my collarbone. That put a damper on things.

When people talk of 1992, McGuinness just smiles with an insider's knowledge. What they went through that summer after the Fermanagh match only insiders like the Glenties man can really appreciate. For McGuinness, still in his teens, the experience was as good as it got:

> We lifted it after Fermanagh. It was unbelievable. We trained really hard and we knew we were bound to win the Ulster final because we had

so much done. We lifted it again and I remember coming home with Michael O'Donnell and saying to him that we couldn't be in better shape, but then I remember thinking to myself three or four weeks later when we were heading into the All-Ireland final that I was at a level higher again. There was serious competition, serious training and all the players were deadly serious about it. I was 19 and as fit as I was ever going to be. I've never seen a team as fit since. The effort was unbelievable.

❀ ❀ ❀ ❀

The hotelier from Bundoran is on a mobile 'phone, pacing the carpark of the McEniff Skylon Hotel in Drumcondra. The hunt is on for a Donegal manager and McEniff, the outgoing manager and county chairman, is orchestrating the search. It's a few days into September 2003 and the events of the previous Sunday, when McEniff guided another Donegal team to the very brink of an All-Ireland final, loom large.

Talk of football invariably straddles several generations of players. But one manager. When McEniff finally ended his involvement with Donegal in the summer of 1994 that should have been it. That it wasn't says something of McEniff and his unquenchable thirst for Donegal football.

Chairman of the County Board, McEniff was acutely aware that no replacement had been found for Mickey Moran as 2002 faded into 2003. With the national league on top of the team, McEniff finally declared that he would take on the job in a caretaker capacity. With him he brought PJ McGowan and Michael Oliver McIntyre. Anthony Harkin would, in time, come back as coach. PJ McGowan laughs as he recalls how McEniff and himself found themselves back in management:

> It was most unexpected. It came about because I was vice-chairman of the County Board and we were operating without a chairman at the time. Brian McEniff and me got the lads together in December because they had done nothing. Every other county was deep in preparation and we met in Biddy O Barnes and persuaded Anthony Harkin to come in. We got the boys together and picked a squad. Anthony didn't want to get involved at all but we got a wee bit of training going and then found that we couldn't get out of the damn thing!

Martin Gavigan was amazed. Back again! The Old Man was something else:

> I don't know how McEniff does it. Those winter nights standing around a training session for an hour and a half – the motivation that takes. It's one thing having glory days in the summer time, but he puts it in on

those winter nights!

There was little time to do anything other than get a team on to the field and fulfil fixtures. The results were inevitable – Donegal had no training behind them and lost to Galway, Dublin, Armagh, Tyrone, Kerry and Cork. Although the last match against Roscommon was won at the beginning of April, Donegal had relinquished Division One status for the first time in 15 years.

The championship was around the corner. McEniff and Harkin were making progress with the squad but June 1 in Enniskillen arrived too quickly. Fermanagh 0-10, Donegal 0-6. Disaster. A new low in Donegal football. "We just fumbled and footered and didn't play well against them," says McGowan. McEniff never liked being beaten by Fermanagh. He let the boys know and told them a thing or two about pride. It was back into the qualifiers. And slowly but surely it all came together. The next game turned out a little differently to what PJ McGowan or anybody else expected:

> The crowd that turned out to see us play Longford in Ballybofey was unbelievable. We were expecting to see a couple of hundred and to be able to hear every foul comment that was thrown at us, but it was actually the opposite. They gave us great support.

Sligo were then brought to and beaten in Ballybofey. Ditto Tipperary in Croke Park. McEniff's new boys were getting better all the time. Anthony Harkin was working his magic. "It was no coincidence that Donegal's fortunes improved when Anthony got at them," suggested Martin Gavigan. They demolished Down in Clones at the end of July, 3-15 to 2-10. Then the adventure really began. This was All-Ireland quarter-final territory.

They met Connacht champions Galway in Croke Park. A McEniff team once again caught the imagination of Donegal folk. They flocked to Croke Park in their thousands and witnessed an enthralling encounter that finished 0-14 to 1-11. The replay was fixed for Castlebar – perhaps Tuam wasn't available. It didn't matter to McEniff's boys, they held Galway off to secure a famous 0-14 to 0-11 win in the heart of Connacht. The scenes afterwards hadn't been seen since the heady days of the boys that brought Sam to the Hills. McEniff was onto something. Again.

And for 70 minutes of the All-Ireland semi-final Donegal stood toe to toe with reigning All-Ireland champions Armagh. Joe Kernan's men would triumph in the end but not before Donegal put them to the wire. That Donegal were outnumbered for most of the second half and that the absence of the dismissed full-back, Ray Sweeney, was crucial in the end leaves McEniff with a huge 'if' hanging over the outcome. He'll never know but he'll wonder just the same. Even so, the whole country had been impressed. What was it about McEniff? "Five decades of turning water into wine," declared Tom Humphries in the *Irish Times*, adding, "There is no story like McEniff's."

Nothing will ever replace the feeling of that Sunday in September 1992 and five Ulster championship victories but, as he says himself, "this year was as sweet as any." Eleven years on he still talks of the 1992 squad with great affection, "A great camaraderie existed between not only the players but their wives and families, or girlfriends as they were, and we all attended the weddings. That stays there. It was a special time."

No one knows more about the boys than McEniff. And there are those who say that no one knows more about Donegal football than the hotelier from Bundoran. "He has forgotten more about football than the whole lot of us ever knew," the Follower once wrote about McEniff.

McEniff's football curriculum vitae is so vast and packed with incident that it undoubtedly merits a book in itself. Perhaps someday McEniff will tell his story. He has come a long way from that day in September 1980 when he took on the Donegal job from Sean O'Donnell. And set about building a team of champions.

There is nothing left to achieve. He really has done it all. Including managing his country – steering Ireland to victory in the Compromise Rules series in Australia in 2001. There are those who speculate that the icing on the cake would be the GAA presidency. He dismisses it out of hand. Nonsense he says. Time will tell. McEniff, as always, is far too shrewd to declare his hand before the timing is absolutely right.

And so, at the end of August 2003, with Donegal football revitalised and back where it belongs, McEniff stepped down one more time. "If I was ten years younger," he told these authors on September 5, "I wouldn't have to think twice. I wouldn't be looking for a manager." It seemed then that the journey really had come to an end. Not so. A little over a month after that conversation the hotelier from Bundoran was confirmed as the Donegal manager for another year. He evidently found a new lease of life and his is a football story destined to run and run. Could it be that he will go a step further in 2004 and lead another band of Donegal men to the promised land? Can he work his magic one more time and bring Sam back to the Hills? Now *that's* another book.

❊

Epilogue
(October 12, 2003)

In the end, that Sunday in September 1992, Keith Barr's repertoire of street-wise aggression was to prove a paltry match for the silken genius of a little man from Kilcar. McHugh did have "the balls" to do it. And all around McHugh, on the lush sward that was Croke Park, Donegal men poured vast knowledge – garnered on a journey that started way back in 1980 – into one afternoon of devastating football. Nothing could divert the boys from their mission. Certainly not Dublin who wilted in the glare of such intensity. Donegal *would* return to the Hills with Sam Maguire. It was written in their destiny.

In doing so they became history-makers. Legends in their own lifetime. The goodwill of a nation descended on them and when that receded they still had the veneration of their county. A hundred years from now when football is talked about in the Hills, their names will be revered. And even if others in green and gold emulate their feat, the boys of 1992 will remain *always* the boys who brought Sam to the Hills. Their kind of history can be copied, never equalled.

The sacrifices those men made on that incredible journey have long since been forgotten by those who packed stadiums across the land to watch their story unfold. All-Irelands are hard won and easy lost. The men who win them are usually men who have paid their dues at the high altar of sacrifice. Donegal worshiped long and hard on the steps of that cruel altar. Scars which cut deeper than the eye can see or the hand feel were accumulated en-route. They carry them still.

And for every ball they pulled out of the clouds, every graceful solo and magical side-step, every crunching tackle landed, every point that spilt the posts, there were those who stood by the boys and facilitated their dream-making. Their sacrifices ran just as deep. The renown achieved by boyfriends, husbands or sons could never recompense those special moments missed. And, in the dark days when yesterday's heroes bore the brunt of the strange fickleness that is the supporter, it was families and friends who heard it all.

Eleven years have passed since the boys brought Sam to the Hills. Let's rise one more time and salute those heroes and those belonging to them. In the pursuit of their destiny they realised the dreams of thousands and made an entire county walk tall.